Christmas 1989.

Love and best wishes c
We'll see you next year.

Simon + Carolyn

A DAY IN THE LIFE OF
Australia

A DAY IN THE LIFE OF
Australia

Keith Dunstan
The Complete Collection of his *Age* Column

M

First published 1989 by
THE MACMILLAN COMPANY OF AUSTRALIA PTY LTD
107 Moray Street, South Melbourne 3205
6 Clarke Street, Crows Nest 2065

Associated companies and representatives
throughout the world

National Library of Australia
cataloguing in publication data

Dunstan, Keith.
 A day in the life of Australia.

 ISBN 0 7329 0185 5.

 1. Australia — History.   2. Australia — Centennial
 celebrations, etc.   I. Title.   II. Title: Age (Melbourne,
 Vic.).

994

Set in Plantin by Setrite Typesetters Ltd, Hong Kong
Printed in Australia by The Book Printer.

Contents

Introduction

Creighton Burns, Editor of the *Age* in Melbourne, had the original idea. He said: 'Why not celebrate Australia's Bicentenary this way? Take events that you find interesting, then go through the diary day by day in 1988 and match them with the same day in some year during the previous two hundred.

'Just move at random, one day 1802, the next 1888 or 1938. You could even come as close as 1975, but keep out of immediate memory, like four or five years ago.

'But don't' he continued 'just dully record what happened. Go back, say, in an H.G. Wells Time Machine, and carry on as if you were actually alive and kicking at the time. Wherever you can, use contemporary sources.'

So that is what we did. I had the help of Colin Dawson, a former librarian at the Herald and Weekly Times Ltd, a man who had the reputation that when given a clue he could find anything, and find he did. He did much of the incredible research, making particular use of the marvellous collection of newspapers and journals at Melbourne's La Trobe Library.

I tried to stick to the rules, not to get out of the time warp and make use of tempting events that took place perhaps a week or years afterwards. There were traps, because often information was withheld, censored or unknown right on the date. For example, I got into trouble over the World War 2 raids on Darwin. The Australian public at the time was innocent of what really happened. I stuck faithfully to the mood and message of the day. Here and there I have added a 'Note' to give further information.

Creighton Burns said: 'We will run it for a month or so to see if anyone finds it interesting'. Well, many did, so it ran for the whole year in many newspapers around Australia. We were overwhelmed with correspondence, particularly from grandchildren and great-grandchildren of people mentioned.

There were letters from schools, signed by every class member; letters from all sorts of amateur historians. Invariably they said: 'We are pasting your daily series into a scrapbook but we have lost February 23 and August 18, so it is not complete. You *do* intend to bring it out as a book at the end of the year *don't* you?'

In answer to those questions, here it is.

JANUARY

Celebrating the new Commonwealth

A Brand New Commonwealth

1 JANUARY 1901

Celebrating the new Commonwealth

What an extraordinary day it has been, a new century, a new unity, a brand new Commonwealth. There were hymns in the churches, patriotic songs in the theatres, singing in the clubs.

One could hardly move in Sydney, every available tram, every harbour ferry, every horse-drawn bus carried all loyal citizens into the city for the launching of the Commonwealth of Australia. They had only been trying to do it for the past 50 years. The six colonies were so jealous of each other I thought they would never get there.

Best of all, though, was the procession. It started at 10.30 a.m. and moved through streets all decorated with marvellous triumphal arches; Venetian poles; Japanese lanterns; and every kind of flag, crown, painting and symbol of loyalty. The noise was uproarious: gongs, whistles, bells, accordions, rattles, people beating tin dishes.

There were grandstands all along the route and you could pay anything from 5 shillings to 25 shillings a seat. Some grandstands even had carpets and bands.

In the procession there were all the trade unions: the Australian Workers Union, the Shearers Union, the gold miners, the timber workers, the coal miners, the metal workers. There were the fire brigades, gleaming brass hats, and wonderful fire carts pulled by superbly groomed horses. On one float they had a bust of old Sir Henry Parkes, beard and all. We will remember him as the father of Federation. There were judges, there were premiers and our first prime minister, Edmund Barton.

The procession wound through to Centennial Park, and a choir sang 'O God our help in ages past, our hope for years to come'. The Church of England Archbishop of Sydney, William Simaurez Smith, said the prayers. The Catholic representative, Cardinal Patrick Moran, was not there. Some say he was miffed because Archbishop Smith won precedence in the procession. So Cardinal Moran had his own ceremony outside St Mary's cathedral.

Our new Governor-General, Lord Hopetoun, was there. Had he been Admiral of the entire British Fleet, he could not have looked more impressive. There was a reading of a proclamation from Her Majesty Queen Victoria: 'We do hereby declare that on and after the First Day of January One Thousand Nine hundred and One, the people of New South Wales, Victoria, South Australia, Queensland, Tasmania and Western Australia shall be united in a Federal Commonwealth under the name Commonwealth of Australia'.

It will be difficult to get out of the habit of talking about States instead of colonies, and I wonder whether they will be any more friendly to each other. At least there will be one advantage. It will be splendid being able to send goods from one State to another without paying customs duties.

Eighteen Wickets to Fall

2 JANUARY 1861

We have just been beaten, thoroughly, by the first touring side from England. It was an XI led by Mr H.H. Stephenson, captain of Surrey, and they arrived at Port Phillip on the steamer, *Great Britain*, just before Christmas. What a vessel! It carried 44 000 soldiers to the Crimean War, and regiments to the Indian mutiny.

The cricket match took place all because of Messrs Spiers and Pond, owners of the Cafe de Paris in Bourke Street. Originally they wanted to bring out Charles Dickens. This great man was unavailable, so they chose a cricket team instead.

Immediately there was a crisis. The plan was for Mr Stephenson's XI to play a Melbourne and Districts side of 22, but Mr Stephenson objected. There had been no time to train. His team had been at sea for 60 days, so the Melbourne side was cut to eighteen. Even so, it was impressive, a fielding side of 18 was something to behold.

On New Year's Day the Melbourne Cricket Ground was in perfect condition and there was a new grandstand, 700 feet long. The whole of the underneath was given over to publicans, and they advertised they would have 500 cases of beer. Outside the ground, there were Aunt Sallies, shooting galleries, hurdy gurdies and photo souvenirs of the teams.

By 11.00 a.m. the roads to the MCG were packed with every kind of vehicle, from buggies to bullock wagons.

George Marshall was captain of the Melbourne team. His men wore strawberry coloured shirts with red spots, and round dove-coloured hats trimmed with magenta ribbon. The Englishmen wore white shirts, blue belts, and white caps with blue stripes.

The Australian XVIII was all out for 118. There were six ducks. Griffith bowling round arm took 7/30 and 'Terrible Billy' Caffyn bowling 'considerable' breaks, took 7/53. When there are 18 wickets to fall, it helps bowling averages.

Mr Stephenson's men, untroubled, made 305, then bundled the XVIII out again once more for 91, this time with ten ducks.

The match did not go the full prescribed three days, so we had a delightful innovation. Messrs Spiers and Pond organised a balloon ascent, the first ever in the colony. The balloon was called 'All England' and it was immense. On the outsides were pictures of Queen Victoria and the English cricketers.

The Melbourne Gas Company supervised the inflation and while a band played 'See the Conquering Hero Comes', off it went. The aviators aboard were Mr and Mrs Brown and Mr Deane. Their cruise was most notable. They hovered over the Botanic gardens, Hawthorn, Richmond and, after 35 minutes, came down in Albert Street, East Melbourne.

Mr Stephenson said he enjoyed the cricket match very much and there is no doubt more teams are likely to come from England in the future. Roger Iddison, a professional, who made 31 runs, commented on the Australians: 'Well, o'i doant think mooch of their play, but they are a wonderful lot of drinking men'.

Thoroughly beaten by the Englishmen

Bridge Disaster Divides Hobart

6 JANUARY 1975

Hobart is a divided city today. The *Lake Illawara*, a 10 000 tonne bulk carrier rammed the Tasman Bridge over the Derwent River. The ship sank and 70 metres of the bridge crashed into the river.

Five people, including four seamen, are reported dead, and 15 missing. Inspector A.D. Parker, officer-in-charge of the Bellerive Police Station, said at least three cars plunged into the river when a whole span collapsed. 'God only knows how many people were in those cars' he said. 'They could have been filled with women and children. We do not know how many people we have rescued. The area around the bridge and the sunken ship is filled with light craft, a lot of private boat owners rushed to the scene to help. It is pitch black out there and we are trying to get some lights but the visibility is terribly bad.'

Frank Manley, 44, of Cambridge, his wife Sylvia, daughter, Sharon, and brother-in-law, John Fitzgerald, had the most terrifying escape. Manley said:

I thought I saw a car broken down and I slowed down. My wife screamed 'There's no bridge!' I hit the brakes, but it was too late and we went over the edge. The centre of the car grounded and we just hung there. It's a two door car, I opened my door looked down and there was nothing but a sheer drop. I scrambled out with my back pressed against the pillar of the car then ran down the road, screamed at a bloke in a yellow car. He was going too fast, he slammed into the back of a car beside us and pushed him over the edge so that his car was hanging like ours.

Police however do not really know how many cars went over the edge. Reports have come in about cars that have not returned home, but there is nothing they can do until ten navy and police divers have covered the area.

What will Hobart do now? It is divided in half. Police have received calls from milkmen and breadcarters asking how they can supply their customers in East Hobart. Forty thousand people are all but cut off from supplies and their work. Bellerive, Montague Bay, Robe Bay, Lindesfarne and Risdon are fast-growing dormitory suburbs.

The only alternative now is to travel by ferry or a 51-kilometre, winding gravel road, which the Government has decided will take traffic only one way.

The police have said there is one blessing — the accident took place at 9.45 p.m. on a Sunday night. One can only speculate on the number of deaths had it been at a peak hour or on a Saturday night.

Cars teetering on the edge

The Garbage Symphony

7 JANUARY 1907

Mrs Webb slates Sydney

We have become very irritated by visitors who come to our beautiful cities and make disaparaging remarks. In 1898 Sidney and Beatrice Webb, those English intellectuals, visited Sydney. They talked of us with awful contempt. They found Sydney inhabited by a lower-middle-class population, aggressive in manner and blatant in dress. We have now received Mrs Webb's *Australian Diary*, and she describes her visit to the Sydney Lord Mayor and Council:

There seated in his robes, sat a large, red-faced, black-bearded man with an expression of worried stupidity, fingering the printed report he was about to lay before the Council with ardent nervousness. He was illiterate in speech and awkward in manner, and extraordinarily muddled in answering our enquiries; an aroma of whisky scented the air...The aldermen were the same sort as the Mayor, heavy common persons; ripples of whisky laden atmosphere reached us whenever one of them moved or spoke.

At one o'clock we adjourned for lunch, an elaborate 'dinner' with a plentiful supply of wine. I tried to extract information from the Mayor, but all I got was an assurance that he was a very rich man, and that he had no occasion to bother himself about the affairs of the city.

But today's copy of the *Australian Star* I find disturbing. Jack London, the famous American author, is in Sydney and he writes:

I live in a flat on Phillip Street. The sidewalks are cement. The streets hard macadam, the buildings on either side are of brick and iron. The acoustics of Phillip Street are splendid. Phillip Street is a combined boiler shop and lunatic asylum. I am fairly credulous, but I should never have accepted on mere faith that several garbage men could produce such a vast quantity of unnecessary noise. I am a good sleeper, but morning after morning by four or five o'clock the last shreds of sleep are routed. It has always been my boast that I could sleep anywhere. I have slept in noisy Asiatic cities. I have slept alongside batteries in wartime. I have slept in the black Arctic night while a thousand wolf dogs bayed at the moon. I have slept in the silence of snow and sea, or sweet country and remote peaks. The throbbing roar of great cities is an anaesthetic to me, the 'shouting of a backstay in a gale' is a tender lullaby. I have slept everywhere until I came to Phillip Street.

I know now the licence of brutal thoughts and the lust for blood, the desire to kill. As I lean wan-faced and angry from my window at 5 a.m. and gaze at a certain garbage man.

Oh, yes, we have read *Son of the Wolf* and *Call of the Wild*, unquestionably Sydney's garbage men will be the inspiration for Mr London's next piece of violence.

Mad Jack Berry

8 JANUARY 1878

We are calling today 'Black Wednesday'. Why? You will remember on 6 February 1851, Victoria was set aflame by bushfires, and by 11.00 a.m. the temperature in Melbourne had reached 117 degrees, so we called it 'Black Thursday'.

Black Wednesday is worse. Our Premier, Mr Graham Berry, has just sacked 278 public servants. Mr Berry is an ex-grocer and a radical. He has fought for protection, a land tax for monopolists and, in particular, he has tried to break down the privilege and exclusive power of the upper house, the Legislative Council.

His present aim is to get payment for politicians, an extraordinary move really. Many people believe if you actually pay politicians you will get all sorts of riff raff in Parliament. The Honourable W. Degraves put it very well in the Legislative Council:

> I intend to vote against the Bill and if I have a seat in the House for the next 10 years I will vote against it. I look upon it as nothing more nor less than an encouragement to a parcel of political loafers to come here and do as they please. If we had payment for members I have no doubt we should have political loafers introduced in larger numbers, and they would keep the country in a state of uproar from one year's end to another and I look upon it as a downright attempt to loot the Treasury.

Mr Henry Wrixon MLA said 'Give money to politicians and you get the poor and meansless, who have not succeeded in prosecuting any business successfully'.

Mr Berry, very slyly, slipped payment for members on the end of the Appropriation Bill. The Legislative Assembly passed it but, on 20 December, the Legislative Council rejected it. The members were to get £30 a year.

Mr Berry did not resign or call for an election. If there was no money to be had, he took other measures. He just sacked all these public servants. The 278 include departmental heads, police magistrates, county court judges, coroner and crown prosecutor, architects, gold field wardens...

Sir George Bowen

The *Age* is sympathetic to Mr Berry in his plight, but other leading articles are blistering. They are calling him 'Mad Jack Berry' and 'Jerry Bunkum'.

Melbourne *Punch* so disapproves of this idea of paying members of Parliament, it has produced a song that it calls 'The Lay of the Liberal MLA':

Three hundred a Year!
Three hundred a Year!
What a glorious grab is 300 a year.
To the loafer, and beggar and bankrupt how dear
Is the chance of a clutch of 300 a year.

The Governor, Sir George Bowen, is coming under terrible criticism for agreeing to Mr Berry's action. But I'm worried about all these public servants. They have only discovered their plight this morning. Most of them, I fear, will be destitute, whereas I am sure the unpaid politicians will survive.

The Wonder of 'Listening In'

11 JANUARY 1924

The new craze is 'listening-in' to the wireless. Station 2FC opened yesterday. It is owned by Farmer and Company, hence the FC, and they have it on the roof of Sydney's Farmer's store. Oh, it wasn't the first; 2SB owned by Sydney Broadcasters opened there in the Smith's Weekly building on 23 November last.

But it is expensive fun. You see, you have to buy a wireless, which is sealed to the station, and you pay a licence fee of three guineas. Ten shillings goes to the station, the the rest to the Government. But if you belong to 2BC, it is only 10 shillings. The people who make the wireless sets are subsidising 2BC to encourage you to buy their wireless.

At 2FC they began with an announcement, saying who they were, and then they gave out chimes from tubular bells. This was to help your tuning. Next they gave a complete transmission of the musical comedy, *The Southern Maid*. This was by courtesy of J.C. Williamson and Messrs J. and N. Tait. *The Southern Maid* is the big show at Her Majesty's.

Putting that on was a huge achievement by the wireless engineers. It had never been done before. People heard it quite clearly all over New South Wales.

We are wondering now what the limits are to the wireless. There is a story in the *Sydney Morning Herald* today about Mr A.K. Wright of Scarborough. He reports that on Sunday he tuned in to California. He has just an ordinary two-valve set, and he heard quite distinctly the music from a pianola and a baritone solo. The time was between 8.30 and 10.30 p.m. and there was an announcement that it was the California Electric company.

According to the *Herald*, many leading experimenters were inclined to regard the reception somewhat sceptically, but they refrained from contradicting Mr Wright's report. Mr Wright plans to contact the Electric Company and gain confirmation. If he does, this will be not only an Australian record but a world record for wireless telephony.

The *Herald* says experts are puzzled. It is not uncommon for people with quite ordinary equipment to gain reception over long distances, even with crystal sets. But they are puzzled how it happens on odd occasions. One night the reception is fine, the next you get nothing. Why is this so? asks the *Herald*. No authority can give a satisfactory explanation.

Some wireless experimenters in New Zealand have also listened in to programs from America's West Coast, but then they are closer than we are.

The prospect is really wonderful. New stations are coming on line soon; 3AR in Melbourne and 6WF Perth. So far about 1400 licences have been issued, but it's ridiculous that you have to pay a licence for each station. How are they going to police these sealed sets? Half the magazines are now giving instructions on how to make your own crystal set.

Oh Woe! A Cash Amateur

12 JANUARY 1952

Frank Sedgman

An unbelievable situation has arisen over young Frank Sedgman. There is a national panic that he might be planning to turn professional.

We have had national tennis heroes before — Brookes, Patterson, Crawford, Quist and Bromwich — but nobody to equal 'Sedge'. It was Sedgman who was the star when we won back the Davis Cup in 1950 for the first time since 1939. Then just after Christmas at Sydney's White City courts, we had the real sensation.

In the first rubber, Mervyn Rose lost to Vic Seixas in straight sets; then Sedgman evened matters by beating Ted Schroeder 6–4, 6–3, 4–6, 6–4. Sedgman and McGregor easily won the doubles, but Rose went down again in straight sets to Schroeder. So the score was two-all with Sedgman to play Seixas. The *Herald*, in Melbourne, reported that the city utterly stopped work. Everybody was listening to the radio. Collins St was jammed. There was one fellow sitting with his portable in the gutter, and he had a huge crowd all around, ears bent down.

Well, Sedge won 6–4, 6–2, 6–2. The comments: one paper said of it, 'One of the most magnificent exhibitions of tennis ever seen in any country'. Another said Sedgman was 'one of the best players who ever lived'. But there were rumours everywhere that he was going to turn pro.

Sedgman is getting married next week, so Melbourne's *Sun News Pictorial* had an idea, to

give him a wedding present. They wrote: 'Ping, Ping, Ping, Ping — Everyone who listened to the Davis Cup matches must remember these sounds. And the final ping was always Sedgman's. All Australia is grateful to him'.

Donations flowed in. The Lord Mayor, Sir Thomas Nettlefold; Gladys Moncrieff, the singer; Edgar Coles of Coles Stores; John Wren; Harry Hopman; Bill Dooley, the bookmaker; all sent cheques. The City of Brunswick staged its own special show at the Padua Theatre. Outside in the foyer there was a big placard: 'Local Boy Makes Good. Let's Buy Him a Wedding Present'.

There have been cries of pain from New York. The *New York World Telegram and Sun* has demanded an investigation into Sedgman's amateur status. It wrote:

Oh yez, Oh yez, we have our hassles over eligibility, expense accounts and 'what is an amateur anyway?' over here in the good old USA. But in the land of the marsupials and the duckbill platypus, Down Under, things are more simple — for example, the case of Frank 'Stirling' Sedgman, the world's greatest amateur tennis player pound for pound... Have you made your contribution to the Keep Frank an Amateur wedding?

Sir Norman Brooks thinks the fuss of no consequence, nor do the rest of us. Let's start a fund of Frank's honeymoon.

Victoria Ablaze

13 JANUARY 1939

The most appalling bushfires in the history of Victoria swept the State today.

Thirty-six people have been reported burned to death, at least 35 are missing and many more in hospital.

Whole townships have been wiped out, thousands of cattle and sheep have perished, and the damage to timber and property runs to many millions of pounds.

The worst area was in the Matlock Forest. There 15 men and one woman died. Borne across the mountain tops on a tornado-like wind, fire demolished five mills in the area — James Fitzpatrick's where the 15 men died; Yelland's where the woman died; Porter's and W.P. Fitzpatrick's, which had been evacuated.

An *Age* reporter has telephoned:

Courage almost beyond belief was displayed by the four women who survived the disaster at Yelland's. Aided by the men they dashed through the flame from a brick house when the roof collapsed and they were forced to stand on the fire-blasted ground until the heat subsided sufficiently for them to find other shelter.

The entire company at Yelland's assembled in one brick home. Through the windows they watched terror stricken as fire struck first the wooden home of Mr H. Henderson, managing director of Yelland's, then they heard their roof cracking overhead. Smashing the windows the men seized the women and children and threw them into the open, except Mrs Maynard, a cook, who was in a state of collapse and refused to leave.

There was no time to save Mrs Maynard, she died. Four children have been burned to death at Barongarook, 9 miles from Colac. It is believed a mother and her baby have been trapped on Mt Hotham. At 7 p.m. Mr D. O'Connor received a call from a woman at Hotham Heights hostel. She said 'The house is on fire; I must save my baby'. A scream followed . . . and then silence. Every effort is being made

Omeo is devastated

to communicate with the hostel, but the line is down and the hills are ringed with fire.

At Bairnsdale, workmen and refugees from Cobungra Station, including seven children, plunged into the Victoria River and remained there until rescued. Ernest Richard, 30, set out on horseback to go to his wife who had recently returned home with a baby. He was overcome by flames. He and his horse were burned to death.

Erica township is surrounded by flames. More than 50 houses have burned around Warrandyte but the main township may have been saved. Fifteen fire fighters are missing near Stawell. Sale is totally blacked out in a pall of smoke. The Christmas Hills have been devastated, and Mansfield, Warburton, and Healesville are all in peril. The township of Lorne, so far, is unharmed, but the area known as little Colac is right in the line of fire, and the swing bridge over the mouth of the Erskine River has burned.

Melbourne broke all records for heat today. From early morning the city simmered under a smoke-clouded sky. Early risers gasped for breath, then got a taste of what was to come. At 12.50 p.m. in the shelter of the Weather Bureau the temperature was 114.1 degrees. This beat Tuesday's record of 113.5 degrees.

A Body Blow to Cricket

14 JANUARY 1933

Bill Woodfull's bat knocked form his hand by Larwood

We are wondering what will happen, whether there is any future for Australian cricket. This whole business of bodyline or leg theory bowling has come to a crisis in Adelaide.

It is all because of Bradman. The Englishmen want to win at any costs. In the Third Test at Adelaide, the Englishmen made 341 runs. On Saturday Fingleton was out to Allen for only one run. Then on came Larwood. He hit Woodfull a tremendous blow. The ball was just over the heart and it if it had been any closer it might have killed him.

The crowd shrieked and hooted. It took Woodfull several minutes to recover. But did Jardine decide to ease his mayhem tactics? No, indeed! When Larwood started his run for the first ball of his next over, Jardine stopped him. He moved the off-side fieldsmen over to the legside for the bodyline attack. The crowd went mad. Even the quiet Adelaide gentlemen in the members stand were hollering abuse. It wouldn't have taken much for the crowd to have jumped the fence.

Bradman went out for just 8 runs, and Woodfull was hit several times again until he was bowled by Allen for 22.

Every time Larwood touched the ball they hooted him. But the climax came when the English team managers, Pelham Warner, and Lionel Palairet, called on the Australian dressing room. Woodfull had taken his shower and he was receiving treatment for his bruises. There was a livid red mark right under his heart.

Warner said 'We have come to say how sorry we are and to offer our sympathy'.

Woodfull replied 'I don't want to see you, Mr Warner. There are two teams out there. One is trying to play cricket and the other is not. The game is too good to be spoilt. It is time some people got out of it'.

You can imagine the play this got in the London press. But Larwood is not bowling leg theory all the time. When he bowls off theory he gets a cheer from the crowd. But today things have gone from bad to worse. Oldfield tried to hook Larwood. He was actually bowling off theory at the time. The ball hit him right on the forehead and he went to hospital.

The Adelaide crowd went mad. They hooted Larwood, counted him out, gave him derisive slow handclaps.

Now the Cricket Board of Control has sent a cable to the Marylebone Cricket Club which says:

Bodyline bowling assuming such proportions as to menace the best interests of the game, making protection of the body by the batsman the main consideration. This is causing intensely bitter feeling between the players, as well as injury. Unless stopped at once it is likely to upset the friendly relations existing between England and Australia.

There has been no reaction as yet from the MCC, but one asks how can cricket sustain this sort of thing. Perhaps it might be better, in future, if Australia played England at safer pastimes, like bridge or ping pong.

A Woman Hanged

15 JANUARY 1894

Mrs Knorr

At 10 a.m. precisely, Mrs Frances Knorr was hanged at the Melbourne Gaol today. Her crime? She was a baby murderer.

Mothers who did not want their babies took them to her, paid her money as a foster mother, then she put them to death. It's a common enough crime these days. Two years ago there was a case in Sydney. John Makin and his wife Sara were convicted of murdering 12 babies. They hanged him. His wife got 12 years.

There has been a big fuss about this one with some very emotional stories in the press. We haven't hanged a woman in Victoria since 1863.

There have been demonstrations by anti-hanging groups and a particularly strong petition to the Premier, Mr Patterson, signed by ten women. They called the hanging an 'abominable, fiendish injustice'. The evidence was circumstantial and the crime due to poverty and the struggle for existence. They claimed men had the entire management of the law and it was the acts of men that caused starvation.

Through nearly all yesterday, Frances Knorr lay huddled in her cell in a state of collapse, hardly speaking a word. However she regained her composure in the evening.

A *Herald* reporter witnessed the execution this morning. He described it as a fearful and horrifying spectacle. First he heard sobs coming from the condemned cell where she was attended by the Reverends Scott and Wilson. Voices rose softly then impressively. She was singing her favourite hymn, 'Safe in the Arms of Jesus'.

There was silence. It was thought Mrs Knorr had collapsed or would refuse to move. But she emerged with a firm confident step, the attending doctor, Dr Shields on one side, matron on the other. She looked very pale, but was quite composed. It was thought her hair might have been shaved. This was the custom with the men, but her hair was just pulled back.

One of the warders murmured 'Surely there will be reprieve any minute'. He could not believe Mr Patterson would allow a woman to be hanged. But no reprieve came.

The sheriff asked her 'Have you anything to say?'.

'Yes. The Lord is with me. I do not fear what men may do to me. I have peace, perfect peace.'

The hangmen put a noose around her neck and a drawstring was fastened to the bottom of her dress to prevent ballooning when she dropped. Immediately after the bolt was shot, there was a sob, a moan, then a shriek and a series of hysterical groans.

The matron who had attended Mrs Knorr and tried to comfort her was so shocked at the dump of the body she fainted and, according to the *Herald* reporter, moaned pitifully for several minutes.

The body hung at the end of the rope for the prescribed time, at the expiration of which the rope was cut. Then the body was removed to the mortuary to await the formal inquest.

Clipping Coupons

18 JANUARY 1944

Now we have meat rationing. It started yesterday. Another damned coupon to be acquired, observed, clipped, and moaned over.

Senator Keane, the Customs Minister, the God who presides over these things, allows us $1\frac{1}{2}$ pounds to 4 pounds a week, according to the type of meat we buy. If you are under nine years old, you get a half-ration.

Poultry, rabbits, bacon, ham, tripe, brains, and pigs' heads are not rationed.

I suppose we will survive, but it is just another agony which supposedly will help us to defeat Adolph Hitler. The first was petrol rationing. That came in October 1940 and the ration tickets give us enough to drive a miserly 16 miles a week. Our family has a gas producer, which runs on charcoal. The car coughs along as if it has a severe case of emphysema.

You have to light the gas producer early in the morning, a frightful business. There's a story about a young female who set out from Adelaide as a platinum blonde and arrived in Melbourne as a brunette. The gas producers are expensive. You'd never get one under £70, then you'd wish you'd never bought it.

Clothes rationing and shoe rationing came in June 1942. Most of us are wearing the Victory suit in honour of Mr Dedman, the Minister for War Organisation. Frightful thing: two buttons, no cuffs, no waistcoat, no buttons on the sleeves, hardly any lining, and if you go for a Victory job, it costs 38 coupons out of your annual ration of 112 coupons.

He's tough, Mr Dedman. Women are now being advised to paint their legs rather than wear stockings. Tea rationing began in July 1942, but it would be better if they had beer and whisky rationing. At least you could get some then. If you want tobacco or cigarettes you have to love the man at the local kiosk. My aunt claims she has now bought 2000 packets of Life Savers just so the man at the kiosk will keep supplying her with cigarettes.

Sugar rationing came in August 1942. You have a whole book of coupons. Every time you go into a shop you have to cut out the wretched things. Just another item to lose, another thing you have to find in the morning.

Meat rationing, however, is the last straw.

The butchers are furious. Amstrong has a lovely cartoon in today's *Argus*. It shows a butcher and a customer crying in each others arms. 'Coupons is offal' says the butcher. 'And no coupons is offal' says the customer.

A Sydney butcher has put a sign up in his window: 'Wanted — One Thousand Men To Build an Asylum for Mad Butchers'.

This will lead to all sorts of black market activities. All the week-end there was a mad rush to butcher shops to get last supplies. There have been warnings, too. The betting is that there won't be a horse left in Perth, Adelaide, Hobart or Melbourne. Every nag will be slaughtered to go into sausages.

There are suggestions, too, that like the Poms, soon we will be eating whale meat.

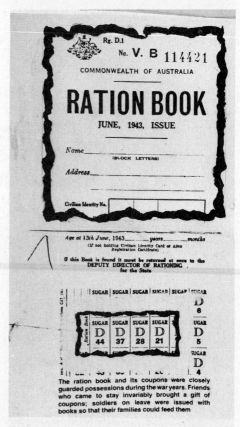

Ration books during the war

12

Plane Travels Faster than Horse or Automobile

19 JANUARY 1911

Mr P. Hammond, chief pilot of the British and Colonial Aeroplane Company, has been making some excellent flights in his Bristol machine. There has been talk of little else here in Perth this past fortnight.

He challenged, by advertisement, to beat any racehorse or motor automobile over a distance of 5 miles, and convincingly won.

His Bristol aeroplane has two wings and a small, but powerful, Gnome engine, which is installed immediately behind Mr Hammond, with a propeller. The engine makes a noise far greater than any motor in full blast, and one can hear it for miles about.

He made two flights on 7 January at Belmont Park racetrack at 7 o'clock, a time chosen to avoid the wind. A small army of motorists, cyclists and others went there to witness the event. There were crowds with field glasses out in backyards and on every hill top.

Mr Hammond gave a wave of his hand, the engine started immediately and his little aeroplane dashed across the turf at express speed and leapt into the air.

The *West Australian* reporter was most lyrical:

Horses leisurely munching grass quickly pricked up their ears as they saw the machine and galloped in all directions. Birds of the air also took fright and flitted out of sight as they saw the Bristol with a human figure seated in it.

A finished pilot he got the machine safely over the journey on which he had directed by the application of a brake like apparatus and with the movement of an eagle swooping down on its prey he made his descent at much the same spot from which he started. Among the spectators was Mrs Hammond, who watched her husband's flights through space and his return among the ordinary mortals who have not sipped of the pleasure of flying with a feeling of feminine pride that could not be hidden even behind a veil to protect an English complexion from the sun's hot rays.

On the second flight, Mr Hammond flew to a remarkable 1000 feet. He tried again the next day with the idea of flying immediately after the

Sir Gerald Strickland

race meeting, but winds were gusting at 20 mph. Many race goers were unnecessarily angry and demanded their money back.

But several days later, Mr Hammond went to Fremantle and his flying was witnessed by His Excellency the Governnor, Sir Gerald Strickland, the Earl and Countess of Harrowby and Lady Frances Ryan. Our *West Australian* reporter said Mr Hammond amply proved to the Governor the possibility of human flight and the excellence of his machine. At times he flew close to 60 mph and there is no question that anything on rail or road could have exceeded his speed. To prove the stability of the Bristol, on one occasion he actually had it at an angle of 45 degrees.

He flew all around the Belmont and Maylands districts and soared above the Canning Bridge. Upon his return, Lady Frances Ryan 'paid him the pretty compliment of asking him to stand for a photograph'.

Yesterday he dismantled his aeroplane and he is arranging its transport to Melbourne. Mr Hammond said he would look into the possibility of actually flying from Melbourne to Sydney, a feat nobody else has even contemplated.

Last Ride for Captain Moonlite

20 JANUARY 1880

'Captain Moonlite'

George Scott, alias Captain Moonlite, was hanged along with his accomplice, Thomas Rogan, at the Darlinghurst Jail this morning.

Was there ever such a man. He claimed that he fought with Garibaldi's red shirts in Italy, and was wounded in the battle against Maori tribesmen in the Waikato war.

He was born in Ireland in 1842, the son of a Church of England Minister. He arrived in Sydney in 1867 and, with forged letters, became friends with the famous churchman, Dr John Dunmore Lang. He was so charming and glib, everybody trusted him. Next he turned up as a lay preacher at Egerton near Bacchus Marsh.

This nice lay preacher, dressed in a mask, robbed the local bank of £697 in notes, and gold worth 503 pounds. The manager at the Union Bank, Ludwig Brunn, immediately recognised the voice.

'Why, Mr Scott, surely you're taking the joke too far'.

'Who's Mr Scott?' Scott roared, 'I'm Captain Moonlite'.

So the name stuck, and even though he almost pinned the crime on Brunn, eventually the police hounded him down, and he was tried before Judge Redmond Barry. His eloquence was something to behold. 'I appeal to God and my country' said he 'that I am the victim of circumstances arising from a base conspiracy. I solemnly appeal to the God of Heaven, as I pass from this dock to my living tomb, that I am not guilty'.

Judge Barry was unimpressed and gave him ten years. He was out in seven and for a time he gave public lectures on prison reform and the horrors of Pentridge. But lectures started to become dull stuff because already he had a rival in Ned Kelly. On 14 November 1879, with a gang of four young men, he raided Wantabadgery Station between Wagga and Gundagai.

The station was under seige. Anyone who came near was herded into the living room, until 30 people were taken prisoner. The eloquent Captain Moonlite never stopped talking. He got the station manager, William Baynes, down on his knees and threatened to shoot him through the head, while the tearful women pleaded for his life.

Falconer MacDonald, one of the station owners, managed to slip away and inform the police. Five troopers arrived and they called on Moonlite to surrender. 'Surrender be damned' he said. 'Come on and fight.' There was a great shoot out in which 120 shots were fired. One trooper, Constable Bowen, died of wounds, and two of the bushrangers were killed.

At the trial, Moonlite pleaded for postponement on the grounds he wasn't getting a fair trial: 'I require time to prepare my defence, the press has teemed me with abuse. Every penny-a-liner, every little writer who itched for notoriety has heaped abuse on me'.

But he got nowhere. Judge Windeyer sentenced Scott and Rogan to death. The *Sydney Morning Herald* thought the sentence entirely appropriate.

If there is at times a danger of extreme severity in dealing with criminals, there is at times a danger on the side of leniency. Under the old system mercy was seldom accorded to criminals, but in place of this there is now a feeble humanitarianism which sometimes thinks of nothing but mercy.

So the hanging took place today, and Mr McGill, the celebrated phrenologist, took casts of the deceased's heads. He commented:

Moonlite's head was so peculiarly formed that it was impossible he could speak the truth, or be honest; that it was devoid of all moral courage and hence would keep up to the last what he once said. . .he had such a love of life and its pleasures he cared not how he gained his ends.

A Hollow Affair for Burke and Wills

21 JANUARY 1863

We buried Burke and Wills here in Melbourne today.

It was a solemn, deeply moving, but in many ways awful occasion. The *Argus* claims it was a hollow affair; a useless piece of pageantry designed to glorify the Exploration committee rather than the explorers.

After the tragedy of their terrible expedition, Alfred Howitt brought back the bones of Burke and Wills just after Christmas. Their remains lay in state at the Royal Society from 31 December until this morning. Everyone went up there to pay their respects: the Governor, Sir Henry Barkly and Lady Barkly; Lady Bowen; Baron Von Mueller; the Lord Mayor; the Premier; Mr King, the survivor, still terribly thin looking and weak, just stood there and wept. Mr Burke's old nanny was another visitor.

But there's a lot of anger in the town, that it was a class affair and they didn't bring back the bones of old Charley Gray. You'll remember when the expedition was on its way through Swan Hill, Mr Burke befriended Charley Gray — who was a rouseabout at one of the pubs — and asked him to join the expedition. Charley died two months before Burke and Wills. Just a common man, nobody wanted him for the great funeral.

Today was hot in Melbourne, not infernally hot like it can be, but dusty and uncomfortable. We have never seen a funeral like it. It started from the Royal Society with the solemn firing of guns, went down Nicholson Street to Parliament House and through the city. The procession was so long it reached from Parliament House down Bourke Street all the way to Elizabeth Street.

There were units of cavalry, infantry and police, all magnificent in their uniforms. The band of the Castlemaine Rifles played the 'Dead March in Saul'. There were no orders put out, but all the shops were closed out of respect to the explorers, and the shop fronts were draped with black banners and black crepe.

The crowd, there has never been anything like it in Melbourne. They were up on buildings, on the top of Parliament House, and there were so many people they came off the footpath on to the road, leaving a narrow path for the carriages.

The funeral car was designed to resemble the huge affair used in the procession of the Duke of Wellington. The *Argus* says caustically, it is a poor reflex of that magnificent work of art, but the four wheels are bronzed and the panelling of the car descends in graceful curves almost to the ground.

The inscriptions on the coffins say simply: 'Robert O'Hara Burke, died 30th June 1861. Aged 40. William John Wills, Died 30th June, 1861. Aged 27.'

The burial took place at the Church of England section of the Melbourne General Cemetery, just near Sir Charles Hotham's monument. With the utterance 'Dust to dust, ashes to ashes', the coffins were lowered into the vault. The crowd of 40 000 people uncovered their heads.

Tonight there was a public meeting at St George's Hall, which was addressed by the Governor and dignitaries of the Exploration committee. It was a rowdy affair. The distinguished speakers frequently were interrupted with cries of 'Where's Charley Gray?'.

Everybody knew where he was, precisely where King and Wills buried him in the hard earth at Massacre Creek.

Mr Burke and Mr Wills

Stuart Crosses the Continent

22 JANUARY 1863

John McDouall Stuart

Yesterday John McDouall Stuart returned to Adelaide in triumph after, at last, crossing the Continent both ways.

An extraordinary coincidence really. Stuart returns in triumph to Adelaide on precisely the same day that they hold the funeral for Burke and Wills in Melbourne.

Adelaide is calling it a triumph, but Stuart is an incredible sight. He is only 48, yet he is a human skeleton, a white-haired old man and almost blind with scurvy. Until the party reached Mt Margaret, he was so weak they had to carry him on a stretcher slung between two horses.

I guess you have to be mad or at least driven by some insane urge to do what Stuart did. It is said that he was a drunkard, an alcoholic, that he would even drink the alcohol out of his scientific instruments, his craving was so awful.

A surveyor by calling, he has made many exploratory trips to the Centre. In March three years ago, he set out with two men and 13 horses, found the centre of the Continent, planted a flag and called it Mount Stuart. He then travelled another 200 miles north, but couldn't get further because of the scrub. He suffered from scurvy so badly he lost the sight of one eye.

That would be enough to stop normal humans, but not Mr Stuart. In January 1961, the South Australian Government was worried because Burke and Wills had already set off to cross the land mass, so away Stuart went again. This time he nearly made it, but almost out of food, clothes in shreds, he turned back. Well, he had only returned two months when in October 1861 he tried again.

This time he succeeded. Yesterday was a public holiday. The buildings were covered with flags and bunting. Crowds lined the streets. There was a great procession, a cavalcade, which included members of Parliament, members of the Demonstration committee, backers of the expedition and, of course, Mr Stuart and his party.

The *Adelaide Advertiser* today says it all:

It is not merely the fact that Stuart has crossed from shore to shore, which entitles him to be placed among the heroes of discovery; — of still greater significance is the fact that he, and he alone, wrested from the interior its long hidden secret. What was the map of Australia in our school days? It was a vast blank, having no line traced upon it? The interior of Australia was unknown. Was it a region of burning mountains, a desert of shifting sands? Was it a sea, or a lake, or a forest? Was it the domain of wild beasts was it the home of savage tribes? Did the rains of heaven fall upon it, or was it doomed to eternal sterility and drought? Who could answer these questions? No one; but Stuart said he would go and see; and he went and he returned to tell.

Stuart was modest in his comments. He said yesterday:

I have received more commendation than I deserve. I did the best in my power. For five years with the assistance of my friends I have been endeavouring to penetrate to the coast. I determined to do or die. When I left the northwest coast I was at death's door. I dared not tell any of my party how ill I was...I thank the Almighty Giver of all Good, that he in his infinite goodness and mercy, gave me the strength to overcome the grim and hoary-headed king of terrors.

Further reading: *The Heroic Journey of John McDouall* Stuart, W. Hardman.

Duke Makes Sport in the Colonies

25 JANUARY 1868

His Royal Highness, Prince Alfred, the Duke of Edinburgh, 23 years old and the second son of Queen Victoria, has been having a fine old time on his tour of the colonies. He arrived here as captain of *HMS Galatea*. Rumour has it that accompanied by Melbourne's Chief of Police, Captain Standish, and other dignitaries, the Duke visited the Saddling Paddock at the Theatre Royal.

Begging your pardon, but everybody calls it Saddling Paddock because that is where the most notorious women of Melbourne gather. It is a small bar presided over by a man, and it is here the girls gather for their pick-ups. On no account would you ever take your wife or daughter to such a place.

From there they went to Sarah Fraser's house of ill repute in Stephen Street. According to the police reporter, J.M.Forde, one young lady, one of the most handsome, followed the Duke to Sydney and set up house in Castlereagh Street.

The Duke has also visited a public ball in Melbourne's Exhibition building. Is this proper? Bishop Perry immediately pointed out that the love of balls is indicative of a poor condition of Christian health. The theatre, balls and racing are on the same level as drunkenness, fornication and racing.

However, best of all, His Royal Highness has enjoyed shooting; killing animals. In South Australia the Governor took him to the Government Farm in the Adelaide Hills. The ideal situation for possum shooting was a moonlight night. One looked up through the trees, silhouetted the possum against the moon and fired. The Duke shot 52 possums, 43 of which he brought home. The rest he left in the trees.

He went on numerous kangaroo shoots, but one of his more spectacular expeditions was to Mr Thomas Austin's property at Barwon Park. Mr Austin introduced the rabbit to Victoria and is now doing a splendid job by breeding them in cages. The Duke killed 86 on his first day, and found it such good fun he asked for a second shoot the following morning, thereby entirely upsetting his carefully planned tour of the Western District.

A dozen guns went out and together they killed 1000 rabbits. The Duke used two Wesley Richards' breech loaders, and he killed 416 of the animals. In one place where the rabbits were trapped in a corner, he shot 68 in ten minutes. He had a man standing behind him, who loaded while he shot, but even so the guns became so hot they blistered the hand. Finally he could hold them only by the stock.

Sydney *Punch* comments today:
> The Duke of Auld Reekie
> Pray, don't think me cheeky
> To nickname is one of my habits—
> Has been out with his gun,
> And shot every one of 416 rabbits.
>
> 'Tis with certainty stated,
> They died quite elated,
> Being shot by a live prince, you see;
> And I hear 'tis said now,
> That the Upper Crust vow
> Their chief diet shall rabbit pie be.

First Fleet Anchors in Sydney Cove

26 JANUARY 1788

The First Fleet in Sydney Cove

Governor Phillip and the first fleet arrived today at Sydney Cove. Probably it will receive little notice in London, nothing like the cheers of a victory against Spain or even the eclat that followed the voyages of Captain Cook.

But it was a remarkable achievement. Eight months ago, 11 somewhat indifferent ships set out from Portsmouth. They carried 1360 people, sailed 5021 leagues, visited both the American and African continents, came in touch with every kind of disease and pestilence, yet only 32 of the entire complement died since leaving home.

As Captain David Collins pointed out, many of the convicts were in wretched health before they left Britain. They were better off below deck than in the streets of London.

Yet survival was not easy. Morale was at its lowest leaving the Cape of Good Hope. No more comfort, no more luxury, only coarse fare and hardship and the prospect of hostile natives. Ralph Clark, second officer of the marines, wrote in his diary: 'If I thought I should have been so unhappy at leaving my family behind I should never have come away from them...all the gains in earth should never have made me leave them'.

Christmas was particularly full of longing and nostalgia. The First Fleet was battling round Van Dieman's Land in ferocious gales. Plum pudding did not sit at all well. There had been high hopes with the last voyage across the Indian Ocean. The ships had been loaded with horses, sheep, pigs, fowl, all sorts of plants, including exotics from Brazil. Captain Phillip's cabin was like Kew gardens. The humans might have survived, but many of the animals perished in the storms.

The first ships arrived at Botany Bay on 18 January. Botany Bay, even from the ship, looked flat, marshy, bereft of fresh water; as dreary as Gravesend. Phillip went on, found Port Jackson and then ordered the convoy to move north.

The entrance to Port Jackson was a revelation, the true approach to a promised land. Governor Phillip, euphoric, called it the finest harbour in the world. A 1000 sail of the line could ride here in perfect security, said he.

There is a nice little cove with deep water, Sydney Cove. Ships can come in so close they can tie up to a tree. The advance party landed early today. Lieutenant William Collins of the Marines took possession in the name of the King. The officers drank the health of Their Majesties in porter. Everyone gave three cheers, and the marines fired a salute.

The troops are choosing flat areas, clearing spaces for tents and huts. Phillip has the best hut. It was prefabricated in London, made entirely of timber and canvas. It is a standard model used by senior officers on many campaigns. It cost £130, truly a tremendous sum.

The troops thought the Australian trees slim and fragile, easy to fell. How wrong they were. Clearly Antipodean timber is composed of iron, and all the tools are blunt on the first day.

Further reading: *Australians to 1788*, Fairfax, Syme and Weldon; *History of Australia I*, C.M.H. Clark.

Mace Disappears during Drunken Freak

28 JANUARY 1893

It's absolutely disgraceful and I don't know how Parliament will ever live this one down. Victoria's Legislative Assembly sat late on 8 October 1891. The Sergeant at Arms took the mace and locked it in an oak box.

It is a beautiful mace, an exact copy of the gold mace in the House of Commons, and it cost 300 pounds. It has been in use since 1866. At 2 p.m. that afternoon, the Clerk of the Assembly discovered the oak box had been broken into with a chisel and the mace had gone. The police were called, but all employees at the House were sworn to silence.

There were no statements from the Speaker, Sir Matthew Davies, and not a word from the police, but as they made their inquiries, soon there were rumours all about town. There had been women up at the House, there had been parties.

The first we heard something was amiss was on 22 October. Melbourne *Punch* said it was an open secret at the House that the mace disappeared after a member had a 'drunken freak'.

A year went by and more papers got into the act. Just before Christmas, *Table Talk* suggested the mace was being kept in a brothel. The *Ballarat Courier* went further:

After many days the joke is leaking out. The mace was not stolen but was taken from Parliament by some festive cusses for a lark, and is even now, so it is freely stated, in a bawdy house in Melbourne, where it is freely exhibited to clients, and where it has been used in low travesties of Parliamentary procedure. The authorities have winked at the scandal and the police have been restrained by those in authority

. . .

The *Courier* added a nice hint for those who knew their brothels. The theft at one house was being 'viewed as a joke equal to anything in Boccacio'. Boccacio House was a wonderful luxurious bawdy house run by Annie Wilson, and very conveniently, it was just over the road from Parliament House.

This story caused a great fuss. On 12 January, Mr Robert Clark, proprietor and publisher of the Ballarat *Courier* was called before the bar of the House. He gave an abject

Victorian Legislative Council mace similar to the one that disappeared

apology. He said the story was untrue and his apology was so red-faced and humble it was embarrassing.

Mr Clark's apology was accepted, but this week Sydney's *Bulletin* says the editor of the *Courier*, Major Wilson, was in the precincts of the House at the time. Had he been called he would have been prepared to assert the truth of the article and have been prepared to let Parliament do its worst. Now the whole matter would remain undisturbed.

So they haven't found the mace, and I doubt if they ever will. It is not surprising that these sort of things happen. There are 43 brothels in Melbourne, and 3000 prostitutes. There are between 23 and 30 brothels in Little Lonsdale Street alone. Fancy ones, like Madame Brussells, go right through from 36 Lonsdale Street to Little Lonsdale. You can leave discreetly by the back entrance.

Nothing would surprise me about Bocaccio House. Last year it had installed one of Melbourne's first telephones. How did they get that?

A Pirate in Melbourne

29 JANUARY 1893

Captain Waddell

It's like something out of a romantic novel. The American States are in the midst of a bloody civil war, and look what happens, a Confederate cruiser, *Shenandoah* has arrived in Port Phillip and the citizens are falling all over the place.

Shenandoah's master, Captain Waddell, is a handsome six-footer from North Carolina. Had Prince Albert himself arrived from Buckingham Palace, the social lights of Melbourne couldn't have done more fawning.

Shenandoah sailed from the Cape of Good Hope. On the way Waddell sank and burned 11 of President Lincoln's ships. As he did so he took prisoners, and the best cabins on the *Shenandoah* have been occupied by captains' wives.

There is a big difference of opinion. The *Age* is thundering. It accuses the *Shenandoah* of being nothing more than a pirate, preying on peacefully voyaging ships of the American Republic, and filling the pockets of the crew with prize money.

The *Argus* thinks very differently and, one suspects, has the sympathy of most Melburnians who look upon the South as the underdog. It says:

'The United States is a Government which has kept no faith with her enemies and has broken every promise to its friends — a Government which under the pretext of a Crusade against slavery, has committed crimes against civilisation more detestable than any slavery'.

Mr Blanchard, the U.S. Consul, is furious and has protested to the Governor, Sir Charles Darling. But the *Shenandoah* is anchored just a few minutes row from the pier at Sandridge. Everything that can float, every little sailboat, has been out to inspect her. One gentleman, far from young, sailed up to the *Shenandoah*, then made a mad leap aboard, whereupon he declared he, too, was a Confederate.

Every licensed boat has been made available to run a courier service. There has been a stiff breeze out on the Bay. A lady and two gentlemen were in a whale boat. They were rounding *Shenandoah's* stern when the wind caught them and they capsized. The men were helped on board, but the lady went off with her rescuers. She felt she was not a presentable sight in her dripping crinoline.

Captain Waddell threw his ship open to the public and on Sunday the Victorian Railways put on special trains. The *Argus* reported that 7074 people went to Sandridge by train. As they left the vessel, they gave it hearty cheers, showing they were all for the Southern cause.

Captain Waddell and his crew have been invited to Ballarat for a special dinner and, would you believe, there is a private dinner at the Melbourne Club, attended by Judges of the Supreme and County Court. Captain Waddell and his officers were guests of honour.

The *Age* again is angry. It says:
That the soft headed flunkeys who are recognised as leaders of the Melbourne Club are capable of any misdemeanor against common sense and good taste, there can be no doubt. Success to the Confederate cause will, of course, be drunk in gin cocktails which the gentlemanly pirates are said to be good at brewing.

Under the terms of Victoria's neutrality, *Shenandoah* is supposed to be here for only 24 hours to gather provisions. The way things are shaping it could be here for ever.

Further reading: *Rebel Down Under*, Cyril Pearl.

FEBRUARY

John Pascoe Fawkner:
an incredible colonial

Race Riots in Kalgoorlie

1 FEBRUARY 1934

We have just seen some of the worst riots in the history of West Australia.

The truth is the local gold miners in Kalgoorlie are not keen on foreigners, never have been. These past few years many Italians and Yugoslavs have moved into town. They are keen, they are young, and they work very hard.

On Australia Day, of all days, there was a fist fight between a local miner and an Italian barman. The miner hit his head on a concrete gutter, was knocked unconscious and died later.

For two days we have had riots. Squads of special police have come up from Perth and, Kalgoorlie, half-wrecked, looks as if it has been in a civil war.

The miners attacked the camp where the foreign miners have been living; one Yugoslav was shot and killed and several wounded. They have been through Kalgoorlie, and any business premises owned by a foreigner has been either burned or wrecked.

The rioting began up at the west end of Hannan Street in the places with the sweet names, Home From Home Hotel and the All Nations Boarding House. Both establishments have been burned to the ground, looted and destroyed.

The mob swarmed into the Rex Cafe, owned by Mr G. Kalafatas, and destroyed the interior beyond repair: broke the refrigerators to pieces, and smashed all the furniture. They smashed the window of the jewellery shop next door; wrecked the Kalgoorlie Wine Saloon, and threw a piano out into the street.

They set the York Hotel on fire, and while the Kalgoorlie Fire Brigade was battling with the flames, they set alight the Oriental. At one stage there was the danger the entire business block would go up in one blaze.

The worst feature has been the looting, the pillaging, the stealing. There are smashed bottles, broken plate glass, china, linen, broken pieces of chairs and tables, glass, remnants of boxes of chocolates, and debris all over the footpaths. The pavement is stained with wine, and heady with the smell of spilled liquor.

Some of the Italians, Greeks and Yugoslavs have lost everything they possess in the fires. The rioters carried a large iron safe out of the Kalgoorlie Wine Saloon, and it is still unknown where it went. The owners claim it contained 50 pounds.

The *West Australian* reports that hordes of looters swarmed through Kalgoorlie in the early hours of the morning. Some were laden with goods they had taken from destroyed buildings. One man just filled a tablecloth with chocolates and fruit that he took from a wrecked fruit shop. In Hannan Street, for hours, bands of men walked up and down smashing shop windows.

So what will happen now with the mines? The Lake View and Star, the Great Boulder Proprietary, the Boulder Perseverance, the South Kalgurli and the North Kalgurli are all closed. There are 2500 miners working on the Kalgoorlie fields, and of these, about 600 are foreigners.

There was a mass meeting yesterday of about 1000 men. It was quiet, orderly, no fights, but they decided they would not return to work until all foreigners were dismissed.

Further reading: *An Eye Witness History of Australia*, Harry Gardon.

Mr Dean Navigates the Air

2 FEBRUARY 1858

Most people were very sceptical. Dr. William Bland of Sydney, in 1851 designed an 'atmotic', steam-driven, semi-rigid airship in which he proposed to fly from London to Sydney in five days, with a payload of 1½ tons. He exhibited a model at the Crystal Palace in London and the Paris Exhibition. He wrote to Queen Victoria and President Lincoln seeking help, but did not get a reply.

The Frenchman, Pierre Maigre, made an attempt at flight in a balloon from the Sydney Domain, but did not get off the ground. So there was great interest when the *Herald* announced, on Monday, the attempt from Melbourne's Cremorne Gardens. Mr George Coppin, the entrepreneur, imported the balloons and aeronauts at vast cost.

The *Herald* said: 'In order that our readers may be furnished with full particulars, fatal or otherwise, one of the gentlemen of our reporting staff will occupy a seat in the car'.

From 8 a.m. to 5 p.m. the roads were jammed with vehicles, the paths filled with walkers, and the Yarra packed with boats and steam vessels. 'Every eminence from which a view of the gardens could be obtained was dark with human beings' said the *Argus*.

Early in the morning, the balloon was partially inflated with coal gas at the Melbourne Gas Works, conveyed by horse and cart and 80 men to the gardens, then further inflated from Mr Coppin's own gasometer. Alas, due to a fault in a valve, a considerable quantity of gas escaped. So much so, it was possible for only one aeronaut to ascend. Not only did the *Herald* reporter not get a ride, but there was a contenti-ous debate between the visiting aeronauts, Messrs Brown and Dean, as to who would be the first 'to navigate Australia's air'.

Mr Brown argued that it was he who built the balloon. Mr Dean claimed it was he who had the experience. Fortunately Mr Brown graciously gave way to Mr Dean. Meanwhile the huge balloon, nearly 59 feet high, was swaying back and forth in the breeze, as the *Argus* put it, 'impatient to soar into the element'.

At last the signal was given to go, and the machine slowly rose amongst the cheers of the multitude, which were repeated and re-echoed by spectators in more distant localities. As the balloon rose, it went close to buildings at the end of the gardens, but William Dean hastily threw out ballast and it soared up towards the north-west.

Said the *Argus*:

In 20 minutes she had become a mere speck, a homeopathic globule in the far distance, serenely and steadily sailing onwards, as though native to and rejoicing in the buoyant element. Those who had declared that the gift of a fabulous sum of money would not induce them to hazard their lives in such a desperate enterprise, might now be heard speaking of the entire safety of such aerial excursions.

About half past six, the balloon appeared to be coming down somewhere on the other side of Heidelberg. Mr Coppin was offering a reward of £5 to any carter or other person who would convey the balloon back to the Cremorne Gardens.

Can we expect to fly like this?

23

Brisbane Paralysed by General Strike

3 FEBRUARY 1912

Brisbane is paralysed today with 34 unions taking part in a general strike. There have been processions and riots; and the Premier, Mr Denman, has appealed for volunteers to help the police.

A special mounted corps has been formed. As the Brisbane *Courier* puts it: 'Many hundreds of sturdy sons of the soil have left their farms to take a hand in preserving the peace in the capital city. They are coming from many quarters of Southern Queensland, usefully mounted'.

It all began when Mr Badger, chief of the Tramway Company, refused to recognise the Tramways Union, and dismissed employees for wearing union badges on the job. Mr Badger is an American. Everyone calls him 'Boss Badger' and he is known as a union breaker.

Most of the shops have closed, the theatres are closed, the hotels are closed, and if you want to get to work you have to walk. The problem now is getting food. There was an incredible scene in the West End yesterday. A great crowd of women and children was gathered outside a bakery clamouring for bread.

The workers have formed a bicycle corps. They tour the city and demonstrate in front of any shop or cafe that should decide to stay open. There was a riot in the city yesterday. A privately owned sulky was coming up from wharves along Mary Street towards Edward Street. It contained merchandise. A crowd of a 1000 workers, wearing their defiant red ribbons, followed it.

Outside the Savoy Hotel, the crowd became threatening, and mounted police rode to the rescue. The workers retaliated with a volley of wooden blocks. One constable received a blow that left him permanently incapacitated from the force; two others had their helmets smashed in.

Soon afterwards, a brewery firm was trying to remove barrels that had been exposed to the sun in the Roma Street sheds. The lorry was surrounded by a huge mob, which refused to let it pass. Foot police and mounted police intervened and there was a battle with sticks, stones and battens of wood.

At the height of the melee a shot was fired and a man with a revolver was arrested. The police on horses rode down the mob and used batons. The crowd, according to the *Courier*, was sullen and angry, and the Commissioner of Police, Major Cahill, appeared in a motor car. After this event the police kept order in the streets, carrying swords.

The Premier, Mr Denman, has appealed to the Prime Minister for help from the Army. He has even asked for a British battleship to patrol the coast. Our Labor Prime Minister, Mr Fisher, is not sympathetic and is likely to send money to the Unions instead.

Mr Denman says that nowhere else on earth could this happen, where the Army cannot be called upon in times of trouble.

Further reading. *From the Dreaming to 1915 — A History of Queensland*, Ross Fitzgerald.

Sydney Turns Out to Welcome the Queen

4 FEBRUARY 1954

The Queen becomes the first reigning monarch to visit Australia

Her Majesty the Queen landed at Farm Cove at 10.33 a.m. yesterday and received the most tumultuous greeting Sydney has ever given any visitor. It is the first time a reigning monarch has ever visited Australia.

Police estimate that a million people lined the city streets. At least another half-million manned every foreshore vantage point from the Heads to the Bridge. Sydney's worst traffic jam developed during the evening, as more than a million people moved to and from vantage points around the harbour for the fireworks display.

Nine people ventured nine miles out to sea on surfboards and surf skis just to greet the Royal couple. There was a Royal salute by the RAAF from two formations of six Vampire jets and six Mustangs.

From the time the Royal car moved off from Farm Cove until it reached Government House one hour and twenty-five minutes later, the Queen and the Duke of Edinburgh were cheered to the echo. Crowds all along the route literally camped by the kerbside all night.

But it wasn't enough just to see the Royal couple once. Without waiting for cars following the Queen to pass, Many dashed headlong down Martin Place, carrying boxes, chairs and ladders that they had used earlier in Macquarie Street. A man dressed in full morning suit, and accompanied by a fashionably dressed woman, sprinted along carrying their fruit boxes.

Actually some smart fruiterers did very well indeed. They were hiring out their fruit boxes at 4 shillings a time. However so many people clambered aboard, many boxes collapsed at the very moment the Queen was passing. Ambulance officers treated 2075 people. The majority were treated for fainting attacks, but there were also numerous cases of heart seizure and broken legs.

Every building, every house along the way, no matter how humble, was decorated with bunting and flags. St James Church and St Mary's Cathedral pealing their bells, quickened the excitement.

Then, last night, there was the greatest fireworks display Sydney has ever seen. A million people packed the foreshore to see it. For more than 70 minutes there was a brilliant panorama of stars, rockets, and Roman candles, which even outdid the illuminations of the city. It ended with a 50-feet square portrait in fireworks of the Queen and the Duke. So precise were the details the crowd could even see the Queen's earrings.

And what was it really like? His Royal Highness, the Duke of Edinburgh, is very handsome, but the women's editor of the *Sydney Morning Herald*, best described Her Majesty's beauty:

> She stepped ashore, matching the golden day — every woman's dream of beauty. Her figure is girlish, and sometimes she seems taller than she is. Tricks of light give new radiance to her face, and there are dreams still in her clear blue eyes. The Queen's complexion is flawless, and paler than the impression gained from paintings and colour photographs. Many a suntanned woman yesterday must have regretted those extra hours on the beach.

Touring Aboriginal Side Leaves for England

5 FEBRUARY 1864

The Aboriginal cricket team leaves New South Wales for England tomorrow, aboard the wool vessel *Parramatta*. The team's rise to cricket prowess has been one of the most extraordinary episodes of our time.

It all began four years ago when Mr Tom Hamilton of Bringalbert station near Edenhope, Victoria, began teaching the game to Aborigines in his employ, and, together with Mr William Hayman of the Edenhope club, began to build a team . Mr Tommy Wills, the marvellous all-rounder of the Melbourne Cricket Club, even went to Edenhope to give the team coaching.

The Melbourne *Herald* commented: 'The men are well built and most intelligent looking fellows, far superior in appearance to the natives whom we have been accustomed to see from time to time'.

Now the incredible has happened, they are off to England: the first Australian touring side. They have just completed their farewell match, which took place at Sydney's Albert Ground — both days in the distinguished presence of His Royal Highness, Prince Alfred, Duke of Edinburgh, and His Excellency, the Governor, the Earl of Belmore.

Prince Alfred, driving his team of four greys, arrived at 3 p.m. and the grandstand was specially fitted out for his reception. As soon as HRH appreared, the blacks were mustered in front, gave three hearty cheers, and concluded with their peculiar yell of victory.

As you know, Prince Alfred is the commander of HMS *Galatea*, now in port. Many of his crew played in the Army and Navy team, and the band of HMS *Galatea* provided popular music with great taste during the afternoon.

There was a very large crowd, over 4000 people. The Aboriginals had fascinating names, Bullocky, Tiger, Redcap, King Cole, Dick-a-Dick, Twopenny, Jim Crow, Mullagh...Then there was Cuzens, an absolute 'capital bowler and batsman'.

The Military and Naval team was all out for 64 runs. Cuzens took 8 wickets for 23 off 72 balls. Then when he went in to bat, he made 86 runs before he was run out. The team made 237. The *Sydney Morning Herald* reported that both Cuzens and Mullagh made hits that frequently hit the fence.

The match ended in a draw, and then there was a sports meeting. There was some somersault leaping over a horizontal bar by King Cole; then there was the running high jump for a prize of one pound. Mullagh distinguished himself with an astonishing jump of 5 feet 7 inches. We don't think this has been beaten anywhere in the colonies.

Dick-a-Dick appeared in his clever trick of dodging the ball. He defended himself with the narrow shield, and though some expert throwers kept up an incessant fire at a distance of only 20 yards, none succeeded in hitting him. For the first time, the team appeared in their new and picturesque costume; a black closely fitting overall, a doublet of possum skins, a headdress of cabbage-tree plait with a crest of lyre-bird plumage.

They staged a mock fight, all armed with spears, boomerangs and throwing sticks. One would give anything to see them stage this at Lord's.

Further reading: *Cricket Walkabout*, D.J.Mulvaney.

*First Aboriginal
Cricket Team*

An Incredible Colonial

8 FEBRUARY 1839

John Pascoe Fawker published the first issue, this week, of the *Port Phillip Patriot and Advertiser*.

It is just another of his astonishing activities. Was there ever such an incredible colonial? His father was a convict, and young Fawkner arrived with his parents in 1803. In 1814, he was doing well in Hobart as a shop keeper, baker and farmer. He took pity on seven convicts and helped them build a boat so that they could escape to the mainland.

The convicts were caught and Fawkner was sentenced to 500 lashes and three years of labour. When he was freed in 1817, he took up baking again. He had trouble with the law, selling shortweight loaves and running a hotel without a licence. He was constantly in strife.

But he had unstoppable energy . He was a bush lawyer; he ran a nursery; he continued his hostelry; and in 1828, launched the *Launceston Advertiser* and used it to castigate the administration. He attacked capital punishment, saying the Government treated men's lives as less than sheep. He was the champion of liberated convicts.

As you know, in 1835 he was one of the founders of Melbourne. Once again he was a hotel keeper and now he is a rich man. Some say that in his first four years in Port Phillip, he has made 20 000 pounds.

Last year, with no licence and practically no equipment, he started the *Melbourne Advertiser*. It was handwritten on four pages of foolscap, and used to come out weekly until it was suppressed. Then a Sydneysider, Thomas Strode — and in the eyes of Fawkner nobody is worse than a creature from Sydney — started the *Port Phillip Gazette*, which has the slogan 'To Assist the Enquiring, Animate the Struggling, and Sympathise with All'.

As a result, Mr Fawkner could not wait to get his paper into action, so the first issue has just come to hand.

It has eight pages of three columns, half of it handwritten. Obviously he has the same equipment that he used with the *Melbourne Advertiser*: an antique wooden press, and a collection of battered, over-worn type, and extremely poor-quality paper.

There is a considerable number of advertisements, and details of ship arrivals and departures, but little news. One reads in the police reports that a man has been fined £30 for the illicit sale of spirits, 'keeping a sly grog shop', according to the *Patriot*. Three drunkards have been fined 5 shillings each; two alcoholics have been confined for 24 hours, solitary, on bread and water. One man has been fined £5 for riding his horse furiously through the city; and another has been fined 5 shillings for riding his horse on the footpath.

The *Gazette* has made it clear that it does not wish to indulge in politics. Mr Fawkner says there will be no such restraints in his newspaper. In his first issue, he lashes out at the administration and the land sales of 1 June 1837.

He implies that we have a system designed to encourage the rich. He points out that there were 100 individuals, artisans and working men, who would have been happy to purchase an allotment for under 20 pounds. 'And thus' said he 'we would have had a class of householder amongst us of the real yeomanry'.

But they resticted the number of lots available, so prices ran from £95 pounds, land which had been taken from the Aborigines and cost the Government 'nothing' said Fawkner.

For a man utterly self-taught, this Fawkner has a gift. He thunders: 'Let the British reader mark this, for as far as the poor man, or working Trade man, is concerned they might as well have been sold in Nova Xembla'.

Why, he even quotes Defoe with the lines: For Governments from Heaven might first appear But Governors came from LORD KNOWS WHERE.

The End of the Six O'Clock Swill

9 FEBRUARY 1966

Six o'clock closing has come to an end. It is a very strange feeling. I can walk into a Melbourne pub at five to six and dally on, maybe even keep on drinking until 10 p.m.

Oddly enough, I don't want to. It's not very interesting when it's legal. Sydney has had 10 o'clock closing since February 1955. NSW towns like Wentworth, Albury and Deniliquin did a lovely nocturnal trade as desperately parched Victorians surged across the border. How they will miss us.

It all started so long ago, there are few around to remember the reasons. Six o'clock closing came to us during the First World War. The feeling was that the early closing of bars would help us to defeat the Kaiser. There was a wave of anti-drink fervour. In April 1915, King George V banned wines, spirits and beer from the Royal Household for the duration of the war. Lord Kitchener and the Archbishops of Canterbury and York followed suit.

The *Bulletin* commented sadly: 'Soldiers with their tongues hanging out will be singing: "It's a long way to Tipple-ary".'

In 1915 the Victorian Chief Secretary introduced the Temporary Restriction Bill. Before the pubs closed at 11.30 p.m., now they had to close at 9.30.

South Australia was first in with 6 o'clock closing, NSW took to it in June 1916, then Tasmania. By October 1916, clearly the war was not going satisfactorily, Victoria needed tougher measures, there had to be an amendment to the Temporary Restriction Bill, so 9.30 p.m. closing to had come back to 6 p.m.

Mr D. Smith, the Labor member from Bendigo, deeply moved the House with an article about pubs in *The Worker*:

Unhappy mothers, mourning for their drunken sons; haggard wives listening for the staggering steps of drunken husbands; frightened children cowering from the fury of drunken fathers. The agony of innumerable desolated lives would stare at you from your eyes like a pallid prisoner through the window of his cell. We would like to sweep away the death traps altogether...that taint the air with disease, and inflict the soil with blighting leprosy.

When the Licensing Bill came up for debate, it was thought six o'clock closing might be removed. No, that charmingly named Act, the Temporary Restriction Bill, remained in force for precisely half a century.

So we invented the 6 o'clock swill. It became a world phenomenon. Journalists from London, New York and Paris came to Melbourne, Sydney, Adelaide and Hobart to write about it.

Most of us can never get away from the office until nigh on 5.30 p.m. This left just a desperate half-hour for action. I guess our school was no different to any other. We had a system. Five of us would all approach the bar at dead on 5.30 p.m. Each of us would buy five beers. That was our only hope of getting a decent serve, the crush was so awful.

Well, you know our bars: no comforts, no tables, no chairs. We either had to park our glasses on window sills or mantelpieces, or put them between our feet on the ground. Very delicate business.

Then we had to down our five beers in 30 minutes. That closing time was deadly. At six, the publican rang his bells and hollered 'Come on fellers, fair go. Drink up'.

Then we would all spill out onto the street. The city was always full of drunks at 6.15 p.m.

The Temperance people said that instead of a 6 o'clock swill, there would be a 10 o'clock swill. No husbands would go home to their wives and there would be absolute carnage on the roads.

Well, nothing's happened. The city has been like a morgue and the pubs practically empty. Our school has lost all its drive. None of us fronts up and orders five beers each any more.

The Cheek of Ned Kelly

10 FEBRUARY 1879

Edward 'Ned' Kelly

There has been another outrage by Ned Kelly and his gang. When it is going to stop?

On 8 February, Kelly and his men rode by moonlight into Jerilderie, a little one-street-of-a-place in New South Wales, and performed the perfect stunt.

Melbourne's *Argus* says Kelly rode straight up to the police station at full gallop, shouting 'Devine, there's a drunken man at Davidson's hotel, who has committed murder. Get up at once, all of you'.

As soon as Devine appeared, Kelly 'presented two revolvers at the policemen'. Thereupon, he took Senior Constable Devine and his deputy, Constable Richards, and locked them in their own lock up. Next he made Mrs. Devine, in her nightie, go round the entire premises, gathering up all the firearms; and they all spent the night in the Devine's sitting room.

Devine complained his wife was in an 'interesting' condition, so Kelly was considerate and lifted heavy loads for her. She complained she had to convert the courthouse into a church, so Kelly sent his brother Dan to help her. Dan even arranged the flowers.

The gang dressed in police uniforms and made the unfortunate Constable Richards take them around the town and introduce them as visiting police, who had come to investigate the Kelly affair.

Today Ned stuck up the Royal Mail Hotel, and told the owner he needed the dining room for his prisoners. While two of his gang took charge of the pub, Ned and Joe Byrne held up the Bank of New South Wales next door and, at the end of a barrel, relieved the establishment of £2140 in cash and gold.

Dan Kelly and Steve bailed up anyone who came into the hotel and made them prisoner. Now Ned Kelly had his own captive audience. He bought them all drinks with money he had robbed from the bank. He told them of his career, how innocent he was, how the police had hounded and terrified his family.

He was alternatively fierce and magnanimous. One moment he threatened to shoot Constable Richards, until the crowd pleaded for his life; the next, when the Rev. Mr Gribble complained that Steve Hart had stolen his watch, Ned insisted that Steve give it back, plus a watch and a horse stolen from the hotelier.

Before they departed from Jerilderie, the Kelly gang gave an exhibition of their horsemanship, jumping fences and bushes. They galloped down the main street singing and shouting 'Hurrah for the good old days of Morgan and Ben Hall'. Then they warned that anyone who attempted to follow them would be shot.

There is just one consolation in this dreadful business. The New South Wales police have been particularly contemptuous of the inability of the Victorian police in their attempts to track down the Kelly Gang, now they have something to think about in their own area.

Kelly has left behind with Mr Living, the accountant he held up at the bank, a very curious letter. Among other things he says:

I have been wronged and my mother and four or five men lagged innocent and is my brothers and sisters and my mother not to be pitied also who has no alternative only to put up with the brutal and cowardly conduct of a parcel of big ugly fat-necked wombat headed big bellied magpie legged narrow-hipped splay-footed sons of Irish bailifs or English landlords.

Further reading: *Ned Kelly, The Authentic Illustrated Story*, Keith McMenomy.

General Gordon and Khartoum Fall to the Mahdi

11 FEBRUARY 1885

The news arrived this morning that General Charles 'Chinese' Gordon has been killed in Khartoum.

The newspapers have brought out extraordinary editions, and the whole nation is in a state of grief. Never before have we grieved so much over the passing of an Englishman. Not the death of the Duke of Wellington, not even the end of Albert, the Queen's consort, affected us so much.

It was just five days ago that we learned that Khartoum had been captured by the Mahdi, the Arab rebels in the Sudan. Gordon and his troops had been there under siege for nearly a year.

Some newspapers, this morning, stated the Mahdi had captured the city, but Gordon was entrenched there and still alive. But now the dreadful news has arrived by cable. General Gordon was stabbed as he was coming down from the Palace. A number of his troops who remained faithful to their commander rallied and resisted the attack, but they were overpowered by the rebels, who massacred all those who had remained loyal to General Gordon.

General Charles Gordon

The grief being displayed for a man so far away is remarkable. Today's Melbourne *Herald* runs excerpts and comments from newspapers all over the country. There is even a column of verse. One begins:

> Died at his post with the face to the foe.
> Our Gordon is dead in Sudan.
> It is hard that we lose such a soldier
> Anguish to mourn such a man.
> One more of England's gentlemen
> Died where his duty lay;
> But never from the nation's heart
> Shall Gordon pass away.

The tragedy, according to the *Herald*, is that the relief expedition under Lord Wolseley would have arrived just two days too late. There is considerable fury with the Gladstone administration for its dilly-dallying, do-nothing attitude. Had it acted quickly in the first place, Gordon would have been saved.

One contributor to the *Herald* says today: The citizens of Victoria should arise to a man and pronounce a decisive and unmistakable opinion to the world, strongly animadverting upon the pusillanimous, mealy-mouthed, peace-at-any-price policy of the Gladstone administration. There was a time when Gladstone was deservedly a mighty power in the land, but now in the days of his dotage, the 'grand old man' should take a back seat...What about our boasted prestige now-a-days? Merely the ribald jest and scoff of nations.

However William Bede Dalley, Premier of New South Wales, certainly does not want Britain to be the ribald jest and scoff of nations. He did not even wait for consent of Parliament. After reading this morning's newspapers, he consulted with his Cabinet and this afternoon he has sent this cable to London:

This Government offers to Her Majesty's Government two batteries of our Permanent Field Artillery, with 10 16-pound guns, properly horsed: also an effective and disciplined battalion of infantry, 500 strong. Can undertake to land Force at Suakim within 30 days from embarkation. Reply at once.

Yes, we can teach the Mahdi a lesson they will never forget.

Further reading: *The Rehearsal*, K.S. Inglis.

Voyager Sinks during Naval Exercise

12 FEBRUARY 1964

The destroyer, HMAS *Voyager*, has been cut in half after a collision with the aircraft carrier, *Melbourne*.

The disaster took place during manoeuvres off the New South Wales South Coast. The *Voyager* sank immediately. The destroyer had a crew of 321, now 82 are feared dead and the chance of finding more survivors is slight. The bodies of three men, including the captain, have been recovered, but 79 are still missing.

The collision took place in calm sea, 20 miles off Jervis Bay at 9 p.m. The *Voyager* was just acting as a rescue ship. Her job was to stand by to pick up the crew of any aircraft that might fall into the sea during take-off or landing from HMAS *Melbourne*.

Voyager was half a mile astern of *Melbourne* when the carrier reversed her course. It was necessary then for *Voyager* to move quickly from being ahead of *Melbourne*, back to the rear position again. While performing this manoeuvre, *Voyager* cut across the bows of *Melbourne* and was cut in half.

The forward part of *Voyager* sank almost at once, the after part remained afloat for three hours.

Allan Cameron, Chief Engineroom Artificer on *Voyager*, said 'full steam ahead' was rung to the engine room seconds before they were hit. He went on to say:

There was a crash and the ship heeled about 60 degrees to starboard. I went for'ard to the machinery spaces and found three men injured lying on the deck. They were being treated. Then I went on to the upper deck, but I couldn't see any part of the ship forward of my engine room. We had been cut right in half. We stayed on deck until we couldn't stand upright because of the slope. Then we jumped and paddled the floats away so that we wouldn't be drawn down with the ship if she sank suddenly.

Wessex helicopters from HMAS *Albatross* went straight to the scene. Commander Ivan Bear had almost 17 hours in the air:

We let a strap down to survivors, but they were too shocked to help themselves. The helicopters picked up three or four by lowering a man down into the water. The man strapped himself to the survivors and they were pulled up together.

HMAS *Melbourne* is sailing slowly back to Sydney. A reporter who flew close to the ship says that a gaping hole in her bows appears to be 30 feet long and it extends well under the waterline. She is making about 6 knots. An oil slick a mile wide covers the area where *Voyager* sank.

The Prime Minister, Sir Robert Menzies, said yesterday:

It is a shocking disaster, unparalleled in the peace time history of Australia. I want to announce at once there will be a prompt and thorough investigation of this tragedy. I have decided that the normal machinery for naval investigations is inadequate... There will be a full public investigation, conducted by a judge.

The executive of the RSL has launched a nationwide *Voyager* fund to help those suffering from the disaster.

Badly holed,
HMAS Melbourne
heads for Sydney

NSW Quarantined as Epidemic Worsens

15 FEBRUARY 1919

The Victorian Government issued a proclamation yesterday that closes all hotels until further notice.

Over 800 hotels are involved, and it means immediate unemployment for thousands of men and women. The crisis began last month when the troop ship *Sardinia* arrived in Sydney. Eight of its passengers had died from pneumonic influenza.

Since then, daily, the newspapers have been filled with death lists. New South Wales has been worst hit. The State has been quarantined. On 27 January, the NSW Government closed all places where people gathered: theatres, picture shows, racecourses, libraries, billiard saloons. The Government has warned against all sorts of mass gatherings indoors.

People are now disturbed about travelling in trains and trams. The Victorian racecourses have been closed, and the Board of Health has suggested that all citizens, when moving in public, should wear face masks. The staff of the Commonwealth Bank, and employees of many large shops in the city have adopted this practice.

All the schools are closed. Christmas school holidays now will be extended for at least a month. But in some areas it is almost impossible to check the spread of the disease. On Monday, eight boys at the Christian Brothers Orphanage in South Melbourne went down with influenza, complicated with pneumonia. Last night, this number had increased to 80 in little over 24 hours.

The Railways Commissioners have cut out all their Saturday and Sunday picnic specials. The public is being asked to travel to the city only if absolutely necessary. Funerals are taking place directly from hospitals rather than from funeral homes; and the Health Department advises that funerals should be as speedy as possible.

Other States are taking precautions. All passengers embarking from ships in Tasmania are being carefully examined. In West Australia, passengers on the Trans Continental train are examined at Kalgoorlie.

Makers of various beverages have not let the flu plague pass unnoticed. Dr Morse's Indian Root Pills now advertise 'Keep clean inside and out and minimise the risk of influenza with Dr Morse's Indian Root Pills'. It is suggested, too, that we will escape the 'Spanish Flu' if we imbibe Bovril or keep our blood pure with Clement's Tonic.

There is a mass inoculation taking place. You get an injection of 'A' vaccine, and a second inoculation a week later. Melbourne *Punch*, in its current issue, reports:

Inoculation parties are all the rage. The idea is that one should collect a nice gathering of young men, preferably with a sprinkling of those still in khaki, and about an equal number of girls with good arms. When the doctor comes along with his little bag and gets to work, the operation, which proves trying to some of us, becomes as excellent joke.

But it is not too much of a joke to the hotelkeepers today. The secretary of the licensed Victuallers Association, Mr A.D. Grant, is complaining bitterly. He says the liquor trade has suffered from war time restrictions more than any other, and just when they were hoping for some relief, this happened. 'If the closing of the hotels is going to lessen the ravages of the diease', he says 'then the trade will bear this great burden, but I only hope it will be confirmed by actual results'.

However it is generally feared the epidemic will be much worse before it gets better.

Captain Armstrong 'Crucified'

16 FEBRUARY 1921

There has been a matter of earth-shaking importance this week, Mr W.W.Armstrong, captain of Australia, was dropped from the Victorian side to play England.

It was a disciplinary measure by the selectors. Armstrong did not turn up for practice in the NSW-Victoria match nor did he inform the selectors that he was unfit until the match was about to start.

We are shocked. Mr Armstrong, the great all-rounder, 20 stone plus, the biggest boots in cricket, not playing! As one newspaper put it, if the world were choosing a team to play against Mars or Venus, he would be captain of the interplanetary XI.

The devoted Armstrong admirer, Mr H.D. Westley, immediately called an 'Indignation Meeting' at the Athenaeum in Collins Street. He did not get the idea until 5 p.m. but still the hall was packed to overflowing. Mr Westley said he had come to raise his voice against the most dastardly outrage in the history of cricket, and he moved: 'That this meeting of lovers of sport expresses its condemnation at the treatment handed out to Australia's greatest cricketer'.

He held another 'Monster Indignation Meeting' outside the Melbourne Cricket Ground at 3 p.m. on Saturday. The Victorian Cricket Association was ruthless. There were no pass out checks. There was a crowd of 17 000 inside, and it was a fearful matter of conscience. Patsy Hendren of England was playing like a man inspired; one of the most beautiful exhibitions of batting ever seen on the MCG. He scored 271 — his first 50 in 38 minutes.

What was a man to do? Miss this historic opportunity? Or watch Hendren inside then, very correctly 'indignate' outside on behalf of Australia's greatest hero, and have to pay to go in again?

It is good to be able to report that a great many went outside. The unofficial count was eight thousand. Mr Westley said:

I desire to apologise to the English cricketers for the indignity placed on them by the holding of an indignation meeting outside the ground on which they are playing. But the Englishmen are true sports and I am sure they are in entire sympathy with the objects of the meeting. (Hear, Hear.) Dirty washing is being washed in the presence of the visitors, but Armstrong is being crucified without trial, and such a thing is opposed to the ethics of British justice. (Hear, Hear.)

Meanwhile Patsy Hendren was murdering the Victorian bowling, and all day the MCG crowd kept up the ironic chant 'PUT ARMSTRONG ON!

Mr Westley, you will be pleased to hear, has not let up. He called a third Indignation Meeting and it took place tonight in the Melbourne Town Hall. He had a projector and showed slides of the splendid meeting we had outside the MCG. There were slides, too, of leading Australian cricketers, and when Armstrong's picture was flashed on the screen there were cheers and everybody sang 'He's a Jolly Good Fellow'. Mr Westley called for the sacking of all the cricket selectors and said this would give new life to Australian cricket.

I am sure Mr Westley has done immense good. How can they fail to select the big man for the next tour of England?

The Fall of Singapore

17 FEBRUARY 1942

Mr Winston Churchill has announced the fall of Singapore.

A Tokyo report, through Berlin, says Japanese warships entered Singapore harbour on Sunday. All Japan is jubilant at the news.

The fall of the fortress is the greatest blow Australia and the Empire has received. The Japanese threat to Australia has now increased immensely. It has not been disclosed in London what Allied troops remain in Singapore, but a Japanese report says there are 60 000 still there, made up 15 000 United Kingdom troops, 13 000 Australian and 32 000 Indian troops. There is no official news of the number of garrison in the final stages of the battle. It is believed we have lost heavily in material and equipment.

The last message received from the Singapore GOC Lieutenant-General Percival, was sent to General Wavell on Saturday afternoon. It said that because of heavy losses of water, food, ammunition and petrol, it was impossible to carry on the defence longer. There was no policy on evacuation. The intention was to fight to the last.

Mr Churchill, in a world broadcast, said last night:

I have never promised sure and easy things and all I have to offer now is hard and adverse war for many years to come. I must warn you that many a misfortune, torturing loss and gnawing anxiety lie before us. One thought, however, one crime — and one crime only — can rob the United Nations and Bristish people of victory. It is the loosening of our purpose, the weakening of our unity. That is the mortal crime.

The Australian Prime Minister, Mr Curtin, left Canberra today for Sydney where he will meet with the War Cabinet to prepare for Friday's emergency meeting of Parliament. He said before leaving that Australia's immediate problem no longer was that of a contribution to a world-wide war, but one of resisting an invasion of Australia. There was a new phase of the war, a new frontier, and it did not mean just the fate of Australia, but the fate, too, of the United States and the English speaking world.

Mr Curtin said:

He would be a very dull person who does not accept the fall of Singapore as involving a completely new situation...Our honeymoon has finished. It is now work or fight as we have never worked or fought before and there must not be a man or a woman in this Commonwealth who goes to bed at night without having related his or her period of wakefulness to the purposes of war.

The Melbourne *Sun* says today that new defence measures are before Federal Ministers. The measures mean a virtual dictatorship by the Executive, with general supervision by Federal Parliament.

The Federal Treasurer, Mr Chifley, announced the Prime Minister would officially open the £35 million Liberty Loan in Sydney tomorrow. Members of the services and representatives of all our Allies would march from Macquarie Street to Martin Place. Mr Chifley said the loan was taking place under the shadow of the fall of Singapore, one of the greatest national disasters that had ever befallen the British Empire.

Lola Montez Horse-whips Editor

18 FEBRUARY 1856

The notorious Lola Montez

There has been a most unpleasant altercation in Ballarat. This evening Miss Lola Montez horse-whipped a newspaper editor.

Miss Montez, of course, is not a lady to be trifled with, and she has been cocking a snook at convention for some time. She hails from Ireland, born in Limerick, Irish mother, Spanish father. She was Liszt's lover in Poland, and it's well known she was the mistress of Louis of Bavaria. She smokes cigars and has a fiery temper.

She arrived in Victoria last year and she has been putting on her, now notorious, Spider Dance at the Theatre Royal. Nothing is left to the imagination, I can assure you. The Diggers, of course, love her. That Irish writer, William Kelly, says their faces are radiant and every eye skinned in watchfulness. That's an understatement.

The *Argus* on 20 September last was terribly disapproving. It said:

We feel called upon to denounce in terms of unmeasured reprobation the performance in which that lady (Lola) last night figured. We do not intend to enter into details. The crowded attendance at the theatre will understand our motives for not doing so... They have no right to insult respectable ladies by inviting their attendances, and if scenes if this kind are to be repeated, we consider that the interference of the authorities is imperatively called for...

Lola thought this was just 'piety and ultra-puritanism', saying it was a national dance witnessed with delight in Spain by all classes and both sexes.

Well, Miss Montez has been on tour, first to Bendigo and now to Ballarat. Two days ago there was a letter in the *Ballarat Times* under the pseudonym 'Civis'. It said that Lola was notorious for her immorality. Who was Civis? None other than Harry Seekamp, editor of the *Ballarat Times*.

Lola, in replay, made a speech from her stage at the Victoria Theatre. She said:

The great gentleman attacks poor little innocent me. I am called notorious for my immorality. While he was at my house the sherry and port and champagne were never off the table. You all know Mr Seekamp is a little fond of drinking. I was a ten-pound note out of pocket by Mr Seekamp but I was a little green at the time...

This evening Harry Seekamp called at the United States Hotel, where Miss Montez is staying, right next to the Victoria Theatre. As soon as she heard Mr Seekamp was in the building, she came downstairs with a riding whip in her hand.

She laid into Harry Seekamp across his shoulders to no mean order. But he came prepared with his own horsewhip. When Lola attacked him he hit her back. This was too much for the Diggers in the bar, and they drew their revolvers. Harry Seekamp might have been killed if the police had not arrived.

Nor is that the finish. I believe Lola is laying libel charges against Seekamp and the *Times*. Meanwhile it is not doing businesss any harm at all. You haven't a hope in life of getting a ticket at the Victoria. The Diggers are all in the front rows and they are showering the stage with golden nuggets.

They can't wait for her to come on and show her charms, hollering out 'Come on, Lola; damn it, come on, ole girl, afore the moon goes down'.

Embarking for the Boer War

19 FEBRUARY 1902

NSW Lancers before sailing for South Africa

The first battalion of the Federal Contingent, aboard the great vessel, *Custodian*, leaves Woolloomooloo for South Africa at 4 p.m. today.

There are three companies from New South Wales and one company from Queensland. The occasion was a little subdued really. When the first New South Wales contingent left back in October 1899, there was marvellous enthusiasm, a real outpouring of patriotic fervour. There were huge crowds in the streets, fine sermons in their favour from the pulpit. They sang 'Rule Britannia', 'Soldiers of the Queens' and 'Auld Lang Syne'. The whole country seemed joyous at going to war.

Henry Lawson wrote a special piece of verse, designed to inspire the boys as they charged the Boers with fixed bayonet:

For up the country and Out Back — from
the Darling to the Quay;
And let some old familiar sound your
cheering war-cry be:
Sing 'Sydney! Clontarf! Manly Beach!
Bondi!' and 'Coogee!' too,
For the honour of old New South Wales
from a worldly point of view!

The Labor member for Waratah, Mr A.H. Griffith, has been attacking the war, saying British forces had no right to be in South Africa. A meeting of the electors of Waratah was called yesterday in protest and the Mayor, Alderman Braye, presided. Mr Alfred Edden MLA said no Britisher had any right, by word or action, to disparage his own country or encourage those of foreign nations which were jealous of England's greatness.

The Premier, Mr John See, and the Acting Lieutenant-Governor, Mr Justice Owen, said farewell to the troops yesterday. There was a very sad mix up when the soldiers did not get their customary 30 days pay in advance. The Commanding Officer, Brigadier General Finn, said 'I quite believe that if I asked you to follow me into a pretty tight place you would all follow without a word. I want you then to try to swallow the nasty taste caused by this disappoinment'.

The Troops very decently did not protest. The battle was more important than the pay.

The work of taking the horses down to the wharf was marred by a fatality. Number 58, Private H.L.G. Gray, while leading his horse along Green's Road towards Oxford Street, was killed when the animal took fright. Gray had the halter rope turned twice around his wrist and lost his footing. The horse bolted, dragging him behind and injuring him terribly. An hour later he died of a fractured skull, smashed face and broken nose. He was 21 and the last remaining son of his parents who live in Maitland. His brother already has been killed in the South African war.

At 24-hours notice, Lieutenant Tedbar Bradshaw Johnson has joined the contingent to fill the vacancy caused by the illness of Lieutenant Innes. Johnson, says the Sydney *Morning Herald*, has had a good deal of bush experience and 'needless to say, is an excellent rider and a good shot'.

Further reading: *A History of Australia V*, C M.H. Clark.

Japanese Bomb Darwin

22 FEBRUARY 1942

The Japanese have carried out two bombing raids on Darwin. The known casualties so far are 43 — 19 dead.

In the first raid, 72 bombers attacked the town, the wharves and shipping. In the second raid, 21 bombers, unsupported by fighters, attacked installations of the RAAF.

The Prime Minister, Mr Curtin, said tonight:

In this first battle on our territory, the forces defending Darwin and the civilians in the town comported themselves with the gallantry that is traditional of our race. While our information does not disclose details of the casualties it must be obvious we have suffered.

We must face with fortitude the first onset and remember that whatever the future holds for us we are Australians and we will fight grimly and victoriously. Darwin has been bombed, but it has not been conquered. We in every other city in the Commonwealth can face similar assaults.

There has been criticism of lack of information. One newspaper says, today, it is a sorry record. The Japanese made a surprise attack, even in daylight. The alert was sounded only just before, if not after, the bomb fall. There were aircraft damaged on the ground. Only six of the 92 enemy planes were brought down. The official report was both delayed and wrong.

Mr Curtin, however, says an open discussion of Australia's war position is impossible for security reasons. There was a joint session of both Houses of Parliament yesterday at 4 p.m. but Mr Curtin said afterwards, 'All matters discussed were of utmost secrecy'.

Douglas Lockwood, a correspondent for Melbourne's Sun has filed a report from Alice Springs. He says 'Blitzed Darwin is now a ghost town from a military point of view. Although four miles of the Commonwealth railway line were damaged in Thursday's raids, repairs have now been completed and everybody not essential to defence has been evacuated'.

He says there are bomb craters in the streets, and the marks of armour-piercing bullets around the wharf and hospital are grim reminders that the enemy may return. Lockwood said the first evacuee train from Darwin arrived at daybreak. It contained nearly 500 women, children and aged men. Among the women was Mrs Abbott, wife of the Northern Territory Administrator, who was wonderfully calm and did what she could to help the wounded.

Other evacuees reached Sydney yesterday by flying boat. Arthur Rudman, boarding house manager, said:

Exploding bombs were our alert. They were the first warning Darwin received. The Japs must have had extra special information about our defences. They did not waste time on unimportant targets. The post office was the first place hit and they plastered it with everything they had.

One bomb completely engulfed the postmaster's residence and left a crater 30 feet deep. This bomb killed nine postal employees, including the postmaster, his wife and daughter.

Mr Rudman said he sheltered under a tree. Fighters and bombers were swooping down to 100 feet. 'I could just get a glimpse of one of our AA batteries: and were those boys letting them have it. I saw one Japanese plane whirl down with a cloud of smoke bursting from it. There was no one with me to cheer.

Note: Australia learned almost nothing about the devastating effect of the raid in which eight ships were sunk, 243 people were killed, and countless millions of pounds worth of damage.

Darwin after the raid

Sydney-Wellington Telegraph Link

23 FEBRUARY 1876

At last we have established the submarine cable between Sydney and Wellington, New Zealand.

There have been some exquisitely polite first messages between the two colonies.

Sir Hercules Robinson, Governor of New South Wales, cabled to the Marquis of Normanby, Governor of New Zealand:

I congratulate Your Excellency on the establishment of telegraphic communication between Sydney and Wellington , and at this time I would express the hope that this great work, in the construction of which New South Wales and this colony have so cordially united, may tend not only to facilitate the transaction of business but also to strenghten the good feeling which exists between the two colonies.

His Excellency, the Marquis, was equally generous in his reply. But of course, sending cables is ruinously expensive and not for the likes of us. It is only for big business; the rich; and the newspapers, which get a special cut rate. The prices to New Zealand, announced today, are 9s 0d for ten words and 11d for each additional word.

From London the cost is even worse, nine shillings and elevenpence a word for you and me. Two shillings and ninepence a word for press messages.

But they are thrilled in New Zealand. We know exactly the feeling. At last they are connected to the world. A copper wire now goes all the way around the globe from London to Wellington and on to Auckland. Should there be outbreak of war with Russia, rebellion in India or even news of a Derby winner. They will know in six hours.

The revolution in our lives began only four years ago with the completion of the overland telegraph between Port Darwin and Adelaide, and the submarine cable between Darwin, Java and Singapore. You can imagine what it was like before. All the news came by sea and the competition to be first with news from the London newspapers was intense. For example, in Melbourne, the *Age* and the *Argus* would pick up the papers as soon as the London merchant ship arrived off Queenscliff. Then there would be the race by coach, horse, railway or fast steamer — whatever was the quickest — to be first with the news to the Melbourne press. No matter that this news was six to eight weeks old, it was still fresh and unknown. New Zealand was thus until this Monday. It was remarkable really. It took only two months to lay 1370 nautical miles of cable. The core is made of seven copper wires, insulated with three coatings of gutta percha, alternating with three coatings of what is known as Chatterton's compound. The laying was done by two steamers, the *Edinburgh* and the *Hibernia*. The *Hibernia* is the larger ship, 3180 tons, and an absolute marvel, with the most complete devices for cable laying that modern science has devised. She took on board 1200 miles of cable — enough for the entire distance from Sydney to New Zealand — and it was all stored amidships in three enormous tanks.

One-third of the cost is being met by New South Wales, and two-thirds, very rightly, by New Zealand, which will reap the greatest benefit.

Although we feel that the telegraph has brought us as close to home as Sussex or Exeter, the cable, to be honest, remains a delicate affair. It is so subject to the corrosive action of the sea, and to the effects of hurricane and monsoon on land, there are frequent breakdowns. The cable goes, and suddenly all Europe and the civilised world has gone. Once again we are alone, like back in the days of Governor Bligh.

Indeed, today's *Sydney Morning Herald*, still carries news from London, dated 7 January, brought by the P & O ship *Avoca*, from Suez to Adelaide.

Hinkler 'The New Lindbergh'

24 FEBRUARY 1922

Bert Hinkler

Bert Hinkler has flown from England to Australia in 16 days.

All England, all Australia is agog. Not only has he beaten the record of 28 days set by Ross and Keith Smith, he has done it in a tiny, flimsy biplane single-seater, made of fabric and wire. It is the longest solo flight ever made. We are calling him the new Lindbergh.

The *Herald's* London correspondent says 'London has been moved as rarely before. Everywhere the flight is heralded as a striking answer to the pessimists who say that British prowess is waning'.

What a change has taken place. A week ago we were told that the Federal authorities officially were taking no notice of the flight, which was purely a private venture and did not have the blessing of the Commonwealth Government. It did not regard Hinkler's machine, an Avro Avian light aircraft with a 60-horsepower Cirrus motor, as suitable for such a hazardous undertaking. The Government was afraid it would encourage less experienced fliers to attempt the same flight and lose their lives.

Aren't politicians marvellous. The Prime Minister, Mr. Bruce, interrupted a no-confidence debate in the House today to announce that, with the approval of all parties, Federal Parliament had decided to recognise Hinkler's great lone-hand flight by making him a gift of 2000 pounds. 'We are all thrilled by his wonderful achievement' said Mr Bruce; and Bert Hinkler will be invited to Canberra to receive his cheque.

All Darwin went out to Fannie Bay to see Hinkler fly in, and waited for many hours. Many had given up hope when suddenly, at 5.30 pm, the sound of an engine was heard over the jungle to the north. A few seconds later the plane was sighted, 2000 feet overhead. Hinkler came in to make a graceful landing. He had eaten nothing since taking off from Bima ten hours before. Darwin is in the throes of a beer strike, but nevertheless a bottle was rushed to Fannie Bay for Hinkler to enjoy.

There were 400 telegrams waiting for him at the hotel, and messages of congratulation are still pouring in. Said the Darwin Mayor: 'It is marvellous for you to land here today after sleeping 1000 miles away last night. It shows the possibilities of the future of aviation'.

Now Hinkler flies on to Cloncurry, to Rockhampton, and then to Bundaberg, his home town. The welcome will be something beyond belief. All Bundaberg, including the school children, is taking a holiday. The church bells will start chiming and the fire sirens will go into action as soon as he passes overhead. The Mayor has ordered that the recreation ground at North Bundaberg be prepared for his landing.

There will be a triumphant procession through town. Before he left to begin the journey, Hinkler said his ambition was to taxi his little plane right up to his widowed mother's front gate. This is precisely what he will do.

Some newspapers are now calling him 'Sir Bert', and a new word has come into the language, 'to Hinkle'. This means that you move very quickly. Good heavens, a new hat, the Hinkler helmet, is all the rage amongst the ladies in Sydney. Sometimes it has the ear pieces, but always it looks like the Hinkler flying helmet. Chin strap is optional.

Ex-convict the Rothschild of Botany Bay

25 FEBRUARY 1838

We buried Samuel Terry in Sydney today. What a funeral! Unquestionably it was the grandest in the history of a colony. We are still trying to work out what he was worth. What with all his houses, land and business interests, it comes to over half a million pounds. How could anyone become so rich, particularly an ex-convict. They had a name for him in Sydney — the 'Rothschild of Botany Bay'. Terry began his career as a labourer in England and received his free passage to this colony for stealing 400 pairs of stockings. He arrived in 1801, when the colony was only 13 years old. He worked in a labourers gang, building the Parramatta female factory and gaol. So he learned to be a stonemason under the command of the very well-known Reverend Samuel Marsden, the flogging parson.

Sam Terry learned quickly what it was like to be flogged. But he was diligent. His time expired in 1807 and quickly he looked round for opportunities. First he was a soldier, next a self-employed stonemason, then he became a farmer with land on the Hawkesbury.

In 1810 he moved to acquire a licence and became an innkeeper. Then he married. This was the smartest thing he ever did. He married Rosetta Marsh, a widow with three children. She, too, was an innkeeper with a hotel in Pitt Street, so they combined forces.

Terry's influence spread everywhere. He had a farm at Mount Pleasant, he had farms at Illawarra, he had breweries and a flour mill. He produced enough flour and meat to be a purveyor to the Government. As for the Botany Bay Rothschild, he seemed to own a considerable portion of the centre of Sydney. Some say he was more secure than the Bank of New South Wales. This is highly probable, as a shareholder, he owned a considerable proportion of that, too.

His residence is in Pitt Street. He has built the Terry buildings opposite. He has a reputation for being tough and ruthless. Fail to pay your debts and Sam Terry would have you in court as fast as you could say ninepence.

But then Sam Terry has been a great public benefactor. He has put his hand in his pocket for almost everything. He has given money for the Sydney Public School, the Bible Society and the Benevolent Society. He has been a trustee of the Wesley Church, and it was Sam who promoted the big 1828 birthday celebrations for the fortieth anniversary of the colony. He was in the chair for the civic dinner.

Particularly fascinating is the fact that he was a mason, a member of Lodge number 548, the most prestigious lodge in the colonies. At first the lodge tried to bar ex-convicts from membership, however, a ruling came back from the mother-lodge in Dublin that this type of behaviour was 'un-masonic'.

So before he died, Terry asked if he could have a Masonic funeral, and this worthy man went to his grave today with full masonic honours. There was a tyler and inner guard carrying drawn swords, there were deacons with wands of office, there were senior and junior wardens, there were masonic banners everywhere and, out front, was the band of the 50th Regiment playing the 'Dead March in Saul'.

Mr Samuel Terry very definitely made his point about convicts and masons.

Further reading: *Australian Dictionary of Biography*.

Farewell to Dame Nellie Melba

26 FEBRUARY 1931

The entire world is paying tribute to Dame Nellie Melba. She died just three days ago at St Vincent's Hospital in Sydney.

Dame Nellie had been in a critical condition for some days, and knew she was dying. Early in the morning she took a turn for the worse. At first she declined to see any minister, but at 5 a.m. she whispered 'Let me see a churchman'.

Canon Lea of St Mark's Darling Point came immediately and they prayed together for some time. After this she sank rapidly and a little while before she died, faintly she sang two bars from Gounod's 'Ave Maria'. The *Age* says the scene was a most poignant one. Dame Nellie was in her seventieth year.

Dame Nellie's casket was of massive English oak. Her remains were sent by Sydney Express to Albury, and from there the Victorian Government provided a special funeral train for her last ride to Melbourne. The train stopped at Wodonga, Chiltern, Springhurst, Wangaratta, Benalla. . .at almost every train stop along the route.

At little country platforms, always there were big crowds — men, women and children, most of whom had never seen Melba when she was alive, but now many of them were in tears. The doors of the funeral carriage opened and hushed people filed past the coffin, laid wreaths, and some went down on their knees.

Yesterday her body lay in state at Scots Church in Melbourne and the casket was open for inspection from 9.30 until 11.30 a.m. Dame Nellie had a simple piece of frangipanni on her left breast. Thousands passed through. Some said she looked beautiful in repose, just like the famous portrait by Sir John Longstaff.

The funeral service began at 1 p.m., and the funeral cortege, a mile long, set out for Lilydale at 2 p.m. There were crowds in 'tens of thousands' all along the 24-mile route. Flags everywhere were half mast. At every window, at every sill, on tops of lorries, on tops of trams and buildings, people were there to pay tribute.

A halt was made, just for a moment, at the Presbyterian Ladies College the diva attended as a girl. A long line of girls in school uniform emerged from the school and added to the

Dame Nellie Melba

tributes yet another wreath.

At Lilydale the casket was lifted from the hearse, placed on a gun carriage, and from there moved slowly to the cemetery.

Tributes are being reported from around the world. One of the best came from Sir Landon Ronald who broadcast through Britain:

With the death of Nellie Melba the day of the great coloratura soprano has gone. . . There is not another Melba. Hers was the most glorious voice ever put into the throat of a woman. It was not its size, for it was not really a big voice, but it was of amazing purity and golden liquidity.

Calling her 'dear chum, so full of fun' he played her last gramophone record, *Addio from La Boheme*, recorded at Covent Garden when she was 64 years of age. She was buried beside the grave of her mother and father. She lies under a stone bearing Mimi's words 'Addio, senza rancore' — Farewell, without bitterness.

The Demon Counter Lunch

28 FEBRUARY 1918

The free counter lunch in Melbourne officially comes to an end tomorrow, banned. It is something one can report only with tremendous sorrow. It has been so beautiful. It all began back in the 1870s. First they would give you just bread and cheese. But then the competition developed, one against the other, and the free feed became utterly noble, with huge plates of roast lamb, roast beef, turkey, goose, and hot dried fish, salads, bread and cheese.

Here is a recent report of how lovely it used to be:

A leading Swanston Street hotel makes a great feature of the counter lunch. It is but 11 o'clock, yet biscuits and cheese, Fritz sausage, cold corned beef, salads, pickles and white puddings, and bread are spread out for the benefits of the morning supper.

At midday the regular lunchers begin to arrive. If they patronise the front or the side bars they are welcomed by the appetising odour of hot pigs' cheek. In the back bars hot roasts or boiling joints are on the table...At 1 o'clock hot fried sausages and saveloys make their appearance...this kind of thing goes on until closing time.

Well, an extraordinary alliance developed between the temperance people. The Reverend A.R. Edgar told in church how evil the counter lunches were. They were a dangerous bait for the younger generation. A young man would go into a bar to get his free counter lunch; he would ask for a glass of ginger ale or lemonade, next it would be a shandy, next he would sink to a beer, and then he was hooked.

As Melbourne *Punch* put it, the problem wasn't so much the demon drink as the demon lunch.

The powerful Brewers Association has cracked down. Mr Montague Cohen has decreed that any hotel that provides a counter lunch will get no beer. Until now some of the breweries have actually been subsidising hotel counter lunches provided the hotel sells their beer alone.

Now Mr Cohen shares the ugly news that the counter lunch has experienced 'an insidious growth' and hundreds of people have actually been living on the food provided. These people would have a substantial meal at 11.30 a.m. and

Mr Montague Cohen

another at 5 p.m. Some leading hotel-keepers were paying out £3000 a year on lunches. 'I don't know any part of the world where this sort of thing goes on.'

True, that's what made our city so wonderful, so unique. They banned them in Sydney and Brisbane, way back in 1912.

The *Bulletin* summed it best with some tragic verse:

The corned beef torn as if by dogs
The slashed and riddled cheese,
The gnawed and nibbled feet of hogs,
Farewell! Farewell to these.

We thought he liked to see us eat—
To watch us daily stuff
With crumbs and bones about our feet
Until we'd had enough.

But now we know that ev'ry plate
We piled with bread and ham
Was sauced with bitter rage and hate
And poisoned with a 'damn'.

MARCH

The first NSW Cabinet

Smith's Weekly

1 MARCH 1919

A very curious newspaper has its first issue on the news stands this week. It is called, *Smith's Weekly*, and is packed with cartoon, jokes, lively stories, impudent criticism, all for twopence. From what one can gather it is passionate about White Australia, it adores Billy Hughes, the returned Digger can do no wrong, blacks are a menace to white women, there is no greater evil than a Communist, and we should look out for the Yellow Peril to the North.

The brains behind it is a very clever journalist named Claude McKay. He did all the publicity last year for the Eighth War Loan. So good was he, that the Lord Mayor of Sydney, Sir James Joynton Smith, a millionaire who began work as an apprentice to a pawnbroker, agreed to back him with £20 000 to start this newspaper. So in honour of Sir James, it is called *Smith's Weekly*.

Also on the team is a young newspaper friend, Robert Clyde Packer, and the famous former editor of the *Bulletin*, J.F. Archibald.

The first issue is remarkable indeed. It has a thumping editorial, signed by Smith, where he says the country has men of initiative and skill in every field except politics, where we are governed by 'weakness and ineptitude'. Smith says:

> Already...the returned soldier, the cavalier, the cream of our country's manhood has become the sport of the politician. Our soldiers fought for freedom in the broad sense of world affairs. Now it falls for them, again in patriotism to fight for real majority rule, the essence of democracy.

Claude McKay was a friend of Billy Hughes, the Prime Minister. He had the courage to cable Hughes, who was in London for the peace talks, and ask him to approach the celebrated Rudyard Kipling for a story on how the glorious Australians saved Amiens. Fee: £500; an unbelievable 5 shillings a word.

Hughes cabled back: 'Will approach Kipling if you wish, but as he declined our invitation to visit Australian battlefileds, he can hardly write effectively. Conan Doyle knows all about it. Shall I approach him?' McKay sent back: 'Exhaust Kipling. Doyle unwanted'.

It was not to be. Hughes replied: 'Kipling declines'.

There is a whole page devoted to the problems of the returned serviceman. There is a complaint from a returned Digger, a non-returned military policeman had hit him with a baton. So *Smith's* says, with some fury, that no non-returned MP should ever be allowed to lay his hands on a true Digger.

Some of the jokes are not too good. As you know, Sydney and Melbourne are in the midst of a killer influenza epidemic. So we have the gag: 'At last NSW Health Minister is happy. His position lately has been most influenzial'.

One cartoon already has caused trouble. It shows an Irish mother, gesturing towards her darling son Patrick:

> Mrs Ryan: We'll make little Patsy a praste, plaza God.
> Ryan (decisively): We will make Patsy a praste plaza God or not.

I believe the Irish Self-Determination League is furious. It has called on Irish everywhere to boycott the paper.

McKay is pleased. He thinks this will improve circulation no end.

Further reading: *Remember Smith's Weekly?*, George Blaikie.

Billy Hughes

Dawn Fraser Expelled

2 MARCH 1965

Dawn Fraser, 27, triple Olympic champion, was expelled for ten years last night by the Amateur Swimming Union of Australia. This means that the world's number one swimmer and Australian of the Year will never swim competitively again.

Three other girls who swam for Australia at the Tokyo Olympics, also have been expelled: Linda McGill, 19, four years; Marlene Dayman, 15, three years; and Nan Duncan, 17, three years.

The entire swimming world is stunned at the severity of the sentences. No Olympian before has ever been expelled. The ASU did not give the charges against the girls and there is no appeal.

Both Dawn Fraser and Linda McGill intend to take legal action. Dawn Fraser's solicitor, Mr Edward France, has briefed Mr Clive Evatt QC. Linda McGill's solicitor, Mr Carl Melvey, has briefed Mr A Goran QC. Mr Melvey said he had read the charges against Linda McGill set out in a letter to her by Mr W. Berge Phillips. ASU secretary-treasurer. 'They are too trivial for words' Mr Melvey said. 'We consider that the action of the Australian Swimming Union is complete contravention of both Common Law and Equity'.

Last night Dawn Fraser said:

'I'm not going to take it lying down. I have the right as an individual to stand in front of the Amateur Swimming Union committee and face it and fight it. My name has been slandered right across the world. I am not going to let it be slandered without an explanation. All I did wrong in Tokyo was to march in the opening ceremony and to wear a wrong swimsuit in my races. The official swimsuit was too tight and uncomfortable.

Linda McGill says from Rome:

I will do everything I can to fight this slur. Please tell Australians we did everything we possibly could for Australia at the Olympic Games in Tokyo and what has happened to us now seems a very poor reward indeed. I can assure all Australians we did nothing we need be ashamed of.

This morning's papers are filled with angry letters. 'Disgusted' (Footscray) writes: 'What a

Dawn Fraser leaves court with Clive Evatt, QC

narrow minded lot of officials we must have in the Amateur Swimming Union, condemning these swimming champions without a trial. Swimming will be a thing of the past for our girls before long'.

'Mother' (Dromana) says 'If the chaperone appointed by the ASU could not control a 15-year-old girl, then it is she, and not Marlene Dayman who should be banned'.

And 'Be Fair' Carnegie insists 'The treatment meted out to our girl swimmers will quench the enthusiasm of future swimmers. The sentences are more in the nature of those for murder and should, in all fairness, be reduced'.

So what will happen now. Even Mr Bolte, Premier of Victoria, is angry. He says insufficient explanation has been given for the suspensions. He would give careful consideration before the State again gave money for Olympic funds. The Victorian Government gave £5000 to the appeal for the Tokyo Games.

The Purity of our Sunday
3 MARCH 1874

The Cerberus *opened on Sundays caused a fearful row*

There has been a deplorable case of desecration of the Sabbath, and the entire Presbyterian world is up in arms about it. There is no question the Melbourne Sunday is in danger.

The battle to keep our Sunday pure really began back in 1854; until then we had bar sales of liquor on Sundays. Despite the fact that 15 000 citizens petitioned and wanted the bar sales to go on, the Sabbatarians staged a splendid onslaught to get their way. The Moderator of the Free Presbyterian Church wrote to the *Argus*, 28 November 1855.

We do solemnly declare, testify to you this day, Beloved Brethren, that the blessing of God can never rest on the temporal gain or profit that may be made by profaning the Sabbath. Woe unto him that striveth with his Maker. Who hath hardened against himself against Him and hath prospered?

There was a fearful row in 1871 because the flagship of Her Majesty's Victorian Navy, *Cerberus*, was thrown open for public inspection on Sundays.

Two years ago, a certain Mr Fairbrother hired the Town Hall for an evening of sacred readings interspersed with instrumental music. The Melbourne Society for the Promotion of Public Morality thought this was just a disguise to provide entertainment, and the members waited on the Mayor to express their utmost indignation at the 'unholy prostitution of a public building'.

Last year we had complaints about boys flying kites at Emerald Hill on Sundays. 'It's high time public attention was directed to such iniquities' said a letter to the *Argus*.

However there has always been a bitter battle about railway trains running on Sundays. Most respectfully, the Railways have only what they call 'church trains' which convey people to church in the morning.

Absolutely the worst affair took place last week. It was the occasion of the Sunday Railway Picnic to Mount Macedon. Over 1500 railway workers went to the bush by train. They had sports, they had four brass bands, they had dancing and there were booths where liquor was served. Melbourne *Punch* reported that everybody had such a good time that some had to be left behind when the trains left that night, yet they still turned up at work the next day with the excuse 'lost in the bush, all night, Sir, and couldn't make anyone hear'. Today at the monthly meeting of Presbytery of Melbourne, the Reverend Dr Cameron called the picnic one of the greatest outrages ever carried out under the sanction of Government, and called for a deputation to the Chief Secretary.

The Reverend J.C. Symons has prepared a memorial, which will be read to the Chief Secretary at this deputation next week:

We believe...that no man should, under any circumstances, be required to work on the Lord's Day for the mere pleasure of others; and that especially the State should not require, or permit any of its employees to engage in their ordinary work except when absolutely necessary; nor should it hold any inducements to them, nor afford the facilities for violating the rest and sacredness of the Lord's Day.

Yes, if we are not careful even the art gallery, the zoo and cafes will be open on Sunday.

Divorce in NSW

4 MARCH 1874

The Matrimonial Clauses Bill, which permits divorce, became law in New South Wales today.

Heaven knows what trouble this will cause. Many fine citizens are worried that it will mean a complete breakdown in marriage. But then, of course, it is tilted in favour of men, which may preserve some morality. Again you must understand, in our society we do not consider that women have the power to understand all problems.

Males have the right to vote for the Legislative Assembly and the Council, but we do not give that right to women and Aborigines. And so far we do not admit them to institutions of higher learning. Furthermore, in the law courts males have the right to the earnings of a wife.

As it is now, divorce is extremely rare and I don't think I have ever met a divorced person. Here in the colonies there is still a preponderance of men. In New South Wales, roughly six women in a 100 go unmarried, whereas you will find twenty-five in a 100 males unmarried.

Under the law, given assent by His Excellency today, males can sue for adultery, but for women it is a different matter. The New South Wales Parliament decided to follow the standard precepts of British justice. A woman will be able to sue for divorce only if her husband has been guilty of incest, bigamy with adultery, rape, sodomy, bestiality or adultery associated with extreme cruelty.

There was much discussion about this. Mr Hay, for example, said:

I do not wish to take the soft sex from their proper quarters. I am no advocate of the so-called 'Women's Rights' but I do think that the feebler sex should not be oppressed. I do not see any reason to fear the effect of giving such power to women, considering it has been in effect in Scotland, and I would affirm that there it has never been abused.

Mr John Campbell intervened here. There was no one with a greater regard for women's rights than he, but those rights in this regard were not the same as those of men, he said.

We must legislate for the children...A woman can always demand maintenance and a separate establishment and no more can be desired than that. But if the women are allowed to prosecute the husbands for adultery a very large door is opened and there will be no end to the divorce cases brought into court. The barristers will be overwhelmed with work.

He pleaded with the House to show proper sense on this question. Sir William Manning said that when first the Bill came before the House he thought there should be an equity of justice between men and women, but now he had thought about it more deeply.

I believe there is an opinion prevailing largely among both men and women that a wife who commits adultery is lost, and could not be a good wife; whilst a man who commits this grievous wrong in a moment of weakness might otherwise be a good husband and father.

Mr C. Campbell proposed a new clause, that after a marriage had been dissolved, the adulteress should never be allowed to marry the person with whom 'the crime had been committed'.

However Sir William Manning was dead against this. The result would be that persons who might otherwise have married and lived honestly for the rest of their days, would live together in immorality and, finally, that woman would be thrown on the streets.

So the clause was rejected. However the adultery clause brought down in favour of the men was a close one. It was decided on the vote of the Speaker, who said 'Aye', giving the edge to the men. Of course, there were no women in the House to say Nay.

Runners Unwelcome at MCG

7 MARCH 1870

Viscount Canterbury

Mr George Coppin, the celebrated theatrical entrepreneur, has brought to Australia, the champion sprinter of the world, Frank 'Scurry' Hewitt, who hails from Limerick, Ireland.

Mr Coppin's idea, of course, is to match Mr Hewitt against John Gregory Harris, the champion colonial athlete. Hewitt is 25 years old and 5 feet 8 inches. Harris is 24 and 5 feet 10 inches. Harris is the perfect physical specimen, and, we like to think, the pure local product. He was born in 1846 in Collins Street, no less; Melbourne's oldest street.

The *Australasian* has been philosophical about this. It says many Australians believe that the colonial climate is more favourable for the perfect development of the human frame. But there is also the suggestion that the colonial youth, while bigger and more precocious in his development, might not have the stamina of the product from 'home'.

The organisers arranged five races from 100 yards to 440 yards, and there were all sorts of rumours about the sprinters' capabilities. Harris's team said he could run 150 yards in 14 seconds, while Hewitt's backers counter-attacked with a rumour that that he had done it in 13 seconds.

The races were at the Melbourne Cricket Ground, and on Saturday we had 20 000 people, the biggest crowd since the days of Mr Stephenson's cricketing XI. There were attempts to climb over the outside fence, and 15 men climbed on the roof of the stable inside the reserve, causing it to collapse. The *Argus* reported that a horse inside the stable escaped injury, but the paper did not concern itself about the fate of the spectators.

Harris, the local boy, won the 150 yards by three yards in 15¼ seconds; he won the 220 by three yards in 20½ seconds and the 300 was a dead heat in 33¼ seconds. The races continued today. His Excellency, Viscount Canterbury, was present and the *Australasian* commented:

Even the most sanguine of admirers of muscular christianity could hardly have expected such a crowd...However the day belonged to Hewitt. He won the 100 yards in 9¾ seconds, and the 440 in 51¼. Harris was angry. He said the 100 yards was a dead heat and he had accusations about the umpires. One of them was a 'well known heavy bettor'.

Nor was the Melbourne Cricket Club overpleased. There was a very disdainful letter to the morning press:

Amateur pedestrianism and athletic sports are all very well, but the professional element is not wanted. We don't want our ground rushed by roughs, our pavilion invaded by members of the ring, trainers etc. The ground was granted for cricket, all cricketers, and although we tolerate amateur pedestrianism it is toleration only.

Why should the dressing room of private members be rendered unbearable by a steaming mob of runners.

A member of the MCC.

So what happens now. It looks as if the next race will be in the Friendly Society Gardens by the Yarra opposite the Botanic Gardens.

A Cricket Selectors' Brawl

8 MARCH 1912

It is almost with tears in one's eyes that one reports the terrible plight of Australian cricket.

It all began when the Cricket Board of Control failed to appoint Frank Laver as player manager for the tour of England. Laver was so popular the players thought they could appoint their own man. So six players, the absolute cream of Australian cricket, Clem Hill, Warwick Armstrong, Victor Trumper, Vernon Ransford, A Cotter and H. Carter, sent a telegram to the Board, saying in effect, no Laver, no trip for them.

But the real trouble erupted on 3 February. The selectors all got together in Sydney. Not only was there the problem of the Laver affair, but the selectors had to pick teams for the Fourth Test in Melbourne and the team to leave for England next week.

The *Sydney Morning Herald* hinted next morning that there had been a fist fight, but when the selectors, Peter McAlister and Clem Hill, arrived in Melbourne by the Sydney Express, it was obvious what had happened.

McAlister had a great black bruise under his left eye and there were numerous scratches on his face. McAlister said Hill had made a cowardly attack on him while his arms were folded. 'I wouldn't have minded so much if he had invited me to step outside, then I would have known what to expect'.

Clem Hill said:

As I entered the room he started insulting me. I told him if he didn't stop I would pull his nose. But then he told me I was the worst Australian captain he had ever seen, and as he aggravated me beyond endurance, I gave him a gentle slap on the face. He rushed at me like a bull and then I admit, I fought him. Iredale and Smith held him, and I, as I went out he shouted that I was a coward.

Of course, this did not improve anything at all. The illustrious six have been left out of the side, they are not going to England. Can you imagine a side without Hill, Armstrong and Trumper? Gloom has spread across the nation. One man sent £100 to the *Argus*, saying this would start a fund to send an independent side to England. In a couple of days the fund has grown to £1000.

Frank Laver, 352 not out

There have been public meetings right across the nation. They had one in Sydney Town Hall. At first the idea was just to have it in the vestibule, but they filled the place to overflowing. In Adelaide there was a huge meeting that overflowed the Adelaide Town Hall; the Mayor, Mr. Bonython, was in the chair. In Melbourne the meeting was in the Athenaeum Hall. The doors were advertised to open at 7 p.m., but at 6.45 p.m. the crowd poured in, sprinting for the front seats. The place was so jammed they filled the upper and lower halls, then had a third meeting in Baptist Hall next door. There was a band which played a parody on a popular tune: 'What's the matter with Laver? — He's all right'.

Mr W.L. Baillieu, the financier was in the chair, and on the committee was Norman Brookes, the tennis champion.

The protests have been fantastic, but what can they do? A miserable, uninspired official team has its farewell on 19 March.

Menzies Thwarted

9 MARCH 1951

Dr Evatt: absolute denial

Today the High Court of Australia ended Robert Menzies's dream of banning the Communist Party.

In his policy speech on 10 November 1949, R.G. Menzies said: 'Communism in Australia is an alien and destructive pest. If elected we shall outlaw it. The Communist Party will be declared subversive and unlawful, and dissolved'.

Soon after he became Prime Minister, Menzies was a good as his word. He introduced the Communist Party Dissolution Act. He described it as a 'Bill to outlaw and dissolve the Australian Communist Party, to pursue it into any new or associated forms and to deal with the employment of Communists in certain offices...and to give the Government power to deal with the King's enemies in this country'.

Six judges declared the Act invalid. Only the Chief Justice, Sir John Latham, dissented.

Mr Menzies tonight was defiant and his antipathy to Labor's Dr Evatt rose to the surface. Mr. Menzies said:

I say on behalf of the Government that this is not the end of the fight against Communism; it is merely the beginning. One thing is quite clear. In spite of the Communists, and in spite of the Chifley–Evatt section of the Labor Party at Canberra, the commu-

nity must either have or get power to defend itself against internal wreckers.

There was an extraordinary blow up today in the House of Representatives. Mr W.C. Wentworth, Liberal NSW, accused Dr Evatt of having for a long time furthered the interests of Communists. He said his statements had been made only after careful examination of Dr Evatt's activities and associations over many years. He said it was in the public interest he should say this.

Amidst a total uproar, he continued:

I have no proof that Dr Evatt has ever been a member of the Communist Party and I have never accused him of being a member; but I do accuse him of long association with Communists and of having too often adopted policy in the Communist interests.

His voice was drowned in shouts from the Opposition benches, and he said he would repeat his charges on the steps of the House, which he did at 2.30 p.m., immediately after the House rose. He was flanked by MPs, attendants, reporters and photographers. The only Minister present was the Postmaster General, Mr Anthony.

Immediately after question time, Dr Evatt, in a personal explanation said:

In my absence insinuations were made that I was acting in this House on behalf of and in the interests of the Communists. I give that statement an absolute denial. It is a compelte and absolute untruth and a monstrous statement. If it does not spring from an honest mistake, it is the outpouring of a distorted mind and a black, malevolent heart.

So what will Mr Menzies do now in his passion to dispose of the Communists. Commentators say a national referendum will take place to put the Communist question to the Australian people.

One thing, the Australian Communist Party and the Communist unions do not have to pay for the challenge through the High Court. The Court ordered the Commonwealth Government to pay for the cost of the action, which will be more than £30 000, and if there is a referendum, that will be just the start of the expense.

The Desperate Dollar Shortage

10 MARCH 1952

The heaviest import restrictions in Australia's history are now operating.

Import of thousands of types of goods has been cut from 80 to 40 per cent. The overall effect will be to halve present imports. From now on virtually all goods, including those from England, can be imported only under licence.

It has all come about because of a record trade deficit, which has been growing in an alarming way for many months. Unless the drift is stopped, this year's trade deficit will be £600 million.

The Prime Minister, Mr Menzies, said yesterday:

This decision was not an easy one to take, because we dislike controls and, in particular, are most reluctant to impose restrictions on goods from the United Kingdom, whose exports at this time mean so much to her, and to her own balance of trade. But a crucial position must be met and overcome.

The plain fact is this...our import expenditure is so far out-running our export income that, unless special measures are taken, our overseas funds, so vital to our solvent international trade, will be seriously threatened.

Unquestionably everybody will feel the brunt of this. The flow of fully-asssembled imported cars has been reduced to 20 per cent, and unassembled chassis to 60 per cent. Tobacco to be processed here is cut 40 per cent, and cigarettes 80 per cent. Textile and clothing imports are so heavily reduced that Lancashire business men have declared that the order 'strikes a body blow'. They say their loss will be £2 million a month.

Imports worst hit by the cuts are: beer and spirits, manufactured tobacco, cigarettes, cigars, foodstuffs, confectionary, textiles, footwear, lawnmowers, washing machines, refrigerators, radios, fans, cutlery, lamps, perfumes, toys, jewellery, clocks, gramophones, fountain pens, motor cycles, cars and musical instruments.

The Leader of the Opposition, Dr Evatt, is castigating the Government. He says:

Again we find the Government openly admitting that it has allowed a situation to

Mr Menzies: increased wheat production and import cuts

develop towards economic crisis and then been forced in panic to adopt stringent and savage measures. The whole thing is fallacious because the export side of our trade is being discouraged by record taxation and lack of a positive plan to encourage Australian primary industries.

Actually Mr Menzies has made a 'Make Australia Solvent' appeal to wheatgrowers. Wool, meat and butter exports could not be suddenly increased, he said. Wheat was the one large export industry that could make a substantial production increase. Every additional bushel of wheat exported after the next harvest would save dollars for the sterling areas — just about two bushels for every bushel. 'I most earnestly urge that all wheatgrowers do all in their power to achieve maximum planting this season'.

The Sydney Stock Exchange reacted quickly yesterday. There was a strong rise in textile shares and a fall in highly-priced motor distributor stocks. There was little panic buying of imported goods, but warehouses withheld stocks of Scotch and imported gin until they could work out new quotas.

There is talk of heavy restrictions on overseas travel, particularly to the dollar area. Dollars will be supplied only for essential reasons.

Gaslight for Hobart

11 MARCH 1852

*Gas lamps in Flinders
Street, Melbourne*

Liverpool Street Hobart was crowded on Monday evening to witness the first introduction of gaslight.

To those who have never seen the effect before, the splendind appearance, which it imparted wherever it was used, must have been most striking. Seeing that it was a brilliant moonlight night, only a limited number of street lamps were lit, and the effect of those was somewhat modified.

Most of the shops were closed, but in some where gas was introduced its superiority was so obvious that it made the oil lamps look completely dull and lacking in cheer. Several of the hotels, butchers and, especially the shops of Messrs Atkins, Spurling and a few others, really looked beautiful.

The Gas Company's fitting establishment drew a great concourse of people. Various descriptions of burners were lighted, and their effect was certainly grand. In Elizabeth Street, Mr Henry Cook astonished the natives with a star illuminated with gas.

Some little time, of course, will elapse before the town is entirely lit, as much caution has to be used in case of gas escape. With proper care and by attending to the published instructions of the Gas Company, no serious accident is likely to arise. To expect that the pipes are perfectly gas tight in every instance would be to expect too much, but the escape of gas, where it is found, is easy to fix. We have heard of only one accident, and that was due to incredible negligence.

The light itself burns beautifully pure and is so superior in every way to the dim lamps hitherto in vogue, that we imagine the number of those who fail to switch to gas will be few indeed.

The Hobart *Mercury* has published safety instructions, which it hopes all gas users will observe. For example:

Before turning on the main for lighting see that all your small taps are turned off. Then in first lighting turn it but slightly on, so that your glasses may get gradually heated, afterwards turn it to the strength you require. If turned on too strong at first, your glasses and chimneys will be filled with gas and when the light is applied cause a loud report and probably not only shatter the glass but cause injury.

As for the cost, Alderman Thomson has told the Council that the Gas Company has arranged for 180 lamps in the city. They will each cost £11-5s a year, and the lamps will be lit on 305 nights. This will cover all costs, lamplighter and maintenance.

Alderman Thomson pointed out that this was very reasonable. Cheaper than Sydney, where they had coal right nearby; and infinitely cheaper than Melbourne.

The *Mercury* is delighted with everything that is going on. It says:

In wandering through the streets of the city the pedestrian cannot but perceive the great improvements which have been made in the condition of the principal thoroughfares. The footpaths are well-formed, the carriage road is levelled and rendered available for the passage of vehicles. Several useful works now in progress will render Hobart Town a very pleasant place to live in, especially when the city is lighted with gas.

HMAS *Perth* and *Yarra* Feared Lost

14 MARCH 1942

HMAS *Perth*, one of Australia's six-inch gun cruisers, and HMAS *Yarra*, an Australian built naval sloop, are missing after leaving Java for Australia, and are presumed lost.

This is a grievous blow. Only last November, HMAS *Sydney*, our finest cruiser, after an heroic battle and sinking a German raider, went down 200 miles off the West Australian coast. It is feared the entire complement of 645 men is missing, and we have news only of enemy survivors.

The Prime Minister, Mr Curtin, said last night:

It is with deep regret that I announce HMAS *Perth* and *Yarra* must be presumed lost... With so much of the area in enemy hands, communication is naturally difficult. It may be some time before additional news, if any, of possible survivors is received. Any information that does arrive will be made public immediately. The next-of-kin have been informed. My Government and the Naval Board extend to them our sincere sympathy in their anxiety. They know that with it is joined the sympathy of the whole nation.

From Washington comes the news that the naval battle of Java Sea is being regarded as the fiercest and biggest sea contest since Jutland, waged with odds that were regarded as suicidal even before it began. According to American reports, the Allies lost 13 ships and the Japanese seven. Washington circles expected heavy losses, though the actual extent came as a shock. Apparently most, if not all, United States warships operating in the Java Sea were lost. Yet there is reason to believe that the Allies estimate of Japanese ships lost is conservative.

The casuality lists in today's neswpapers are terrible. There are 833 names of those missing, 682 from the *Perth* and 151 from the *Yarra*. There is another official statement from the Army Minister, Mr Forde that total Australian casualties in Malaya and Singapore so far are 17 031, including prisoners of war. Mr Forde said figures were based on calculation. It is known 287 officers and men were killed in action, or died before the real battle for Singapore began. Some parties of men and officers escaped, but 16 744 officers and men were not accounted for.

The *Sun* says today:

All Australia will grieve for their loss and share something of the acute personal sorrow now being experienced in so many Australian homes. Pride in the nobility of their lost ones and faith in the splendour of the cause for which they gave their lives will in time assuage the anguish of the bereaved, but its present poignancy will be fully appreciated only in other homes across whose thresholds war has cast the same dark shadow. Heavy indeed is the price of admiralty that Australia has been called upon to pay, but we shall not falter or complain, but shall continue on our way strong of purpose and with undimmed vision.

Meanwhile the Air Ministry is boosting local morale by issuing communiques of heavy RAAF attacks on Gasmata in New Britain. All our bombs fell on the target area. Our aircraft beat off attacks by Japanese Zero fighters, and returned safely with most of their ammunition exhausted.

HMAS Sydney

Madame Pavlova

15 MARCH 1926

Madame Pavlova, the greatest ballerina the world has seen, is in Malbourne performing at Her Majesty's Theatre.

She gave an interview as soon as she stepped off the Adelaide Express. Reporters were impressed that she was so natural, so easy to talk to. Her hair not bobbed or shingled, no pet dog and no story about her legs being insured for half a million. They aren't insured at all.

Madame Pavlova is small with a toothy smile, all expression; and as she talks she uses her hands and conveys a mood, a feeling, with huge meaningful eyes. She left Russia in 1914 and has never been back. 'If I returned I do not know what would happen to me'.

Yet she spoke of her Russia with great love. For 150 years, she said, the Russian Government had subsidised the Imperial College, where all branches of art were taught. This century the Government had spent £300 000, and the benefit to the world was so obvious.

'They tell me that you are lovers of art, that the power of appreciation is greatly developed in you. You have given the world its greatest singer, well,' and there was an expressive shrug of the shoulders, a snap of dainty fingers, a roll of the eyes 'why do you not do the same, subsidise the schools of art?'.

She told how art was a tradition, how it evolved, and with great feeling mentioned her old maitre de ballet who, after 50 years, attained the position of master. Money meant nothing. People like him worked for art alone.

The reporters asked her about jazz and modern dancing. Jazz, she said, was decidedly crude and graceless. Vile noises emanated from the orchestra, and frogs, cans and other things seemed to be the main feature of such crude music. It seemed that the kitchen and not the orchestra was making the row.

She said:

My favourite dance is known as 'The Dying Swan' It is the best dance I have. M. Fokine created it and Saint Saens composed the music. After the first performance of that dance Saint Saens came to my dressing room and said, 'I never realised that I had written such beautiful music'.

When asked what she would do in Melbourne, she said:

Madame Pavlova

I am so anxious to see your famous bush, Melba told be to go into the country and so I shall. In London I have eucalyptus tree I grew myself. It was presented to me in the form of a bouquet, a tiny thing, and now it is quite large.

Three thousand people went to the opening performance at Her Majesty's to see *Fairy Doll* and *Chopiana* Tickets are one guinea, 12s 6d, 10s 6d and 7s 6d.

The *Age* critic, normally a reticent gentleman, has excelled himself. This morning he writes:

Perhaps no form of artistic experience could make a more direct appeal than the overwhelming spell of abstract beauty made visible; of the infinitude of intermingling lines of loveliness that Pavlova brings before her enthralled audiences. Pictures motionless, as well as silent, music with all its promise of something divine beyond life's horizons does not tell us all its secrets Words fall back, baffled from the radiance of the terror of supreme experiences.

Canberra to be National Capital

16 MARCH 1913

Good heavens, the name of the National Capital is going to be Canberra.

You appreciate that for some time the whole business has been in the hands of that extraordinary, Canadian-born, parliamentarian, King O'Malley. In the first Parliament it was King O'Malley who moved a recommendation that the Government should buy 585 square miles of land from the State of New South Wales for the establishment of a Capital Territory.

Oddly enough, having done this, he mocked the idea of a capital in NSW. He felt they were very comfortable using the Parliament House in Melbourne and he claimed 'We old roosters will never see the new site'.

In 1908 the running favourite spot for the capital was Dalgety in the Snowy Mountains. King O'Malley asked the Prime Minister, Mr Deakin:

> In view of the fact that the Honorable Gentleman has announced that next week we shall deal with the question of the Canberra site, I wish to know whether he has any photographs or pictures of Dalgety, showing the immortal Snowy River, the heights of Kosciusko and peaks covered with perpetual snow, so that we can see these features when forming an opinion of the beauties of the situation.

Come 1909 the site switched to Canberra, and O'Malley said 'There is a proposition to establish the capital in a district which is so dry that a crow desiring to put in a week-end vacation would have to carry its water bags'.

He then suggested to the House the attractions of Tasmania for the capital. It was well known, he said, that through all history all the brilliant brains and diligent workers came from frigid climates.

But since becoming Minister for Home Affairs, he has been a very different, diligent character, and for weeks members have beseeched him for the name of the new capital. Not only did he refuse to give information, neither did he give members the privilege of voting on it. All he would concede was 'The name I prefer is Shakespeare'. He never said why. Perhaps it is because the very name personifies drama. comedy and tragedy.

But names have come out of the sky like rain. Sir George Reid wanted Pacifica; Andrew Fisher liked Myola; Austin Chapman, Austral; and Hugh McMahon, Radiance. The *Star* newspaper in Sydney ran a competition and offered a gold watch worth £20 to the citizen who could find the most appropriate name.

Amongst those published were Sydbourne, Melba, Washington City, Palladium, Paradise, Bee-hive, Coo-ee, Dulce Domum, Jumbuck City, Eucalypta, Cookhaven, Thirstyville, and even Syd-Melb-Ad-Per-Bris-Ho, which was an inspired combination of all our State capitals.

This week King O'Malley handed a gold card-case to Lady Denman, wife of the Governor-General. She read out the name from the card inside it: not Coo-ee, Kookaburra or Dulce Domum, it was just dull, predictable Canberra, the name that had been there all the time.

King O'Malley lays the third foundation stone of Parliament House

Problems in Picking an Australian XI

17 MARCH 1877

We have just held...shall we call it?...the First Test match against the Englishmen.

Mr James Lillywhite's team of professsionals has been in the colonies, so it was decided to match him for the first time with an inter-colonial XI, six players from NSW and five from Victoria.

By heavens, it has not been easy. First the great Sydney bowler, Evans, announced he couldn't play because of business. Then the famous 'Demon' Spofforth, another Sydney player, said that Murdoch was the only wicket-keeper who understood his bowling. Unless Murdoch was picked he wouldn't play.

The Victorians said they would not give up John Blackham, whom they claimed was the greatest wicket-keeper in the world. So Spofforth did not play. Then Frank Allan, the top Victorian bowler, who worked for the Lands Department in Warrnambool, said he was not available. He wanted to go to the Warrnambool Fair that week-end. So they had to pick a Richmond bowler named Hodges, who at the beginning of the season was playing for a minor club in Collingwood.

It was a disaster. England was the out-and-out favourite. Finally interstate rivalry was appeased, the match was at the Melbourne Cricket Ground and Dave Gregory of Sydney was the captain.

The English bowlers were Shaw, Hill and Ulyett, the latter a hefty Yorkshireman, considered the fastest bowler in England. Australia lost wickets early, but Charles Bannerman stood firm. Soon the news spread; the Sydney batsman was still there; maybe there was a chance; and crowds flocked to the MCG. By Stumps Bannerman was still there on an absolutely prodigious 126 not out in a total of 6/166. The next day 12 000 people were present to see Bannerman continue his innings. He went on to make 165 before a rising ball from Ulyett hit him on the hand, split his fingers, and he was unable to continue. Our total score was 245. No other batsman made more than 20 runs.

The *Argus* was so excited, yesterday it called for a Bannerman subscription, saying 'We should not grudge him a jot of the honours even if he did come from Sydney'.

England replied with 196, Jupp 65, Ulyett 36. The Australian all-rounder, Billy Midwinter, took 5/78. The Australian second innings was a disaster. Bannerman tried to bat with his hand in bandages, but could not stand up to Ulyett, and was clean bowled for four. The speed trio of Shaw, Hill and Ulyett was formidable, and they went through the Australian side for 104 runs.

It all looked pretty hopeless, but today was one of those days when a bowler was born for the occasion. Tom Kendall, a left-hander, bowled practically unchanged through the match, and took an incredible 7/55. Hodges, the new boy took two wickets, England was all out for 104 and Australia won outright by 45 runs.

Melbourne *Punch* is so thrilled, it is putting the whole match into verse. Here are a few lines:

> There came a tale to England,
> 'Twas of a contest done;
> Australian youths in cricket fields
> Have met the cracks and won;
> They fell like sheaves in autumn,
> Despite the old world dodges.
> Their efforts vain the runs to gain
> Off Kendall or off Hodges;
> Then rose a shout Australian
> That echoed to the main,
> 'Twas confident, not 'blowing',
> "Again we'll do the same!"

Bare Knuckled Fighters Take to the Bush

18 MARCH 1879

The Marquess of Queensberry

We have just held the boxing championship of Australia. Very tricky, it was.

Abe Hickin, a celebrated fighter in England and USA, is here and he wanted to fight our great champion, Larry Foley. What's more, he said he wanted none of this Marquess of Queensberry rubbish. 'I want a fight, not a pillow fight' he said. 'I'll cut this fancy dancer to pieces if he'll only stand up and fight like a man.'

So they arranged a bout at £500 a side, but the old-style bare-knuckle fighting is illegal. Well, first they decided to have the bout out in the bush; the police got wind of that. Then they hired a bay steamer; the police beat that one, too.

Then they thought, why not stage it on the dividing line between the two colonies, on the Murray, then they could escape the police forces of NSW and Victoria. The Victorian fans hired a special train to Echuca, which should have been signal enough, but they tricked the police into thinking it was taking place in Goulburn, and finally settled on a glade of red gums, just below Dead Horse Point near Echuca.

There were three wretched little punts to ferry Victorians across the river, the fee an outrageous half a crown a time. Most people got their trousers ruined in the mud.

The time 6.55 a.m. The Echuca Police arrived in the nick of time and tried to stop the bout, but Jem Mace, Foley's manager and former heavyweight champion of the world, said the Victorian Police had no jurisdiction here, they were in NSW territory. According to the *Argus*, if the police really wanted to stop the fight, they weren't over diligent about it.

The betting was six to one on Hickin, even though Foley was taller and looked beautifully muscled. The first round went for 23 minutes. Hickin was a charger, a bar-room brawler, but Foley was cool, a classic scientific boxer. He landed all his punches on Hickin's 'illuminated' face with ease. Soon it was clear Hickin was hopelessly outmatched.

The *Riverine Herald* man reported:
When time was called for the 12th Hickin presented a horrible spectacle. Both eyes were nearly closed, his lips were cut and blistered, his nose knocked out of shape, and his whole face pounded almost to a jelly. During this round one blow brought streams of blood from his mouth. He continued to respond to calls of 'Time', although he received more punishment. During the 14th his face was in a sickening condition, he was weak, muddled in the head. Still he fought on with dogged determination which evoked administration, even from those who were disgusted with the brutal nature of the affair.

In the sixteenth, bleeding, on his knees, almost unconscious, his second threw in the sponge. The crowd took up a collection in appreciation of Hickin's courage.

A tall, dark bearded man came up to congratulate Foley. Some say it was Ned Kelly, and very likely, too. He had been in Jerilderie a month earlier.

Foley is now returning to his hotel in Sydney. His loving admirers are taking up a testimonial. They will present him with one thousand pounds and a gold watch.

De Groot Opens Harbour Bridge

21 MARCH 1932

The Sydney Harbour Bridge, one of the wonders of the world, at last is open.

They started building it back in back April 1923, and the final cost is 9 577 507 pounds. It has been an enthralling experience watching the great arch grow: one piece from the north shore, the other from the south, and finally it all came together like the two arms of a tiara.

The actual opening was a sensation. Eric Campbell, head of the New Guard, a private, semi-military organisation that is opposed to Lang's Socialist Government, announced last week that Lang would never do the opening. The New Guard would beat him to it.

But how? Who could ever get past Lang's police army? Captain Francis de Groot was the man. When the Governor-General, Sir Isaac Isaacs, drove up in an open coach, he had with him a military escort of the New South Wales Lancers. De Groot, in full uniform, craftily tacked on behind. He wore a military cap and not a cocked hat like the lancers, but nobody noticed the difference.

When the military escort reached Bridge Street, de Groot's horse slipped on the damp pavement. A policeman held up the traffic so that de Groot could quickly regain his place.

As they passed the Governor's stand, de Groot saluted, the Governor saluted back. When de Groot took up a position rather too close to the ribbon an official asked if he was sure he was in the right place. Yes, he was absolutely sure.

Just as Mr Lang finished his speech, de Groot spurred his horse and with an underhand swish of his sword at the ribbon, he shouted 'On behalf of decent and loyal citizens of New South Wales I now declare this bridge open'.

At first people thought the horse was out of control and de Groot would jump the ribbon. However he missed with his first sword slash, then severed it with the second. Police rushed forward and dragged him from the saddle. He caught his foot in the stirrup and fell to the roadway.

You can't touch me, I'm a Commonwealth officer said de Groot. 'So am I' said a policeman, who hauled de Groot to his feet and immediately

Captain de Groot prepares to slash ribbon

placed him under arrest. He was taken to the Darlinghurst Police Station, where he is being charged with being a person deemed to be insane and not under proper care and control.

Mr Eric Campbell told the *Sydney Morning Herald* that de Groot acted with the full approval of the New Guard, but the idea was entirely his own. Campbell said the New Guard had been depending on the Federal Government to live up to its promise to suppress Communism and to deport all Communists. The Guard had a number of alternative schemes to make sure the Government kept its promises.

Meanwhile Sydney is more concerned about celebrating, than worrying about de Groot. Everybody wants to be the first to drive over the bridge. Last night the queues of the cars backed up all the way to the Town Hall, and on the north side they went back for a full mile.

An ecstatic *Sydney Morning Herald* asks: 'Was there ever such a jewelled 24 hours?' It describes the event as a wedding — a marriage of the north and south sides. The first time the city is one, a great symbol for the future and a hope that the dark days of the depression are over.

The Theatre Royal Burns

22 MARCH 1872

The Theatre Royal burned to the ground yesterday in an absolutely shocking fire.

I know a lot of people are clucking their tongues and saying that the Lord has merely visited justice on sinners. Only a few years ago, that great Presbyterian, Dr Adam Cairns, pointed out that no good ever came out of stage playing. Once a youth was tempered by this diversion, he absented himself from church, his imaginations was excited, and the risk was imminent of his becoming a slave of lust.

However the Theatre Royal in Bourke Street, as the *Herald* put it, was Melbourne's most famous refuge of the Thespian art. It was just after midnight that the 'first handful of flame' appeared to come somewhere from the back stage of the old theatre. Minutes later, the roof at the rear fell in.

Fire shot across from end to end with a speed that resembled the ignition of a train of gunpowder. According to the reporter of the *Herald*:

The building was enveloped in rose-coloured flames. The mere heat of which was sufficient to ignite the wooden seats in the pit, then the box-circle and the galleries which reached to the ceiling.

The iron roof lasted after this but a second or two and then there rose to the sky such a vast volume of bright fire as made the few thousands of people in the

Mr George Coppin: severe loss in theatre fire

street yell in their mad excitement.

Next some of the fittings were exposed and our man wrote:

...unconsumed pantomine masks leered hideously on the scene and in one portion of the dress circle the crimson damask fittings seemmed to offer a convenient seat for a demon fresh from the last act of *Don Giovanni*.

The United Insurance Brigade came into action and poured out hissing jets of Yan Yean water, but it only seemed to make the blaze roar more furiously.

The firemen now could only try to isolate the fire. The owners of buildings around piled their belongings into the street. Worst hit was Pain's Museum, which contained a vast collection of Australian and Polynesian curiosities, unique and 'never to be replaced'. Among them was a 'petrified man, the dried remains of an Australian native which had been found in a tree'.

But pilferers were everywhere and Mr Pain's loss cannot yet be estimated. Looters also raided Mr McDonald's photographic establishment at St George's Hall, and the Cafe de Paris next-door, also suffered terrible damage.

Mr George Coppin, lessee of the Theatre Royal, was called out of bed. His loss is severe indeed, in scenery, dresses, fixtures, wardrobe. He had been insured for three policies, over £1000 pounds each, but three months ago he decided not to renew.

Worse still, 150 actors, actresses and stage-hands are now out of work. As the *Herald* points out, there are 'Priests and Levites' amongst us who declare they are unworthy of assistance, but it is not the time to take a holier-than-thou attitude.

An entertainment is being organised to raise funds to help the fire sufferers. There will be a number of amusing events, including a cricket match at the Melbourne Ground with races in theatrical costume. There will also be a sacred concert on Good Friday night at St George's Hall where gas will be provided free. Mrs Gladstone, a great favourite with Melbourne audiences, will sing. We hope all will attend.

General MacArthur Arrives

23 MARCH 1942

General MacArthur (right) welcomed by Lord Gowrie

New manpower regulations come into force today. National service offices have been opened in all States, and everyone must register and have an identity card.

The Director-General of Manpower, Mr D. Cameron, said yesterday that he had appointed a staff of expert investigators. They will visit all places of employment to make sure that every able man and woman is in his or her effective war-time job. The staff appointed at manpower offices are all public servants over combatant age.

Every man called for medical examination must report. If he claims exemption on grounds of hardship, the Army will decide. If he is a conscientious objector to the bearing of arms, the case will be referred to a magistrate. Only in extreme cases will exemption from military training be recommended by manpower authorities.

Australians have been slow in their response for registration. More than two million cards have yet to be collected. All those over 16 must register by 25 March or the penalties will be very severe.

There will be Air Raid Precaution (ARP) tests in the cities on Friday. First there will be the warning of a single siren, followed later by an 'All Clear'.

Now it is official. General MacArthur and his party have arrived in Melbourne after a dramatic dash from the Bataan Peninsula. The Supreme Allied Commander in the South-West Pacific gave his first press conference yesterday.

He told reporters:

I want your help. Without it we cannot get the maximun out of the situation, and we need the maximum in order to win. To that end my main purpose is not to suppress news, but to get news for you. Men will not fight and men will not die unless they know what they are fighting for. In democracies it is essential the public know the truth.

General MacArthur, according to US headquarters, defied the best advice available on the Bataan Peninsula when he made his dash. When told it was impossible, he replied 'We go with full of the moon; we go during the Ides of March'. The MacArthur party, in 12 powerful PT boats, sped through the Japanese defences, even sighting enemy destroyers on the way. They took a continual pounding from heavy seas, and many of the party were ill. On one occasion, another PT boat, convinced that the General's oncoming boat was an enemy, cleared the decks for action. Only by the merest chance, they identified MacArthur's boat in time to avoid opening fire with .50 calibre machine guns.

Meanwhile in Melbourne, there is a heavy beer drought. Many hotels have signs up: 'No More Beer on Draught until April Fool's Day'. Brewery executives denied yesterday that a deliberate attempt had been made to restrict supplies to provoke public agitation against the Government regulations.

Air-liner Crashes in NE Victoria

24 MARCH 1931

The Australian National Airways air-liner, the *Southern Cloud*, carrying six passengers and two pilots, is lost somewhere in north-eastern Victoria.

The machine left Sydney for Melbourne at 8.30 a.m. the day before yesterday and has not been seen since. ANA has suspended all services so that every available aeroplane can take part in the search. Normally the service is non-stop to Melborne, but in accordance with company regulations, when there is bad weather the aircraft can land on a flying field at Bowser, 5 miles north of Wangaratta, where there are refuelling arrangements.

There are reports that the aircraft was heard in the area on Sunday and it appeared to be flying through driving rain. There has been widespread rain throughout Victoria in the worst storms for many years.

The missing airliner is a three-engined Fokker, piloted by F.W. Shortridge and his co-pilot, C.W. Dunnel. All pilots engaged in the search yesterday agreed on one point, if anyone could land the Southern Cross safely in difficult country, it was Mr Shortridge, the chief pilot of Australian National Airways. He was the most skilful pilot in the employ of the company, and he could handle the big machine better than anyone else.

At 6.15 a.m. yesterday, a dawn patrol gathered at Essendon airport to take part in the huge search. The first to leave were Mr Charles Ulm and Captain Johnston in an Avro Moth. They made for the Eildon district. Next was Mr Allan who piloted the *Southern Star*. He left with three observers and a parachutist.

Then at 7.45 a.m., Air Commodore Kingsford Smith piloted the *Southern Sun*, carrying three observers, a doctor, an assistant pilot, a parachutist and a photographer. Kingsford Smith left Sydney immediately he heard the *Southern Cloud* was missing. There was drama here, too. He landed at Holbrook, the wheels of the *Southern Sun* stuck in soft mud and the aeroplane tilted forward onto its nose, smashing the air screw of the centre motor. Miss N. Lyle, one of Australia's most competent air women, flew to Holbrook in an aero Club Moth carrying a new propeller, so that Kingsford Smith could continue his journey.

The tireless search went on all day. An *Age* reporter who flew with the Air Commodore, said:

> Returning to the Essendon airport Kingsford Smith after a morning's search held a hurried consultation with the other pilots and observers, who had taken part in the search. All had the same tale to tell. 'No luck' But the indomitable Air Commodore just smiled that irrepressible smile of his, encouragingly remarking, 'Well, we must try again, that's all.' Without waiting to snatch any lunch once again he set out on another sustained and intensive search. He continued for 10 hours and his final words were 'We shall continue. They must be found. They shall be found dead or alive. But the time has come when I must confess that I feel seriously disquietened.

The RAAF, under the command of Wing Commander Cole, is also searching with front-line aircraft, ten Westland Wapitis.

Air Commodore Kingsford Smith (second from left)

61

'Red Raggers' Turn Out in Brisbane

25 MARCH 1919

Brisbane is in the midst of an anti-Bolshevik, an anti-Red, furore.

It all began on Sunday when the Deputy Premier, E.G. Theodore, better known as 'Red Ted', gave permission for a rally to demonstrate against the continuance of the War Precautions Act.

As the Brisbane *Courier* put it, every kind of 'Red Ragger' turned out, members of IWW, trade unionists, Sinn Feiners, Socialists and Russians. They unfurled red banners and made revolutionary statements.

In the evening there was another gathering at North Quay of 5000 people. A brawl broke out when the Returned Soldiers invaded with cries of 'Come on Diggers. Down with the Bolsheviks'. They threw the speakers platform in the river, and then a group of 500 decided to march on the headquarters of the Russian Association at the corner of Russell and Merivale Streets.

The terrified Russians in the club rooms opened fire with rifles over the heads of the crowd, and a 'terrible tragedy' was only prevented by the intervention of the police.

'Red Ted' Theodore

Yesterday the events were particularly ugly. There was a gathering of 7000 people at North Quay. A great Australian flag was unfurled and they passed a resolution:

We the returned soldiers and sailors of Queensland demand direct action by the police and federal authorities to prevent further meetings and demonstrations held by Russian Bolsheviks in this State, and we solemnly declare that if such action is not taken we will take the law into our own hands and by force quell disturbances made by the Russian Bolsheviks at once.

So to cries of 'Down with the Bolsheviks' and 'Who let you down at the war?', they decided once again to attack the Russian Association, and they marched across Victoria Bridge with the Australian flag flying at their head. A returned officer of the Light Horse, wearing ribbons and three wound stripes announced 'The whole crowd will have to be wiped out. I know I have got all you men with me'.

When they reached the Russian Association, there was a line of 50 or 60 foot police across the road — with fixed bayonets — plus mounted police. From verandahs nearby, women cheered on the soldiers to attack the police. Men ripped palings off the fences and they threw missiles at the police. Horses panicked and there was a mad melee. Then there were shots fired, and crackers exploded.

One mounted policeman was shot in the side; several soldiers were wounded; the Commissioner of Police, Mr Urquhart, was severely wounded by a bayonet in the left shoulder; in all there were 19 casualties amongst police and soldiers.

Tonight in Albert Square there was one of the largest outdoor meetings seen in Brisbane. It demanded that the authorities intern or deport all Bolshevik Russians and their sympathisers.

One man in the audience did not take his hat off during the National Anthem. He was given an 'upper cut' on the jaw, and with a fist 'fairly planted in his face', said the *Courier*, he did finally sing 'God Save the King'.

Convicts Murder Inspector-General

28 MARCH 1857

Mr Price set upon by felons

There was a hideous outrage at Williamstown yesterday. An angry mob of prisoners charged the Inspector-General of Prisons, John Price, and virtually stoned him to death.

Melbourne now is torn between feelings of conscience, guilt, fear and savage desires for revenge. With the gold rush and huge immigration, the city is desperately short of prison accommodation, so we are using four hulks, the *Success, Lysander, Sacramento* and *President* to house convicts.

There are more than 500 convicts, most of them in leg irons. They are held in such inhumane, dreadful conditions, that several weeks back a Citizens Committee was formed to do someting about it. Some branded the Committee a bunch of naive simpletons.

Whatever one thinks of the Citizens Committee, the Inspector-General, Mr. John Price, had a reputation for unrelenting harshness. At 3 p.m. yesterday, a large group of prisoners was working on a tramway and earthworks at Gellibrand's Point.

Mr Price, unarmed, went amongst the prisoners with some of the warders to listen to complaints. One prisoner by the name of Kelly said he had sent in his application for a ticket of leave; he had done three years there; and when was he going to get his freedom? He had been in solitary, unjustly, for three days. Price called on an overseer, Wilson, who told him that Kelly had been caught in his tent with writing materials. Price then refused Kelly's request and told him to go back to work.

Kelly in a fury stepped forward shouting 'You white-livered b———— wretch your race is run'. More men gathered in a circle. They were calling out 'Down with the b———— tyrant! Kill the b———— wretch'.

One man hit Price with a clenched fist. Others were picking up stones and hurlung them at him. Price ran down the side of the embankment with the prisoners after him. Price tried to fight them off shouting 'Don't! Don't'.

As he lay on the ground, Kelly dropped a great stone on his head. A prisoner named Bryant , took a shovel and bashed him with that then announced 'He's cooked, he wants no more'.

Meanwhile Captain Blatchford, Inspector of Hulks, was stunned by a blow on the neck, and Warden Wilson was knocked to the ground. Then the convicts gathered for a mass break out. They knocked off their irons with their quarrying tools and, but for the arrival of the police and the artillery corps, a very ugly situation could have eventuated. Two of the prisoners had dug an ingenious underground shelter complete with air holes, the whole arrangement obviously pre-meditated. They would never have been found had the police not been tipped off by one of their fellow convicts hopeful of receiving kindly treatment.

Several prisoners carried Price away on a hand barrow and took him to the lighthouse; he died later at the house of Dr Wilkins. Fifteen men have been charged with murder. Unquestionably at least seven of them will hang.

Price was 48 years old. He leaves a widow and nine children. According to the *Herald* they are most inadequately provided for.

Melbourne is frightened of these prison hulks. What if there is another break out next week?

Annette Kellerman, the Perfect Woman

29 MARCH 1933

Mrs James Raymond Sullivan, better known as Annette Kellerman, arrived in Sydney aboard the liner *Orsova* yesterday. It is the first time we have seen her in ten years.

Frankly I don't think Australia has produced any females more extraordinary than Miss Kellerman. She was born in Sydney in 1886 Her father was a violinist and her French mother was a pianist.

Little Annette used to have steel braces on her legs, and she learned swimming to strengthen her unformed muscles. By the time she was 16 she held every swimming record in NSW from 100 yards to the mile.

She became famous as a long-distance swimmer, and in 1905 her father took her to London. She swam 13 miles down the Thames; and 7 miles down the Seine in a race against male competitors, she came third. She raced the Baroness Isa Cescu in a challenge race 22 miles down the Danube and won.

Annette Kellerman has been a fearless campaigner for sensible swim wear for women. In her early days she startled Europeans with her eye-popping gear. She wore a male bathing costume with black stockings stitched on to the legs. Back in 1907 she was arrested on a beach in Boston for wearing a one-piece bathing suit, showing rather too much leg. That event attracted very satisfying publicity.

She married her manager, James Sullivan, in 1912, and became famous around the world in vaudeville and movies. It's hard to put one's finger on what Miss Kellerman did not do. She did aquatic acts, tightrope walking, ballet, acrobatics, male impersonations. One of her better efforts in New Zealand was diving 60 feet into a pool of crocodiles.

Annette Kellerman has been in more than half a dozen movies, and won a competition in the USA from 10 000 contestants for being the 'perfect woman'. She is now touring the world lecturing on physical fitness and diet. She does this speaking English, German, French, Danish, Dutch and Norwegian.

She told the *Sydney Morning Herald* yesterday that she had never known a nation so interested in physical culture and yet so ignorant of diet as the Germans. They ate too much food; their food was badly cooked; and they used too much vinegar.

As for her own diet, she said she had been a vegetarian for 20 years, but recently her doctor had ordered her to take some meat and coffee. Never had she drunk alcohol, and never had she smoked a cigarette. She believed in plenty of hot water, and she drank eight glasses a day.

Danish girls, she claimed, were the prettiest in the world, but there was nothing to compare with the figure of the Australian surf girl. While in Australia she would get into a bathing suit and stay in it.

Now she is off to Java and the South Seas to make travelogue films. She specialises in under water effects. She told everyone yesterday that she can stay under water without ill effects for 3 minutes 14 seconds.

Quite impressive for an acrobatic lady of 47 years.

Further reading: *Australian Dictionary of Biography*.

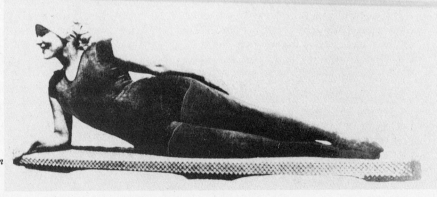

Annette Kellerman in an 'eye-popping' swimsuit

The Russian Scare

30 MARCH 1885

HMVS Nelson

Ever since the outbreak of the Crimean War, we have had this curious fear that we are about to be invaded by the Russians.

Every time a Russian ship has put to sea in the Pacific, we have presumed that it has had in its sights those choice morsels, Sydney and Melbourne. In Sydney Harbor back in 1854, they armed Pinchgut and Fort Denison. Steadily Melbourne has been mounting guns at Queenscliff and Point Nepean.

We had a scare when the Russian ship, *Bogatyr*, visited in 1863, and another in 1882 when the Russian ships came our way. The *Age* published what it claimed to be 'an intercepted despatch' from Admiral Aslanbegoff to the Russian Minister of Marine. The whole thing turned out to be a complete hoax, but we trembled in our beds, I can assure you.

Well, this week-end there has been another. Russia has been mounting forces on the border of Afghanistan. England's 'jewel', India, is under threat, and according to the *Herald* Britain and Russia are like 'two gladiators with swords drawn and shields advanced'. Mr Gladstone has demanded that the Russians pull back.

A Russian Fleet was at Cape Town in January, only 19 days steam from Australia. As a result, the Government of Victoria took dramatic steps. It has proclaimed that no foreign or overseas vessel will be allowed to enter the heads between sunset and sunrise.

Crewmen of HMVS *Nelson* have been called back from leave. It has been rumoured that HMVS *Cerberus* has been despatched to the Heads. Chains are being installed in the Western Channel, mines and torpedoes are being laid. The battery at Queenscliff is being readied for action. It has guns capable of penetrating 14 inches of armour at 4 miles. There are three guns at the Point Nepean Battery, but it is to be strengthened by two more.

All Melbourne is talking about the threat. It has been decided that in the event of enemy attack, bells will be run. At 5 o'clock this morning, the Footscray fire bell rang out and practically every local resident rushed outside, believing Russia had decided to fight.

A Warrnambool correspondent complains today they are virtually at the Russian's mercy. The value of business and property there is worth 'well over a million', but what do they have to defend themselves? Nothing but two ancient pieces of ordnance.

The *Herald* has been rather cynical. It says the Defence Department has been indulging in great secrecy yet:

> if Russia intended without doubt to send a force specially for the bombardment of Melbourne the Czar's Government could not possibly transfer its ironclads to this part of the world before our mosquito fleet could reach the Heads. Your Defence Department is incased in an armour of dullness more dense than the plating of the *Cerberus* and as impenetrable to plain common sense as the iron plates of the *Nelson* would be to a popgun.

However it is puzzling why the Russians, so far off, should find 'Marvellous Melbourne' or even Sydney or Warrnambool, so inviting.

The Labor Split

31 MARCH 1955

Mr Cain can command only 25 votes

The Australian Labor Party is in ruins and it is very hard to see its future.

Last October the Federal Leader, Dr Evatt, launched a bitter attack on an inside group in the party, which was trying to take over ALP policy.

So much of this has been innuendo, nobody coming out in the open. From what we can gather, inside the Labor Party there is a group known to some as 'The Movement'. Now the Movement has a very close alliance with the Bishops of the Roman Catholic Church, which has been distressed over the ALP's soft line towards Communists. The Movement formed industrial groups to fight Communism within the unions.

Headquarters for the Movement has been in Victoria. Dr Evatt moved in, sacked the Victorian ALP executive and appointed a new one. The old executive refused to resign, so we have experienced the ludicrous situation where both the 'old' and the 'new' executives went to the Hobart ALP conference.

Yesterday we had one of the most dramatic days in the history of State politics. Twenty-four parliamentarians who attended a meeting of the 'old' executive have been suspended. There are seven federal members: Joshua, Cremean, Keon, Andrews, Bryson, Bourke and Senator Devlin.

Amongst the 17 State members, four are ministers: Mr Barry (Health), Mr Hayes (Housing), Mr Coleman (Transport) and Mr Scully (Honorary Minister). They have been sacked from Cabinet. Mr Coleman has been selected as leader of the breakaway group, with Mr Barry leader in the lower house. They call themselves the State Parliamentary Labor, so now we have two Labor parties.

Mr John Cain, the Labor Premier, has called on the Governor, Sir Dallas Brooks, tendered his resignation and has received a commission to reconstruct his Government. But it is all a very bad dream. Now Cain can command only 25 votes of the 65 in the House. The leaders of the new party, Coleman and Barry, have written to the Premier saying that in no circumstances will their party support any further vote for supply.

On the Federal side, Mr Arthur Calwell, has remained loyal to Dr Evatt and the traditional ALP. He is still convinced there will be a reconciliation, but it is difficult to see how it can happen; feelings are running deep. Supporters of the sacked old executive are saying they are pledged to fight Communism, but this new Evatt executive had a non-aggression pact with the Communist party. The Communists were holding John Cain a prisoner.

Dr Evatt says the unholy, secret anti-Labor alliance backed by Mr B.A. Santamaria will soon 'be shattered by public exposure and the growing determination of the rank and file of Labor'. Commentator, Clive Turnbull, has a despairing story today. He says:

Stable Government becomes a dream...
Victoria becomes a kind of little France –
not the France of French cooking or oo-la-la, but the France of chaotic politics, blown one way or another while the country slides still further down hill.

It is inevitable as the start of the football season that we will have an election and neither of the two Labor parties will have a ghost of a chance. The Liberal–Country leader is a man named Henry Bolte, whom nobody knows much about.

Many people see him as a very unlikely prospect as Premier.

Further reading: *The Movement*, Paul Ormonde.

APRIL

Landing at Gallipoli

Phoenix Foundry Proudly Delivers 'Engine 83'

4 APRIL 1873

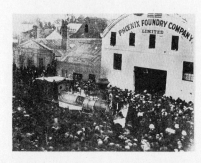

Engine 83

There was a huge celebration and banquet in Ballarat this Wednesday to honour the delivery of 'Engine 83', the first of 25 locomotives ordered by the Victorian Government.

The new locomotive brought a crowd of dignitaries including two ministers, four members of the Legislative Council and 20 member of the Lower House. I think everyone was impressed with the power and speed of the new engine. It pulled three carriages and a tender. It took just 2 hours to travel from Melbourne to Geelong, and then it sped on to Ballarat in 1 hour 35 minutes.

There was bunting and flags all over Ballarat. The Ballarat *Courier* pointed out yesterday that a jealous 'contemporary' in Melbourne had made sneering reference to this event, describing the engine as 'Ballarat's Chick'. Ballarat did not mind the epithet, everyone was aware of the fecundity of the species. Here was a new path of industrial skill, but Ballarat had shown it could triumph in the production of machinery of almost every description.

Free-traders, said the *Courier*, looked askance at this experiment and pooh-poohed, but now they had seen the folly of their doleful doubts.

The guests had a two-hour inspection of the Phoenix Foundry, then 200 sat down to the banquet in the Ballarat Town Hall. The chair was occupied by Mr Smith MLA; supported by the Hon. A. Fraser MLC, Commissioner of Public Works; and the Hon. Duncan Gillies, Commissioner of Railways.

The viands, supplied by the caterer, Mr George Thompson, according to the *Courier*, were of the 'most recherche description'. One felt they needed to be. There were 26 speeches and they went on for three hours. There was one comfort, almost every speech, including the honour to Her Majesty Queen Victoria and HRH the Prince of Wales, required a formal toast, so nobody went thirsty.

Maybe the best speech came at the end when Mr. W.C. Smith responded on behalf of the workers. He explained that the co-operation between capital and labour had been unique. The workmen had agreed to take only half wages, then at the end of every quarter a balance sheet was made out, and the profits divided. Only once since the formation of the company had these profits not given the men full wages.

Yes, they were producing engines as good, if not better than those imported from 'home'. The imported articles cost £7000 alone, just to put together. Now their new engine they put on the rails one day, and that very same day it took carriages to Lal Lal and had done 1000 miles before they handed it over.

All the Phoenix workers are going on a celebratory picnic to Geelong on Saturday. There's a picnic display of the beef, mutton and lamb today in Mrs Paterson's shop in Bridge Street. The *Courier* says: The meat is of 'the finest possible description and no doubt will be consumed with great gusto by the hearty fellows of the foundry when their appetites have been sharpened by a few whiffs of the sea air.'

The Cremation Outrage

5 APRIL 1895

There is no question most people have a deep mistrust of cremation. It is un-Christian and disrespectful of the dead. There is the feeling that if there is a second coming and the trumpets blow, the dead will still be found at their original address and will rise up in front of their elegantly carved headstones.

The *Bulletin* said recently, devoted souls believe in the Almighty's ability to reclothe a skeleton, but doubt his ability to reform from ash.

Melbourne *Punch*, on the other hand, said optimistically it would mean the end of all funeral expenses. Well, on 30 October 1892, the Melbourne Cremation Society was formed and Professor Kernot of Melbourne University presided. He said cremation could be done decently for £1, and relatives could be kept in urns on the mantelpiece.

The *Argus* was very distressed at the Professor's comments and said 'One has but to walk into a Melbourne cemetery and see the fresh flowers placed on graves to wither, and then one will understand how completely the sentiment of the living has adapted itself to the custom of burial'.

It took another three years to get round to a genuine cremation, and the subject was so appalling all newspapers ignored it, but I have found a report in the undertakers' trade, journal, *The Light*. When Mrs Henniker of 8 William Street, Richmond died, aged 83, she said in her will she wished to be cremated. Mr J.R. Le Pine of Richmond agreed to do it at moderate cost. He picked a remote spot on the sea shore between Half Moon Bay and Black Rock.

Light reported they used 3 tons of firewood and a keg of kerosene. A curious mob of spectators gathered when they saw the 'unwonted spectacle of a hearse drawn up in the midst of the sandy scrub'.

The body, enclosed in an elaborate coffin, was put in position with logs piled all around it and brushwood sprinkled with kerosene placed amongst the logs. No clergyman was present, but the mourners carried white flowers and stood around the pyre. Mr Frederick Henniker, Mrs Henniker's only son, bent down on his knees and set fire to the heap of wood.

The *Light* reported:

The heat was intense and the onlookers had to retreat some distance off but they watched the progress of the flames with unflagging interest. As the fire gained strength and crept around the coffin, a little band of mourners, among whom were half a dozen elderly ladies and young girls, sang very softly a few verses of Moody and Sanky's hymn, 'Shall We Gather At the River'. The hymn 'There's a Land That Is Brighter Than Day' was sung, then mourners climbed the cliffs again, and an empty hearse rattling away at a brisk trot told all was over. The undertaker left the scene at 9.30 p.m.

The event at Sandringham Beach has been described in Parliament as 'a scandalous and horrible occurrence', but as there is no law against it at the moment, no penalty is likely to be imposed.

Mr J.R. Le Pine and his wife

Hobart Leads the Way with Parking Meters

6 APRIL 1955

Hobart has traffic devices called 'parking meters'. It is leading the way, the first Australian city to try them out.

To me, they turn the city into a cemetery, little tombstones placed at body-length intervals all along the pavement, ticking away the death of the freedom of the motorist.

The Lord Mayor set in motion the first parking meter, appropriately on 1 April. Inappropriately, perhaps, the Mayor's name was Mr Park. He performed the ceremony near the intersection of Elizabeth and Collins Streets. He drove up in his private car and fumbled for a couple of threepenny pieces, which gave him the right to sojourn there for half an hour.

He said Hobart was making history because it was the first city in Australia to install these devices. Wherever the new invention was tried, there was always criticism, but it came only from people who were not fully informed.

The parking meters, said he, would be a boon. Not only would they raise money to pay for themselves, but the extra cash would go to pay for off-street parking centres. In Auckland, the pioneer parking meter city in Australasia, they found it was the selfishness of motorists that drove business out of the city. Now the man who parked all day was gone, and business was coming back again.

The parking meters have been in action now for a week, and certainly they have had an effect. The Hobart *Mercury* reports streets that normally were jammed with cars, now have empty gaps all over the place. People think having to pay threepence for 15 minutes is a terrible slug.

Others are crafty; they wait until they find a meter with unexpired minutes then they nick in and get free time. The *Mercury* did a survey of opinion. A couple of people thought it a good idea, several said they resented paying the money, and one character when asked just growled 'Rotten'.

The Mayor says the meters will pay for themselves in a year, and will meet the cost of building off-street parking to boot. But one wonders about his accounting skills. The revenue for the first week is 200 pounds. That

Mr Park sets the first meter going

is only £10 400 in a full year. The meters cost £20 000 pounds and, as one correspondent pointed out, the Mayor is not taking into account the cost of attendants, the costs of installation, and the costs of servicing; and if he thinks those threepences will provide us with the price of off-street parking stations, maybe they will...some time around 1990.

Incidentally there were 43 offenders in the first week who went over-time. Fines from these tardy folk scored £21 10 shillings.

The *Mercury* is not enthusiastic about the meters. It wonders whether the City Council is not just hell bent on making things more difficult for the motorist.

But unquestionably Tasmania is something of a trail blazer. Launceston is acquiring automatic telephones. No longer will subscribers have to lift the receiver and wait that eternity for the exchange to answer. The 3600 subscribers are being visited by Postal Department staff to change their telephones across to the automatic type. Isn't that something?

Phar Lap Dies in California

7 APRIL 1932

Phar Lap died yesterday at Menlo Park, California.

The shock is too much to bear. Only last week we were told he had won the Agua Caliente Handicap and he was the greatest galloper in America. Phar Lap was the one beautiful Australian thing happening in this awful depression. Now this.

First reports said the horse died of colic and indigestion. But Dr Neilsen, the Australian veterinary surgeon, has gone further. He claims Phar Lap was poisoned.

Today's newspapers tell the tragic story. Tommy Woodcock, Phar Lap's attendant:

...threw his arms around the horse's neck and wept unrestrainedly. Mrs D.J.Davis, wife of the part-owner, was hurriedly summoned and tried to comfort the trainer. Finally he was dragged away from the horse. Woodcock said: 'My friends in Australia know how much I loved the horse. He was almost human and he could almost speak. At home they will realise what his death means to me'.

The artist Daryl Lindsay said:

Phar Lap

It's like the Prince of Wales is dead. I went to the store and bought a paper. It was a long time before I could take in the significance of the headlines. People were standing about the store with long, stunned faces. Phar Lap was dead.

The *Sporting Globe* says Harry Telford, the trainer who stayed at home, is suffering the greatest grief.

Poor Telford. He is quite distracted. He walks around Braeside like one in a trance. The tragedy has been a terrible blow to him. Listlessly he wanders about the place — into the huge stables, out again into the exercise yard and down on the track, following a phantom, or perhaps listening for some spirit voice that will tell Phar Lap is not dead. Telford said: 'He was an angel. A human being couldn't have had more sense. I've never practised idolatry but I loved that horse. He was to come back and end his days in these paddocks. I wish to God he was coming back'.

In Sydney, flags at many public and private buildings in the western suburbs and Parramatta are at half-mast. In Melbourne, a pavement artist has produced a picture of the horse draped with an Australian flag and the inscription 'The Late Phar Lap RIP'.

At the City Court there was an offensive behaviour case. Two men came to blows over which was the greatest horse — Phar Lap or Carbine. The Magistrate commended that it was an argument unlikely to be settled, not even in 50 years.

All the newspapers have leading articles on Phar Lap's greatness and importance to our national culture. The *Sun News Pictorial* has gone further. It burst into verse:

Phar Lap farewell; your race is run.
And 'tis not in defeat that Death has won.
Your victory is that extinction came
While yet the world was ringing with your name.
To swell your country's fame you've done your part—
Your name is graven on Australia's heart.

But I am worried about our relations with the United States. First Les Darcy, now Phar Lap. It could be the end.

'Yes' to WA Secession

8 APRIL 1933

West Australia held a referendum today to decide whether it should secede from the Commonwealth and the answer is an overwhelming YES!

The counting isn't over yet, but so far 79 523 have said yes, and 42 724, no

Oh, the feeling is natural enough. The depression has been appalling. Of a population of 440 000, there are 70 000 men, women and children living by earnings from relief work; a sustenance allowance of 7s 0d a head per week.

The obvious thing is to blame all troubles on the villains out 'East' who are sweating the innocent, gullible creatures of the Golden West.

The Prime Minister, Mr Joe Lyons, came here last week in a desperate last ditch effort to swing the vote, but he had a shocking reception. His first speech was at the Theatre Royal. There was so much noise the only way they could quieten the crowd was to play the National Anthem.

He told those at the reception that he would have a convention to revise the constitution, and he would appoint a special body to examine the whole question of State Grants. As it was, the Commonwealth collected £4 700 000 from West Australia, but WA benefited by £1 million over what it paid.

Next he had the rowdiest meeting ever heard in Fremantle. Abusive remarks were hurled at him. He was counted out repeatedly. There were shouts of 'Judas' and 'You knocked old age pensions'.

The secession movement is run by the Dominion League, which wants WA to be a dominion in its own right. The League says it is utterly loyal to King George, but it is desperate to get away from Canberra domination. It had a great counter meeting in the Perth Town Hall to Mr Lyon's affair, and they opened it with a song which had such lines as:

The same old songs, the same old speech,
Dear old Groperland is good enough for
each,
We'll stand together boys,
If the East wants a flutter or a fuss,
And we're hanging out the sign,
From the Leeuwin to the line,
This bit of the world belongs to us.

The Lord Mayor, J.T. Franklin MLC, said that 33 years ago he voted against Federation, and was still against it. He wanted to see a change so that children in the State would be able to find employment and make goods for West Australians to consume.

The Dominion League made a number of last minute appeals before the election. Mrs F.A. Pratt, for example, on behalf of the mothers of WA said:

I send out an SOS call to be true to our British traditions on April 8. Our ship of State is sinking fast, overloaded with a cargo packed in the interests of the Eastern State monopolists, providing work for the children of the East but leaving your sons and daughters helpless.

Colonel Noel Brazier, Vice-President of the Dominion League, said:

When the future history of the British Empire is written, April 8, 1933 will be revealed as the day that a beacon of light first shone which led the people of Western Australia into the paths of justice, truth and righteousness.

Well, they have been given the beacon of light, but one wonders whether the West Australian Government, when it discovers all the costs, will have the courage to go ahead.

Mr Lyons: counted out and called Judas by a hostile crowd

'Mad Dog' Morgan is Dead

11 APRIL 1865

Mad Dan Morgan is dead and there is considerable pleasure and satisfaction around Beechworth today.

Some say he was the most bloodthirsty monster who ever roamed the Australian bush. On the other hand, he never had much chance. His parents were convicts. His father was a costermonger and his mother was a prostitute, Kate Owen.

His parents could not do anything with Dan. He grew up as a petty thief and was flogged savagely in gaol. So he took to the bush and his life was like an act of revenge on society. He actually enjoyed killing, and for the past three years he has been the terror of the Riverina and the Monaro, making a practice of shooting down unarmed and sleeping men.

He has always sneered at the police as 'a sour milk lot', and for a long time he has been threatening to cross the Murray 'to take the flashness out of the people and the police of Victoria'.

This time he did it. For four days, mounted on a celebrated race mare, Victoria, he terrorised the district. He went to Evan's property at King River, where he fired the granaries. This was an act of revenge because four years ago Evans shot off Morgan's finger while the latter was thieving.

Morgan held up carriers on the Melbourne road between Benalla and Wangaratta: he shot cattle, robbed travellers and finally he invaded Peechelba Station on the Ovens River, and bailed up the entire household.

The word went around very quickly that the villain was in the district. The police were on his track and every civilian within 50 miles was armed and ready. According to the *Sydney Morning Herald* correspondent, the excitement was intense.

Meantime Morgan proceeded to enjoy himself. He gathered what he thought was the entire company of Peechelba in one room, and tea being ready, he made Mr McPherson, owner of the station, his wife and other ladies, all sit down together. He became very chatty, spoke of all the hardships he had had to endure, and of his father and mother, whom he said were still alive.

He made one of the ladies play the piano and allowed them to retire at bed time. Alice MacDonald, a nurse maid, asked to be excused to look after the children. She immediately ran out through the bush to a neighbouring station, where all the men were immediately mustered with firearms.

Police came from Wangaratta and the house was surrounded. It was decided not to rush in for fear that Morgan might start a massacre. They waited in ambush until the dawn. Meanwhile Alice MacDonald kept the McPhersons advised of what was going on, and even took out a can of coffee to the men in the ambush.

Morgan was sleepy. He nodded off occasionally, but he kept a revolver in his hand. In the morning Morgan washed, combed his hair very nicely, and apologised for eating so much breakfast. There had been few meals lately.

At 8 a.m. he had half a glass of whisky. He ordered McPherson and three men out before him, then, with a revolver in each hand, he told them to get the horse.

There were 14 men with 14 guns waiting. As McPherson and the others went for the horse, Quinlan, an Irish workman on the property, came out from behind a stump. McPherson jumped to one side and Quinlan fired. The bullet entered Morgan's back and came out through his neck.

The police ran forward and disarmed him. Morgan thought it was a cowardly attack. 'Why not challenge me, and give me a chance?' he said.

Morgan was shot at 8.30 a.m. He died at 1.30 p.m. Two loaded revolvers, £86 in notes, and a bank draft for £7 were found on him. One revolver belonged to a police sergeant he shot several months ago. The inquest will be held this evening.

Ironclad HMVS *Cerberus* Arrives

12 APRIL 1871

Captain Panter celebrated with champagne

Her Majesty's Victorian ship, *Cerberus*, has arrived in Port Phillip.

She is the first ironclad, unassisted, ever to circumnavigate the globe. As she made her triumphant entry to the Port of Melbourne, Hobson's Bay absolutely came alive.

According to the *Argus*:
The boys of the HMVS *Nelson* crowded into the rigging of their ship and made the air ring with peels of boyish cheers... nearly every vessel in the bay hastened to add the compliment of dipping colours. Captain Panter dropped his anchor at precisely 1 p.m., and immediately celebrated with frothing champagne.

It is four years since we got the first intimation that we should have her for our protection and at last she lies at anchor in our waters, one of the most powerful vessels for harbour protection in the world.

Built at Jarrow-on-Tyne, she is 335 feet over all, with a 45 foot beam, and 2108 registered tonnage. She has two steam-powered turrets with 18-ton Woolwich muzzle-loading 10-inch guns, which have a range up to four miles. Impressive indeed, and what's more, she has solid armour-plate on her sides 8-inches thick.

As the *Argus* says, she is not regarded as a handsome ship by any means, just a huge, long, square box, cut down straight at both ends, and surmounted by a funnel, turrets and stunted masts, no topgallants at all.

She came up the Bay at 9 knots, but her average speed out was four. She is billed as one of the finest vessels afloat, but frankly, her voyage out sounds disturbing. For a start nobody wanted to sail on an ironclad. Captain Panter had to 'rake the back slums of London to get a crew'.

Cerberus left Plymouth on 7 November and how she survived the trip through the Bay of Biscay is a miracle. She had coal piled high on her decks. She doesn't really have a keel and her indicators, which go to 35 degrees, ceased to function when she rolled at 40 degrees and her bottom was actually out of the water. At one stage, a man was thrown from one side of the captain's cabin to the other without ever touching the deck. Everyone on board was convinced she would capsize. It's a wonder she did not, she had 1900 tons above the water line and only 1800 below it.

At Malta two-thirds of the crew went on a drinking spree, as a result of which Captain Panter left 25 of them behind in prison. He says he was not sorry. He found his sails useless, therefore he did not need so many men.

In the Red Sea, the heat was unbearable, pitch boiled through planking on the deck, and the iron sides could not be touched. The thermometer stood at 130 degrees. In Batavia it seemed even worse, and everything aboard ship was mildewed.

However there were some good points. Captain Panter bought no fresh meat on the way out, the men ate Australian preserved meat, which was excellent. His engines worked admirably, and throughout the voyage there was never more than a 10-minute stoppage at any time.

It is interesting that in combat not a single person is shown to the enemy, there are voice pipes and telegraphs leading to every part of the ship, and the *Cerberus* can present to the enemy a surface impregnable to any but the best class artillery in the world. She cost £140 000 pounds of which this colony will pay £25 000.

We Weep for Carbine

13 APRIL 1895

You appreciate, of course, that Carbine is practically a God. He is, just simply, the greatest horse that ever trod the turf.

Good heavens, when Carbine won the 1890 Melbourne Cup the *Argus* devoted 16 huge columns to the event, more than it gave to the bank crash, the outbreak of the Crimean War or anything else I can think of.

Quite rightly so, after all, Carbine carried 10 stone 5 pounds, a weight never previously borne to victory in a Melbourne Cup, nor has it been carried since. What's more he ran it in record time for the race, 3 minutes $28\frac{1}{2}$ seconds, and beat a record number of starters.

Today Carbine left forever, to go to England aboard the Orient liner, RMS *Orizaba*. Mr Donald Wallace has sold him for £13 000 to the Duke of Portland to go to stud. The grief in Australia at this event is enormous.

Mr John Murray, in the Victorian House of Assembly, has suggested that considering Carbine is an idol, even a god, could he not be made Victorian Agent-General in London? Not a bad idea really. He would be easily as useful as most agents-general.

There were crafty moves to divert the public from Carbine's departure. They slipped him aboard ship very quietly last Friday, but that didn't stop an enormous crowd turning up today at Port Melbourne Railway Pier — over 2000 people. The *Age* says not a true departing agent-general or even a governor could have attracted such a crowd.

Famous writer, Nat Gould, was there. He says:

I never saw a more determined mass of people...They crushed up the gangway and jammed in front of his box, regardless of torn clothes and pickpockets and there were plenty of the latter about...When we cast off from Sandridge there was a mighty burst of cheering and cries of 'Carbine' rent the air. I was near the horse's box and Old Jack pricked up his ears and raised his splendid head at the sound, as though he fancied there was another race to be run. A beautiful wreath was send on board for Carbine. It was in the shape of a horseshoe and had Donald Wallace's colours on, and written on a card attached to it 'For dear old Carbine: bon voyage.' Had Carbine got hold of that wreath he would have made short work of it.

There has been a tremendous amount of verse, but maybe the best is by Oriel in the *Argus*. It begins:

Place your palm upon my shoulder
    Stroke my smooth and glossy mane,
Let me lay my honest muzzle
    In my owner's well-loved hand;
I shall never feel my dear old master's
    Proud caress again,
Beyond the cruel ocean in a strange
    and distant land.

And now good-bye. To each and all a last and fond farewell.
Yes, pat me, Hickenbotham, trusty trainer, truest friend,
And unbuckle this old headstall, while I turn my head to tell
The people of Australia that I'll love them to the end.

Carbine winning the 1890 Melbourne Cup

'The Lion of Athens'

14 APRIL 1896

Edwin H. Flack, a handsome young man from Melbourne, is being called 'The Lion of Athens'.

Flack has competed in the modern Olympics, the first Olympic Games staged for 1503 years. There were 311 athletes from thirteen nations, and most of them went to Athens at their own expense.

King George of Greece opened the Games. His pronouncement was followed by the firing of guns and the singing of hymns; and doves of peace were released into the air. An orchestra played the Olympic Anthem and it was sung with great emotion by a large choir.

Edwin Flack, a former Melbourne Grammar boy and Australian mile champion, was in London studying accountancy with Price Waterhouse. He heard about Baron de Coubertin's plans to revive the Olympics, so he decided to visit Athens and compete.

He battled his way there by train. He says 'the food was damnable', he was ill on the way, and because of his studies, there had been hardly any training.

Then he was shocked by the Panatheniac Stadium: the track was so rough it was even dangerous. It was long and oval with sharp turns. Runners had to slow down in case they ran into the grandstand. Edwin Flack didn't give himself much chance.

Yet he had lost none of his speed. He won his heat of the 800 metres in 2 minutes 10 seconds, a time 6 seconds better than any other competitor.

The next day he ran in the 1500 metres. The man favored to win was an American named Blake. Blake was alleged to have a brilliant fast finish, so Flack decided to take the lead and dashed to the front after the first 30 yards. The finish was a thriller, they were shoulder to shoulder all down the final straight, but Blake ran out of power and Flack won in 4 minutes 33.2 seconds.

Flack was an instant hero. All the other track events had been won by Americans, and this was the first break through. An Australian win was so unexpected the officials did not know what to do. Australia was a mixture of colonies. They believed there was an Australian Federation Movement flag, but no such item

Edwin Flack: feted in Athens

was to be had in Athens. Ultimately they did the next best thing. They flew an Austrian flag.

The winner at the first modern Olympics gets a silver medal, a diploma and a crown of olive branches. Second prize is a bronze medal and a laurel branch. Third man gets nothing.

The next day Flack won the final of the 800 metres in 2 minutes 11 seconds. 'I had a very easy race' he said 'and I never had to exert myself in the least'.

He has been a very busy man, he also ran in the marathon, a race he had never run, and one for which he had done no training. He was out in front when he had to give up at the 37-kilometre mark.

He also competed, unsuccessfully, in the tennis, playing both singles and doubles.

The final ceremonies all take place tomorrow. Meantime Flack, he is only 22, is a hero in Athens. He has been feted all around Athens, particularly by King George of Greece, who has taken him to the theatre, to the churches, and has shown him the sights.

Further reading: *Australians at the Olympics*, Gary Lester.

Tree Breaks Fall of Famous Balloonist

15 APRIL 1879

Mr L'Estrange's balloon

M. Henri L'Estrange's extraordinary adventure is the talk of the city today.

L'Estrange was advertised to ascend in his huge balloon at 4 p.m. yesterday from Melbourne's Agricultural Society ground, and a huge crowd assembled.

The Metropolitan Gas company laid on a special 6-inch main, and many of us marvelled when the balloon was inflated in just under 30 minutes. However there were some ominous events. The workmen, when they carried the balloon from the Horticultural Hall grounds, made several holes in the calico. M.L'Estrange repaired the holes with a plaster, then decided he would 'chance it'.

Right on time, he gave the signal to go and immediately the balloon shot up into the air with surprising velocity. Yet the aeronaut was not alarmed, he waved his adieux with perfect sang-froid.

When he was half a mile from the earth he threw out handbills, which floated off to a considerable distance. Then, when he had ascended to a still greater height and was barely recognisable without the aid of a glass, he threw out the contents of a bag of sand.

The *Argus* reports:

Suddenly the balloon appeared to open itself on one side and commenced to descend with terrible velocity. Almost instantly the silk parachute attached to the centre of the balloon opened and checked the speed at which the balloon was descending but still it was so rapid that the majority of those looking on were of the opinion M.L.'Estrange would be dashed to pieces. The crowd watched the descent with breathless anxiety, and seeing the direction in which the balloon fell, rushed to the spot.

The balloon car crashed into a fir-tree at the rear of Government House, went through, and L'Estrange disappeared in a pile of wreckage, branches and calico. The crowd, aghast, sprinted across to extricate him. Out he came, miraculously, barely injured.

L'Estrange explained that he went through a stratum of cloud, and thinking he would meet with extra atmospheric resistance, he threw out ballast, which caused him to ascend with remarkable speed and burst the balloon.

As he descended with 'terrible velocity', he was convinced his days as a balloonist were finished for ever. He also attributes the disaster to difficulties with gas. In Sydney he was supplied with gas of very inferiority quality, but here in Melbourne the gas was so good, with such marvellous buoyancy, he miscalculated its marvellous lift.

Unabashed, however, he is appearing on stage at St George's Hall. As the *Argus* points out, ballooning is a most dangerous activity. Various aeronauts have contemplated a dash across the Atlantic. Professor Donaldson recently lost his life trying to cross one of the immense North American lakes.

The only way to discern your height is by the rise and fall of mercury in a thermometer. One needs a remarkable knowledge of air currents, otherwise all movements are extremely erratic. Indeed the balloonist must trust to luck to a very great degree.

Classical Education now Open to All

18 APRIL 1855

Mr Barry: remarkably fluent in Latin

Mr Redmond Barry is a man of uncommon energy. Is there anything for the good of the colony in which he is not concerned?

He is the senior puisne judge, he is President of the Mechanics Institute, a fighter for the Aborigines, a leader in the movement that separated us from the thraldom of New South Wales, and he is working diligently for our new library and museum.

True, he lives with his housekeeper, Mrs Louisa Barrow, the mother of his children. Bishop Parry would be much happier if he chose to marry the lady, but that is another matter. There is no finer gentleman in Melbourne than Mr Barry. Now he is Chancellor of Melbourne University, which opened this week.

The event took place in the Exhibition Building, newly erected to show off the exhibits contributed to the Great Exposition of Paris for 1855. Sir Charles Hotham, the Governor; Lady Hotham; Vice-Chancellor; Registrar; parliamentarians and the first 16 matriculants were present.

Mr Barry, a graduate from Trinity College in Dublin, spoke at huge length with vast erudition. Frequently he switched to Latin, presuming that his learned audience immediately under-

stood every word. He told us how universities originally were restricted to theological instruction, and only later expanded to offer instruction in law. Oxford University went back to the days of Alfred in the ninth century; Cambridge University was established by Edward I in the thirteenth century.

As for Melbourne University, His Excellency Mr La Trobe, granted 40 acres of land favourably situated on the northern boundary of the city, adjacent to extensive parks of 2200 acres. Its endowment was £9000 a year, and Her Majesty's Government generously voted £55 000 for the erection of buildings.

The building for the accommodation of the Professors, the registrar and two commodious lecture rooms would be ready in August. Meantime they would have their lectures right here in the elegant Exhibition building.

Mr Barry announced his professional staff. For Classics: Professor Rowe, MA of Trinity College, Cambridge. For Mathematics: Professor Wilson, MA, of St John's College, Cambridge. For Natural Science: Professor McCoy, Professor of Geology, Queen's College, Belfast. Then for Modern Literature, Professor Bearne LLD of Trinity College, Dublin. Alas, with sincere regret, Mr Barry then had to announce that Professor Rowe, deeply lamented, had already been cut off from among us. The Council had given a donation of £500 to his young widow, so unexpectedly bereaved.

Mr Barry said the University would be open to all classes of Her Majesty's subjects, who were freely invited to enter.

The Governor eloquently told of the importance of a classical education. The students should remember that the Duke of Wellington, in his early life, was scarcely ever to be seen without a book in his hand. They might also remember that Daniel Webster on his death bed asked that Gray's elegy might be recited to him. What's more, Lord Wellesley at the age of 80 still pursued his study of Latin and wrote beautiful poetry.

Mr Barry said it was impossible to underestimate the importance of this day. The students would be free to pursue their own interests on Saturday but studies would commence on Monday.

The Kelly Blood Money

19 APRIL 1881

The full list of the blood money for the capture of Ned Kelly and his gang has been announced.

Now that Mr Kelly has been hanged and in the short space of five months has turned into something like a folk hero, the whole business leaves a disagreeable taste in the mouth.

You see, the reward offered for the capture of Kelly was 8000 pounds. Ninety-two people believed that because of the hardship and peril they endured, they deserved a slice of that very considerable sum of money.

As we always do in this country, we had to appoint a Board. This one had the ambiguous title, 'The Kelly Reward Board'. The members were: Mr Murray Smith, MLA, Sir Charles MacMahon, MLA, and the Hon.J.MacBain, MLC.

Of the 92 applicants, 62 were successful. The list, frankly, is unbelievable. Almost everybody gets a cut: the engine driver, the fireman, and all the railwaymen associated with the train that dashed from Melbourne to Glenrowan; all the blacktrackers who were in the hunt, also receive a cut; and three newspapermen get honourable mention.

There are rewards to 42 policemen, for Heaven's sake. Now there is a general feeling around town that the police took an unconscionable time to capture the Kelly Gang, more than two years, allowing them to terrorise the countryside. Nobody could say that the affair was handled with any competence and when one remembers the final storming and burning of the pub at Glenrowan, for courage, Kelly and his men, definitely won on points.

Then, remember the murder of Aaron Sherritt? Sherritt sat down to dinner with four policemen. Sherritt went to his front door and Joe Byrne killed him. The four policemen, Constables Armstrong, Duross, Dowling and Alexander, all hid under the bed. They even pulled down 15-year-old Ellen Sherritt with them in the hope she would give them some protection.

Glory be, those four constables all shared in the reward. They received £42 15s 9d each.

The man who receives the biggest reward, £800, is Superintendent Hare. He led the police in the battle of the Glenrowan pub and he was the first casualty. A bullet smashed his left wrist and he collapsed from loss of blood.

The next highest on the list is Thomas Curnow, 550 pounds. He was the schoolteacher who escaped from the hotel and ran down the railway line to warn the police train. But the *Argus*, quite rightly, points out that Curnow was the real hero. It was he who talked Kelly into allowing him to slip out of the hotel. Kelly warned him that if he didn't keep faith he would blow his brains out.

But had Curnow not gone down the railway line with his lantern, the entire police train would have been derailed and a terrible disaster would have occurred. Hare, no doubt, was brave and deserved to be compensated, but he was doing his duty. He was put out of action very early and had he remained the operation would have been handled more efficiently.

The native trackers called in from Queensland, men with names like Hero, Johnny, Jimmy, Jacky, Spider and Moses, all receive £50 each. The Board has recommended that this money will be delivered to the Queensland Government to be paid out at its discretion.

However there is to be a Royal Commission into the police force, and its behaviour during the Kelly uprising will be studied in considerable detail. Mark my words, the day will come when the findings of the Kelly Reward Board will cause much embarrassment.

Conscripts Leave for Vietnam

20 APRIL 1966

Mr Calwell: threatening national security

The first Australian conscripts for the Vietnam war left Sydney by air last night.

They are members of an advance party in Australia's new 4500-man task force. The 5th Battalion will march through Sydney at lunch time tomorrow before boarding ship.

One national serviceman, Private Bill Gilders, 20, of Perth, WA, who was conscripted in the first intake in July, said he wasn't worried about going to Vietnam. 'It's great' he said. 'Why shouldn't they be sent? I don't know what all the fuss is about — if they can send regulars they can send us too'.

But it is an affair that has split the nation. Anti-Vietnam demonstrators are rallying. There will be a night-long vigil by candlelight tonight as a 'quiet' protest against Government policy. A prayer vigil by 20 clergymen from all States will also be held in Wynyard Park tonight.

The Leader of the Opposition, Mr Calwell, bitterly denounced the sending away of conscripts. He says that his Government, when it comes to power, will withdraw from Vietnam all these conscripts. Actually he did not call them conscripts. There is a euphemism for that. Officially, they are National Servicemen.

There have been some nasty clashes in the House of Representatives. The Minister for the Army, Mr Malcolm Fraser, made a savage attack on Mr Calwell. He accused him of threatening Australia's security.'This would result', said he, 'in a repudiation of our obligations and commitments in South-East Asia at the present level'.

Then Opposition members laughed and jeered at the Prime Minister, Mr Holt. The clash came when Mr Calwell asked the Prime Minister if he had received a letter, from the editor of a Brisbane Sunday paper, setting out the results of a poll on the conscript issue. Mr Calwell said 10 383 signed ballot papers in the poll, and 9241 were opposed to sending National Serviceman to Vietnam.

Mr Holt produced a letter given to him just before he entered the House. It stated that a left wing organisation bought large numbers of the newspaper and distributed them by wheelbarrow at an anti-conscription rally in Brisbane.

But when asked to name the writer of the letter and table it in the House, he refused. He was jeered and abused by the opposition.

The *Age* says today:

No one can deny the sincerity of Mr Calwell's denunciation of the imminent despatch of national servicemen to Vietnam. Even in the darkest hours of the second world war, he never wavered in his personal opposition to conscription. But his highly emotional campaign and his election promise to bring national servicemen home from Vietnam and elsewhere demonstrates the depth of his feeling rather than the strength of his reasoning.

The Government recognises that many Australians are disturbed by our involvement in Vietnam and the compulsory call up. But, as the Ministers have explained, a defence policy cannot be built on the shifting sands of popular sentiments. It must be firmly based on realities.

However thousands are refusing to accept national service, and some very big demonstrations are planned in all the capital cities.

Eight Hours Labour

21 APRIL 1856

Right here in Melbourne, building workers have become the first in the world to establish the right to an eight-hour working day.

We had a public meeting on 11 April when Dr Thomas Embling coined the slogan 'Eight hours labour. Eight hours recreation. Eight hours rest'.

At that meeting in the Queen's Theatre, there were a number of noble resolutions. The gathering agreed to the eight-hour day and announced that an association should be formed of all trades, professions or occupations, whatsoever, for the carrying out of the much desired reform.

The history-making resolution continued: We fondly hope (eight hours) will prove not only a blessing to us, but a valuable legacy for future generations. We therefore solicit the assistance of every individual that we may go forth in strength — leaving not a stone unturned until the boon be obtained and appreciated through the length and breadth of our adopted country.

So that is what happened. We have had more meetings, demonstrations and — with men in the building trade leading the way — slaters, stonemasons and quarrymen have decided they will not work for anyone who does not recognise the eight-hour day.

Incredibly it looks as if the Eight-hour movement will be accepted. The *Argus*, for example, a newspaper hardly known for its devotion to the working man, has produced several leading articles, in favour of the movement.

It points out that the Anglo Saxon, the modern Englishman, is too hard working an animal. He has a passion for making money. His absence from work during an hour of daylight is like an act of murder.

But eight hours work was enough for an ordinary man, and it was just possible he could do more in that time than ceaselessly toiling for 12 or more hours in a dusty hot Melbourne.

But the worthy *Argus* was careful to point out that the Benjamin Franklins and the Sir Robert Peels of this world did not achieve greatness by restricting their working hours. If men wanted to work night and day, then they should still have the freedom to do so.

There has been some alarm, contractors are withdrawing their tenders on all sides. The Government is hesitating about entering new contracts and is worried about the construction of the new Legislative Council building.

But please take note. On 12 May there will be a grand procession and fete, which will start in the Carlton Gardens. At 12 noon precisely, accompanied by the celebrated Cremorne Band, it will proceed along Spring Street, down Bourke to Elizabeth, up Collins East and then to the Vauxhall Gardens.

Entertainment will include the celebrated Bombardment of Sebastapol with additional and appropriate fireworks. Two large and beautiful balloons will ascend into the air. It will finish with 'Extraordinary Gymnastic Performances' by the brothers Dherang and Stebbing. There will be music and dancing all evening. Every working man, and the public at large, is urged to come forward and support this great movement.

First banner proclaiming the Eight Hour Day

Mrs Petrov Decides to Stay

22 APRIL 1954

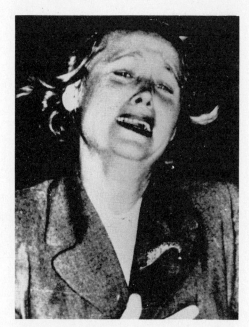

Mrs Petrov leaves Sydney in tears

There have been a series of sensational events. Mrs Evdokia Petrov has decided to stay in Australia. In a dramatic scene at Darwin Airport, police disarmed her Russian guards; now she is returning to be re-united with her husband.

It all began on 13 April. The Prime Minister, Mr Menzies, announced that Vladimir Petrov, the third secretary at the Russian Embassy, had asked for political asylum. Petrov had the rank of Leiutenant Colonel in the MVD, Russian secret police, and was in charge of Soviet espionage in Australia.

Petrov, said Mr Menzies, had handed over a whole series of documents, naming Australian 'contacts' and 'co-operators'. A Royal Commission into espionage in Australia would be appointed as soon as possible. Meanwhile Mr. Petrov's whereabouts were not revealed and he was being kept under strong guard for fear of attempts on his life.

Mrs Petrov did not know of her husband's decision to defect. She believed he had been kidnapped and killed. The Russians took her from her home and placed her in the Embassy.

Their next step was to get out of the country. They booked her on a BOAC airliner with two guards and an official secretary.

The captain of the aircraft reported back that Mrs Petrov appeared afraid of the Russian couriers and would like to stay in Australia.

When the airliner landed in semi-darkness at 4.55 a.m., three Russian officials, with Mrs Petrov between them, stepped off the plane. As Mr R.S.Leydin, the Northern Territory Government Secretary, approached her, the Russian guards tried to intervene.

Police rushed forward and disarmed the couriers, One of them struggled violently and tried to grab his revolver. Mr Kislitsin, second secretary at the Russian Embassy, shouted 'What is your freedom?--a lot of police and gunmen'.

Mrs Petrov was undecided what to do for nearly three hours. She was obviously distressed and weeping slightly while talking to Mr Leydin. Mr Leydin arranged for her to speak to her husband by telephone privately at the top of the hangar. The Russians objected, so she took the call in the customs House while the Russians listened.

She resumed her seat with the Russians, but just as the Constellation was due to take off at 7:15 a.m., she asked to speak to Mr Leydin privately. She had decided to stay.

Douglas Lockwood, *Herald* representative in Darwin wrote:

Her decision made $3\frac{1}{2}$ hours after her arrival — obviously came as a shock to the Russians, who had seemed confident that she would re-board the plane with them.

Mr Kislitsin shouted angrily: 'Why don't you let me talk to her? She is being kidnapped'.

Mr Kislitsin called out 'This is a comedy. My Embassy is going to hear about it.' And the Russians joined the BOAC aircraft and flew off to Jakarta. Mrs Petrov remained in Australia and will soon join her husband in his secret hiding place. The *Age* says Mrs Petrov is 15 years younger than her husband. She is a smart figure among Embassy wives, trim in her dressing and attractive. She does not speak good English and chance acquaintances find her reserved, almost to the point of being chilly.

Australians Bury Gallant Enemy Air Ace

25 APRIL 1918

Captain Manfred Baron von Richthofen is dead. Often called the Red Devil, the Red Baron or the Red Knight, he flew a blood red Fokker triplane, and legend has it that he has shot down 80 of our aircraft.

But who killed the Baron? Already there is controversy about his death. It happened at 11 a.m. on 21 April at Vaux-sur-Somme in France, in an air battle above thousands of troops, including Australians.

It was just after 10.30 a.m. when Lieutenant Wilfred May, a young Canadian with the Royal Flying Corps, was returning to base that Richthofen in his red Fokker saw him from above and dived to the attack. The Canadian, in a Camel, twisted and turned at almost ground level.

A more experienced pilot, and another Canadian, Captain Roy Brown, saw what was going on and tacked on to Richthofen's tail and they wheeled after each other in battle. Brown fired his machine guns and he claims he saw the bullets rip into the triplane.

Richthofen's plane crashed from 150 feet. However many eye witnesses claim that the red Fokker went on flying for another mile, continuing to attack May's Camel, then he rose to cross a ridge, came under fire from rifles and machines guns, swerved eastwards, rose several hundred feet, then dived and crashed.

Some claim they never saw Brown's aircraft at all and there were only two planes in the battle. The strongest claimant to have brought down the Red Baron is Sergeant C.B. Popkin, of the 24th Australian Machine Company, a carpenter from Palmwoods in Queensland. He says that two planes flew very low towards his gun. As soon as he was free from the risk of hitting the British plane, he fired on the German. The Camel banked and gave up the chase. Popkin said:

The German plane banked, turned around, and came back towards me, I opened fire a second time and observed at once that my fire took effect. The machine swerved, attempted to bank, and make for the ground and immediately crashed.

Corporal, W.C. Gamble of the 25th Australian Machine Gun Company also gave a convincing account that his bullets destroyed the Baron. However there is no doubt Australian soldiers risked their lives to rush towards the wrecked plane, looking for souvenirs. Lieutenant Fraser, an intelligence officer, undid Richthofen's safety belt, lifted him out, and on examining his papers, discovered he was the famous pilot. A bullet had entered his right armpit and come out through his chest.

Doctors differed in their opinion, but Colonel Barber of the Australian Medical Corps believed Richthofen had been hit from the ground while his triplane was banking.

The Germans believed Richthofen was still alive when he hit the ground and that the Australians rushed upon him and murdered him. It was not true, the rush merely came from men looking for souvenirs, and one got away with his boots.

The ground staff from No. 3 Squadron, Australian Flying Corps, constructed a coffin on which they placed a plate giving the German's name, and rank. He was buried with full military honours under a hemlock tree, and a guard of honour fired shots across his grave. The grave was covered with flowers, an Australian tribute to a gallant enemy.

Baron von Richthofen, the 'Red Baron'

Heroes in Defeat

26 APRIL 1915

Allied forces have stormed the Dardanelles and are fighting the Turks on the Gallipoli Peninsula.

The first report has arrived from Ellis Ashmead-Bartlett, a British war correspondent, and he devotes it to the Australians and the New Zealanders. Writing in the *Argus*, he says:

The Australians rose to the occasion. Not waiting for orders, or for the boats to reach the beach, they sprang into the sea, and, forming a sort of rough line, rushed at the enemy trenches. Their magazines were not charged, so they just went in with cold steel.

It was over in a minute. The Turks in the first trench were either bayoneted or they ran away, and their Maxim was captured.

Then the Australians found themselves facing an almost perpendicular cliff of loose sandstone covered with shrubbery. Somewhere, halfway up, the enemy had a second trench, strongly held, from which they poured a terrible fire on the troops below. The Australians stopped for a few minutes to pull themselves together, got rid of their packs and charged their magazines.

Then this race of athletes proceeded to scale the cliffs, without responding to the enemy's fire. They lost some men, but did not worry. In less than a quarter of an hour the Turks were out of their second position either bayoneted or fleeing.

The country of the landing is formidable and forbidding. It is ideal for snipers as the Australians found out to their cost. In the early part of the day heavy casualties were suffered in the boats conveying the troops from the destroyers. The enemy sharpshooters were hidden everywhere and they concentrated their fire on the boats.

But then the Australians whose blood was up, instead of entrenching rushed northwards and eastwards, searching for fresh enemies to bayonet. It was difficult country in which to entrench. Therefore they preferred to advance.

Towards dusk the attacks became more vigorous. The enemy was supported by powerful artillery inland, which the ships' guns were powerless to deal with. The pressure on the Australians became heavier, and their lines had to be contracted.

Some idea of the difficulty may be gathered when it is remembered that every round of ammunition and all water and stores had to be landed on a narrow beach and carried up pathless hills and valleys several hundred feet high to the firing line. The whole mass of our troops was concentrated in a very small area, and was unable to reply when exposed to a relentless and incessant shrapnel fire, which swept every yard of ground.

The courage displayed by these wounded Australians will never be forgotten...In fact, I have never seen anything like these wounded Australians in war before. Though many were shot to bits, without the hope of recovery, their cheers resounded through the night. You could see in the midst of the mass of suffering humanity, arms waving in greeting to the crews of the warships.

They were happy because they knew that they had been tried for the first time and had not been found wanting. For 15 mortal hours our men occupied the heights under an incessant shell fire without the moral or material support of a single gun ashore and they were subjected the whole time to the violent counter attack of a brave enemy, skilfully led, with snipers deliberately picking off every officer.

There has been no finer feat in this war...these raw colonial troops in these desperate hours proved worthy to fight side by side with the heroes of Mons, Aisne, Ypres and Neuve Chapelle.

Fatherly Statesman Leaves Young Family

27 APRIL 1896

Sir Henry Parkes dies in poverty

Sir Henry Parkes, five times Premier of New South Wales, the most celebrated statesman the colonies have ever known, died yesterday.

It is hard to believe he has gone; he had this enormous Moses-like beard, the flow of white hair; sometimes he seemed like the father of us all. Constantly lampooned by the cartoonists, castigated by leader writers, he was hardly ever out of controversy.

The gusto of the man was amazing. He was married three times, and the first two wives gave him 11 children. His second wife died in 1895, then only three months later, at the age of 80, he married one of his servants, Julia Lynch. The Bishop of Sydney, F.B.Boyce refused to perform the ceremony because he thought it would injure Sir Henry's health.

Sir Henry Parkes was bankrupt three times and in recent years he has been in a state of penury and has had to depend on public subscription. Last year he auctioned his personal library just to keep going. And what happens now? The *Sydney Morning Herald* says Lady Parkes has five children from Sir Henry's previous marriages, all unprovided for. With tears in her eyes she told a reporter 'I shall have to face the world alone with five young children. It will be years before they are able to earn a living'.

What a remarkable man he was. The newspapers today carry page after page of tributes. They come not only from the other colonies, but every town and hamlet in New South Wales, Glen Innes, Lithgow, Lawson, Narrabri, Gunnedah, West Wyalong, Forbes...

There are even kindly words from one of his old foes, the Premier, Mr G.H. Reid: 'He (Sir Henry) is the one colossal figure in the public life of Australasia. He takes his place in history as one of the master builders of the colonial empire'.

And you wonder how ever he did it. He was born in Warwickshire in 1815, the son of poor English tenant farmers, who put him to work at the age of eight. He had practically no formal schooling and he came to Australia with his first wife on an assisted passage in 1836.

He educated himself by the passionate reading of the classics. He had an enormous and natural gift for words, which not only made him a fine journalist and poet, who published many books of verse, but a spellbinder as an orator.

Oh he was vain, he constantly craved recognition. His bitterest critics claimed he created a charade, an image of the man he would like to be. But Parkes had a great vision, a dream of a united Australia. It was his speech at Tenterfield in 1889 calling for 'a great national government for all Australia' that led to the Australian Convention in 1891. Parkes was President, and an Australian Constitution Bill was drawn up for submission to the colonial parliaments.

If anyone will be remembered as the father of Federation — the birth of the Australian nation — almost certainly it will be Sir Henry Parkes.

The *Sydney Morning Herald* reports today: Sir Henry had just been given some nourishment, and his attendants had settled him on his pillows. He was lying back with his eyes closed, and it was thought he had lapsed into semiconsciousness. It is most probable he was then already in that last heavy death-slumber, for shortly afterwards he rallied for a few seconds, as often happens with those in the shadow of death. His wife was at his bedside, and the dying man clasped her hand in his in the final moments. Sir Henry expired peacefully.

The time was 4 a.m.

Fitzsimmons Takes World Heavy-weight Title

28 APRIL 1897

Bob Fitzsimmons is heavy-weight champion of the world. We reckon, pound for pound, there has been no fighter like him in history. In his career, this 11-stoner has captured the light-weight, middle-weight and heavy-weight world titles.

He's our hero, the newspapers report his every move. The *Sportsman* has burst into verse:

The star of Fitzsimmons has risen
A meteor flaring in sight
Which scatters the clouds that imprison
And curb its impetuous flight
From the land where the kangaroo races
And leaps with prodigious bound
Comes Robert the ruthless and graces
Our glorious ground.

Bob was born in Cornwall. He went to New Zealand when he was two, and as a young man had some amateur fights before moving to Sydney. Unlikely character really, droopy, round shouldered, freckled, knock-kneed, half bald and a very lean six feet. He was asthmatic, and you'd say the most unimpressive fighter of all time. When he first went overseas he didn't even possess the Australian middle-weight title. Jim Hall had beaten him for that on 10 February 1890.

But that marvellous boxer of the 1870s, Larry Foley, taught him how to fight; how to time his blows; and, particularly, how to punch with phenomenal power. Soon he was beating everybody.

His biggest fight came this St Patrick's Day. He fought Gentleman Jim Corbett at Carson City, Nevada, and it was billed as 'The Fight of the Century'.

As you can understand it takes time for full reports to reach us from the USA, but today's *Referee*, our leading sporting newspaper, has brought out a special edition with a Fitzsimmons-Corbett supplement spread across four huge broadsheet pages.

Fitz, known as the Freckled Freak, is announced as 'Champion of all the Champions of the World'. He was in terrible trouble early. Corbett knocked him down in the sixth round for a count of nine. But then Fitzsimmons proceeded to out-box Corbett and the end came very suddenly. He crashed Corbett with a left

Bob Fitzsimmons

to the stomach, and as Corbett gasped for air, gave him the old Foley right king-hit to the jaw and knocked him out.

It is too soon to get photographs from Nevada, so the *Referee* has sketches suggesting how it might have been. There is the romantic sketch of Fitzsimmons knocking out Corbett, Fitzsimmons at the punching bag, Fitzsimmons in fighting stance, and an awe-inspiring sketch titled 'Fitzsimmons' Fighting Face'.

English newspapers are claiming him as an Englishman, New Zealand papers have him as a New Zealander, but we insist he is an Australian because we taught him all he knew and, after all, his fighting career was launched in Sydney.

As soon as the photographs arrive, the *Referee* is offering a 'grand illustrated portfolio in 81 photographs on toned paper, a triumph of artistic taste, no better work of its kind ever been placed before the public'. The portfolios will be available for one shilling and sixpence.

Melbourne is a Cess Pit

29 APRIL 1878

You have to face it, Melbourne is a cess pit. According to the *Argus* 'that fearful scourge, typhoid fever, lurks in evey mucky gutter, drain and cesspool'.

If the population were as dense and under-fed as in London, thousands would be dead. The city is bereft of any adequate sewerage system; what goes into the drains beggars the imagination. There are attempts being made to form a Board of Land and Works, but the problems of reconciling the jealousies between councils seem insuperable.

There was the death recently of Miss Kate Johnson, in Toorak of all places, and unquestionably her demise sprang from bad drainage.

Last night there was an Indignation Meeting held at the Wellington Parade Hotel in Joli-mont. Since 15 April, 20 people in ten different houses in Jolimont have been hit with typhoid fever. There have been two deaths.

Mr T.M. Girdlestone, the Officer of Health for the City of Melbourne, believes the typhoid is spread by infected milk, and he has named the milkman McAuley. McAuley's own son died of the disease. McAuley lives at 3 Jolimont

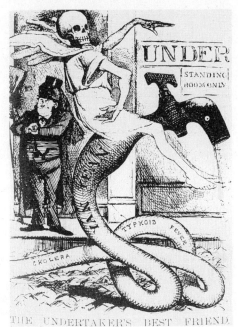

THE UNDERTAKER'S BEST FRIEND.

Melbourne Punch *blames the water*

Place and he has been keeping four or five cows in the confined space out the back.

Nineteen of the 20 people who contracted typhoid received their milk from McAuley.

But it goes further than that. As they said at the meeting, 'there is no more honest fellow than McAuley', and if his milk was getting infected, what was the cause? We heard the whole story. It is the City Council. The corporation has this practice of dumping all its refuse garbage, decaying vegetable matter, night soil, filth of all kinds, on the vacant ground between the Fitzroy Gardens and Wellington Parade.

Mr George Davies said the Council needed educating. The stench was absolutely intolerable. 'The bodies of dead animals are frequently exposed in a putrid state and I personally have seen emptied on the reserve cartloads of putrid fish.'

Theoretically the council covers the refuse with clean soil, but what difference does it make? The stench that comes up is incredible. One speaker said it wasn't safe to take children into the Fitzroy Gardens, it was just a hotbed of disease.

Mr D. Gibson said that in addition to the nuisance in the Parade, the corporation had deposited a 7-foot bank of dirt on the edge of the Yarra. It was composed of dead rats and dogs and vegetable matter, and the southerly breezes produced a stench so bad he frequently lost his appetite for breakfast. If it didn't stop he would be driven out of the district.

One gentlemen at the meeting claimed he was particularly entitled to speak because there was typhoid in his house. Thereupon Mr Walstab inquired if there was any danger of contagion, and he demanded that all windows be opened immediately.

The *Argus* says today:

Is this practice of depositing filth here, there and everywhere to be continued? For Jolimant is not an isolated case — it is only one example of a system which has grown up until it has become intolerable...To continue such practices is simply to court disease.

Further reading: *Governing the Metropolis*, Dr David Dunstan.

MAY

A celestial delicacy

Banks Take an Enforced Holiday

1 MAY 1893

Mr Patterson weighed down by the problems of the unemployed

The Premier, Mr Patterson, has done something nigh unbelievable, through His Excellency the Governor, Mr John Madden, he has declared bank holidays for five days.

He says it is to bring the public to its senses, to create a calming down period and to give the banks a chance to reconstruct.

The final card to bring down the whole pack and cause final chaos is the National Bank of Australasia. It suspended payment and closed its doors on Monday. The Commercial Bank of Australia closed its doors on 5 April and has announced reconstruction.

The English Scottish and Australian Chartered Bank was suspended on 13 April. Then came the London Chartered Bank and the Australian Joint Stock Bank.

The truth is that the citizens of Australia, and those in the colony of Victoria in particular, are in a state of terror. They are rushing to the banks to pull out everything they possess. On 31 March the amount of cash in all points in Australia was 1 450 000 pounds. By closing time on 29 April, it was down to 800 000 pounds.

The National Bank said in its statement: The board of directors announce with deepest regret and concern that, in the exercise of their discretion, they have resolved it is advisable for the bank to suspend payment on Monday morning... The directors are thoroughly satisfied as regards the solvency of the institution, and the present course has been forced on them solely through the persistent continuous withdrawal of deposits...

Two banks have defied the Government order to go on 'holiday', the Union Bank and the Bank of Australasia. The scenes have been astonishing. The footpaths outside the banks in Collins Street, filled with seething pushing crowds have looked like the betting ring at Flemington on Melbourne Cup Day.

The banking chambers at the Union and the Australasia remained frantic from 10 a.m. until 3 p.m. Out on the stairs, men literally pushed and shoved to get inside. Frightened customers were terrified that a minute's delay could cause disaster.

But there was a curious situation. Many people having drawn out great bags of sovereigns did not know what to do with their gold. So while some were fighting in queues to draw out gold, others were fighting to pay it in.

The *Argus* expresses surprise and bewilderment today. It claims that the phenomena we have witnessed in the past few weeks will appear half-tragic and half-ludicrous in Australian history. It adds:

The situation here is unprecedented. And what we have to impress upon the community is that it is altogether an artificial situation — one which can be ended in a moment by a return to calmness and common sense on the part of depositors.

However it is far from artificial for those who have already sunk into poverty. The South Melbourne Court heard the story yesterday of Sarah Watson, widow of James K. Watson, who had died 'very suddenly'. Senior Constable McEvoy said Mrs Watson and her three children had occupied a house in Brook Street. There was no furniture in the house, and not a morsel of food. How they were able to exist he could not understand.

Sergeant Monckton said the Equity Trustees Executors' Agency had removed every article of furniture, including a piano that Mrs Watson had purchased with her own money. Mrs Watson was remanded on vagrancy until the ninth. She was allowed to keep her baby. The other children were remanded to the Industrial Schools for 14 days.

The Complete Week-end

3 MAY 1909

Empty streets on Saturday night

There has been a complete week-end revolution. The Government has just introduced a Half Holiday Act. Would you believe, from now on we do not have to work on Saturday afternoons.

The *Argus* put it very nicely this morning. It said: 'On Saturday, at the magic hour of 1 o'clock, business ceased in the city and suburbs, and something like 20 000 employees, who had hitherto worked throughout the afternoon and evening, were released'.

The Railways department had to go into an entirely new planning phase. It had to get all the workers into the city on Saturday morning, take them home again at midday. Then it had to provide all the excursion trains for the people who wanted to get away for the week-end. Alas, the weather was very unsettled, so the first great holiday week-end was not quite the success it might have been.

Can you imagine what it has done for football? This week-end was the opening of the season. Ordinarily the match of the day attracts 15 000 people, and maybe a couple of other matches draw 10 000. On Saturday, however, there were more than 50 000 at the four big league matches. There was a huge crowd at the Essendon — St Kilda match, and the association games also attracted larger crowds.

Normally shops remain open until 10 o'clock on Saturday nights. Now instead they close at 10 o'clock on Friday nights. It worked quite smoothly, with large crowds in the city and suburbs on Friday, but it was a very different story the next night.

I mean, normally Saturday night in Bourke Street, Smith Street Collingwood or Chapel Street Prahran, is tremendous, bustling with people, street vendors, all kinds of entertainment. On Saturday night the streets were dead, like any other day of the week. People were taking advantage of the great new idea and had gone off for the week-end.

But there is another devil of a problem. Most firms are continuing with Saturday as pay day. Well, what good is this if Friday night is the big shopping time? The manager of a big retail house said yesterday:'The money just doesn't stay intact for a whole week. You must display your goods attractively to the purchaser at the moment when he has the money and is in a humour to spend it'.

Last Friday was proof of this. People did not spend as of old on Saturday. So the big move is on now for a universal pay day. Some firms are paying on Fridays, but Thursday is the obvious day. The worker can take home his pay packet on Thursday night, then his wife has time to think about her Friday evening shopping.

But you wonder where it will all end don't you? Lieutenant Ernest Shackleton, the great Antarctic explorer, arrived in town yesterday. I bet he was not thinking about holidays on Saturday afternoons when he discovered the magnetic South Pole. You wait, next thing Australians won't want to work on Saturdays at all.

Keeping the Chinese Out

4 MAY 1888

There is an extraordinary fear and detestation for the Chinese in the Australian colonies.

The *Bulletin* mocks them with cartoons in almost every issue. It calls them 'the yellow race'...'the Celestials from the Flowery Land'. They are 'pagan', 'un-Christian'. 'immoral'.

You can see the cause of the terror. The Chinese have 114 people for every square kilometre; we have two and a half square kilometres for every one of our three million people. The Premier of NSW, Sir Henry Parkes, said he was fully convinced that the Chinese with their unrivalled population, their unrivalled resources, would be the greatest power in the civilised world. They were obtaining instructors to teach them the art of war, and they had at this moment naval ships as skilfully constructed as any in the world.

Not only is there the fear they will invade, they will take our jobs, everything. A ship called the *Afghan* reached Melbourne on 27 April and it caused the most feverish excitement. Now it is in Sydney.

It has on board 208 Chinese, of whom 67 are for Melbourne, 89 for Sydney and 105 for New Zealand. They all have British naturalisation papers, which puts them on exactly the same footing as British subjects.

According to the *Sydney Morning Herald*, these papers are unmistakably fraudulent, but there is fear of offending Her Majesty's Government, because Britain is on good terms with China. Thousands of people crammed into the Melbourne Town Hall for a big anti-Chinese protest meeting. Mr Duncan Gillies, the Victorian Premier, was crafty. He put the ship into quarantine and refused to let it land.

Last night we had a protest meeting of 5000 people in the Sydney Town Hall. They moved a resolution 'That this meeting emphatically condemns the continued influx of the Chinese, whether they be provided with English naturalisation papers or not, as being fraught with peril to the rights and liberties of the Australian people'.

Then the anti-Chinese mob moved round to Parliament House and demanded to see Sir Henry Parkes. He put them off, saying he would greet a deputation at his office on Friday morning. There was immediate uproar. The mob shouted 'The Chinese must be stopped... We will pitch them overboard...We must see the Premier tonight, the *Afghan* will be here at daylight'.

There were cries of 'Let us show him we are determined'. There was a very ugly scene. The crowd decided to go right into the Assembly chamber. According to the *Herald* today, they were a like a tidal wave and bore the Mayor, John Harris, along with them.

Before the excitement had reached its highest pitch the Speaker had become acquainted with the state of affairs and he at once came to the support of his officers and worked so effectively the outer doors were closed, and Parliament House was saved from a scene of disorder which doubtless would have developed into a riot of great magnitude.

The Mayor then sent a message of direct appeal to Sir Henry to prevent the Chinese from landing. Sir Henry replied: 'The Right Worshipful the Mayor. On the arrival of the S.S. *Afghan* the necessary steps will be taken to prevent the Chinese on board from landing'.

The Mayor then went to the crowd and read them Sir Henry's message. It was quite a triumph for the Right Worshipful gentleman. They gave him three cheers.

The First Agricultural Society Exhibition

5 MAY 1869

Lord Belmore

The first Annual Exhibition of the Agricultural Society of New South Wales opened yesterday. Unquestionably the most impressive display came from God himself.

As the *Sydney Morning Herald* pointed out, the weather could not have been more inauspicious. The Society used 29 acres bounded by Elizabeth and Cleveland Streets. One wouldn't have called it a lake yesterday, merely a covered drain churned into a fine glutinous consistency by myriads of various types of feet.

But this said, there was indeed a fine, spectacular display of almost everything that can be grown, produced and manufactured in the colony. We were particularly taken with Messrs Russell and Company's sheep washing plant, which consisted of hot swim, wash pool and spouting tank. There was also a quite wonderful display of pumps and windmills, and Mr Ainsworth's pony plough received great admiration.

His Excellency, the Earl of Belmore, accompanied by the Society's president, Sir William Macarthur, opened the Exhibition. The Governor and the committee sat down to a generous lunch and a dinner served in M. Courvoissier's best style. At dinner they had some dishes prepared from meats preserved by the Australian Meat Company. Among these were 'Preserved Kangaroos', 'Civet de Kangaroos' and 'Turban de Palais de Boeuf'.

The Society took over the Cleveland School for the exhibits. It will do for 1869 but not for 1870, said the *Herald*. There were 8000 schoolchildren there yesterday, and what a crush. Many who saw the crowd, abandoned, in despair, their attempt to enter the show building. Then some who triumphantly squeezed in began to doubt whether they would get out again, or, if they did, whether they would ever regain their original shape.

What an amazing range of things to see: cattle — shorthorns, herefords; pigs; horses; sheep; fowls; turkeys; and such an array of dogs. There were bloodhounds, Newfoundlands, King Charles spaniels, retrievers, kangaroo dogs, English terriers.

There were reapers, mowing machines, rain gauges, fire engines, preserved fruits, baskets, colonial-made tweeds, and a simply beautiful collection of silver and gold mounted emu eggs. We were delighted with one silver mounted egg that was festooned with native pear and emu heads, with a cover surmounted by an Aborigine in oxidised silver.

There were garden displays and plants, with a particularly tasteful tea-tree covered garden house. Greatly admired, too, have been the boots and shoes by some of our finest colonial makers. There were 50 different kinds of boots for men and women. There were several pairs of ladies' kid elastic-side boots for walking, and the ornamental stitching was exquisitely neat and pretty.

The wine judging was completed yesterday. The *Herald* thought it was a poor representation of the wine growing interest in this country. The prize for the best full-bodied red went to Mr John Wyndham for his Dalwood No. 3.

All in all, the show is a great success. The *Sydney Morning Herald* comments: 'The efforts of the gentlemen who have promoted the Exhibition will be, we hope, fully successful, not only in advancing the prosperity of New South Wales, but by increasing the friendly relations between all the colonies of this hemisphere'.

Ben Hall Cut Down

6 MAY 1865

Finally they got Ben Hall yesterday, cut down near Forbes in a hail of bullets.

Curious thing about the colonies, there is always this contempt for authority, and loathing for the police. Yet there is hero worship, devotion, almost love for every roaming thug, killer and desperado.

Hall saw himself as something of a Robin Hood, a friend of the poor, while he had this hatred for the station owners and the upper class — nicely spoken prissy Englishmen who seemed to get all the jobs as officers in the police force.

True, Ben Hall never actually killed anybody, but he committed 64 robberies and his colleagues were associated with at least two murders. One of his favorite escapades was holding up the mail coach in the Gundagai—Jugiong district.

In July 1863, the Hall gang attacked the house of Henry Keightly, the gold warden and police magistrate at Dunn's Plains, 29 miles from Bathurst. Keightly had killed Mick Burke, one of Hall's men. The gang were wild keen to return the favour, but Ben Hall had another idea.

If Keightly could raise a ransom of £500, precisely the reward that had been offered for Mick Burke, then he would be set free. They gave him 24 hours. A frantic Mrs Keightly rode into Bathurst and raised the money just in time.

Last November the Hall gang rounded up 60 travellers near Jugiong; captured a mounted policeman; then held up the stage coach, which was under police escort with a sergeant and a sub-inspector. Well, John Gilbert, Hall's prize colleague, shot and killed the sergeant. They did very well out of that raid.

On Friday night police heard a whisper about Hall. Sub-Inspector James Davidson, a sergeant, four constables and two black trackers, surrounded him near Forbes, just as he was scratching a hole to go to sleep. They waited until dawn. When Hall went to fetch the horses, Davidson says he called out for him to halt, there was no answer, so they opened fire with a blaze of 30 bullets. Hall grabbed hold of a sapling, called out 'I'm wounded, I'm dying'.

Ben Hall

He died almost immediately. He was carrying £78 in notes, three gold chains, three loaded revolvers and the portrait of a young woman. He was 27 years old.

The *Sydney Morning Herald* reporter says they laid him out in a room at Forbes, and more than 500 people went through to look at the body. There were a number of females and several of them said 'What a handsome face'. Some took the opportunity to steal a lock of hair. He had 'excellent features' said the *Herald* correspondent, 'lofty forehead and fine brown hair...The most remarkable feature in the countenance was a peculiar curl in the right side of the upper lip, indicating ordinarily a feeling of contemptuous scorn'.

The *Sydney Morning Herald* is deeply shocked at this outrageous 'morbid folly'. The same thing happened in Victoria after Dan Morgan's death. The reign of Hall, said the *Herald*, was particularly pernicious, because he was able to win the admiration of many a foolish lad just hovering on the brink of perdition. How terrible it is that there are many who are not repelled by pillage and violence as long as it is accompanied by daring.

Truganini, the Last of her Tribe

8 MAY 1876

Truganini, the last Tasmanian Aborigine, died today. She passed away as peacefully as a child, says the *Hobart Mercury*, and she looked only half her age. And what was that? No one knows really, some say she was born in 1812.

How many people suffered as much as she did? She saw it all, the mass extermination of a race. She was there on 7 October 1830 when the Lieutenant-Governor, George Arthur organised 3000 troops, settlers, any white man who could handle a gun, to hunt out every black Aboriginal as if they were looking for some kind of vermin.

When Captain Cook came to Australia, there were at least 2500 Aboriginals in Tasmania, and perhaps many more. Now it is all over. Truganini, or as she was sometimes called, Lalla Roohk, was born on the west side of the D'Entrecasteaux Channel. Her mother was killed by sailors. Her uncle was shot by a soldier. Her sister was abducted by sealers. Then there was Paraweena. She was to marry him. He was murdered by timber cutters.

After the great murderous round-up, Truganini went to Flinders Island in 1835. This was the great solution, take the Aboriginals away from their homeland and isolate them on a windswept island where they would cause no inconvenience to any one. So 70 odd went there in the care of George Augustus Robinson, a great kindly man, often referred to contemptuously as 'Booby Robinson', who tried to convert them into Christians. The settlement was not a success and many died of disease.

Truganini, with four other Aboriginals, went with a party of whalers to Portland Bay. In 1841 all five of them were charged with the murder of two whalers. Two of the men were hanged and Truganini, too, was under sentence of death. The *Mercury* says always she claimed she was innocent, but she would have been hanged had she not once saved a woman and two children from the fury of the blacks, so her life was spared.

Twenty years ago, Truganini went to the Aboriginal station at Oyster Cove and there she lived with the 16 survivors of her race. The other 15 died, then three years ago Truganini moved to Hobart Town, and there she lived with the Dandridge family.

She was short, stout, wore a red turban, and was known all over Hobart. She was on a pension of £60 a year. She had a glass of beer every day, some tobacco and a nightcap of hot ale spiced with ginger.

In 1869 she and William Lanney, often called 'King Billy', were the only Tasmanian Aboriginals left alive. Lanney's body was mutilated for scientific purposes after his death. Truganini has been terrified of this prospect. She said recently: 'I know that when I die the Museum wants my body'.

Ten days ago she had a presentiment that death was near. Last Wednesday night she called Mrs Dandridge and said the devil was on her hand and she wanted her to catch him. After that she went into a fit and never really recovered.

Her body was removed to the General Hospital, and there are real fears about her last wishes. Her skeleton could end up in the Museum.

Truganini

Federal Parliament Opens

9 MAY 1901

Federal Parliament is now open and working. As the *Age* pointed out, the curtain rose today upon the first act of the great drama of our national life.

It was a scene 'perhaps without precedent in the history of civilised mankind'. It all took place in Melbourne, the present capital of the new Commonwealth.

The bells of St. Paul's Cathedral rang out with the inspiring 'triple bob major', guns fired the Royal Salute in the Domain. There were great triumphal arches across the streets, poles, columns, streamers, flags. As the *Age* pointed out with some enthusiasm, 'the striking festival apparel of Melbourne glowed with a double sheen against the rain-washed circumambient air'.

The crowds began to gather long before dawn, and tens of thousands of people lined the streets all the way from Government House to the Exhibition Building, unquestionably, the only building large enough, fine enough, for the grand occasion, both 'modern and commodious'.

His Royal Highness and the Duchess of Cornwall and York were the first to enter the building. The Duke was in the uniform of a Rear Admiral, and the Duchess wore an exquisitely designed gown of embossed velvet. A string of magnificent diamonds suspended from her neck to her waist, gleamed with every movement. 'Soft tulle was specially becoming to Her Royal Highness's young face and she carried a large parasol of black chiffon'.

There was the grand entry into the Exhibition. First came the Royal party followed by the Governor-General, Lord Hopetoun, and the Countess of Hopetoun. Then came our Prime Minister, Mr Barton, followed by colleagues in Cabinet: Mr. Deakin, Sir William Lyne, Sir George Turner, Mr Kingston, Sir John Forrest and Sir Phillip Fysh.

The assemblage sang the Old Hundredth hymn, 'All People That on Earth do Dwell', and then Lord Hopetoun read prayers for the King and Queen and Federal Parliament. 'Nothing more impressive' said the *Age* 'could be imagined than the hush which fell over the vast assemblage as Lord Hopetoun delivered the prayer'.

There was a telegram from Buckingham Palace that read:

'My thoughts are with you on today's important ceremony. Most fervently do I wish Australia prosperity and happiness'.
EDWARD R.I.

The Exhibition building rang out with cheers as HRH read out this message and his reply:

I have just delivered your message, and in your name declared open the first Parliament of the Commonwealth of Australia. I also read your kind telegram of good wishes, which is deeply appreciated by your loving Australian subjects, and was received with great enthusiasm. Splendid and impressive ceremony, over 12,000 people in Exhibition Building.

It all went on tonight, there was a State concert, 'unlike anything Australia has ever witnessed before'. The concert was divided into three parts, but hardly anyone noticed the third part. 'As soon as The Heir Apparent departed every one by common consent rushed off to sample the comestibles and beverages placed at their disposal by a paternal Federal Government'.

Mr Slapoffski's excellent orchestra provided the music and Miss Nellie Stewart sang Mr Charles Kenningham's 'quasi' national hymn in honour of Australia. It was an item, writes the *Age* critic sourly, that can hardly be said to have done justice either to the musician or the singer.

Parliament Housed in Canberra

10 MAY 1927

The Duke and Duchess of York opened our new Parliament House in Canberra yesterday.

It was a marvellous triumph, but if you look back, it all took an unconscionable time to happen. As the *Sydney Morning Herald* says today, for nine years the politicians discussed where they were going to put this capital. Another four years elapsed before even a stone was laid, then another 14 years went by before it became a reality. Yes, 27 years may not be long in the history of the nation, but it is a long and weary wait in the term of human lives. What a pity it was so; many great and earnest men whose hopes centred around this function, did not live to see it.

The Sydney *Herald* talks too, of the happy crowds, the thousands of people, the event of 'transcendent importance' but not everybody was there. There were special stands allotted for each State: 1750 seats for visitors from New South Wales, 1500 for Victorians, 500 for Queenslanders, 750 for South Australians, 150 for West Australians and 200 for Tasmanians. The Commonwealth and NSW stands were packed to capacity, Victoria's was two-thirds full, Western Australia's and Tasmania's were a quarter occupied, and Queensland's and South Australia's were nigh empty.

Smith's Weekly has the most revealing report. The roads to Canberra are far from fancy. The Lord Mayor of Sydney, for example, spent all Saturday night bogged in Paddy's River. We learn that the Prime Minister's '14 000 pound humpy' is very nice, and the writer wonders whether statues of Dummy and John Taxpayer adorn niches in the wall.

However Canberra's most fashionable two-up ring is in the thick scrub just behind the Bruce residence. But *Smith's* is most impressed with Prime Minister, Stanley Melbourne Bruce.

'His shoes shone sable and comely, his linen was whiter than the soul of St Anthony'. Then while His Royal Highness the Duke of York was making his opening speech 'Mr Bruce stood by with an expression like that of a man who carried a wax impression of St. Peter's keys in his pocket'.

As for HRH, 'My friend the Duke appears slightly more robust than of yore, but the little Duchess is blooming like a rose'. And the little Duchess utterly stole the show. The fashion reporters described her style.

A wrap coat of cloth of silver, lined with vellum coloured mirror velvet, had long cape sleeves, bordered with palest fawn fox fur, which also formed the collar. Under this was worn a gown of vellum coloured satin with embroideries of gold beads, and with a wonderful uncut opal surrounded by diamonds in the V shaped neckline'.

Mr Bruce handed the Duke a gold key, which he used to open the doors of the splendid new Parliament House. He said:

I am commanded by the King to say that his thoughts are with you in this hour. Today's historic occasion brings back vivid memories of that other 9th of May, 26 years ago, when as Duke of Cornwall and York, his Majesty opened the first Parliament of the Commonwealth.

All the clergy were there, from Archbishop Riley and the Apostolic Delegate, Dr Cattanno, through to the Chief Rabbi, Rabbi Cohen.

The *Smith's* man commented:

During the devotional interlude, I noticed the Duke cast several nervous apprehensive glances towards the political gallery. Possibly he had just remembered his ancestor, George the Third's illuminating outburst, 'Politics is a trade for scoundrels'.

The scene outside the new Parliament house in Canberra yesterday

'Chloe'

11 MAY 1883

There has been a devil of a row. The Gallery, Library and Museum are now open on Sundays.

Very carefully, they are not open during church hours, only from 1:30 p.m. to 5 p.m., but on the first afternoon 6000 went through the turnstiles.

The fury is immense. The Sunday Observance League issued a manifesto: 'We assert the supreme majesty of God's Sabbath law against its violators, nation or individual. We will fight to the death for Sunday for every toiler of the nation'.

We have had indignation meetings, deputations to the Premier, yet anger might have subsided but for Chloe. Now Chloe is a painting of a haughty, hippy, naked young lady, painted by Charles Jules Lefebvre of Paris. Chloe came here for the Grand International Exhibition of 1880. Dr. Thomas Fitzgerald, the surgeon, bought the painting and lent it to the National Gallery.

On 7 May there was a letter to the *Argus*, asking how dare the Trustees display such a picture on a Sunday!:

Would any of the gentlemen trustees permit a nude picture of their daughter, or sister, to be hung there; and if not, why anyone else's daughter?...No decent woman with her daughters would dare to stop in front of it? For whose delectation is it hung there? It may safely be said not for female visitors and therefore it must be for males and only those of vicious proclivities.

John Russell, Emerald Hill.

There were many other letters. For example, 'A Mother' wrote 'Can it be right that a mother cannot take her young daughter to a public gallery, never to speak of her sons, without her cheeks tingling with shame?

Now a letter has appeared in the *Argus* signed by eight art students whose names are Thomas Trood, F. McCubbin, Louis Abrahams, Thomas Humphrey, Chas. S. Bennett, T. StG. Tucker, F. Longstaff and Alexr. Colquhoun.

We wonder how your correspondent or his female relatives managed to get so far into the building as the Picture Gallery, considering that there are two nude female figures guarding the entrance...As students and lovers of art are not notorious for their evil and vicious proclivities we do not consider it necessary to make any reply to this particular point...but maintain that in the present case any indecency whatever exists only in the remarks of your correspondent.

Then a gentleman who signed himself simply T.D.I. wrote:

The artist shows us (I write as a bachelor) what a really beautiful thing a young maiden is — a matter that I am sure you will agree with me in stating we can otherwise know nothing of except by hearsay, and I maintain that if anything can fan the incipient sparks of affection into such a flame of love or induce a young man to commit matrimony, it is the sight of Chloe.

Dr. Fitzgerald, we believe, is far from amused by the controversy, and proposes to withdraw his picture from public exhibition. When that happens, the Trustees, undoubtedly, will be relieved to get the 'indecent' problem out of their hands.

Samuel Marsden, the 'Flogging Parson'

12 MAY 1838

Mr Marsden, the 'flogging parson'

The Reverend Samuel Marsden passed on to his eternal reward today. He died in the parsonage at St Matthews, Windsor.

Indeed one wonders what judgement St Peter will make regarding the Reverend gentleman, because there is an extraordinary difference of opinion here on earth. Some see him as a great and good creator, an inspiration to all mankind; others dismiss him as a cruel self-seeking monster.

You will remember, his birth, in 1764, was very humble as the son of a Yorkshire blacksmith. He showed skills as a lay preacher, he was noticed by important Anglicans and ultimately went to Magdalene College in Cambridge.

As a pious 29-years-old, he sailed for the Antipodes to become assistant to the chaplain of New South Wales. He was deeply shocked by the ship's captain who had taken a female convict as his concubine. Then, during a terrible storm, Marsden's wife gave birth to the first of their five daughters. He gave thanks to his Maker for his infinite mercy.

But it was not only as a preacher that he prospered. He owned 4500 acres of land at Parramatta, and became a farmer of sheep and cattle. He was one of the first in his attempts to produce sheep both for quality meat and quality wool. Some say he was even ahead of John Macarthur.

Marsden exported his wool, and when he visited England in 1807, he had a magnificent suit tailored from cloth made from his very own wool. King George III was so impressed, he made him a gift of some Merinos from the Windsor stud.

There were some conflicts with the job of being a pastor to his flock, but then, surely God meant man to be diligent and make the most of his talents.

Marsden was horrified by the vice and sin that was all around him. He fought to make sure that the convicts observed the Sabbath. Governor Hunter in 1795 appointed him magistrate-superintendent at Parramatta, a role which did little for his popularity. Marsden believed deeply that sin could be cured only by ruthless measures.

He was notorious as 'the flogging parson', and he would use the awesome text;'Behold the great day of wrath is come, and who shall be able to stand?' The convicts used to say that he prayed for mercy on the souls on Sundays, but he had little mercy on their bodies on week days.

The Irish will never forget him because of the Castle Hill uprisings of 1800. An Irishman named William Johnston was transported for his part in the Irish rebellion of 1798. He gathered together a group of 33 men; armed them with rifles and pikes; and proposed to march on Sydney. Governor King received a tip from one of Johnston's very own colleagues and the Army cut them to pieces.

Marsden helped prepare the case for the prosecution. He ordered terrible floggings to extract confessions, and the ringleaders were hanged.

But then he worked to ease the lot of female convicts on transport ships, he tried with conspicuous lack of success to turn the Aboriginals into Christians, and he made seven trips to New Zealand conducting missionary work amongst the Maoris. He also did extraordinary work organising relief during the great floods on the Hawkesbury in 1806.

Jack Lang Sacked

13 MAY 1932

Jack Lang, 'The Big Fella' is sacked as Premier of New South Wales. The State Governor, Sir Phillip Game, removed him from office just before 6 o'clock this evening.

Big Fella indeed, 6 feet 4 inches tall. We thought it would be easier to move the Harbour Bridge. He had these famous slogans, 'Lang is right' and 'Lang is greater than Lenin'.

It would be hard to underestimate the drama or the state of chaos in New South Wales. J.T. Lang has been battling to live up to his reputation as the champion of the underdog, the working man, but with 31 per cent unemployed it has been impossible.

The Lyons Government, in order to bring Lang into line, brought down the Financial Agreements Enforcement Act. Lang withdrew £1 million in cash from Sydney banks, but then Lyons used his Federal powers to take over the revenue of New South Wales.

Yesterday Lyons, with his newly packed upper house, pushed through an amazing bill to get cash quickly, a tax on money lenders. All mortagees would have to pay 10 per cent of their mortgages to the Government within 14 days. Estimated return, seven to £10 million.

Then, today Mr Lang issued a circular instructing public servants not to pay any money to the Commonwealth Treasury. The circular was written in amazing terms and began: That as forced labour without payment by the Authority who would use such labour, or in other words, slavery, has been abolished in the British Empire for over 100 years...'

There was an exchange of three letters each between Premier and Governor. The last one from Sir Phillip says: 'I feel it my bounden duty to inform you that I cannot retain my present Ministers in office, and that I am seeking other advisers. I must ask you to regard this as final'.

The news went around Sydney with the speed of light. In one cafe in Castlereagh Street three women cheered lustily. In a small place in George Street a heavily built man stood outraged and challenged anyone to deny that Jack Lang was the best premier the workers ever had.

Another man was told this meant the end of the Mortgage Act, and with great glee he was shouting. 'I'm saved a thousand pounds'. Then in another city restaurant, the orchestra struck up a popular song, 'We feel so happy Hallelulujah'.

The *Sydney Morning Herald* is not shy about expressing its opinion. It says:

A great weight lifted from this people — an incentive to common thanksgiving for deliverance from grave danger — a relief as from a malignant evil miraculously removed from our midst...deliverance from tyranny...menace from the greatest internal danger which can afflict a community.

A *Herald* represensentive managed to see Mr Lang. He was greeted with the remark: 'Well, I am sacked. I am dismissed from office'. Refusing any comment, he added 'Well, I must be going. I am no longer Premier, but a free man. I have attempted to do my duty'.

A squad of unemployed timber workers was waiting outside to protect him. The new Premier is the Opposition Leader, Bertram Stevens.

Further reading: *The 'Big Fella'*, Bede Nairn.

Turning a Sheep Paddock into a City

16 MAY 1912

Walter Burley Griffin

King O'Malley, the Minister for Home Affairs, has announced a winning design for Canberra, our new Federal Capital.

You would think by now that all the jealousies and rancour would be over. Far from it. Many people look upon the idea as the ruin of a good sheep paddock.

Mr Andrew Fisher's Labor Government announced a world-wide plan for the design of the capital. Entries had to be in by 31 January, with £1750 for first prize, £750 for second and £500 for third. The extremely extroverted Mr O'Malley said 'This must be the finest capital in the world'.

There were 137 entries, and the judges pondered over them for three months. They could not agree. Two judges, Mr John Kirkpatrick and Mr James A. Smith, have gone for an American, believed to be Mr Walter Burley Griffin; the third judge, Mr J.M. Coane, has chosen an Australian design.

The Burley Griffin design has two large lakes. The Capitol is right on Camp Hill, with parliamentary and administrative buildings sweeping down to the lake side. The are two roads across the lakes to public gardens, the municipal centre and the University. Government, commerce and administration are all nicely separated, and the roads are concentric curves.

The Australian design also has a lake, and Camp Hill is the central part of the city, featuring the Houses of Parliament, the city hall, the library, the mint, banks, the GPO, the stock exchange and museum, all in there together. On the western side of the lake are the art gallery, university and the Anglican and Roman Catholic cathedrals. The business area is south of the capital site.

Some of the newspapers, particularly Melbourne's *Argus* heap scorn on the whole idea. The *Argus* sees it as mythical Eden with King O'Malley playing the part of a Martin Chuzzlewit or Zephaniah Scudder with 'the twitch and jerk in his throat. . . like the hammers of a harpsichord'.

The *Argus* continues:
Zephaniah Scudder could not produce an eden in a swamp, and King O'Malley cannot conjure a great capital city into existence in a remote, rainless, barren region. It is claimed that the delicate and susceptible nature of our Federal representatives requires that they should be permitted to legislate in some place 'remote, unfriended, melancholy, slow' where the rude clamour of active life cannot penetrate. . .

But what the people should impress upon their representatives is that having sought a lodging in a vast wilderness they must not attempt to rapidly transform that city by enormous expenditure of public money. Population will never flow naturally to it, because the territory will never yield anything beyond a meagre subsistence to a few.

The *Argus* moans that this extravagance could cost us as much as £30 million, sheer inexcusable waste, when the great problem of the Northern Territory remains unsolved.

Let us keep our pretty plans for brooding over, perhaps at the century's close when the Commonwealth shall have a population of 20 millions. But meanwhile, we as a people cannot retain any pretentions to sanity if we throw away in founding a city, money which ought to be laid out in building up a population and establishing our security as a nation.

The Dambusters

17 MAY 1943

In an amazing bombing feat, RAF planes have hit and breached the two biggest dams in Germany.

They are the Mohne and Eder Dams, one containing 134 million tons of water and the other 202 million tons. The attack is the most devastating blow of the war at German industry.

'I have great news for you today' said the Secretary for Air, Sir Archibald Sinclair. 'Bomber Command, the javelin of our armour, struck a heavy blow of a new kind against the sources of German war power.'

Thousands were killed, scores of thousands made homeless and canal communications brought to a standstill. The RAF lost eight Lancasters.

Pilot Officer F. Spafford, DFM, of Wayville, South Australia, was bomb aimer for the leader of the expedition. Wing Commander Gibson and Flight Lieut. David Shannon, DFC, of Bridgewater, South Australia, led the Lancasters against the Eder dam.

Pilot Officer Toby Foxlee, DFM, flew in a Lancaster captained by Flight Lieut. Mick Martin, DFC, of Randwick, Sydney. He said:

Flak was heaviest as we were going in almost at water level. A shell blew the starboard tank from the aircraft and the tank, as it fell, exploded, buckling the main plane. We dropped our mine and after a couple more attacks the wall was breached and water surged out sweeping away a huge power station as though it were made of paper.

In spite of the flak, everyone circled around watching millions of gallons flooding out. It was a vivid and unforgettable sight. We were drawing the enemy's fire from the other attackers. We fired thousands of rounds against the German gunposts, many of which were swept away in the torrent.

Pilot Officer Spafford paid a tribute to Wing Commander Gibson.

He is a marvellous pilot and a marvellous man. I'll eat my hat if he doesn't get a V.C. After seeing the Mohne dam smashed, he flew 50 miles to the Eder dam and gave the course for the attackers, who were led in by the 20 years old Flight-Lieut Shannon.

Wing Commander Gibson

It was a brilliant attack, just as we rehearsed for weeks. Our Lancaster was only holed three times. When the Eder dam burst, Gibson led the formation back to Mohne where the Germans were so filled with consternation that only one gun was operating. In moonlight bright as day we saw rescue cars and trucks rushing to the stricken villages.

Our Lancaster was purposely drawing the enemy's fire at both dams, which is not so suicidal as might be imagined. The fast low flying Lancaster must have resembled a giant swooping eagle. It was hard to tell which was dam and which was flood water, so many millions of tons of water already cascaded over the countryside.

When we returned to our base where Air Marshal Sir Arthur Harris and others were waiting, everyone was so elated that there was no handshaking. We began celebrations at 5.30 a.m.

The Australian participants in the raid were absolute topflighters — brilliant pilots, navigators, bomb aimers, who had already completed a full tour of bombing operations.

Hospital Ship Torpedoed

18 MAY 1943

Two hundred and sixty-eight lives have been lost after the Australian hospital ship *Centaur* was deliberately and callously torpedoed last Friday.

A Japanese submarine was believed to be responsible. *Centaur* was off Stradbroke Island, only 24 miles from Brisbane. The time was 4 a.m. *Centaur* was fully lit according to the Geneva Convention, and most of the victims were in bed asleep. The weather was clear, the visibility was good and the ship was clearly marked with the signs of the Red Cross.

The torpedo struck the oil fuel tank, and *Centaur*, 3222 tons, sank in just over two minutes. Few people had a chance to get out. There were only 65 survivors.

'I cannot express the revulsion I feel at this unnecessary act of cruelty' said General Macarthur. 'Its limitless savagery represents the continuation of a calculated attempt to create a sense of trepidation through the practice of horrors designed to shock normal sensibilities.'

Courageous Sister Savage

The last moments were desperate. Blazing spars crashed on the deck as survivors dashed across it and jumped into the oil-covered sea. The master, Captain G.A. Murray, of Aberdeen Scotland, was last seen desperately trying to launch a boat, then the ship was gone, leaving survivors struggling in the water and clinging to rafts. Captain R.M. Salt, 67 years old and a Torres Strait pilot, got out of the blazing ship by wrapping a blanket around himself and tipping a bucket of water over his head. His hands and face were terribly burned, but he managed to get on a raft. Other survivors salvaged a medical kit floating in the water to treat his injuries.

At dawn the rafts converged some miles from the scene. Sister Ellen Savage was the only survivor of the 12 nurses aboard, and Dr Leslie Macdonald Outridge of Redland Bay, Queensland, was the only medical officer to survive of the 18 on board.

Then began a drift of 36 hours. Most of the survivors were semi-clad, some already ill from exposure. Thirteen survivors, including Sister Savage, were crowded on one raft. One of the men gave the nurse his khaki trousers and another his topcoat. This she shared with the youngest of the survivors, Robert Westwood, 15, of Gardenvale, Melbourne.

To keep up their spirits, the men sang 'Roll Out the Barrel' and 'Waltzing Matilda'. On one of the smaller rafts was a badly injured man, and the doctor asked someone to swim over and look after him. A sailor went over and stayed all Friday night. At 4 a.m. he called 'He has gone'. All the survivors repeated the Lord's Prayer as the dead man was lowered into the water.

On Saturday night, the convoy of rafts was sighted by an RAAF Avro Anson and the survivors were picked up by the US destroyer, *Mugford*.

The courage and fortitude of Sister Savage was remarkable. She led the men in prayers for their deliverance and recited the rosary. 'She was wonderful' said Alex Cochrane of Subiaco, Western Australia, a member of *Centaur's* crew. 'She only complained once. She said to someone "Please don't lean on my side". We thought she was just tired, but it turned out later she had two broken ribs.'

Holden Celebrates

19 MAY 1953

The Australian car industry is a tremendous success. We own a Holden, almost all our friends have a Holden and the Holden FX is absolutely the most popular car on our roads.

Yesterday there was a grand ceremony at General Motors Holden at Fisherman's Bend when the 100 000th Holden came off the production line. It was bright red and burst through a series of huge calendars, labelled '10,000 Feb 1950,' '30,000 Feb 1951', '60,000 April 1952', '100,000 May 1953'.

In January 1949, the daily production rate was ten cars a day, and at the end of this year, GMH will be producing an astonishing 200 cars a day. The business is worth £30 million, and 10 500 people are employed in seven manufacturing and assembly plants.

It all brings back memories. The car was named after Holden Motor Bodies Limited, a firm originally established way back in 1856 to build horse-powered carriages. We first got wind of the new car in 1948. General Motors had their test course at Lang Lang near Melbourne.

They had four or five of these snub-nosed models: windscreen with division down the centre, grill which looked like a shark trying to smile, mudguards all smoothed into the body. The design was obviously borrowed from a small Chevrolet, in other words, modified Detroit.

Newspaper photographers carried out all sorts of espionage. They hid behind bushes and published pictures: 'Is this the new Holden?'

And, of course, it was. The launching was on 29 November 1948. There were 1200 guests at Fisherman's Bend. The place was decked with flowers, and they had a ten piece orchestra. At first we were not permitted to see the car, but then silver lame curtains swept aside, spotlights came on, and lo, there was the jewel, the triumph, an ivory coloured sedan sitting on a sea of black velvet.

The Prime Minister, Mr Chifley, inspected the first car outside the hall. The GMH people had it standing beside a Cobb & Co. coach made in 1870. Interesting how they liked to stick with American origins.

The ceremony was relayed over landlines to public address systems in General Motors plants in Sydney, Brisbane, Adelaide and Perth, and over the radio network. Mr Chifley praised GMH for its initiative in producing an Australian car. He said the war had given Australia lessons in the need for independence in transport.

And it was Australian. Imported parts and components did not exceed 10 per cent of the list price of the car, nor more than 5 per cent of its weight.

Yes, we thought it was a marvel; no proper chassis, this thing they called the monocoque construction, six-cylinder, 21.6 horsepower, overhead valves, top speed 80 mph, independent coil springs (front), semi-elliptic springs in lubricated covers (rear), 3-speed gears — synchromesh in second and top, 35 miles to the gallon, weight 19 hundred-weight.

We can look back with some nostalgia at the price. The first Holden, if you could get one (the waiting list went from Melbourne to Alice Springs) was 675 pounds. At the time a four-cylinder Vanguard cost £785, a four-cylinder Morris Oxford, £778, and an Austin A40, 650 pounds.

These prices were before tax. By the time you got your Holden on the road you were up for around 733 pounds. Progressively it came out in different models. We had the utility two years ago in 1951. There was the standard model and the business sedan. The special came with arm rests and leather trim.

There is a rumour around that GMH will produce a new model, come next October, to be called the F.J. Sleuthing photographers already are in hiding at Lang Lang.

The 100 000th Holden: bright red

103

Mafeking Relieved

20 MAY 1900

Mafeking has been relieved and Australia has gone mad with excitement.

This lonely outpost right on the border of civilisation in Africa, half-way house to Rhodesia, has been held by Colonel Baden Powell and his band of 800 courageous men for seven months, over 200 days of constant siege by the Boers.

The *Argus* reports:

Adelaide received the longed-for message, 'MAFEKING RELIEVED' at 20 minutes past 11, and in an uncontrollable excess of loyal enthusiasm the Adelaide operators sprang from their stools and gave vent to their enthusiasm with tumultuous singing of the National Anthem.

A few minutes later the information was posted at the *Argus* office, and a burst of cheering from the waiting crowd told all the city within earshot. No-one who was lucky enough to be present during the first breathless ten minutes that followed the publication of the news will ever forget the electrical thrill that ran through the community. There have been many street demonstrations and farewells of departing troops during the last eight months. The city has echoed time and again to the hurrahs of a dense packed crowd, hearty and genuine as it was, the dramatic suddenness with which the news was sprung upon the people introduced a new element of spontaneity, and it must have been a dull heart indeed that did not beat faster as the word flew through the city that the gallant little band of our fellow-country-men, penned in the little frontier, had outstayed, outfought, and out-generalled their bitter and remorseless enemy to the last.

The *Argus* said it was amazing how quickly the news spread. A hurricane of sound raged all the way up the street. A hearse, followed by mourning coaches, was coming across Princes Bridge. 'It mattered nothing to the silent occupant of the coffin that he was borne amid salvoes of cheers for a victory won in distant land.'

A dense crowd completely blocked Swanston and Collins Streets. They thundered with sticks on the doors of the Town Hall. They rang bullock bells, blew trumpets and waved Union Jacks. 'Open the doors' they cried. Alderman Ham put his head out the window and said a mass meeting would be held at 7 o'clock. 'No, no, now' they shouted back. 'We are the people — the British people.'

There was only one way to appease the crowd, Mr W.G. Barker, who has a magnificent voice, appeared on the balcony, and sang the National Anthem and 'Soldiers of the Queen'. Rain was pouring down but nobody moved, and they all sang along with Mr Barker. Then an artist pulled out huge sheets of paper and sketched Colonel Baden Powell, Lord Roberts and other idols of the nation.

A meeting of rejoicing did take place in the Town Hall tonight; it was so large they had to remove all the chairs to pack in the crowd.

But that is not all that has gone on. Hotels have thrown open their doors and offered free beer. McCracken's Brewery in Collins Street held open house and rolled hogsheads out into the street. The Carlton Brewery distributed 50 000 photographs of Her Majesty, Queen Victoria; proclaimed a holiday for the staff; and every employee received a gold portrait of the Queen in the shape of a half sovereign.

The Queensland Government has consulted all the other colonies and called for a national holiday. You could almost call it the first real act of federation.

Commander Killed at Gallipoli

23 MAY 1915

Major General Sir William Bridges, commander of the First Australian Division, is dead, killed at Gallipoli

There could hardly be anything more disturbing than this. The casualty lists have been frightening enough, but when the leader's name appears, it is all too much. This must be the new type of war, Generals used to be safe, secure behind the lines.

Bridges, born in Scotland in 1861, was a major with the NSW colonial forces. He fought in South Africa with the cavalry and took part in the great battles at Paardeberg, Kimberley and Driefontein.

He was a well-read cultivated man and most athletic. He loved canoeing on the Yarra, and in January 1908, along with three friends, he went down the rapids of the Snowy River. It was an astonishing feat. They started up near Dalgety in New South Wales and went almost to Buchan in Victoria, nearly 200 miles.

After the formation of the new Commonwealth Army, he had many high appointments. He always believed that just acquiring guns and equipment was not enough. There had to be properly trained officers. He fought for the creation of a military academy at Duntroon in 1911 and was its commandant until war broke out in 1914.

He went away to Eygpt as commander of the Australian Imperial Force. That name was his idea. His troops landed at Gallipoli, and Bridges, always a fearless man, was forever moving about the lines. He would laugh at staff who put their heads down or ran for cover.

On 15 May he decided, with Colonel Brudenell White and his aide Lieut R.G. Casey, to visit Brigadier Chauvel's headquarters. Major William Glasgow warned him: 'Be careful of the next corner. I have lost five men there today'.

They had to make a dash of about 200 yards through sniper fire to get to Chauvel's HQ. There were a number of shots being fired, but they seemed to be the usual wild and unaimed shots. Casey reported they had run barely 5 yards when Bridges went down. He had a huge bullet hole in his thigh. It had cut the femoral artery.

The Turks were good. They stopped their

Major General Bridges

fire and allowed bearers to carry Bridges away. The doctors removed him to the hospital ship *Gascon*. The whole blood supply to his leg had gone. They did consider amputating the leg, but at his age, 54, they believed he would never live through the operation.

The leg became gangrenous and he died two days ago on the way to Alexandria. He knew death was on the way and he commented 'Anyhow I have commanded an Australian Division for nine months'.

He received his knighthood just the day before his death. Senator George Pearce, Minister of Defence, announced yesterday that Colonel J.G. Legge, Chief of the General Staff, will succeed General Bridges.

Senator Pearce said:

Colonel Legge has already left for the front and we have the satisfaction of knowing that we will have in charge of the Australian Division an Australian officer in every way worthy and capable. I extend my sincere sympathy to Mrs Bridges in her trouble, but also to the hundreds of thousands of relatives of officers and men who have fallen in the historic struggle at the Dardanelles in the glorious cause of the Empire.

Amy Johnson

24 MAY 1930

Miss Amy Johnson, the English girl pilot, landed at Darwin at 3.55 this afternoon.

The entire population gave her a rapturous welcome. Today's hop in her Gypsy Moth biplane was over 500 miles of open sea. It was the most hazardous on the whole route from England to Australia, and must have been a terrific ordeal for the 26-year-old girl.

The news has been received in Melbourne with great joy. At the St Kilda football ground, there was tremendous cheering by 27 000 onlookers when the announcement in big letters 'AMY O.K.' was placed on the scoreboard. The Fitzroy and St Kilda players joined in the cheering.

Messages of congratulation have come in from all around the globe. According to the *Herald*, never has a single flight aroused such widespread and sympathetic interest. Everyone calls her 'Johnnie' and the poet, C.J. Dennis, has written special verse for the occasion:

Johnnie's down in Darwin town! Lift your glasses high!
When the tale is told again, in the years to be,
Shall her name ever live, writ across the sky,
The British lass who came to us across the Timor sea

Amy Johnson

Live to be a British boast all the ages thro'!
Gentlemen! I give the toast! 'Johnnie from the blue!'

Dogged by bad luck, she made the trip in just under 20 days, failing to beat Bert Hinkler's 1928 record of $15\frac{1}{2}$ days. She took off from Croydon on 5 May in a green flying suit, and with a bunch of roses in the cockpit.

It was a flight full of adventure. On the way from Aleppo she flew through a driving sandstorm, and it was so bad she came down in the desert. She was so worried by the thought of marauding Arabs she sat with a revolver in her hand, but after two hours, the storm cleared, she picked up the Tigris and flew on to Baghdad.

Near Allahabad she ran out of petrol and landed in a paddock, but the real disaster came at Rangoon. She made a perfect landing but landed in a ditch and smashed her propeller, so she lost two days.

She ran into a terrible monsoon, flying blind in whipping rain, and at Sourabaya she had magneto trouble. All chances of beating the Hinkler record disappeared.

But the last bit across the Timor was the agony. She thought Australia would never turn up. She said the hands on her watch moved so slowly she tried desperately to give up looking at it. 'I would think, I can look now, half an hour has gone by. But it would be only 10 minutes. Terrible!'

But then she saw a Shell oil tanker, *Phorus*, which had been told to look out for her.

Down I swooped towards it and in impulse threw a cake at a man I saw standing apart. I think my aim was bad, but the crew cheered good old British cheers — and when I heard them my heart was pounding with joy. I knew the wireless operator would be flashing his message abroad. Darwin would be thinking of me, and mother will hear too.

The Prime Minister, Mr Scullin, has invited Johnnie to Canberra. The Lord Mayor of Melbourne, Cr Luxton, has called for a 'Royal Welcome' and he says 'In my opinion it is the most remarkable flight in the history of aviation because she had only a short flying experience before leaving for Australia.'

'Mercenary Cads'
25 MAY 1879

There has been a very nasty reaction in England to the riot that took place at the Sydney Cricket Ground on 8 February last.

Frankly, we have never been over fond of English nobility, and the aloof Lord Harris in particular. You will remember Lord Harris and his XI engaged their own umpire, George Coulthard, a professional with the Melbourne Cricket Club.

Coulthard gave a number of outrageous decisions. I mean, he failed to give his Lordship out when you could hear the snick all around the ground. Then when Coulthard, calm as you like, lifted his finger to Murdoch, the Australian hero, *run out*, it was all too much, and, besides, there was a group of bookmakers and punters in the grandstand.

Suddenly there was an uproar. According to the *Sydney Morning Herald*, one of the English professionals shouted 'You're nothing but the sons of convicts'. The Englishmen deny it was ever said, but reputable citizens have written to the *Herald* claiming they did hear it.

Anyway the mob rushed the ground. One larrikin hit Lord Harris with a stick, and A.N. Hornby, the English fast bowler, took quite a mauling and had his shirt almost torn off. Lord Harris, alone and defiant, refused to leave the ground and stood there, an extraordinary figure surrounded by 2000 people. Eventually it was all resolved and the players returned, but the situation was very unpleasant indeed.

Now Lord Harris has written:

I cannot describe to you the horror we feel that such an insult should have been passed on us, and that the game we love so well and wish to see honoured and supported and played in an honest and manly way everywhere, should have received such desecration.

The London journal, *Figaro*, mentioned the warm welcome that had been given to Gregory's XI and said:

The fact is we were too civil and hospitable by half to the greedy gate-money hunting crew of Australian cricketers... Mercenary cads, low contemptible specimens of humanity.

And the *Daily Telegraph* has printed a letter which says:

Everyone must feel the warmest sympathy for Lord Harris and his XI in the outrageous insult offered to them, and it is sincerely to be hoped that we have now seen the last of Australian cricket and cricketers.

The *Sydney Morning Herald* is terribly pained and hurt by all this. After all, Australia has apologised, but other newspapers are not so polite. They accuse Lord Harris of behaving like a spoiled little boy crying to his Mamma, and the *Illustrated Sydney News*, normally a very sober journal, has been moved to satirical verse, and it begins:

Sing we of Lord Harris
    Scion of a noble race
Sick of London, Brighton, Paris,
    And of every other place.
Swore he by the crest deep craven
    On the family silver spoons,
That he'd ne'er be washed or shaven
    Till he'd thrashed the parlous loons.
Came the morning of the struggle
    Thrown aside were vest and coat,
And the 'fizz' went guggle, guggle
    Down his Lordship's lordly throat.

Ah, it is all very worrying. Do you really think that sport is designed to inspire goodwill or is it merely war?

Melbourne's Finest Street

26 MAY 1875

Collins Street

Collins Street, unquestionably, is Melbourne's best street.

Some claim that Collins Street is to Melbourne, what Regent Street is to London. It caters almost entirely for the needs of man. It has the splendid Scotts Hotel, built in 1861 on the site of John Pascoe Fawkner's Lamb Inn.

Down the West End, we have Mr McCracken's absolutely marvellous City Brewery, which lends its comely smell of malt and hops to St James Cathedral and parsonage, almost next door.

There is the Western Market, there is the Stock Exchange, there are the banks with their glistening granite fronts, designed to inspire confidence about the doings inside. There is 'The Block' between Swanston and Elizabeth, where beautiful ladies and their beaux, parade in the afternoon, usually between two and four. It is a time to see and be seen; a time for popping in and out of the fashionable shops.

It is here, too, that you see the hansom cabs, the fine carriages. The great churches are just a little further up the hill and, of course, Burke and Will's noble statue at the corner of Russell and Collins.

Just lately the doctors have started taking up residence at the East end, building some most handsome residences. Many of them have large gardens, planted with vegetables and fruit. Some of them even boast vineyards.

Just a few years back, one couldn't walk in Collins Street without choking in dust or sinking knee-deep in mud. You will be pleased to hear that now we have adequate paving and fine bluestone gutters. It is a street with style and elegance. Indeed, the *Argus* has just reported an event of great significance. The Mayor, Mr Gatehouse, a saddler by trade, planted the first of the shade trees, procured from the Minister for Lands.

The affair, says the *Argus*, attracted considerable attention. A crowd of 300 persons was there at noon to witness the proceeding. The first tree, a healthy flourishing elm about 12 feet high, was placed in a trench by the Town Hall, filled in with earth and surrounded by an iron guard.

The Mayor pronounced that first shade tree in Collins Street well and truly planted. All this was not his idea, said he. Only recently there had been a deputation from the Melbourne Club, which wanted to plant trees in front of their premises. There were many others in Collins Street East who wanted to do the same thing.

Now, this was the beginning. He was willing to lay himself open to criticism from the public and the press on the type of trees selected, but none of the trees planted in front of the Town Hall would cost the City Council anything. All the expense would be borne by the Mayor.

Three cheers were then given for the Mayor. A number of gentlemen present accompanied him to the Mayor's room, bottles of champagne were opened and His Worship asked all to drink the health of the tree just planted.

We do hope that several hundred more trees are planted along the mile of Collins Street. All loyal citizens will be only too delighted to be present and to drink the health of each tree in champagne.

The Prince Removes his Gloves

27 MAY 1920

His royal Highness, Edward Prince of Wales, arrived in Melbourne yesterday afternoon to a dazzling, joyous welcome, but the cheering crowds had a very long wait.

The young Prince came to us aboard HMS *Renown* described as the 'most wonderful battleship in the world' but yesterday we had very nearly the densest fog the city has ever seen. *Renown* should have entered the Heads in the early morning, but that was impossible.

At 1 p.m. the Prince transferred to the destroyer *Anzac*, which at 28 knots and every bolt shaking, made the fastest trip ever recorded down the Bay to the new wharf at Port Melbourne, and from there His Royal Highness transferred to the excursion vessel *Hygeia*, to land at St Kilda where everyone of importance in Australia was waiting to greet him.

Journalist Keith Murdoch, who travelled out with him on the *Renown*, describes him this way: 'Bashful by nature, sensitive in temperament, he always does a little more than necessary. A good-looking youth, very fair and blue-eyed, the mere sight of him is enough to touch many hearts. There is nothing formal about him, according to Murdoch. At a picnic you will see him sharing his hamper with his chauffeur and his equerry, lighting a cigarette, chatting to anyone who passes.

The Governor-General, Sir Munro Ferguson, greeted the Prince at the pier, and then there was a triumphant progress into the city. The crowd was immense, a human sea of faces. The railways alone brought 120 000 people into town. They even fitted temporary seats into wagons normally used for postal parcels, and trains were running every two minutes.

All along St Kilda Road, every building was decked with flags and bunting and there were gay Venetian masts at every corner. There were signs out: 'WELCOME TO THE PRINCE' and, particularly, 'CHEERIO DIGGER' and 'WELCOME TO THE DIGGER PRINCE'.

Yes, the Diggers recognise him as one of their own, and the crowd was full of men in uniform. The *Herald* says:

There were men in uniforms glorious with ribbons and stars — men who had been through the terrors of the campaigns on Gallipoli and in France — men who in the dark days of holding the line on the Somme never wavered in the sight of a merciless enemy.

Last night the Prince attended the State Ball and had the first dance with Miss Beatrice Irvine, daughter of the Lieutenant-Governor and Lady Irvine. Everyone was so interested or perhaps awestruck, nobody else took the floor. The Prince had to take his partner right up the other end of the hall, then others began to make a move.

All the season, Melbourne girls have been dancing with slow gliding movements 'with the body in perfect repose', known as the Toorak glide. But the Prince does not do this. He favours quick steps, his body swaying with the rhythm. So everybody had to change to the new style.

What's more, said the social writers, he took off his gloves and did not wear them all evening. The Prime Minister, Mr Hughes, promptly did the same. This, indeed, promises to be a relaxed Royal Tour.

The Career of a Spendthrift

30 MAY 1936

George Dick Meudell

We have just had the funeral of George Dick Meudell. He died suddenly at St Kilda aged seventy-six.

George was a little fat man, who, along with fellow members at the Athenaeum Club, believed that a rotund girth was a sound insurance against bad health.

Always a gentleman, he wore a top hat, a frock coat, and bought all his clothes in London. He said 'To be well dressed is a better consolation than one of the many religions'.

He also said 'My way of joking is to tell the truth. It is the funniest joke in the world'. His funniest joke was tell the true story of Melbourne's Land Boom and have it suppressed for nigh on 70 years.

Meudell started his career as a banker, then went into the Stock Exchange, but come 1929, he published a book titled *The Pleasant Career of a Spendthrift*. He spilled the lot on all the people he knew during the land boom.

For example, he told the story of Sir Matthew Davies, a politician who owned an enormous mansion in Malvern; a man whose bankrupt companies managed to ruin shareholders by the thousand. Meudell and Davies were living at the Athenaeum Club at the very time when the banks and building companies were crashing.

At breakfast M.H. took his seat looking blithe and debonair, spic and span, smiling while sombre at heart. Hidden behind the *Argus* he would whisper 'How dreadful, another bank closed its doors. Tut, tut, very sad'. Or 'Did you see Lath and Plaster Building on Sand Society has stopped payment? Shocking isn't it? Waiter, a little more buttered toast, very hot and very buttery'.

The book went on sale and caused a profound sensation. After the first release orders came from the board of Angus and Robertson to withdraw the book from sale. The chairman, J.M. Gillespie, was named as one of the land boomers.

Meudell had to sell his book privately, price ten shillings and sixpence. He had his office in the St James building opposite Menzies Hotel in William St. All along the wall, right up to the splendid 18-foot ceiling, he had double stacks of the *The Pleasant Career of a Spendthrift*.

Another edition appeared three years ago, *The Pleasant Career of a Spendthrift and His Later Reflections*, but alas, all the harsh stuff had gone and no longer was there any mention how B.J. Fink had paid a halfpenny in the pound and gone to London after a threat of assassination. Furthermore, there was nothing but the kindliest of references to the Baillieus.

In recent years, he and his wife spent much of their time travelling. He claimed that he travelled 400 000 miles by land and sea on over 400 steamships, and stayed in 600 hotels. He was smart enough not to get stung by the land boom.

He did not think much of Canada and the United States, and as for Eastern countries... 'Travel in Eastern countries is spoiled by the dirt the traveller has to endure. My experience is that travel amongst coloured and uncivilised people is neither instructive nor comfortable'.

His comment on his own life was that he committed the immorality of being far too advanced for his age, and in other times he would have been tortured and hanged.

Further reading: *The Land Boomers*, Jack Cannon.

Blamey's Remarkable Funeral

31 MAY 1951

Field Marshal Sir Thomas Blamey's cortege

Field Marshal Sir Thomas Blamey is dead. His funeral yesterday was the most remarkable this nation has seen.

It was remarkable because of the numbers who wanted to be there. The *Argus* reports today that the ordinary people formed a 300 000 strong, unbroken guard of honour for his funeral procession along the entire route from Melbourne's Shrine of Remembrance to the Fawkner Crematorium.

For nearly an hour, the heart of the city was silent. With flags at half-mast, with blinds drawn in many business houses, and with most shops shut, the eerie quiet of Swanston Street was broken only by the sound of marching feet and the minute by minute crash of field guns in the Domain.

There were 4000 uniformed troops in the procession. Mr W.J. McKell, the Governor-General, followed immediately behind the gun carriage. Then came Sir Dallas Brooks, the Victorian Governor; Mr Menzies, the Prime Minister; members of Parliament, judges, and ten lieutenant-generals flanked the casket.

Earlier over 20 000 people made pilgrimage to the Shrine where Australia's first and only Field Marshal lay in state from 9 a.m. to 2 p.m. Later Lieutenant-Colonel Norman Carlyon, former senior aide to the Field Marshal, laid a bunch of daphne from Lady Blamey on the casket, the only floral tribute it carried. With the daphne were the Field Marshal's scarlet and gold baton and his cap, and his orders and decorations glittered on a purple and gold cushion.

J.H. Rasmussen, his former director-general of public relations, in an *Argus* tribute, tells of the Blamey who served Australia in two world wars:

Two armies know him as Tom — they have hooted him and they have cheered him, and most of them love him. He didn't give a damn whether they hated him or loved him. He had a job to do and did it, and as far as he was concerned it was a case of the devil take the consequences. At times Tom Blamey was the most criticised man in the Army; at other times the most respected.

Rasmussen recalled how Sir Thomas was born in Wagga, the son of a storekeeper. He started his career as a schoolteacher, joined the permanent army in 1906, served at Gallipoli, and became tactician and brilliant 'G1' to General Monash.

His greatest service, says Rasmussen, was the way he kept the AIF together, fought for the rights of the Australian soldier, and refused to be trampled upon by Macarthur.

Interesting that the obituaries carry almost nothing about his career as Chief Commissioner of the Victoria Police. He had the unenviable job of police chief during the depression, keeping order amongst the unemployed. He ran that force like the Army, with total discipline. His departure was the Blamey low point, a tragic and reluctant resignation after a Royal Commission instigated by Premier Dunstan in 1936. That commission was all over a cover up concerning the wounding of a CIB chief in a shooting affray. At the time we all thought Blamey's career was over.

How wrong we were. As R.G. Menzies says today: 'History will give him a very high place'.

Further reading: *Blamey*, John Hetherington.

JUNE

W.E. Hart in his boxkite

Labor Commits Suicide

1 JUNE 1955

Mr Henry Bolte

The Liberal and Country Party in Victoria has swept Labor from office, in one of the greatest victories on record.

The victory, according to commentators, has come about not so much because of voter enthusiasm for the Liberals, but utter disenchantment with the bitter internal strife taking place in Labor. The result can only be described in these terms, Labor has committed suicide.

The official ALP, led by John Cain, contested 49 seats and has been reduced to 20. Five ministers in the Cain Government have lost their seats. The Anti Communist Labor Party, led by Mr Barry, a former Health Minister, was decimated. It contested 44 seats and secured only one, Mr. Scully in Richmond.

The break-away Victorian Liberal Party, led by the former premier, Mr Tom Hollway, was annihilated. It contested ten seats and won none.

The splinter parties caused incredible confusion. Voters at the polling booths kept asking: 'But which is the right party?' Furthermore, there was angry rivalry between Cain and Barry

Labor canvassers. There were fights between canvassers outside the State School polling booth in Carlton, and the police had to be called. The secretary of the ALP branch at Clifton Hill claimed that two Barry canvassers assaulted him outside a polling booth in Spensley Street, Clifton Hill.

Arthur Calwell, deputy Federal Opposition Leader, describes the Victorian election as a disaster. Not for 30 years has the Labor opposition sunk to such small numbers. It looks as if the Liberal Country Party will be able to govern in its own right. This is the probable line up: Premier and Treasurer, Henry Bolte; Deputy Premier and Chief Secretary, Arthur Rylah; Attorney General, Mr Leggatt; Lands and Soldier Settlement, Sir Thomas Maltby; Health, Mr. Whately; and Housing, Mr. Petty.

But who is this Henry Bolte? Hardly anyone knows him. He is 47 and he has been a member only eight years. He has a property at Meredith and he runs 3000 merinos. The *Sun* says 'Bolte's colleagues do not dab him a brilliant leader. They say he has other qualities — calmness, tact and a friendly down-to-earth manner'.

Geoffrey Tebbutt in the *Herald* says: 'It is not easy to write about the new premier, because, externally at least, he lacks striking characteristics and has never aroused public curiosity'. Tebbutt thinks there are some similarities to Thomas Playford of South Australia, also a farmer.

But Tebbutt, clearly is unimpressed. He adds: 'He (Bolte) would, of course, have a long way to go to begin to match the force of character, nimble mind and dominant personality of the 'permanent' premier of South Australia'.

Meanwhile Mrs Bolte, wife of the new Premier, spent all day yesterday answering telephone calls at their home, Kialla, and making cups of tea for visitors. She said she was looking forward to her new role, but she is terrified at the thought of making speeches. 'I have never tried' she said. 'I tremble at the very thought...'

Many wonder whether Bolte will survive a full term, and, further, they wonder how long it will take the ALP to come to its senses and reunite as one party.

Midget Submarines in Sydney Harbour

2 JUNE 1942

Three Japanese midget submarines have made an astonishing attack on Sydney Harbour.

One submarine fired two torpedoes that hit and sank the *Kuttabul*, a Sydney ferry boat that was used as a depot ship. Eight sailors are dead and 11 missing, believed killed.

The first indication of the presence of the submarines was given when an explosion occurred and guns began to fire late on Sunday night. Searchlights swept the water, and ferry passengers had an unnerving experience. Shells whistled around them and they heard the reverberation of machine gunfire.

A seaman who was on watch on the deck of a steamer moored just near the harbour vessel that was torpedoed saw the periscope and conning tower of the submarine. He said:

Bright moonlight was flooding the water and the periscope and conning tower were clearly visible only 50 yards away from where I stood. I thought I must be dreaming and pinched myself to make sure I wasn't asleep. For a moment I thought it must be one of our own submarines but I was quickly disillusioned. While I was still watching the black object, trying hard to identify it, there was a terrific explosion and a vessel berthed a short distance shook violently and began to sink.

Almost simultaneously there was a rattle of gunfire. It was the smartest bit of work I have ever seen. Machine gun bullets were spitting all around us, with tracer bullets shooting stars as the gunners tried to get range.

The submarine remained visible only for a few minutes but in that time the conning tower must have been riddled with bullets. Searchlights were now playing on it and as they picked out the lines the submarine quickly submerged. I reckon that submarine met its Waterloo just where it was. The crew must have got the shock of their sweet lives.

The Minister for the Navy, Mr Makin, says one submarine was destroyed before it entered the harbour, the second which fired the torpedoes was put out of action in the harbour, but there was a third. So far it has not been found, but the Navy is convinced it was destroyed.

Midget submarine hauled from Harbour

Geoffrey Tebbutt writes in Melbourne's *Herald* today:

The cheeky crews of the midgets performed a feat of seamanship even to enter, and deeply to penetrate, the greatest harbour and naval bases remaining to the Allies in the South-West Pacific.

The dead men of two or three submarines, and documents or equipment that may be fished up from the harbour bed, could yield a tale to Naval Intelligence. What the event does further emphasise is the imaginativeness, even the suicidal boldness, of the enemy. It did not come off this time, but it was, as Mr. Churchill said of the sinking of the *Royal Oak*, 'a remarkable exploit of professional skill and daring'.

It does prove one thing. As the *Sydney Morning Herald* comments:

Any lingering popular belief in southern Australia that 'it cannot happen here' should now be completely dispelled. The risks under which Australians live belong no more to the realm of theory, for the enemy has come to announce them in unmistakable form.

The War in South Africa is Over

3 JUNE 1902

The war in South Africa is over. The newspapers today are filled with euphoric expressions of loyalty and satisfaction concerning the evidence of the strength of the British Empire.

The *Argus* carries handsome sketches of His Majesty, the King, Lord Roberts, Lord Kitchener and Major General Baden Powell, set against a panoply of Royal Ensigns and Union Jacks.

There have been rejoicings in the streets, the blowing of fog horns in Sydney Harbour, buildings are bedecked with flags, and we read there was even a riot at Leeds where the Australian XI was playing Yolkshire.

The crowd of 30 000 was utterly unmanageable; local people broke into the ground from all sides. Victor Trumper and Clem Hill were batting at the time, and play was interrupted. However before play resumed, both teams assembled in the centre of the ground and sang 'God save the King' in honour of the declaration of peace. The crowd joined in and finished with three cheers.

Lord Kitchener

It did not do the Australians any good. Their batting was lamentable and the late score is 7 down for 70 runs. Mercifully, Trumper at least, did manage a handsome 38 runs.

There have been services of thanksgiving in all the churches, but one has to say the jubilation has not been as great as we saw after the Relief of Mafeking. The *Argus* says today:

As a result of the ill-instructed ambition which aimed at making the Vierkleur dominant in South Africa there remains only the memory of a brave and stubborn conflict which has drenched the land with blood. Dragons' teeth were sown, and armed men sprang up...the point on which there is miserable certainty is the utter wastefullness of the last 18 months fighting.

Oh, yes, the victory, according to the *Argus*, 'is entirely glorious to the British Empire'. And there is enthusiasm in all the capital dailies over the magnanimous terms of the British peace. Of course, there will be no independence for the Boer republics, and the military occupation of the Transvaal and Orange States will continue. But the burghers will pay no special tax for the expenses of the war, and His Majesty's Government will provide £3 million sterling to restock the burghers farms. (Not a great sum when it is considered the estimate for the job is £15 million.

Dutch will be allowed in the law courts and schools. South Africa will be a crown colony until self-government can be established on a sound basis. The kaffirs will be disenfranchised.

You could say most people are fiercely proud of this British triumph, but there is a minority group in the Labor Party. the trade unions, the Irish and some university intelligencia, that is horrified. Henry Bourne Higgins, MHR for North Melbourne, told the House that the war had spattered shame and degradation on the fair name of England. Left wingers have insisted that Britain was only interested in securing the gold, and the Rand does produce £50 million sterling every year.

We sent 16 175 men to the war and lost 518 killed through war action or disease.

Further reading: *A History of Australia*, Vol V, C.M.H. Clark.

Professor Miller — Champion Athlete

6 JUNE 1883

Larry Foley

The most extraordinary character in all the colonies is Professor William Miller.

He is not a professor in the university sense, he's a professor because he is the greatest exponent of his art. He always signs himself 'Professor Miller, champion athlete of the world'.

He claims he is a world champion at boxing, fencing, wrestling, heavy dumb-bell lifting and long-distance walking. He came to Australia from Cheshire in 1851, when he was five years old. Since then he has been Melbourne's prime example of manliness, physical fitness, strength and clean living.

Table Talk says he is the embodiment of good nature. He doesn't have the scowl usually adopted by your average second-rate pugilist. In 1879 he walked 102 miles in 24 hours. When he trains he rises at 4 a.m. and walks 20 miles before breakfast. He returns to a meal of stale bread, a scraping of butter, a chop and two cups of tea. The Professor believes utterly in stale bread.

He said after his 102-mile walk:
While on the track my drink consisted of good sherry, well dashed with water, while my food off the track was raw oysters, beef tea, calf-foot jelly and a small portion of boiled chicken. Soups or slops of any kind I studiously avoided.

He can do remarkable things. At Cincinatti recently he raised with one hand a 100 lb dumb-bell 20 times; a 201 lb dumb-bell twice, 150 lb bell, three times. He raised in each hand two dumb-bells of 250 lbs, and with both hands, 1550 lbs of solid iron.

He offered to meet any man breathing at Graeco—Roman wrestling or with the gloves on. So this week he met Larry Foley, the magnificent fighter who thrashed Hickin in a secret border battle on the Murray in 1879.

The fight took place in Sydney at, of all places, the Academy of Music. Foley was 32, 10 stone 12 pounds, whereas the Professor was 37, and at 13 stone 9 pound, three stone heavier than Foley. But everyone agreed Foley's boxing skill and dazzling speed would finish off the muscle bound Miller.

The fight was even enough for the first 16 rounds, but the Professor slowly gained the upper hand. By round 27, Foley was shaky, by the thirty-fifth he was exhausted and almost defenceless. The Professor was too kind, unwilling to administer the final blow. In the thirty-seventh he decided it had to be done, he sent a right to Foley's jaw and floored him unconcious. This gave Foley's seconds time to swamp him with water and push him back into the ring.

The Professor was still reluctant but in the fortieth he gave the *coup de grâce* and Foley fell, a motionless heap in the middle of the stage.

The crowd rushed forward, there was an all-in brawl and the referee declared the bout a draw. The *Sydney Morning Herald* commented 'It was just another upheaval of the detestable spirit which gives the inhabitant of another State opportunity to point the finger of scorn'.

But all Melbourne is thrilled. It is looked upon as an absolute Southern triumph. The Fitzroy band has been called out to welcome home the Professor, and there is to be a special benefit at the Princess Theatre where the Professor himself, no less, will give an exhibition of weight lifting.

Making Do
8 JUNE 1943

Now butter rationing has been introduced as the latest idea to help defeat Hitler.

Already we have clothing, tea and sugar rationing. Double-breasted suits and waistcoats are banned. There is a maximum length for skirts. You are not allowed to buy balloon or leg-of-mutton sleeves.

Evening wear is not being made any more, and as a war-time measure, you are prohibited from taking evening gowns, dinner suits, cream trousers and furnishings to the dry cleaners.

Today the not-too-slim Customs Minister, Senator Keane, announces that we need new ration books. So there we go, lining up in queues again. You queue for everything at the moment. Every British subject over 14, or alien over 16, must have an identity card, a completed form CR7, and an old ration book to get the new one.

The E coupons are for butter, and we are told, starting today, every person in Australia, including babies, is allowed half a pound of butter a week. The Senator regrets the rationing but he tells us we are doing it for Britain.

We have to step up our exports to help the people of Britain. If we don't, they won't maintain their ration of only two ounces a week. But the Leader of the Opposition, Mr Fadden, and people like ex-Prime Minister, Mr W.M. Hughes, are far from convinced. They just think we have bungled. The Melbourne *Sun* agrees. It says our exports to Britain are well below those of pre-war years. The fact was, our dairy industry was disorganised by a short-sighted manpower policy.

Some people are not taking to it kindly. The coal miners at Cessnock in New South Wales are planning a pit-top meeting in protest. Most of them claim they take seven slices of bread in their lunch each day. What does that leave for use at home? Butter, they say, is a staple food for miners because of its salt content and they want the Government to double their ration.

We would suggest they read Prudence's column in today's paper. Prudence gives a number of tips for spinning out your butter ration. Instead of sandwiches in lunches every day, why not vary your diet with an occasional pie or pastry? For the making of the pastry use clarified dripping beaten to a cream with the addition of lemon juice.

Then, there are many ways, says Prudence, for saving your butter ration. One method is to cream your butter and blend it with a little milk or full cream powdered milk. Another wonderful method, she says, recommended by dietetic experts, is to add marrow fat. Just buy a shilling's worth of marrow bones, simmer for several hours and skim off the fat.

But this is not all, Senator Keane announces further today, that Manchester goods are being rationed, that is we have to use clothing coupons for towels, sheets, pillowslips, cushion covers, bolster covers and all similar articles. Brides will get a special ration, and young mothers will get 50 extra coupons. There is one slight concession, now you need only two coupons for a pair of rayon stockings.

Prudence is promising further tips in later issues on how to help with Manchester goods.

Smithy Crosses the Pacific

9 JUNE 1928

You could only describe it as an ecstasy of enthusiasm. The crowds went mad and almost ran into the propellers when the *Southern Cross* landed at Eagle Farm airport, Brisbane this morning.

Thousands of radio operators all over Australia, the Pacific and the Pacific islands, had a long all-night vigil monitoring the big Fokker's progress. Crowds in every city waited outside newspaper offices. In Melbourne, loud speakers were set up in the streets, and hundreds waited to hear at the office of 3LO.

In Brisbane, there were thousands at the airport, shivering in the cold, long before dawn. Their anxiety was shared by an entire nation. This gigantic flight across the Pacific by Charles Kingsford Smith, his co-pilot C.P.T. Ulm plus the Americans, Lieut. Harry Lyon (navigator) and James Warner (radio), seemed impossible. They did it in three stages, the biggst hop, Honolulu to Fiji, was the longest non-stop flight ever attempted, nearly 35 hours.

The *Southern Cross* was expected to land at 8:30 a.m. At 8:40 a wireless message came through: 'Batteries low, have not been listening for 30 minutes'.

So six aeroplanes took off to see if they could locate *Southern Cross*. Captain L. Brain, manager of Qantas, was the first to return. He had flown over Moreton Bay at 7000 feet, not a sign of the *Southern Cross* had been seen.

At half-past nine, 4QG, which had a temporary wireless station at the airport, reported that *Southern Cross*, off course, was over the coast at Ballina, NSW, and was heading north for Brisbane.

At 10:13 a.m., *Southern Cross*, its blue body and silver wings glistening in glorious sunlight, flew over the hangar. Simultaneously the horns of more than 5000 motor vehicles of all descriptions shrieked a wild welcome. 'The cheering and tooting' says the *Argus* 'swelled into a deafening crescendo as the monoplane twice circled gracefully over the aerodrome, so low that Southern Cross, the famous symbol of the Southern Hemisphere could be clearly seen'.

The aeroplane, huge, wingspan 72 feet, had three engines and a fuel capacity of 1555 gallons. It had flown to Australia in three days, 10 hours, 42 minutes, at an average speed of 70 knots.

It landed sweetly, but the police were completely inadequate to control the crowd. Before the machine had ceased its progress, the barriers broke down and everyone charged forward with a wild rush, disregarding the whirling propellers.

The *Argus* says:

Captain Kingsford Smith was first to climb out. He acknowledged the cheers of the crowd with a broad smile, and shouted 'Hello Aussies'. He was followed by Mr Ulm. Both immediately demanded cigarettes, and inhaled them with luxurious enjoyment.

The crowd then put up a chant. 'Where are the Yanks?' Out came Lieutenant Lyon, the wit of the party, who said 'Waal Jim, we've travelled 7000 miles to get a drink'.

The party then was greeted by the Govenor, Sir Charles Goodwin, and the Premier, Mr McCormack. His Excellency said that Captain Kingsford Smith and his gallant comrades had successfully completed an achievement which had been watched with breathless interest by the whole world. The flight marked the commencement of a new era of aerial navigation. It would remain throughout all periods as a great event in history.

There is a telegraph message from the Prime Minister, Mr Stanley Bruce. He says Kingsford Smith and his companions are to receive for their triumph a special grant of 5000 pounds.

Alcohol and War Wage Battle

10 JUNE 1916

In new South Wales today there was a referendum to decide on 6 o'clock closing for hotels.

Of course, the Methodists, the Presbyterians, the Congregationalists and the Baptists have been campaigning for this for the past year. The early closing party distributed 11 000 posters, and one, displayed near the railway station at Newtown is 140 feet long and 12 feet high.

The *Sydney Morning Herald* was right behind it. It said 'Six o'clock is the patriotic hour. The call for the greater restriction of the liquor traffic comes for the same reason as the call for recruits. Both are needed to win the war'.

And for those of us who like a beer, the war news could hardly be worse. Three days ago we had the shocking news that Lord Kitchener and his staff had been lost aboard HMS *Hampshire* on the way to Russia, and right now there are reports that a great naval battle, called the Battle of Jutland, is raging in the North Sea, with many ships sunk.

From Bishopcourt, Archbishop Wright has announced: 'In this solemn hour of the Empire's need every true patriot should vote for six o'clock closing'.

The Liquor Trades Defence Union had a final advertisement in the newspaper which pointed out that the armies of France and Britain were supplied with beer, wine and rum and the 'word Anzac was sent ringing around two hemispheres by men who lived under 11 o'clock closing'.

But it looked tame beside the final advertisement from the 6 o'clockers. It started dramatically with some verse by Lowell:

Once to every man and nation
Comes the moment to decide
In the strife of truth with
Falsehood, on the good and evil side.

Then it invoked the late Lord Kitchener.

The late Lord Kitchener's Pledge which the Empire's soldiers are asked to observe:

In order that I may be of the greatest service to my country at this time of national peril, I promise until the end of the war, to abstain from all intoxicants, and to encourage others to do the same.

Then it gave 'The Mother's Point of View'. Drunkards will die out, but with 6 o'clock closing, thousands of young men will never learn the taste of drink.

Sydney's *Bulletin* fought back:

The argument that the business of providing refreshment and entertainment for the public should be limited to the hours when the public is not free to be refreshed and entertained is of the kind that might take place in comic opera. Why not compel all other forms of entertainment to keep within business hours? Why should milk-shake and ice-cream and vaudeville and Shakespearean tragedy and picture show and tea meeting not come under the same rule?

But it's all over. Early closing it is. Six o'clock won handsomely with a majority of 138 485. South Australia and Tasmania also have shown fierce anti-drink patriotism by voting the same way. Victoria has gone from 11 p.m. to 9.30, but the triumphant campaign is on there, too, to switch to six.

Ben Chifley Dead

13 JUNE 1951

Ben Chifley

Ben Chifley, former Prime Minister and Leader of the Opposition, collapsed and died in Canberra tonight.

Mr Chifley had appeared in the House during the afternoon. He was in his room at the Hotel Kurrajong when he collapsed with a heart seizure.

At first he made light of the attack and said it was of no consequence. A member of the staff, Miss Phyllis Donnelly, called a doctor, and at 10 o'clock Mr Chifley was rushed to Canberra Community Hospital. A priest administered the last rites of the Roman Catholic Church, and at 11.10 Mr Chifley was dead.

Most members of Parliament and their wives were attending a Jubilee Ball in King's Hall at Parliament House. The Deputy Leader of the Opposition, Dr Evatt, and the Labor Leader in the Senate, Senator McKenna, went straight to the hospital as soon as they heard of Mr Chifley's illness.

It was after 11.30 p.m. when the Prime Minister, Mr Menzies, called a halt to the dancing in King's Hall, and announced that Ben Chifley had just died. As Mr Menzies spoke many of the guests wept openly. Most immediately went straight home. They did not go on to supper, and the ball was abandoned.

Mr Menzies said:

It is my sorrowful duty to tell you that tonight, during this celebration, Mr Chifley, former Prime Minister and Leader of the Opposition, has died.

I do not want to try even to talk about him, because, although we were political opponents, he was a great friend of mine and yours, and a fine Australian.

You will agree that it is appropriate on this sorrowful occasion that the festivities of tonight should end, and therefore, in the circumstances there will be no more music. I do suggest that you have supper and that we then leave quietly, having in our minds very great sorrow for the passing of a fine Australian.

It does not matter about party politics in a case like this. Oddly enough, in Parliament we get to know each other very well, and we sometimes find we have a warmest friendship among people whose politics are not our own.

I would like Mrs Chifley to know how much we all liked him and how much we shall all miss him. He set a high example of great ability, devotion and industry. He was a good Australian. He was a good man.

Reg Tracy, driver to every Prime Minister since W.M. Hughes, said:

It was a terrible shock. He worked too hard and too devotedly. I knew he could not stand up to it after all those years. He did not rest even at home. Alternate weekends I used to drive him to Bathurst but he would spend all his time there — except for church on Sunday mornings — on electorate work.

Our best times were when he would put his feet up an talk. He would have his pipe — and he would always make sure I had a cigar — and he would tell us about his experiences. He talked often about his overseas visits. He was very loyal to the King and the Princesses. He thought they were great people.

Mr Chifley was 65 years old. There will be a State funeral in Bathurst.

All Change at the Border

14 JUNE 1883

A source of incredible friction between Sydney and Melbourne has been the break in the railway gauges.

Sydney, by Act of Legislative Council on 7 July 1852 went for 5 feet 3 inches and other colonies followed suit. All would have been fine except that, a year later, the Sydney Railway Company changed its engineer and decided 4 feet 8½ inches was for New South Wales.

Victoria already had ordered its rolling stock and refused to change. The Victorian Legislative Council appointed a select committee which warned on the danger of mixed gauges, but very grandly, it still recommended 5 feet 3 inches for Victoria. There was a blissful feeling, the cities were so far apart it did not matter, and besides the main object of a railway was to bring goods into the city. We have always felt that the cheapest and best method for interstate travel would be by ship.

Well, at last, after 31 years the railways have met. For months we have had anxious debates in both Legislative Houses of Assembly, which colony will control the exchange point? — Albury in NSW or Wodonga in Victoria.

Mr Thomas Bent, the Victorian Railways Minister, a very wily man indeed, went to Sydney and worked out a master compromise. Passengers travelling from Melbourne to Sydney would go right through on the 5 feet 3 inches to Albury, where they changed to the 4 feet 8½ inches. Passengers travelling from Sydney would do the reverse. They would go through to Wodonga to change trains.

The celebration for the linking of the cities by rail took place at Albury today with a mighty banquet in an engine shed transformed with bunting for the occasion. It was actually lit by electricity with power provided by a NSW engine. Lord Loftus, Governor of NSW, came by train from Sydney, and the Marquis of Normanby, Governor of Victoria, came by rail from Melbourne. There were 1000 guests and about 20 interminable speeches.

Melbourne *Punch* is cynical about the whole affair. It says:

So determined are the two Governments that everything today shall be done in a half-and-half manner that the caterers have strict orders even to cut the sandwiches with a slice of Victorian bread on top and New South Wales bread on the bottom. The difficulty about the ham has been got over by purchasing the whole of it from stock cured exactly on the border line.

The *Argus* correspondent says the whole through trip from Melbourne to Sydney takes 25 hours. But for red tape you could do it in 18. The Sydney train goes through to Wodonga, all right, but you have to cool your heels for at least 30 minutes in Albury before it moves on.

Then there are darker shades of rivalry. Some say the Victorian refreshment rooms in Wodonga are so superior you would not eat at the NSW refreshment rooms in Albury in a fit.

Then NSW people are complaining that Victoria is a protectionist colony, NSW goes for free trade. So upon arriving in Wodonga there is the humiliation of having one's bags gone through by the Victorian customs officer.

One wonders whether relations are any easier on the border between France and Germany.

Beatle Mania Strikes Melbourne

15 JUNE 1964

Yesterday was 'B-Day', the Beatles arrived in Melbourne.

We have had many popstar airport arrivals lately. Usually they are carefully orchestrated by some PR firm, and if 1000 people are not out there to wave and cheer the visiting czar of popdom does not rate.

Johnny Ray is particularly good at it. He has his special airport arrival suit. It is only slightly stitched here and there. He always expects to lose at least one sleeve. However we have never had an arrival like that of the Beatles.

We were intensely excited long beforehand. The build up has been going on for a month. Radio station 3UZ declared itself 'Beatle Headquarters'. It gave away 400 reserved tickets for Beatle concerts, 100 pairs of Beatle stockings, 100 Beatle wigs.

During the past 24 hours they played 114 Beatle discs. To cover the arrival they had 12 announcers along the route; they had five mobile cars for broadcasting, plus a Cessna aircraft, also broadcasting, to give the overall picture. Altogether they had 40 outside technicians and announcers on the job.

Nobody knows how many people turned out to see the Beatles, but one police estimate was 300 000, and with that 300 000 there were at least 200 000 transistor radios. As radio followed their movements, so the excitement built.

The climax came at the Southern Cross Hotel. Here there was a packed crowd of 15 000, and nothing quite like it has happened in radio before. Don Lunn, of 3UZ, had an outside position at Ireland's florist shop right opposite. He was broadcasting and everyone had their trannies. He called out 'Can you hear me out there?' Back came the roar 'YEAH, WE CAN HEAR YOU'.

So a conversation went on between the announcer and his huge outside audience. 'Let's all sing "WE LOVE THE BEATLES"'. And so it went on. 'We love John, We love George, We love Ringo, We love Paul'.

Then there was the announcement that they were less than half a mile away. They were in Bourke Street. They were just around the corner. The excitement was too much to stand.

The *Sun News Pictorial* reports today that 350 were treated for fainting, hysteria and minor injuries in the foyer of the Southern Cross. The mounted police came through, picking up swooning girls here and there, laying their limp bodies across the saddle.

It all looked more frightening than it was. There were no serious casualties, except that one lady burst a blood vessel in her neck from screaming too loudly. Dr. Ivan Markovics, a Sydney gynaecologist, who was staying in the hotel, said he treated only one girl who was genuinely ill. She was suffering from exhaustion and lack of food from sitting up all night. At least 25 per cent of the others thought fainting was a magnificent way of getting into the hotel to see the Beatles.

As for the Beatles themselves, they take it all with surprising calm. At the press conference we asked whether they were worried by the appalling scenes that took place outside the hotel. 'No', said John Lennon, 'I'm only worried that they might stop'.

Apart from their long hair they are quite nice looking young men.

Shark Disgorges Grim Evidence

16 JUNE 1935

Mr Clive Evatt

The shark arm murder inquest is in its fifth day. The story is even more bizarre than a tale created by Edgar Allan Poe.

Back in early April, an aquarium at Coogee announced it had captured a splendid 14-foot Tiger shark. For a week the shark refused to eat, incessantly, desperately, it swam round the pool. On 25 April it began to disgorge a number of objects including a human arm.

The arm carried a tattoo of two boxers. It was extraordinarily well-preserved and police were able to trace it from fingerprints. It belonged to James Smith, a billiard marker, 45, who had been missing from home since early April.

From then on, the pace of the story accelerated. Smith had been working for Reginald Holmes, a rich boat-builder. Holmes had a luxury yacht, *Pathfinder*, which last year, caught fire and sank. Smith was the only man aboard, and he swam ashore. The boat was worth £11 000 and was insured for much more. The whole affair was very strange and Holmes failed to collect the insurance money.

The police worked on a theory that Holmes was involved in a smuggling ring. Smith never got paid for burning *Pathfinder*, then when he started blackmailing Holmes, he was murdered.

Last month Sydney police arrested Patrick Brady, a well-known forger. He had been seen drinking with Smith on the day of Smith's murder, and was later seen with a bag remarkably similar to one owned by Smith.

The inquest was due to start last Wednesday, 12 June. At 8 p.m. the night before, Holmes, the chief witness for the prosecution, told his wife that he had just received an urgent telephone call and had to go out. At 1 a.m. his body was found slumped over the steering wheel of his car. Three .32 calibre shots had been fired in a triangle just under his heart.

On Friday, Holmes's widow, Mrs Enid Parker Holmes, gave evidence early. She was interposed because she was unwell and wanted to get her ordeal over. Yes, she remembered Brady. He came to their house at McMahon's Point many times, mostly at night.

One time, in early April, he came to their house at 8 a.m. He was very dirty, unshaven, and both of his hands had blood where they had been cut. He was carrying a bag like that of James Smith.

Mrs Holmes was asked had her husband mentioned Smith's disappearance. She said, yes, He told her Brady had murdered Smith, put his body in a tin trunk, taken it out on the harbour and tipped it overboard.

Mr Clive Evatt, counsel for Brady, claimed this was hearsay and inadmissible as evidence. He is now appealing to the Supreme Court on the grounds that an inquest cannot be held on the mere finding of an arm, a body is essential for proper jurisdiction.

So, inevitably, the case will be postponed. However all Australia is agog for the next episode.

Note: Evatt's appeal was successful. The Crown prosecuted Brady, but without the evidence of the murdered Holmes, the police case failed and he was acquitted. Two men were charged with the murder of Holmes. The jury failed to agree at two trials and they, too, were acquitted. The Shark Arm affair remains a mystery.

Sydney's Theatre Royal Burns but the Show Goes On

17 JUNE 1892

Sydney's famous Theatre Royal was destroyed by fire early today.

It is a matter of great grief. Many famous actors and actresses came to the corner of Castlereagh and King Streets today to gaze just once again at the scene of their triumphs.

Many of them wanted to go inside and walk among the charred ruins, perhaps, shed a tear. But the *Sydney Morning Herald* says there is an imperious guard at the entrance. Even if you spin the most piteous tale he will not let you inside.

A very clever show has been performing at the Royal, Mrs Bernard-Beere in *Lady Gay Spanker*. On Thursday night, the lady had elicited great applause and the theatre closed shortly after 11 o'clock.

At 4.20 a.m., the watchman was doing his rounds, he saw flame coming from under one of the seats in the family circle. He rushed to one of the landings, dashed back with buckets of water, but the flames only became bigger.

There were resident firemen actually sleeping in the theatre, they got all their hoses, but the fire just kept leaping in ferocity. They tried to telephone the Metropolitan Fire Brigade; the phone wouldn't work, already the wires were burned through.

But soon every Brigade in Sydney turned out. There was the Metropolitan, the Standard Brewery, the Paddington Brewery, the North City, Woollahra and Waverley brigades.

They had four big steam engines, all around the theatre, pumping water. But soon the whole theatre was just one mass of flame, burning with the utmost fierceness. As the *Herald* put it: 'the devouring element made short work of everything'. There was a whole series of crashes as the roof collapsed and the burning mass of timber and galvanised iron hit the pit floor.

Fortunately there was no loss of life, and through the brilliant work of the fire brigades they were able to save the Criterion Hotel next door. But it is all very sad. This is the third theatre to burn down on the same site.

The Prince of Wales Theatre, the largest and most commodious theatre in the Australian colonies, seating 3000 people, was built there in 1854. It burned down on 3 October 1860. Two people died in that fire, and many other buildings were destroyed. The farce they were playing at the time was called *A Very Serious Affair*.

Well, they rebuilt that theatre, called it the Prince of Wales Opera House, and that was burned down on 6 January 1872 with £50 000 loss of property and a 100 people thrown out of work.

But the Theatre Royal was the best and grandest theatre in the land. Only last July the 'divine' Sarah Bernhardt appeared on its boards, playing her celebrated 'Theodora'. Oh yes, the marvellous shows we all remember, Ada Ward in *Rosalind*, Mrs Scott Siddons in the wonderful revival of *Macbeth*, Louise Pomeroy, the vivacious American, who included Romeo and Hamlet in her repertoire. Then George Ringold thrilled Sydney with his performance of Henry V. The glorious Miss Jennie Lee produced *Jo* in 1883, and ah yes, Patty Laverne appeared as Stella with Miss Nellie Stewart as Griolet in *Fille de Tambour Major*. Then we had all those successes with Miss Stewart in the Royal Comic Opera Company.

So what will happen with the present show? Regrettably the great entrepreneur, Mr George Musgrove, presently is in Melbourne, but Mr Boucicault has been in touch with him by communication of the telegraph.

All is not lost. Incredibly the scenery for *Lady Gay Spanker* was not destroyed. Late tonight arrangements were made with Mr J.C. Williamson, and for the rest of the season Mrs Bernard-Beere's show will switch to the Criterion.

However the Theatre Royal will be sadly missed.

Sharkey Charged with Sedition

20 JUNE 1949

Laurence Louis Sharkey, General Secretary of the Communist Party, was convicted in Sydney's Criminal Court today on a charge of sedition.

Just five years ago, when Stalin's troops were destroying Hitler's finest divisions in front of Stalingrad, the Reds were all heroes. Not any more. Last June the Soviets blockaded Berlin, and the Allies kept it going with an incredible airlift of all supplies.

That blockade ceased only four weeks ago. So where will the Communists infiltrate next?

The Sharkey case is a curious one. Last March the French Communist leader, Maurice Thorez, announced that if the Soviet 'liberators' came to France they would be welcome.

A reporter on Sydney's *Daily Telegraph* was told to get the views of local Communists. So he called Mr Sharkey. Sharkey said he would prefer to give a considered statement the next day.

Sharkey did make his statement:

If Soviet forces in pursuit of aggressors enter Australia, Australian workers would welcome them. Australian workers would welcome Soviet forces pursuing aggressors, as the workers welcomed them throughout Europe when the Red troops liberated the people from the power of the Nazis.

Sharkey added that invasion of Austraila by Soviet troops was remote and hypothethical. The Soviet Union would go to war only if she was attacked.

These words were sufficient for Sharkey to be charged with sedition. Mr W.R.Dovey, KC, for the Crown, warned jurors to put out of their minds that Sharkey was a Communist. The charge was not against a Communist, but against an individual who owed allegiance to the King.

Mr Dovey said a man was entitled to express his views freely so long as he did not use words tending to create disaffection and breaches of the law and order in the civil State.

Sharkey refused to go into the witness box. He said the case was so weak and trivial that it would be preposterous to ask anybody to give evidence against it. His counsel, Mr J.W. Paterson, said the answering of questions over a telephone could not be construed as incitement to produce disaffection against the sovereign or the constitution.

'How could it possibly endanger the peace and good conduct of the Commonwealth?' said he.

Mr Justice Dwyer did not pass sentence today, but when he does it seems certain Laurence Sharkey will go to jail. Meantime he is on £2000 pounds bail.

Every newspaperman in town wants to interview Sharkey, but his attitude is the same as it was in Court, he is not talking.

If you want to know about Sharkey, then you have to buy the Communists' own journal, the *Guardian*. We learn that Sharkey is 50, born on a farm near Orange, NSW. Brought up a Catholic, his education was limited. All his spare pennies went on books, says the *Guardian*. When unemployed he would go to the Public Library, and study everything from the *Encyclopaedia Britannica* to histories of religion. He had a better grasp of philosophy and economics than capitalist university professors.

He never felt attracted to the ALP. He said 'A police baton at an unemployed demonstration under the Labor Government helped considerably to clarify my ideas'.

Oh yes, says the *Guardian*, don't believe the lies of the capitalist Press, Laurence Sharkey leads a life which is utterly blameless.

Note: Sharkey was sentenced to three years hard labour. This was reduced to 18 months on appeal.

Laurence Sharkey

Celebrating the Queen's Jubilee

21 JUNE 1887

Queen Victoria

This is Jubilee Year to celebrate Her Majesty Queen Victoria's fiftieth year on the throne.

An immense amount of money is being spent around the colonies. Both Sydney and Melbourne are getting large and elaborate statues of Her Majesty, holding orb and sceptre and looking more imperious than you can imagine.

City buildings are being decorated with loyal motifs, and every colonial capital is holding levees and Vice-Regal Jubilee Balls. It is absolute social death not to be invited.

Could one quote this week's *Table Talk* from Melbourne:

Throughout the length and breadth of Queen Victoria's dominions, there has been no more dazzling scene of splendour during this Jubilee season than that which His Excellency's guests were privileged to witness at Government House on Wednesday night...It was a blaze of colour, a poem in tones; a glimpse of fairyland.

Sir Henry Loch invited 4000 guests to the Jubilee Ball. The building was lined with crimson, and everywhere the eye rested upon the most exquisite contrast of colour. Shrubs and flowers in all their varied colour of foliage and bloom were lavishly arranged in studied elegance; and the general effect was heightened by the brilliant gleams of electric light...

The carriages commenced to arrive shortly after nine o'clock, and for upwards of an hour a constant stream of gaily attired people poured to the grand entrance. At 10 o'clock the kaleidoscopic grouping of magnificent costumes rivalled in dazzling splendour the gorgeous ornamentations of the vast reception rooms.

Sydney's *Bulletin*, you will be saddened to hear, has been particularly rude. In derision this journal constantly refers to the Queen as Mrs Guelph, the long forgotten German name. This week there is this item:

For many years a painful struggle has been going on to keep up interest in Victoria, but the heaviness of that dead lift has been all too apparent. The whole Empire has been requested to be staggered and awestricken at the fact of her widowhood, which as her late husband died in his bed of a very ordinary complaint and left her well-provided for, seems even less remarkable than the majority of widowhoods.

Her political wisdom which was never proved by a single known act, and her condescension, to a stout, elderly Scotch servant named Brown, and the fact that her secretary sends telegrams of inquiry when any notable person breaks his leg, have also been advertised to the point of weariness. And through it all, there intrudes the vision of a brief, stout, rather cross-looking old lady dressed in rusty black and with a countenance that shows no admirable characteristic whatever.

The *Bulletin* suggests that Victoria's statue of 'the wealthy Mrs Guelph' should be exactly like the original, short, squat, fat, obese and melancholy looking, and then the 'Southern grovellers' might come to their senses.

Regardless of the *Bulletin*, most of us are loyal to the point of total euphoria.

Landy Runs a Four-minute Mile

22 JUNE 1954

All Australia is thrilled, John Landy, the boy from Melbourne, has run the 4-minute mile.

He did it today in Turku Finland, in the world record time of 3 minutes 58 seconds. It is being described as a new golden age of athletics. London's Roger Bannister broke the first 4-minutes mile with 3.59.4 on 6 May.

Conditions were ideal and the track fast. Six thousand Finns wildly cheered the Australian. Landy was kept up to his task over the second half of the mile by Englishman Chris Chataway, who also paced Bannister's world record run at Oxford on 6 May.

Chataway was second in 4 minutes 4.4 seconds, forty yards behind Landy. The crowd sensed the record was tumbling and all through the last lap everyone was standing up cheering. Half a dozen stop watches clicked at 3.58 minutes as Landy pushed himself over the tape.

Officials cried 'You've done it!' as he broke pace and slowed. Officials and other competitors hoisted Landy high into the air, three times. The Union Jack and Australian flag were flown on top of the stadium.

Landy, curly-haired and very modest, gave the credit to Chataway. He said he was instrumental in making it all possible, and he added: 'I've kept my present top shape for more than nine months now. I think an even better mile race can be done but I don't think I'll be able to do it myself — not this year'.

Chataway asked to compare the great runners said:

I will say that Landy and Bannister are dead level. Bannister ran his race on a cold windy May day, but conditions at Turku were ideal. It was a perfect mile race in every way.

A Finnish pace-maker led for the first half-mile then John took over at a cracking pace. I stuck on to him and the 6000 crowd in that little stadium were yelling. On the way John broke the world record for 1500 metres. I was dropping back by then, but I covered the 1500 metres in 3:45.2 my best ever by six seconds. With 300 yards to go John was on his own, streaking out for the post. Everyone crowded around John afterwards, but I saw he was not very distressed; in fact, he looked very fit.

The Australian newspapers have gone beserk. The Melbourne *Sun*, for example, has the Landy family all over the front page. Then there is a centre spread giving a history of Landy's entire career, what he ate, how he performed when at school at Geelong Grammar, how he trained at East Malvern's Central Park.

There is a slow motion picture series of 'the fastest man on earth' with 'his amazing mile-swallowing stride' and there is a photograph showing us exactly what a mile looks like from Flinders Street to Victoria Street.

American officials and sports writers, we are told, are clamouring for a 'mile of the century' in the United States, but this could be dangerous for Landy's amateur status. The big clash with Bannister will come at the next Empire Games.

John Landy

The Great Wheelbarrow Marathon

23 JUNE 1935

What, with the financial depression, there has not been much to amuse lately, thank heavens for the great wheelbarrow marathon.

It all began like this. The road from Beechworth to Mt Buffalo, is 50 miles of loose metal and gravel; a steady climb of 5000 feet. Tony Evans, a local Beechworth publican, weighing 160 lbs. said it was dangerous.

Tom Parkinson of the Beechworth garage said that was nonsense. 'I could wheel you there in a wheelbarrow'. The wager was the impressive sum of 20 pounds.

The great saga immediately became world news, every step covered by foot, radio and thousands of sightseers. In Myrtleford there was a street parade to celebrate, with the turning out of every conceivable object that looked like a wheelbarrow.

However the task became tougher and tougher. The push started eight days ago with bands playing, flags waving and aircraft flying overhead. But then snow set in. The road was slippery, Tom Parkinson couldn't see hidden rocks and sometimes it took two hours to cover two miles.

Conditions were freezing, Tom could not get a grip with his feet, and occasionally the sometimes dozing Mr Evans was capsized into the snow and mud. Dr Alexander, superintendent of Prince Henry's Hospital, gave solemn warning. He said the strain was too much. Mr Parkinson would be wise if he stopped. 'His heart must be feeling the task'.

But yesterday, as if by magic, the weather cleared and the sun shone. It made all the difference. Parkinson and Evans made such good progress they did not want to get into Mt Buffalo too early. They knew the exact time Australians would be coming home from church. Furthermore the ABC, which was covering the event step by step, did not want to disrupt its programming.

So the triumphant pair trundled in today at 12.25 p.m. Skiers formed a triumphal arch of sticks, a crowd of 1500 sang 'There's a long, long trail a-winding'. Mrs Evans hung a blue ribbon around Parkinson's neck bearing the words, 'Parkie, The Pride of Beechworth' and Mrs. Parkinson put another blue ribbon around Evan's neck, 'Tony, Still Smiling'.

Parkinson told the crowd:

When I say I am pleased to be here I am telling no lie. The last three or four days have been the most trying I can remember. My friend has been a true and generous sport during these last terrible days. He could have made things very nasty for me, but he didn't. He always played the game, often at his own expense.

Some people have called me a fool... this barrow has brought the greatest crowds and publicity to Beechworth and Myrtleford that the towns have ever known.

This is true. There is a craze now for wheelbarrow pushes all over the country. The *Sydney Morning Herald* says new pushes are starting in Dubbo, Albury and Adelaide. In Adelaide, a councillor is substituting 'a bourgeois gig for the proletarian barrow'.

What's more Parkinson and Evans are celebrities. They agreed this afternoon to appear at the Princess Theatre, Melbourne, on Monday night and every other night until Saturday. They will also attend the wheelbarrow carnival in aid of Prince Henry's Hospital.

Poet Suicides

24 JUNE 1870

Adam Lindsay Gordon is dead at 37 years. They found him on Brighton Beach this morning, a bullet hole through the top of his skull.

Colonial writers, artists, poets, are a despairing lot. They get little recognition. But Gordon, particularly, was a wild, haunted man. His father was a retired captain in the Bengal cavalry, and his mother, who had inherited £20 000 was comparatively rich.

Young Gordon, from an early age, adored horses, and his horse was nearly always turned in the direction of a farmer's beautiful daughter. The daughter was considered not quite up to the station of the Gordons, so young Adam Lindsay, in 1853, was exiled to the colonies.

He joined the mounted police force of South Australia and for several years was stationed at Penola in the Mount Gambier district, which surely inspired rollicking great poems like 'Wolf and Hounds' and 'From the Wreck'

His mother died in 1861 and left him £7000, which should have been enough to support him for life. However he had a true poet's gift for parting with money. It was a world of race meetings, steeplechases, spectacular leaps on horseback and terrible falls.

He married a woman born in Glasgow. The Gordons back home would not have approved, she had little education but was a first class horse rider. He had a brief period as a South Australian politician, a disastrous period as a farmer, and even ran Craig's livery stables in Ballarat.

Soon he was virtually penniless. In 1867 he published his first book of poems, *Sea Spray and Smoke Drift*, at his own expense; £50 for 500 copies. He sold only 100 of them and, as one writer put it, they remained like a weary load on the publisher's shelves.

There was a good review from *Baily's Magazine* in England, but the only lengthy Australian notice was in the November issue of *Colonial Monthly*, which used such words as 'unimpressive', 'abrupt' and 'totally lacking in the characteristics of Byron'.

His only child Annie Lindsay, was born on 3 May 1867, she died on 14 April 1868. This left him in a state of deep depression from which he never recovered.

He had expected a further legacy from Scotland. It did not arrive. He was in debt for over 350 pounds. Yesterday he met the writer, Marcus Clarke, and had drinks with him. Then he met the poet Henry Kendall, also suffering poverty. They decided to spend the last pennies in their pockets on drink. Kendall produced a very flattering critique he had written for the *Australasian* of Gordon's volume *Bush Ballads and Galloping Rhymes*. It put Gordon on a plane with Kingsley and Swinburne.

But even this was not enough. This morning he rose early, took down his rifle, kissed his sleeping wife, then walked down along the low cliffs to Brighton Beach. A fisherman saw him striding along the sand, but no one saw him alive again.

At 9 a.m., a man named Allen, who was hunting for a cow that had gone astray, spotted a man lying in an open place under the trees. He was wearing tight breeches and a velvet jacket. He thought at first he was sleeping.

It was Adam Lindsay Gordon. He had put his rifle in his mouth and shot himself through the top of his head.

Unquestionably he will get more recognition in death than in life.

Adam Lindsay Gordon

129

Jacka Awarded the VC

27 JUNE 1915

Albert Jacka, 22 years old, has been awarded the Victoria Cross. He is the first Australian in this World War to win the enormous honour.

Jacka comes from Layard near Winchelsea. He is the fourth child of Nathaniel Jacka and his Englishborn wife, Elizabeth.

Jacka left school by the time he was 14, worked as a labourer with his father, then for the Victorian Forests Department. He joined up as soon as war broke out, trained at Broadmeadows, then went to Egypt and Gallipoli with the 14th Battalion.

Back on 19 May, the Turks launched a massive counter attack against the ANZACs. It was about 4 a.m. and the fighting was fiercest in the Mule Valley at a gentle rise called Courtney's Post.

The Turks rushed the Australian trenches and observers could see gun flashes coming from both sides at point blank range.

Albert Jacka, VC

The Turks captured a 12-yard section of trench. They threw bombs, causing terrible devastation. One blast killed two of the nine men inside, and wounded two others. Jacka was left down one end, almost alone, it was Jacka against the enemy.

A young lieutenant ran forward and was immediately shot through the head. Another officer, Lieutenant Crabbe, called out and asked Jacka if he needed any help. 'Yes, I want two or three', he said.

Three men, all from Bendigo, arrived. Jacka asked them if they would back him up. They said. 'yes', so Jacka led them forward into the captured trench, with fixed bayonets. Jacka kept close to the wall and he wasn't hit, but all three men coming from behind were shot. It was impossible to go back, and now he was left once again completely unsupported.

It was still dark. Jacka jumped out of the trench, and while the rest of the party provided cover by throwing grenades, Jacka went through a communication trench to attack the Turks from the rear.

In the midst of smoke and noise from the grenades, Jacka leapt over a parapet, shot five of the Turks and bayoneted two more. The rest of them fled.

The trench was filled with the dead from both sides. Lieutenant K.G.W. Crabbe of St Kilda entered the trench. He found Jacka there with an unlighted cigarette in his mouth. 'I managed to get the beggars, Sir'. said Jacka.

Well, there is considerable excitement. Jacka is a national hero. John Wren, the Melbourne businessman, racing and boxing promoter, promised £500 and a gold watch to the first Australian to win a VC. Jacka will get that.

Jacka is only a private and it is going to be interesting. You always salute a VC winner, no matter what his rank. But you can bet he won't be a private for long. They will have to promote him very quickly, at least to Corporal.

This VC is just the tonic everyone needs. The daily casualty lists could not be more depressing and the war is at a very low ebb. There is talk of using Albert Jacka's portrait, sporting his VC, on all recruiting posters.

An End to the War to End All Wars

28 JUNE 1919

The Treaty of Versailles is signed. It is on paper. Officially the war is over.

The Australian Press Association cables: Crowds cheered Monsieur Clemenceau and Mr Lloyd George madly as they emerged from the Palace of Versailles, soldiers joining in. Aeroplanes swooped overhead.

The Germans before leaving made the following statement: We are signing without any mental reservation. The German people will use every means to meet the terms of the treaty. We believe that the Entente will not insist on the delivery of the ex-Kaiser and other high German officers for trial.

However reactions were not good in Berlin. According to a Copenhagen message, several German newspapers appeared with black borders. They attacked the Entente bitterly. The Treaty was described as having been dictated by Satanic hate. 'The Germans' they went on 'must teach the children retribution and revenge before they learn to say "mother" or "father"'.

Mr W.M. Hughes, Australia's Prime Minister, is back in London after signing the Treaty, and there was a remarkable incident. Between 200 and 300 Australian soldiers waited for him at Victoria Station and rushed the platform. The Australians picked up Mr Hughes from his wife's side, placed an Australian hat on his head, and carried him shoulder high through dense, cheering crowds up Victoria Street to the Anzac buffet. Then 50 Australian soldiers, acting as a bodyguard, put him in a motor car and escorted him to his residence.

Meanwhile Sydney awoke to a wonderful sight, the greatest naval force ever seen in our waters. As the *Sydney Morning Herald* says 'never before in our history have we seen together such instruments of British sea power, the battlecruisers, *New Zealand* and *Australia*, plus the cruisers, *Brisbane* and *Encounter* and the submarine *J2*.

Today flags flew from city buildings, crowded ferry boats in Sydney Harbour chorused their shrill whistles, passengers cheered, street bands played patriotic airs, guns — 101 of them, boomed out a tremendous salute and at 6 p.m. there was a brilliant scene. The warships played their powerful searchlights across the sky; they sent out rockets in a spray of beautiful colours; and Admiral Jellicoe's flagship, *New Zealand*, illuminated a crown suspended between the two masts.

Admiral Jellicoe, when interviewed aboard said:

All I can say is that I rejoice, as I know every Britisher and every one of our Allies are rejoicing today, over this last act, which marks the end of the most terrible war in the history of the world.

However the *Sydney Morning Herald* offers some sobering thoughts:

Australia is on the side of the victors and in getting there has won a remarkable place in history...The price of it has been 57,000 young lives yielded up, tens of thousands of other lives permanently broken, casualties by the hundred thousand, treasure consumed by the hundred million, and all the unscheduled dread and heartache and desolation left at home.

If Australia is to write a fair story upon the new page it will have to be done more courageously, with a greater regard for unalterable principles and with much less resort to doubtful or mischievous political expediency than has characterised the control of affairs during the past five years.

May we not hope that this will be so?

Fire at St Mary's

29 JUNE 1865

Archbishop Polding

St Mary's Roman Catholic Cathedral, the finest Gothic edifice in all the colonies, is blazing tonight.

It was really only just completed. It had been being built since His Grace, Archbishop Polding, laid the foundation stone in 1829.

A huge crowd has been watching the fire with many people down on their knees weeping with grief.

The *Sydney Morning Herald* says 'The intelligence of this deplorable catastrophe will cause a thrill of sorrow in the hearts of the Roman Catholic population throughout the country'.

The cost of it all is awful. The value of the building alone was 50 000 pounds. There were some immensely valuable old masters over the altar. For example, there was one painting, representing the death of St Benedict, which was valued at 1000 pounds. That went up in flames.

Then there was the magnificent organ, worth £2000 which the newspapers tell us cannot be replaced and was 'unmatched in the colonies for volume, compass and sweetness'.

Everything was uninsured. Presumably the Lord is meant to look after these things.

However they did manage to save the chalices in the vestry, plus all the valuable vestments. But the *Herald* says:

It was melancholy to see the wreck of so much valuable property which was unavoidably damaged by removal. There were piles of furniture, books, pianos, pictures, and other costly articles, strewn about in the most confused manner. A great many persons were concerned in the removal of the furniture, and there is too much reason to fear that some dishonest fellows were not deterred by the presence of so fearful a catastrophe, from sacrilegious speculation. Two young men were taken into custody by the police.

No one knows what caused the fire. There was a service for the festival of St Peter and St Paul at 7 o'clock that finished at eight. There is a theory that there was a gas escape, because suddenly the whole cathedral was filled with fire, then the shingles on the roof caught alight.

The fire engines of the Insurance Company Brigade and two volunteer fire companies did their best, but they were hampered by a total lack of water. Captain Heselton of the steamer, *You Yangs*, which has just arrived from Melbourne, says you can see the blaze 20 miles out to sea.

The *Herald* in its leading article says:

No spectacle ever beheld by the city exhibited such magnificent desolation. No spectacle ever beheld by the city exhibited such fearful grandeur — such magnificent desolation — the Gothic size — the clearness of the space around it — enabled the thousands of spectators to see the breadth and splendour of the conflagration, shaped and designed by the tracery of the walls. These dreadful forces of nature show the impotence of man and the vanity of all his works...

Without yielding to any in our predilections for the Protestant religion, we recognise in this unfortunate case for universal sympathy and friendly aid. We should expect of our Roman Catholic fellow-citizens a similar sentiment and equal generosity.

We have no doubt that a new and more magnificent edifice will rise phoenix-like from the ashes of that which has fallen. In fact, the great pioneer of renovation is the inexorable flame.

Dentist's Boxkite Disturbs the Cows

30 JUNE 1912

W.E. Hart beat 'Wizard' Stone, the American, in Australia's first air race yesterday.

Mr Hart is a Parramatta dentist. He bought himself a Bristol Boxkite last year and taught himself to fly. He qualified just last November for the Royal Aero Club's Aviator's Certificate, the first Australian to do so.

I am sure you are familiar with the Bristol Boxkite. It is not vastly different from the aeroplane built by the Wright Brothers. It does actually look like a huge boxkite, two wings, and the pilot sits way up front as open to the breezes as an eagle; the engine is behind him with a propeller that pushes, and there are four large wheels like bicycle wheels.

Mr Hart has had his adventures. He crashed in a Chinese market garden and had to pay compensation to the far from delighted owners. Also he was sued by a Waterloo dairy farmer. The complaint was that he propelled his machine over the farmer's land, frightened, disturbed and stampeded his cows, with the result two cows were killed and others injured. He had to pay the heavy fine of £20 damages.

Hart challenged the visiting aviator Wizard Stone to a race from Sydney to Parramatta for a prize of 250 pounds. The idea was that one aeroplane would take off 10 minutes before the other and the aviator who achieved the fastest time won the race.

The *Sydney Morning Herald* described the weather as 'very pocketty, as the aviators say' cold, with an occasional spurt of rain. Not good for flying, but the two men considered they had a debt to the public, and were determined to pay it off, regardless of the risks.

The Australian Aerial League was in charge of proceedings, with Captain Stowe as time-keeper. Hart won the toss and took off, flying low at an altitude of 200 or 300 feet. His plane rocked a good deal in the winds. When he left Botany, the wind was blowing at 30 miles an hour. He used the breeze to carry him towards Parramatta, but several times he had to take evasive action against some nasty rain clouds.

He struck a particularly nasty gust over Rookwood, but cleverly he manoeuvred his plane so that the winds did not blow him past his destination. He landed at Parramatta Park, 20 miles covered in 23 minutes. At one time, he believes, he actually reached 70 miles an hour.

And what of the American? He took off after Hart. He climbed to 3000 feet and he could see Hart way off in the distance, but he got into cloud and lost sight of him entirely. His guides told him to keep the river on his right, but when he came out of the cloud he picked up the wrong river.

So the Wizard got himself lost. Immediately he looked for a good landing place and came down safely and without injury at Lakemba.

The *Sydney Morning Herald* in its leading article is delighted with the event. It says even the marvel of wireless has not the fascination of this new aerial science. There has been a tragic loss of life amongst fliers in the air, but human ingenuity and human courage will overcome the forces of the air as it has done over so much of 'Nature's guarded inviolate mystery'.

The *Herald* continues:

It is only a few years since the spectacle of a man directing the course of a heavier-than-air machine was a startling pheno-menon, and Bleriot's world-stirring flight across the Channel is but a recent exploit. Nowadays aviators are numbered by the hundred, races over vast distances are re-gular sporting fixtures and the use of the aeroplane as an ordinary vehicle of transit no longer calls for surprise.

JULY

Bishop Moorhouse

Les Darcy Dies Unfairly Condemned

1 JULY 1917

Les Darcy

The immortal Les Darcy, Australia's greatest fighter went into his grave today, aged twenty-two.

Ah, what a pugilist he was. During 1915 and 1916, he beat all the fighters that mattered, and although the title was not recognised, we believed utterly, that he was the middleweight champion of the world.

According to one report, 700 000 people lined the three-mile route from the Darcy home in Maitland to the cemetery. Even if you make that 100 000, it's still one of the most remarkable funerals Australia has seen.

Officially, of course, he was a shirker. He should have been fighting with a rifle, not his fists. The truth is he tried several times to enlist, but when under 21 his mother refused to give her consent. So secretly and illegally he caught a boat bound for New York.

There was an awful furore, and he was bitterly condemned by the newspaper. Stadiums Ltd stripped him of all his titles. Well, on 24 May in Memphis, Tennessee, he came down with a streptococcus throat infection and died of blood poisoning. His broken teeth had been rivetted by primitive methods, and he often complained of sore teeth and gums. That was the official version, ordinary Australians believe he died of a broken heart.

In Memphis undertakers embalmed his body, put him in a magnificent coffin made of pure aluminium, upholstered with white satin. An inner glass case contained the body dressed in a brown Carmelite habit.

So out it came in the American steamer *Sonoma*. Last Wednesday, a horse drawn lorry took it ot the Mortuary Chapel of Wood, Coffill and Company in George Street, Sydney. The public grief has been unbelievable. Estimates on how many people went through the chapel to view the body vary from one to two thousand. They moved through, men, women and children at the rate of 60 a minute, then stepped up to 200 a minute before closing time at 6 p.m.

Four police inspectors and 50 policemen controlled the crowd, but in the push, even then, they broke the plate glass windows of Wood, Coffill and Company. Trams could not move in George Street, and the crowd did not disperse until 10 p.m.

The funeral took place in Maitland today. From a very early hour every kind of vehicle was on the road from Sydney, and there were special trains from Sydney, Newscastle and the coalfields. Maitland and Singleton bands played the funeral march in the cortege.

Father Cody of Maitland said at the service: The doctor said he died of blood-poisoning, the result of a complication of diseases. Those who loved him and knew him best, and I am one of them, say that he died of a broken heart...The pack that howled at him for those few months past had doubtless new and many more insidious snares laid for him, and the Almighty in his tender mercy called him to his reward, before their malice could be further exercised.

One wonders had he been a poet, a great inventor, or a mere prime minister, whether he would have received such a fine send off.

Anti-Chinese Feeling Sparks Racial Riot

4 JULY 1861

We have just witnessed the most repugnant racial riot ever seen in the colony of New South Wales.

Anti-Chinese sentiment has been building on the goldfields for some months. The whites have looked upon the Chinese as interlopers, rivals, invading hordes who take the gold from under their noses. They describe them as 'Mongolian locusts', 'filthy, immoral, heathen Celestials'.

At Lambing Flat near Yass, the diggers formed a Miners' Protective League. They have a sweet name for assault on the 'heathen'. They call it a 'Roll Up'.

Last Saturday night and Sunday morning, they had the greatest Roll Up of them all. Between 2000 and 3000 diggers assembled. They had English, Irish and American flags, they had bands. They played 'Rule Britannia' and the 'Marseillaise'. There were banners, too, with 'NO CHINESE! ROLL UP! ROLL UP!'

The scene that followed was pitiful. They went to camp after camp. They rounded up the Chinese as if they were cattle, striking them with bludgeons, whips and spades. Some of the Chinese went down on their knees and pleaded for mercy, but it gave the diggers satisfaction only to hear them yell. One poor Chinese with blood running down his face was put up against a tree.

They cut off the Chinamen's pigtails and one man returned with eight pigtails attached to a flag, glorying in his work. A *Sydney Morning Herald* correspondent says he saw 'one tail with a part of a scalp, the size of a man's hand attached, that had been literally cut from some unfortunate creature; another had his back broken.'

The diggers gathered everything the Chinese possessed, rice, stores, butchers' shops full of meat, scales, clothing and nigh on 300 tents. They made them leave behind all their swags and set up six or seven immense fires. The scene, says the *Herald* man, defies description.

Now the Chinese have gone to Roberts Station. Many are seriously injured, two are in a very dangerous state and all are destitute. It is raining and extremely cold.

The dreadful part in all this is the lack of action by the authorities. As today's news report says: What have the authorities done? Nothing. 'From a force of upwards of 300 men, our executive wisdom in one week reduced it to some 20 policemen...there was no force at all to cope with such an excited mass of men.'

The *Sydney Morning Herald* in a leading article says:

The Chinese in this colony have been insulted, hunted, defamed. Calumnies of the most atrocious kind have circulated with authority. The common laws of Christianity have been trampled underfoot... The Chinese population have inflicted no injury. They have appeared for a few hours in our streets, in peaceful contact to the same number and rank of Europeans. They are gone to occupy land which they alone can use and to employ by their earnings, hundreds of shopkeepers and mechanics and European labourers.

The *Herald* wishes that no Chinaman had ever entered the colony, but it abhors the tyranny and oppression that has taken place.

It is a very dangerous situation. Unquestionably more Roll Ups are planned on the goldfields.

Anti-Chinese riots at Lambing Flat

'Diamond Jim' Dies

5 JULY 1891

'Diamond Jim' Beaney

James George Beaney, better known as 'Diamond Jim', eminent surgeon of Collins Street, is dead, aged sixty-three.

James was a short pudgy man with his hair brushed up either side to look like a pair of horns.

There is tremendous competition amongst doctors to have the best vehicle, but it was always hard to beat Diamond Jim. He had a glorious open barouche, pulled by two horses and filled with the most expensive rugs.

He dressed himself in velvet and the purest of linen, but his special delight was to cover himself with jewels. He would wear anything up to £10 000 worth at the one time, rings with diamonds like pigeon eggs, diamond-studded watch with diamond-studded chain, diamond cravat pin, and three diamond studs would hold together his amply filled vest.

Beaney was honorary surgeon at the Melbourne Hospital, and he would send invitations to his friends to come and watch him perform. He wore all his rings as he operated and his hands would flash and sparkle.

He earned an incredible £12 000 a year. He always liked a bottle of claret for breakfast and a small bottle of champagne for lunch, then a decent bottle for dinner. He believed deeply in prescribing alcohol for most ills. During the month of August 1883, Dr Beaney worked on 63 patients at the Melbourne Hospital and during that time he prescribed 122 ounces of brandy, 101 bottles of ale or porter, 14 bottles of lemonade and soda water, and two bottles of champagne.

Beaney suffered a series of embarrassing court cases, any one of which would have been sufficient to destroy more sensitive mortals. There was Mary Lewis, 21, a barmaid at the Terminus Hotel, St Kilda. She called to see Beaney. He was alone with her for an hour and she died the next day. Beaney on the death certificate said the cause was 'a malignant disease of the uterus'.

All around Collingwood they said it was a plain old-fashioned abortion, and Beaney was tried for murder. At the first trial, the jury did not agree; and at the second trial he was found not guilty. But Inspector John Sadlier, who was at the Ned Kelly capture, always claimed Beaney missed hanging by one vote.

Beaney enhanced his reputation by giving lectures and producing 18 books on everything from lithotomy to syphilis. Actually Bailliere, the Collins St medical bookseller, produced most of them under his name, and how many he wrote himself is problematical.

It is hard to tell how good a surgeon Beaney was, although *Lancet* gives him high praise and says he has had over 400 hernia cases without a single death, and few surgeons can boast that.

J.L. Forde who writes under the title 'Old Chum' says imaginative persons made excuses about accepting invitations to meals at his house, because he was probably the champion carver of the world.

A few touches of the knife would make the most stubborn turkey fall into suitable joints and slices; and his artistry is so reminiscent of the dissecting room that those possessed of weak stomachs stare at the table cloth until he is finished.

His estate is said to be worth £60 000 and then there are all the jewels. He spent over £20 000 on those. But then with the disastrous state of the economy, times are very bad. Who know what they will bring.

Politics Takes its Toll

7 JULY 1945

The funeral of John Curtin, 60, Prime Minister, takes place in Perth tomorrow.

He died in Canberra at 4 a.m. last Thursday. Mrs Curtin had a cup of tea with her husband shortly before midnight when he said 'Go on, Mrs Curtin, it's best that you go off to bed now'. She did not sleep, and Mr Curtin died without awakening.

The newspapers are filled with tributes to this remarkable man. The son of an Irish police sergeant, he left school at 13 and was, by turn, printer's devil, page boy, trade union secretary, journalist, politician and leader of a great political party.

He took over as Prime Minister in 1941, at the time of our greatest crisis, and had the mental toughness to make decisions which altered the course of history. He campaigned against conscription in World War 1 but he introduced it with no referendum in World War 2 and sent conscripts to battle in New Guinea.

He defied Churchill and demanded the return of Australian forces in the Middle East and, perhaps, changed for ever our relationship with Great Britain when he made his famous New Year message of 1942. 'Without any inhibitions of any kind, I make it quite clear that Australia looks to America, free of any pangs as to our traditional links of kinship with the United Kingdom'.

Undoubtedly the strain of office killed John Curtin. Two former prime ministers, both older than Mr Curtin, James Scullin and W.M. Hughes, appealed for greater Australian respect for the working worries of Australian leaders.

Mr Hughes said:

For nearly four years John Curtin led this country through its darkest days. By his unwavering courage, wise leadership and winged words he roused the people of Australia to action. The Prime Minister died as he would have wished, at the post of duty. Of no man could it be said more truly that he gave his life to his country.

Mr Scullin said:

It is not hard work, physical or mental that kills men, it is anxiety and worry. The hardest struggle in leadership is the making of vital decisions in crises. Misunderstand-

John Curtin

ings and misrepresentation also take their toll.

General MacArthur, Commander-in-Chief, South-West Pacific, cabled Mrs Curtin:

Mrs MacArthur and myself send you our deepest sympathy in the death of your noble husband. He was of the great of the earth.

The newspapers tell of his simplicity and modesty. Recently he startled a bank teller when he appeared at the counter and applied for a War Bond. After he spelt out his name the amazed teller said 'The Prime Minister!'

'Yes' replied Curtin. 'I'm just an ordinary bloke'

The *Sun News Pictorial* writes:

His love of plain living, of ordinary amusements, was reflected in his love of home cooking, his conservative — almost drab — mode of dress and his enjoyment of common entertainments like Western novels, football and cricket. Yet Curtin was a cultured, widely-read man with a fine literary sense and a polished literary style.

A flight of Boomerang and Kittyhawk fighters escorted the aeroplane which carried his body to Perth.

Mr Forde is acting Prime Minister. The choice for a new leader is between Forde and Chifley, but Mr Chifley is regarded as having the greatest support.

AIF Scores a Superb Victory

8 JULY 1918

There have been appalling bloody battles all along the Western Front. The casualty lists, making familiar names like Bullcourt, Messines, Ypres, Passchendaele and Villers-Bretonneux, have been nothing but a misery.

But at last there is some good news. The Australians have been recognised for being the great fighters they are. They have been formed into a single corps under the brilliant Lieutenant-General Sir John Monash. A civilian, volunteer, but battle-hardened Army it is, and they have scored a superb victory.

The *Age* reports:

The Australians aided by other troops with tanks, swept forward at dawn attacking along a front of four miles from the Somme to Villers-Bretonneux. They captured Hamel, with Vaire and Hamel woods. The Germans were completely taken by surprise. About 1600 prisoners were taken.

It was a perfect battle, hardly any casualties to the Australians and it all worked like clockwork. First the RAF night bombers went in harassing the enemy. Next at 3.10 a.m., the artillery laid down a heavy barrage and immediately after the falling shells the infantry moved through the fog.

The bombardment was so clever the Germans did not know where the main attack was coming from. The tanks were splendid, and only three, temporarily were put out of action. They carried forward ammunition and supplies, a brilliant new idea and for the first time aeroplanes parachuted ammunition to the Vickers gunners.

Mr Philip Gibbs of the *Daily Chronicle* writes:

The Germans were utterly surprised and the whole battle was completed in an hour. Under a widespread flight of shells the tanks started forward. Smoke screens sent before the tanks made dense clouds which lay on the ground and hid the tanks from the German anti-tank guns. So the tanks nosed their way forward and three or four men were sitting on top of each tank fully exposed, with their legs dangling over the sides, like boys having a joy ride. Thus they rode into hell fire.

The infantry followed in waves. As they came close to the barrage, the Australians chose to risk wounds from their own bullets rather than give the German machine gunners time to work. Dawn was just breaking through the trees when the Australians made the final charge, shouting for the enemy to surrender. In most cases the Germans gave no trouble. They meekly held up their hands, and came out out the trenches without their weapons, showing no sign of fight. The Australians were through them and beyond them before they were able to organise a defense. So the Germans submitted to their inevitable fate. They were glad to follow their escorts to our lines before their own artillery could annihilate them.

Monash has proved today that the Germans are not invulnerable and that attack rather than the old idea of defense can bring enormous results.

Sir Douglas Haig, on Thursday, warmly congratulated Sir John Monash and all ranks of his command.

Further reading: *John Monash, A Biography*, Geoffrey Serle.

Lieutenant-General Sir John Monash

Velocipedes — the Latest Craze

11 JULY 1869

Mr Finlay and his velocipede

Velocipedes, you must understand, have become the rage of Europe, and the absolute sensation of the 1867 Paris exhibition.

Yesterday Melbourne became the first city in all the Australian colonies to stage a velocipede race. It took place at the Melbourne Cricket Ground.

The *Argus* says:

All the world of Melbourne flocked to see the novelty, and the meeting was regarded as a sort of velocipede fete at which these machines were to have their first introduction to the public. It remains to be seen whether the latest mania of the change-loving Parisians will be successfully acclimatised here. The new locomotive luxury, when applied to the deep water storm-channels and stone crossings of the streets of Melbourne, will be scarcely as enjoyable as on the smooth macadam and asphalt of the French metropolis, and it is not probable that the velocipede rage here will ever pass beyond club circles.

However the *Argus* pointed out that the crowd must have numbered 12 000 and there had been no such brilliant scene at the MCG since the visit of the All-England XI.

It was apparent from the great numbers attracted to the ground that great interest has been aroused in the subject, and judging from the reports which have been circulated for the benefit of a credulous public as to the extraordinary capabilities of bicycles the Melbourne crowd could hardly wait for this opportunity to see them in action.

Mr J. Finlay of Fitzroy was the only gentleman who appeared to have properly acquired the knack of propelling one of these machines, and he carried all before him.

Mr Finlay built his own velocipede and he called it the Barb, in honour of the 1866 Melbourne Cup winner. What's more, he dressed in black and gold, the colours Davis, the jockey wore, when he rode Barb to victory.

Finlay rode his machine in the way a cavalryman bestrides a horse and seemed able to economise his forces on the pedals much better than the other riders. In the final heat he covered his two miles in 11 minutes 29½ seconds attaining a speed of nearly 11 miles an hour. Seeing that we have had some very heavy rain this week-end, this was a remarkable speed on such a soft track.

The velocipedes far outshone the bicycles, and Finlay fairly walked away from his competitors. J. Ivey of Ballarat was doing well for a time, but he got in front of a tricycle, they had a collision, and he broke off one of his treddles.

But what is the future for bicycles? Very little, say many of the journals. The *Australasian* says:

Velocipedes have had their trial and the verdict is that as a means of creating sport they are a failure. The universal opinion is that they won't do . . . Unicycles, when their management is understood, will soon take the shine out of bicycles, as I am told that in competent hands they can be worked up to the rate of 40 m.p.h. I suppose that the next thing we shall hear of some mountebank running across the falls of Niagara on a single rope.

Bradman Out at Last

12 JULY 1930

Donald Bradman, the 21-year-old wonder, is out at last, for 334 runs.

The entire cricketing world is spellbound at his skill. Mr P.F. Warner, the former English captain, says today:

Bowling to Bradman is like throwing stones at Gibraltar. There has never been another batsman who, match after match, claimed such a huge proportion of runs. You may talk of Alexander the Great, Hercules, Trumper or Macartney, but this young Australian is equal to anyone.

That great bowler Arthur Mailey is also agog. He says 'If I were the Prime Minister, Mr Scullin, I would get Bradman to open the Sydney Harbour Bridge'

Bradman made 254 in the last Test at Lord's, now in the Leeds Test he has made 334, and here, in only early July, he has made over 2000 runs for the Tour. The headline in the *Daily Sketch* says 'BOY BATTING ROBOT SURPASSES ALL MARATHON SCORERS'. and the *Manchester Guardian* says pathethically: 'Can we ever get him out?'

All through the match, the English captain, Chapman, received advice from a stentorian voiced Yorkshireman, who shouted 'What about Leyland?' When Leyland came on, Bradman hit 13 runs off the first over. So the Yorkshireman changed his cry to 'What about Larwood?' When Larwood came on Bradman was so merciless the fast bowler had to be removed after four overs. The next man to get the treatment was Tate.

All this has caused an entirely new pattern of behaviour in Australia — 'listening in'. It has been impossible to go to bed while Bradman has been at the wicket. The sale of wireless sets has been slow until now, but this past two weeks sales have increased over a hundred. Some people who cannot afford wirelesses even listen in the cold through the night outside wireless shops.

The Melbourne *Herald* reports barbers are doing a tremendous trade. After listening in all night, men have been unable to find time to shave before going to work. So they are going to barbers in the city.

In Bowral there have been cheers in the streets where people have stood outside shops

Don Bradman

listening to the scores, and local hotels have reported marvellous business. Don Bradman's mother said that if the records continued much longer she did not know how she could stand it. She was so worked up with excitement when the big matches were on, she did not know what she was doing. His amazing scores followed each other with such regularity that it was hard to realise that it was her boy who was being acclaimed as the greatest cricketer in the world.

Mr Arthur Whitelaw, a wealthy Australian merchant, sent a telegram to Leeds today saying: 'Kindly convey my congratulations to Bradman. Tell him I wish him to accept 1000 pound as a token of my admiration of his performance'.

Whitelaw has lived in London for 16 years and made his fortune from a patent soap-making process.

Everyone wants to get into the act. Gifts will be showered on Bradman. Melbourne's *Sporting Globe* says:

Don Bradman is the cricketer of the hour. The *Sporting Globe* has decided to open a shilling fund as a testimonial. Send along your shillings to the *Sporting Globe*. Subscriptions will be acknowledged in these columns.

Campaign against Barmaids

13 JULY 1896

You must appreciate that for many years now there has been a campaign for the abolition of barmaids, one of the great evils that beset our society.

The moralists object to barmaids on two grounds: they lure young men to drink, and things take place in a hotel bar that make it no fit place for a woman.

In 1884, Dr Moorhouse, the Anglican Bishop of Melbourne, led a deputation to the Chief Secretary, and told him that on visits to country districts, frequently he had to sleep in public houses where the partitions were so thin he could hear the conversations in the bar. These conversations, said he, were often of such a character that they were not fit for a decent man to listen to, let alone young girls.

Archdeacon Boyce of Sydney, pointed out recently:

A barmaid spends her time in serving out intoxicants which weakens people's moral restraints...Can this possibly be a fit business for any pure-minded girl? Again a pretty girl is frequently engaged to attract soft young men, and keep them hanging about the bar, and when nature's bloom has left her cheek paint is often used.

The Archdeacon quoted this verse:
Wanted, a beautiful barmaid,
    To shine in a drinking den
To entrap the youth of the nation,
    And ruin the City men;
To brighten destruction's pathway,
    False gleams with dark fate to blend;
To stand near Despair's dark gateway,
    To hide Sin's sad bitter end.

The best anti-barmaid man of all is King O'Malley, whom the *Bulletin* calls 'a glorified Yankee bagman'. Actually he is a Canadian who emigrated to South Australia. He has a great shock of unruly hair and he likes to be known as the bald-headed eagle of the Rocky Mountains.

In 1896 he stood for election for Encounter Bay in South Australia, and the chief planks of his platform were: children out of wedlock should be legitimised; railway carriages should have lavatories; and barmaids should be banned. He had done well on all three.

No man on earth has a richer turn of phrase. Here is a little of his barmaid speech today to South Australian Parliament:

All Government bills for the regulating and limiting of the drunk traffic are so much waste paper as long as the barmaid system continues. They might as well try to tame and manage a huge rattlesnake, an Indian cobra, or an Australian rattlesnake, without extracting the fangs and the poison pouches, as attempt to regulate and limit the drunk traffic while the barmaid system remains in force, bespattering with mud the golden mantle of the loving moon-eyed goddess of democracy — South Australia.

Mr O'Malley quoted an advertisement from a Melbourne publication:

Wanted two barmaids for Adelaide only those coming up to the following physical requirements need apply — Fairly tallish with well-defined hips and extra-developed bust; small reachy waist, long fetching neck, dimpled chin, attractive face with a permanent bewitching smile, and all round artists at bewitching men.

He would never say where he found the ad.

Note: South Australia abolished barmaids, except those in present employment in 1908 and did not repeal the Bill until 1967.

Cawarra Breaks Up in Heavy Seas

14 JULY 1866

The paddlesteamer *Cawarra* has sunk off New-castle in a fearful storm. Sixty-three people have perished and there is only one survivor.

The *Sydney Morning Herald* says today:
The storm through which she passed was of terrific force. No one could listen to its rage even on shore, without thinking of those whose lot it is to face the dangers of the deep. How sad to think that so many who left our harbour a few hours before were doomed, in sight of shore, to sink unaided into the boiling waters.

Some details have arrived by telegram from Newcastle.
On Thursday afternoon a fearful sea was running, blowing almost a hurricane from the north-east. At 2 p.m. *Cawarra* could be seen moving slowly towards North Head. At about 3 o'clock she struck on the Oyster Bank and became unmanageable.

The passengers and the crew were seen huddled together on the rigging. Extra-ordinary as it may appear, the lifeboat had not gone out up to this time. A few minutes after the funnel went over the side, and a minute after that the mainmast went over, carrying with it every living soul in that part of the ship to eternity. At 3.25 the foremast went, on which some three or four men were seen climbing. In a few minutes not a vestige of the ill-fated *Cawarra* was to be seen.

A lifeboat went out to the rescue, but the sea was so heavy, eight out of 14 oars were broken, and she was compelled to return.

A telegram, which arrived at 5.30 p.m. reports
One man has been saved from the wreck, a seaman named F.T.Hedges and he has been taken to Winche's Hotel where he is suffering from immersion.

4.15 p.m. Friday. Following informa-tion obtained from Frederick Valliant Hedges. He believes the Captain intended making for the port at the time. *Cawarra* was hit several times with tremendous force by the waves. She went down at the head, the fires went out, and she was unmanageable.

Captain Chatfield ordered the boats lowered which were immediately occupied by some Chinamen. He ordered the China-men out to make room for the females on board. The boat on being lowered imme-diately capsized. Hedges got into the main rigging but he had not been there long when the funnel went over the side carrying him and others with it.

He managed to get hold of a plank and drifted towards a buoy where he was rescued. He believes all the others perished in the surf. Up to the time Hedges was washed off the steamer, the Captain ap-peared perfectly self-possessed and cool; in fact, all stood at their posts to the last.

The *Cawarra* had a large and valuable cargo and was one of the finest steamers on our coast. The devastation in the storm is awful. A large ketch, the *Caroline*, has gone down and every soul on board has perished. The schooner *Sea Gull*, has foundered at the Heads, all hands perished. The barque has been swamped, the mate and a seaman drowned. The schooner, *Lismore*, is washed ashore at North Beach. It is believed the crew is being rescued.

There must be an inquiry into these dis-asters, says the *Sydney Morning Herald*, to 'satisfy us that nothing has been done recklessly to imperil life, and that the misfortune, which has fallen upon so many families is solely from the hand of God'.

Flemington Crowd Turns Savage

15 JULY 1906

*Flemington Racecourse
marred by murder*

Yesterday we had the Grand National Steeple-chase at Flemington. It was a lovely day, as perfect as the good Lord could make it.

Table Talk pointed out that all the right people were there. Lady Northcote wore a handsome sapphire blue velvet coat, toque and large muff, and Lady Talbot was in a pale mauve frieze, with velvet toque of a slightly darker shade with dark green wings.

However on the Flat things were far from perfect. Donald John McLeod, only twenty-three, 15 stone and muscular, better known as 'Big Mick', was taking small bets. On the first race Big Mick thought Lady Dorris had no hope, so he accepted more than 20 bets. Dorris won at a canter.

Mick was unable to pay. He advised his clients he would pay in front of Wren's Collingwood Tote on Monday morning. Then he returned their money. Mick was a 'scaler'. If you return the money you're a scaler. On the other hand, if you skip with all the money, you're a 'welcher', a sin on the Flat worse than rape or murder.

On the second race, the same thing happened. Mick scaled, and he was becoming very unpopular indeed. Then came the Grand National and Mick took seven bets on the favourite, Decoration. Decoration broke the course record and won by quarter of a furlong. Mick bravely called out 'I'll pay the winner', but he did not pay.

Immediately the mob gathered round Mick. One man shouted 'He ought to be arrested'. Another shouted 'Tear the bag off him'. McLeod was jostled and struck, very red in the face he dropped everything and ran. There are various reports about the size of the crowd. Some say 400 to 500, but the police make it 2000. Anyway the mob steamed after him like a wedge, with the fastest runners in front. Down he went in a cloud of fists and kicking feet.

According to an *Age* reporter, he managed to struggle to his feet, slumped on a fence by the outer carriage paddock, and screamed for mercy. 'I haven't the money. Give me a chance boys'.

There were shouts of 'kill him. I'll get my value out of him'. One young man climbed on the fence and dealt him a mighty blow on the neck. Then the mob proceeded to kick him to death. Edward Martin, who had been assisting McLeod, found him lying on the ground. 'I raised his head' he said, 'asked "How are you Don?" But there was only a gurgle from his throat'.

The *Age* in a leading article says:
No more horrible tragedy has ever occurred in Victorian history than that which Donald McLeod was a victim at Flemington. His assailants immediately surrounded him and giving rein to their primeval savage instincts, they wreaked their vengeance on the poor wretch who had cheated them by kicking him to death...every man who took part is legally and morally a murderer.

Dr Clarke, Archbishop of Melbourne, says: I bow my head in shame for the city in which it is possible for such a tragedy to take place...If there is any manliness left in Victoria it must be roused into indignation over this unspeakable horror.

The *Age* racing writers say welching has become common and flagrant at Flemington, and something like this was bound to happen. Today, however, police have charged two men with murder.

144

Bluebird Captures Land Speed Record

18 JULY 1964

Donald Campbell, forty-three, broke the world land speed record in his Bluebird yesterday. His triumph was at Lake Eyre. In his marvellous streamlined machine, Campbell had two runs in either direction at exactly 403.1 mph.

Campbell, of course, has always been haunted by the memory of his record breaking father, Sir Malcolm Campbell. Now he has achieved his ambition. Donald Campbell becomes the third man to have held both the world's land and water speed records. The other two were his late father, Sir Malcolm, and the late Sir Henry Seagrave.

Conditions for Campbell yesterday were far from easy. Bluebird tore deep ruts in the salt-pan. His second run nearly ended in tragedy when the razor-sharp salt crystals ripped all the rubber tread off his right rear tyre before he reached full speed.

Campbell said that he gave 'thanks to the Almighty that he was still alive. My first reaction is a prayer of thanksgiving' he said. 'This is the end of a long, hard road. We have achieved what we set out to achieve. My second reaction is one of tremendous admiration for the machine, that it was controllable and for the tyres that stood up to the terrifying treatment'.

Tonia, Campbell's wife, threw her arms around her husband, and shouted 'Darling, we've made it'. Joyfully she kissed him. Campbell held in his hand 'Mr Woppitt', his good luck teddy-bear, which travelled with him in the cockpit.

It has been a long haul for Campbell. He first inspected Lake Eyre in 1960, and since then he has been closely associated with Elliott Price and his family at Muloorina Station. This year Campbell and his team spent four months at Muloorina. A small army of mechanics, officials, technicians, police, army men, tyre experts, and reporters, all have been at Muloorina, waiting patiently for the right day.

Yesterday at dawn the weather was perfect and the wind died to only three miles an hour, blowing from the West.

Campbell was disappointed that he did not do better than 403 mph. He believes he could

Donald Campbell

have improved his speed by 40 mph, but the lake was the trouble. The salt, dampened by last year's heavy rain, has never fully recovered, and every run has torn deep ruts. Campbell says the track is finished and cannot be used again.

He is disappointed because he did not beat the 407 mph set by Craig Breedlove in Utah last year. Breedlove's speed was not recognised as a record because the power for his three-wheel vehicle was not transmitted through the wheels. It was jet propelled. But Campbell wanted the unofficial as well as the official record.

Now Campbell wants to set a new water speed record in Australia. Already he holds the world water speed record of 260.35 mph. But he wants to break the triple century out here on water.

Asked yesterday if he still planned the water venture, Campbelll replied 'You betcha'.

Note: Donald Campbell was killed attempting the World Water Speed record on Coniston Watu, England, on 4 January 1967.

The Perfect Co-operative Society

19 JULY 1893

The *Royal Tar* has sailed out of Sydney Harbour and is off on its 130-day voyage to Paraguay to create the 'New Australia'.

The leader is 32-year-old journalist, William Lane, who has a dream that if a group of pure-minded artisans can find the right remote area, free of alien influences, then they can create the perfect co-operative society, the ultimate utopia.

Now it has happened. Aboard the *Royal Tar* is the first contingent, 239 men, women and children, off on the great social experiment. The *Sydney Morning Herald* says nobody but Lane could have achieved this in such a short space of time. Lane is rugged in appearance with irregular features, he has a club foot, thin gold-rimmed spectacles and honest blue eyes which seem to look right through you, says the *Herald*.

He was born in an English gardener's hut, and saw very early the sordid poverty which prevailed in the English peasantry. At 16 he worked his way to Canada, and became a printer then a journalist. He sailed to Australia in 1885, became associated with the Labor movement and was the first editor of the *Worker*. But he decided true socialism was impossible in this selfish Australian society.

As the *Herald* says, he has this gift, his spell-binding oratory with a Yankee twang. Never has he had any trouble finding an audience, particularly amongst those seeking escape from the drudgery of bushlife. He formed the New Australia movement, and now he has over 1000 members.

The 1000 members, says the *Herald*, include every trade and calling, but first and foremost, there are small selectors, cockatoo farmers, who have given up their single-minded struggle with nature to try cultivation on a co-operative basis. There is no lack of money; £60 000 has been raised. The rules of the constitution are equal share of all property and capital, equal voting power, equality of sex, a director to be elected by two-thirds majority, the community to be racially white, and total abstinence from alcohol for all members.

The ban on drink is interesting. The captain of *Royal Tar* said during the preparations for the voyage, with everyone pledged to temperance, he did not have the slightest trouble from the crew.

Lane is heavily under the influence of Edward Bellamy and his utopian romance. *Looking Backward*, but the pessimists claim, there have been attempts before of a similar kind and they have ended in failure. Only some fanatical religious order would have the power to hold such a group together.

However Lane says this group will have unique power. He is relying on the fact that his men are trade unionists who have been trained to habits of discipline and obedience. In his splendid eloquent language he said:

The world will be changed if we succeed. And we shall succeed. We cannot help succeeding. For what do we expect? Not mansions, but cottages; not idle luxury, but work-worn plenty, for each a home, and marriage — honest, lifelong marriage — with sturdy children growing all round to care for us when we are old. We expect that the earth will yield, and that the flocks will increase...

Note: Lane and his followers settled on 187 000 hectares, 176 kilometers south-east of Asuncion, provided free by the Government of Paraguay. The colony only just became self-sufficient, suffered under Lane's despotic puritanical rule and finally broke up through internal strife.

Dr Bell Checks Out our Telephones

20 JULY 1910

Alexander Graham Bell

Dr Alexander Graham Bell, the inventor of the telephone, has been visiting Brisbane and Sydney.

He is amazed at our cheap rates. He said 'Perhaps that is the result of the Government service. The idea is to give the people cheap service, but perhaps it interferes with efficiency and the cheapness might not be altogether a good thing'.

Dr Bell said a call on a public telephone in the US cost 10 cents or about fivepence. In Australia you could get a call for a penny. He tried out our telephones in Brisbane and found that the instruments worked very well. But the service was slow. Sometimes you would wait an eternity before the operator put you through. In America the telephone service was run by private companies, and he was very keen to see who could do it best, Government or private enterprise.

Dr Bell added :

I notice that the telephone has not entered into the life of the people here as it has in America. There are telephones fixed in every bedroom of an hotel. You don't ring for a boy when you want anything. You have a telephone in your bedroom with a little central office down in the hotel, and you just ask for what you want. If you want to talk to someone in town, you ask to be put on to the exchange, and you can talk to anywhere you want from your bedroom. They charge outside calls to you in the bill.

Dr Graham Bell's comments on the cheapness of our telephones has caused a furore. The Postmaster General's Department has just devised a new method for charging for calls, called the Thomas system. Before, we had Chapman rates: rent £5 a year and 2600 free telephone calls. Now, unbelievably, under the so-called Thomas system, we will have to pay four pounds a year and we get only 2000 calls, at a rate of two a penny.

One letter writer to the *Argus*, 'W.A.M. St Kilda', is livid. He wants to know whether the Postmaster General considers that he is an 'insouciant millionaire'. He says that a telephone is not quite a luxury, nor is it quite a necessity, but it is a convenience, and he adds: 'To pay ground rent and the cost of five calls a day at the rate proposed is far more than the convenience justifies, and I, for one, would rather smoke really good cigars (like Ministers and pugilists), and let the convenience go'.

There are protest meetings all over the country. In today's newspaper there are such headlines as :'Dissatisfaction in Sale', 'Indignation at Yass' and 'Anger at Ballarat'. A Ballarat subscriber, with careful mathematics, has worked our that before the Thomas system was introduced, he paid a halfpenny for a telephone call, now it will be more like two pence three farthings. 'This excessive charge', says he 'becomes so much a luxury, I shall have no alternative but to cease subscribing. This, I fear, will be the reaction of many other small subscribers'.

But the *Argus* warns of a fresh danger. There are few mechanical recorders. At most exchanges every call has to be recorded tediously by hand. Imagine, under the Thomas system, what will happen at peak hour.

We know only too well. Try and call your girlfriend at 6 p.m. and it might be tomorrow before the exchange puts you through. As Dr Bell says, maybe a better system is worth more money.

Angry Penguins Embarrassed

21 JULY 1944

All this month controversy has raged over the remarkable Ern Malley hoax.

It all began last October with a letter to the editor of *Angry Penguins*, an Adelaide literary journal. It was in a lovely, sweet round hand. Ethel Malley said she had been going through the things of her late departed brother, Ern, and she had found these poems. Would they let her know if they had any literary value?

The editors, Max Harris and John Reed were impressed indeed: 'here was a poet of tremendous power, working through a disciplined and restrained kind of statement in the deepest wells of human experience'.

Ernest Lalor Malley, *Angry Penguins* learned, was born in England. An orphan, he never had many breaks, and worked as a mechanic and an insurance salesman. Finally with failing health, this lonely man struggled to make a living repairing watches.

So *Angry Penguins* brought out a special Ern Malley issue with 16 poems titled *The Darkening Ecliptic*. In a series of issues, *Fact*, a supplement to Sydney's *Sunday Sun*, has given the tip off. It's all a hoax. There was no such person as Ern Malley. He is the creation of two Sydney poets, both in the Army, James McAuley and Harold Stewart.

Max Harris

In a letter to *Fact* they said that for years they had observed with distaste the gradual decay of meaning and craftmanship in poetry. What we wished to find out was: Can those who write, and those who praise so lavishly this kind of writing, tell the product from consciously and deliberately concocted nonsense?

They said they concocted Ern Malley's life work in an afternoon. For example the first lines of 'Culture As Exhibit' came straight from an American report on the drainage of breeding grounds of mosquitoes. It went:

> Swamps, marshes, barrow pits and
> Other areas of stagnant water serve
> As breeding grounds....Now
> Have I found you, my anopheles!
> There is a meaning for the circumspect
> Come we will dance sedate quadrilles
> A pallid polka or a yelping shimmy
> Over these sodden breeding grounds

The newspapers have had a fine old time passing comment. The *Herald* in Melbourne says 'There is a great lesson to be had in this exercise. If alleged experts can be so easily taken in then how is the layman to detect the good from the bad? The *Advertiser* in Adelaide thinks there should be a fitting academic award for the poetasters and quidnuncs who take the academic fictitious Ern Malley to their bosoms swearing he is a genius after their own hearts. The *Advertiser* suggests a wooden spoon on a leather medal. The *Bulletin* this week, in its illustrious Pink Page, says the editors of *Angry Penguins* are so completely the victims of the moment they have made complete fools of themselves.

But most of the gleeful comment has come from journals that normally would not print poetry in a fit. Others are not so sure. There have been comments by people like Geoffrey Dutton, Adrian Lawlor, and A.R. Chisholm, saying they too would have been taken in. After reading the poems they think McAuley and Stewart, the next time they feel like composing poetry, perhaps they should co-opt the help of their gifted phoney, Ern Malley.

Eureka Hero Elected Speaker

22 JULY 1880

Mr Peter Lalor

Mr Peter Lalor, the hero of the Eureka uprising, was elected today Speaker of Victoria's Legislative Assembly.

An incredible turn of history, when you think of it. At one time, the Governor, Sir Charles Hotham, offered a reward of £200 for the apprehension of Lalor, and charged that he did use 'treasonable and seditious language and incite men to take up Arms with a view to make war against Our Sovereign Lady the Queen'.

Well, he was acquitted of all that, but some people have not forgotten. Mr Thomas Bent, member for Brighton, opposed Peter Lalor's appointment, and his speech in the House today was astonishing.

Mr Bent said:

Mr Lalor has been known here for six and twenty years, but as a native of this colony I am sorry to think that to obtain the distinction of being Speaker of this House, it is absolutely necessary that a man should be a rebel against the British crown'

(Opposition cries of 'Shame' and 'Disgrace' were heard.)

Mr Bent continued

I am quite sure that the teetotal members of this House will be gratified and very pleased to go back to their constituents and say that they voted for a man who was drunk on the floor of the House while chairman of committees.

(Further cries of 'Shame. Shame'.)

I think it is a disgrace to this country to elect Mr Lalor as Speaker and I am one who will oppose the election...I am ashamed to think that for party purposes honourable members will vote for a man who is not fit for the post.

The Premier, Mr Service, was shocked. He said Mr Bent had allowed his feelings to get the better of his judgement and he added:

I do regret that he (Mr Bent) should have thought proper to have referred to a very old passage in the life of the Honourable Member for Grant — a passage which I venture to say reflects no disgrace upon the Honourable Member.

Actually it has been downright fascinating to follow the career of the rebel leader at the Eureka Stockade. Sometimes he has acted like the rebel of old, as other times he has been more like a an old-fashioned Toorak Tory. One time he even supported plural voting for those with property, and it is said that he has even employed 'scabs' to force wage cuts at his mines.

But then, he has fought to get rid of these awful Customs Duties between NSW and Victoria and, incredibly for a good Irish boy and devout Roman Catholic to boot, he denounced State aid for church schools.

Nor, naturally, did he want State money to go to a monument to Sir Charles Hotham. He said there was sufficient monument already in the graves of the 30 individuals slain at Ballarat.

Some say it was Lalor who was behind the famour 'Black Wednesday' of 1867. The Council would have no part of payment for members, and Graham Berry sacked 300 civil servants in retaliation. It was Lalor who attacked the arrogant power of the Legislative Council.

Maybe he will make a good Speaker. 'The first duty of a Speaker' said Lalor 'is to be a tyrant. Remove him if you like, but while he in the chair obey him. The Speaker is the embodiment of the corporate honour of the House. He is above party. He is the greatest representative of the people'.

Note: Lalor proved to be a good, impartial Speaker until illness overtook him two years before his death in 1889.

Melbourne Welcomes the Fleet

25 JULY 1925

The American Fleet, 43 ships, the greatest naval force ever to visit our waters, sailed through Port Phillip Heads on Friday.

All Melbourne was agog. From 5 a.m. people gathered all around the Bayside — Portsea, Sorrento, Rosebud, St Kilda, Williamstown — to witness this extraordinary scene. At Dromana, 500 cars were waiting at daybreak three hours before the ships were due to arrive.

But what a fleet it is. To make it even more dramatic, the big ships are equipped with 'piston driven catapults' that project seaplanes into the air. For two hours, six American seaplanes flew over Port Melbourne giving an exhibition of formation flying such as we have never seen before.

As for the ships, there was Admiral Robert E. Coontz aboard his flagship, *Seattle*. Then there were the battleships, *Pennsylvania*, *Oklahoma*, and *Nevada*. There were the cruisers, *Trenton*, *Marblehead*, *Richmond* and *Memphis*, plus 28 destroyers and other auxiliary and supply vessels.

Regrettably Melbourne turned on one of its most frightful days, and the ships looked awesome grey shapes as they moved up the Bay. The *Argus* said: 'Sullen in appearance, the sea itself seems to toss with a mournful restlessness...Is this the best we can show the great American fleet?'

Everything was very nicely organised, the State Party with the Premier, Mr Allan, his Cabinet, Lord Mayor, Chief Justice and all, was to greet the fleet aboard the steamer *Hygeia*. The Commonwealth Party, with the Prime Minister, Mr Stanley Bruce, was to welcome the Americans aboard the *Weeroona*. 'Owing to the disgraceful conduct of a few firemen and greasers' said the *Argus*, the *Weeroona* trip was cancelled.

This happened because the Seamen's Union objected to the Prime Minister. They said that if Mr Bruce made a humble apology for his recent 'malicious and blasphemous' attack on the Union, then it might consider taking him to sea aboard the paddle-steamer *Weeroona*.

At 12 noon, Captain Booth and Captain Ramsay assured the firemen that the Prime

Mr Bruce banned by Union

Minister was not aboard. Then the firemen announced they wouldn't take the word of 'any nob who did not work'. So they demanded a guarantee of 100 pounds in cash that Mr Bruce was not aboard. The impudence of these men, thought the *Argus*, was unforgivable.

The Minister for Defence, Senator George Pearce, was firm. 'Never' said he 'would they listen to such an outrageous demand'. So the *Weeroona* and all the Commonwealth dignitaries failed to leave the dockside.

It was almost beyond belief how quickly Melbourne was engulfed with American sailors. 'Two sailors from the *Seattle*' says the *Argus* 'stepping jauntily down to the pier kissed two girls giggling at the ship's side'.

Squadrons of taxis homed in on Port Melbourne. Some sailors wanted to get to a baseball game. When told cricket was the sport in Melbourne, a gob from the *Omaha* asked 'What is cricket?' Others wanted a drink and were startled to hear that the hotels closed at 6 p.m. and the city was utterly dry until the following morning. Further, discovered it was difficult to buy cigarettes in sedate Melbourne after dark.

But the hospitality and the warmth of the welcome is marvellous. The sailors are being greeted with big smiles on every street corner. The YMCA is turning on dancing and parlour games; the Hoyts De Luxe and the Hoyts Gaiety Theatre is giving free admission to sailors; there's a ball at Whernside, Toorak; a Mayorall ball in Ballarat; and St Patrick's Cathedral is providing cars on Sunday for a special outing for Roman Catholic officers and men.

M. Blondin Risks his Neck

26 JULY 1874

Monsieur Blondin, tightrope champion of the world, 'Blondin the Magnificent', performed in Brisbane yesterday.

It is a marvel that this extraordinary man has chosen to come here. But you see, his manager and publicity agent is Henry Percival Lyon, an Australian.

Blondin, a Frenchman, went to North America 15 years ago and announced that he would cross Niagara Falls on a tightrope. American sportsmen said he was mad. He was certain to kill himself, but they were happy to accept his challenge. He sent a rope 1100 feet across the falls by rope, winched it tight, held it by guy ropes and crossed easily, scooping up much money in bets. He then did it in every conceivable manner, on stilts, pushing a wheelbarrow, and finally for $15 000, he said he would carry a man, pick-a-back.

Any volunteers? He would give $100 to any man who would make the journey. The offer was taken up immediately by Lyon, a barnstorming acrobat, cornet player.

Blondin warned him: 'If you panic I'll dump you on the rope to look after yourself'. Lyon replied cheekily: 'What are we waiting for?' So off they went and even when Blondin pretended to fall midstream, Lyon just sat there like an amiable monkey. From then on they were a team.

Yesterday he set up his rope in the Brisbane Botanic Gardens. The rope was specially made for him in Spain, and as thick as a man's wrist. It was 250 feet long, set 80 feet high, and he had an immense mast at either end with two small platforms.

'Nothing will draw like the probability of a man breaking his neck' said the *Courier*, and draw he did. The crowd numbered 3500, with some even watching from across the river at Kangaroo Point.

Now, this man is 50 years old, stout, muscular, but very neat and dainty on his feet. First he appeared as a Knight in Armour, but he just danced down the rope to the tune of a band. Next he came out as an acrobat, and for 10 seconds, way aloft, he stood on his head. Next, and we could hardly believe it, he actually lay down on the rope.

His star turn was to go across blindfold. As the *Courier* says, how he managed to accomplish this, only M. Blondin himself knows. But he did cause a sensation when he came down full length, then managed to recover himself, balancing his huge pole.

His next act, perhaps not so hazardous, was to carry a stove, all the utensils, then midway, he washed his dishes, lit his stove, mixed his omelettes, cooked them, then sent them down below to anyone who wanted to test his culinary powers.

The applause of the spectators was immense. What next? He took up an ordinary chair, balanced it on one leg, then deliberately got up and stood upon it. Just one puff of wind would have sent him to his doom. Finally, and perhaps most picturesque of all, he rode across on a bicycle.

The *Courier* insisted that no one should fail to see this man. 'We consider Blondin to be one of the greatest living arguments against the charges made of the effeminate and degenerate character of the age'.

*M. Blondin
defying death*

Our Troops off to Korea

27 JULY 1950

The Acting Prime Minister, Mr Fadden, announced tonight that Australia will send a ground force to fight in Korea.

A simultaneous announcement came from the Prime Minister of New Zealand, Mr Holland. A Kiwi contingent will be there and it will be the Anzacs all over again.

You will remember that when Japan surrendered at the end of World War 2, Russian and American forces met at the thirty-eighth parallel, which became the border between the two countries. On 25 June the Communist Government in North Korea decided to unify the nation and invaded across the border.

Of course, with the Cold War there has been great disillusionment. Mr Menzies was elected to Government in 1949 in the wake of the Communist threat, and there is a Bill before the House to outlaw the Communist Party. The invasion of South Korea only confirms Mr Menzies's suspicions. There is real fear now of an outbreak of another global war between the Communist and non-Communist countries.

General Douglas Macarthur, the great American General, is commander of a United Nations Force, mostly American, which is now launching a counter-attack. On 29 June, almost immediately after the Korean war started, Mr Menzies announced two of our ships, the destroyer *Bataan* and the frigate *Shoalhaven*, would be at the disposal of the United Nations. Lieutenant General Robertson, our commander with the occupation forces in Japan, ordered 77 Squadron RAAF into action. So Australia was the first non-American nation to give support.

Mr Menzies, right now, is on his way to the United States and he expects to have lunch this week with the American President, Mr Harry Truman. Mr Truman already has asked the US Congress for $10 billion to put the United States on a war footing.

Mr Fadden says the Australian forces will be part of a British Commonwealth unit. It is likely that we will send 5000 men, all volunteers, all fully trained. We will be looking for officers and ex-officers under 40, NCOs and former NCOs, aged 21 to 38 and others between the ages of 21 and 32 years.

General Macarthur is delighted. He has issued a statement:'As you know the Australians

Mr Fadden

are my blood brothers. I have a degree of confidence in them that cannot be excelled'.

Unquestionably the conflict will be dangerous. Already the North Koreans have occupied large areas of the South, and Mr Fadden has given warning of the menace. He says it is just one of the chain of Red activities that constitute 'a finger pointing at Australia'. We are resolved to play our full part in Korea, says he, but we may yet be called upon to play a much larger part in a much larger conflict.

The response has been amazing. All round the nation people have rushed to join up. In Brisbane there were 500 inquiries. In Sydney there were 497 direct applications plus another 200 telephone inquiries and in Perth there were 197 applications. In Sydney three-quarters of the applicants were ex-servicemen, and many of them said they would not enlist unless guaranteed action abroad.

Mr Menzies, in the United States, says Australia is ready to become 'the arsenal of the Pacific', but one wonders what we can really do. At this point we have only one fully-equipped battalion and that is in Japan. But apparently America really wants the gesture, our presence, rather than vast numbers of troops.

Horse Racing Returns to Adelaide

28 JULY 1888

Praise the Lord, it looks as if the fine old sport of horse racing might revive in South Australia.

Back in 1883 the Parliament of South Australia decided that betting on horses, and with bookmakers in particular, was the source of all evil. Part of the problem was the bookmakers who swarmed over from Melbourne. One member claimed 'They come here like hawks seeking what they can devour'.

Well, the Attorney General, Mr J.W. Downer, brought down a Bill stating that any person who bet or offered a bet in a public place would be considered a rogue and a vagabond under the Police Act and would be convicted and punished.

That was the end of the Tote, end of the bookmakers, everything. In the past three years horse racing has just withered and died. The *Christian Colonist* pointed out recently:

It is seriously asserted by racing men that unless the use of the betting machine is legalised racing as a sport must become extinct. It appears that the great attraction of the racecourse has not been to witness the legitimate trial of speed between two or more horses, but the excitement of gambling.

The *Colonist* said the South Australian Jockey Club was £1500 in debt, and unless the Tote returned, it was impossible for the SAJC to continue.

There was a marvellous cry of pain from opposition member, Mr John Crozier. He said:

Adelaide is such a priest-ridden, poverty-stricken, farinaceous village that we can neither hold a jubilee exhibition or maintain a racecourse.

Then he added:

A leading newspaper in Manchester found that we were a priest-ridden, Salvation-Armyised, canting, hypocritical snivelling country. Another newspaper had a description of South Australia : If ever there was a parson-ridden country it is South Australia. They come in hordes on all occasions...they swarm over everything like bluebottles.

Mr W.B. Rounsevell was another who fought again and again on behalf of the racing clubs for the return of the Tote. The *Colonist* this time wrote:

The blood of these souls will be upon those who voted with Mr Rounsevell, who, although they may be able to retain their seats in Parliament, cannot escape the judgement of God.

Mr Rowland Rees told the House that in 1884 Morphetville had 98 horses in training, not including the Adelaide racetrack. Now there were only 20 horses altogether in training. Horse breeding in the State was practically ruined.

At last there has been a breakthrough. Mr Rees has pushed through the Second Reading of an amendment to the Totalisator Bill. He pointed out that now there was no horse racing in Adelaide, it was merely one of the pleasant reminiscences of the past. For example, on Ascension Day at the Adelaide Racecourse there was no race meeting. Instead a few hundred people congregated for a 'kangaroo hunt', a disgusting sport.

The new Bill permits the return of the Tote, but it bans bookmakers.

Note: South Australia remained pure and utterly free of bookmakers until Christmas 1933 when bookmakers became legal again. Sixty bookmakers fielded at Cheltenham, and the *Advertiser* described it as the most successful meeting in 40 years.

Lord Casey New Governor-General

29 JULY 1965

Lord Casey is our new Governor-General. There was a joint announcement yesterday both from Buckingham Palace and Sir Robert Menzies.

Lord Casey was the obvious choice, but there was still an element of surprise. The Liberals, until now, have never appointed an Australian as Governor-General. Only Labor has done that with Sir Isaac Isaacs and Sir William McKell.

Then there was all the Menzies – Casey rivalry. Sir Robert was never a friend to Casey. Casey had aspirations to be prime minister, and Menzies always seemed to get him out of the way with illustrious appointments overseas.

But the remarkable thing is that the appointment has met with universal approval everywhere, not a cry of pain from either side of the House. Arthur Calwell, leader of the Opposition approves. He says Casey as Governor-General is 'wise and welcome'. Sir William McKell who suffered an orchestration of Liberal protest when he became Governor-General in 1947 said today:

Lord Casey

> It is an appointment that gives me a great deal of personal pleasure. Lord Casey is a great Australian and he has rendered very faithful devoted service to Australia. I am sure that he will carry with the greatest distinction the responsibility of his high office.

The newspapers today are practically Casey special issues. We have shots of Lord and Lady Casey drinking tea at their city house in East Melbourne. We have pictures of Casey with Eisenhower, Casey with Nehru, Casey with Churchill, Casey with Eleanor Roosevelt, Casey shooting eagles from his Cessna, Casey with the skin of a tiger he shot in Bengal...

The *Sun* has writtten him an extraordinary open letter:

> We can think of no one who would have more claim to this title. We know you are 75 next month. Everyone does. We know that until recently you were famed for shooting down eagles from aeroplanes. Your eye must be straight. One of the great things about your appointment, Lord Casey, is that you have broken through the Liberal Party ban on Australians heading their own country. This is a great achieve-ment....P.S. If you and Lady Casey want to shoot some of those cocked hats and funny swords, the way you shot down the eagles, we will doubly bless you. It would make it feel more like the Australia we like.

Lord Casey told the Press:

> This is a very great privilege — the pinnacle of my life, the crowning moment. I am delighted but very humble that the responsibility of this great honour has been conferred on me. Lady Casey and I are quite shaken. My emotions are very mixed. Sir Robert Menzies told me I had better be prepared for the announcement. I think my first words to him were, 'Good heavens!'.

Lord Casey said both he and Lady Casey were pilots and they would be taking their Cessna to Canberra. 'Yes, you can call me the flying Governor-General if you like'.

Lady Casey apologised to the Press. She had only half a bottle of beer in the house, and that was probably flat.

However, it was obvious, everything else in the Casey house today is very effervescent. The retiring Governor-General is Viscount De L'Isle, who left Australia on 6 May.

AUGUST

Football under electric lights

Miners Entombed by Explosion

1 AUGUST 1902

The most dreadful mining disaster in Australia's history took place at Mount Kembla yesterday afternoon. The explosion killed 26 men outright and over 100 men are still entombed.

It was like an earthquake. Just after 2 p.m. there was an explosion as if thousands of pounds of dynamite had been exploded, windows of houses rattled, doors moved, kitchen dressers shook and the earth moved.

There was an instant rush to the mine said the *Argus*.

At the tunnel mouth, there was a terrible scene of devastation. All buildings including the office and the engine house had been blown into an unrecognisable mass. The entrance to the main shaft was wrecked and gangs of men were set to clear away the debris. Under the mass of timber and rocks was the body of lad named Nelson, only 17. A few minutes later a human leg was discovered.

Wives, mothers, sisters, waited at the mouth of the mine all night.

The grief of one woman and three children was at once turned to joy, for in a tattered and blackened figure they recognised a husband and a father. It was painful, almost heart breaking to hear the joyful exclamation of the wife and her children.

Some of the men when they reached the open air became delirious. Many of them could not walk, and they had to be brought on stretchers. Some stated they were knocked down as if by a blow. In each case the miner said he felt almost choked to death with smoke. The only way they escaped suffocation was by lying flat on the ground.

However the real tragedy came when body after body was carried out of the mine, followed by the screams and suffering of the relatives. The tragedy goes further when you realise so many families here near Wollongong are interrelated. As the *Argus* says:

Grey-headed men have been discovered lying side by side with their sons and nephews, while two brothers were found locked in each other's arms. There were seven brothers named Egan at work in various parts of the workings. Only three escaped. There were the Purcells, four of them were killed, the Uncle, James Purcell and three nephews, Tom, Jack and Jim.

The mystery of course is the cause. The general impression is that the explosion was due to gas. The remarkable thing is that gas has never been known to exist in the mine before. Only yesterday, the manager, Mr Rogers, said there was not a whiff of gas in the whole works. So never was it thought necessary to use safety lamps. The men always used naked lights.

Death to many of the miners came from what they call 'after damp'. This is the dreadful irrespirable gas, consisting chiefly of carbonic acid gas and nitrogen, that comes after explosion. It is an even greater terror than the explosion itself. Says the *Argus*: 'When overcome by these poisonous fumes the men are practically paralysed. The lower limbs, it appears, give way first, and, in this helpless condition, they sink to the floor, where almost certain death lurks'.

Note: The final toll of miners at Mount Kembla was 94 dead.

A One-word Sermon

2 AUGUST 1967

Arthur Stace at work

Arthur Stace is dead at eighty-three. Maybe you didn't even spot the notice in yesterday's *Sydney Morning Herald*.

Arthur Stace is the man who used to write 'ETERNITY' on the pavements. Always he started early, usually before dawn. Every morning he was somewhere else, Wynyard, Glebe, Paddington, Randwick, Central Station. As he said, he went where God directed him. Every night the message appeared in his head.

As he walked, every so often he would stop, pull out a crayon, bend down and write on the pavement in large, elegant copperplate — ETERNITY. He would move on a 100 metres, write it again, ETERNITY, nothing more. For 37 years he chalked this one-word sermon, more than half a million times.

He did not like publicity. For a decade he was a mystery, and all columnists speculated on who possibly could be the author. The mystery was solved in 1956, and the man who cracked it was the Rev. Lisle M. Thompson of the Burton Street, Baptist Church. Stace was actually the church cleaner and one of their prayer leaders.

One day Lisle Thompson saw Stace take out his crayon and write the famous Eternity on the pavement. Thompson said : 'Are you Mr Eternity?' and Stace replied, 'Guilty, Your Honour'.

Tom Farrell of the *Sunday Telegraph* won the first interview. Stace was born in 1884 in a Balmain slum. His father and mother were both drunkards. Two sisters and two brothers also were drunks and lived most of their time in gaol.

Stace learned to drink like the rest of his family, and lived in a fog of alcohol. He went to gaol for the first time when he was fifteen. He became a metho drinker and a derelict.

In the depths of the depression in 1930, he went to a prayer meeting at St Barnabas's Church on Broadway. You endured a sermon so that you could get tea and rock cakes at the finish. He noticed, up front, some nice clean-looking people, a remarkable contrast to 300 grubby-looking unemployed. 'Who are they?', he asked another character, a well-known criminal.

'I reckon they'd be Christians', he replied.

Stace thought, 'I'm going to have a go at what they got'. He got down on his knees and prayed. After that he found it possible to give up the drink. Some months later he heard the give-'em-hell preacher, Rev. John Ridley cry 'I wish I could shout eternity through the streets of Sydney'.

That set him off

I felt a powerful call from the Lord to write 'Eternity'. I had a piece of chalk in my pocket and I bent down there and wrote it. Funny thing, I had no schooling and I couldn't have spelled 'Eternity' for a hundred quid, but out it came in a beautiful copperplate script. I couldn't understand it and still can't.

He was nearly arrested 24 times for defacing the pavement, but eventually everyone came to love him, including the Sydney City Council.

He has bequeathed his body to Sydney University. One hopes Eternity treats him kindly.

Note: In 1977 Ridley Smith, architect of Sydney Square placed the message ETERNITY in cast aluminium, near the Sydney Square waterfall. No garish presentation, one word only, ETERNITY, in copperplate, just as Arthur Stace would have wanted it.

Walter Lindrum Dies

3 AUGUST 1960

We had the funeral in Melbourne yesterday of Walter Lindrum. He died of a heart attack at Surfers Paradise aged only sixty-one.

St Pauls Cathedral was packed: every sportsman you could think of was there — Harry Hopman, Doug Bachli, Ossie Pickworth, John Coleman, Hubert Opperman, Ian Johnson, Lindsay Hassett, Doug Ring, Jack Purtell, Jock Sturrock, Laurie Nash, Frank Sedgman, Lou Richards, Jack Dyer....

The newspaper reports say today:
The hundreds of magnificent floral tributes were a fitting last tribute to the man who raised at least three million pounds for charity. He was not only the world champion billiards player, but without doubt the most unchallenged champion of all Australian champions in any particular sport. He was such a master of the game that no one bothered to challenge his supremacy.

Of course he came from a family of billiard champions. When he was only 13 or 14 years old his father had him training from 10 a.m. to noon; 2 p.m. to 5 p.m. and then 8 p.m. to 10 p.m., six days a week. When he was beginning to look tired his father would say:
'Well, son, is your back aching?'
'Yes, Dad'.
'Then, son, it's time you did a little more'.

Lindrum's career did not really take off until 1929. He recalled how he went to John Wren, the sporting man's patron. Wren had a billiard table in his large Melbourne mansion at Studley Park. Wren asked Lindrum if he would demostrate a few shots. Walter said he wanted to do more than that, so he asked Wren to time him while he made a break of one thousand.

Wren did not believe anyone could make a break of 1000, and he looked on incredulous while Lindrum made a 1000, then another 1000 in an unending display of dazzling, high-speed scoring.

He held 57 world records but perhaps his greatest was the break of 4137 that he scored against the reigning world champion, Joe Davis on 20 January 1932. The London representative of the *Herald* reported on that occasion:
Lindrum smiled, chalked his cue and executed the shot which broke the record. A great roar of applause followed, interspersed with coo-ees and shouts of 'Good old Walter'. Hats were thrown in the air. The demonstration lasted for five minutes. At 4137 he missed a cushion cannon by a whisker and it was all over. His record break took two hours 56 minutes.

He was so good the controllers of billiards changed the rules, putting a check on nursery cannons, but even that was not enough, he remained in a class above all the others.

He was president of the Victorian Sportsmen's Association. Doug Bachli, the vice-president said 'He was the greatest professional amateur in the world. Other men become professionals to earn money for themselves. Walter was a professional who raised money for others'.

The Sportsmen's Association plans to put a special memorial over his grave at the Melbourne General Cemetery. It will be like a billiard table in marble.

Walter Lindrum had no equal

Army Goes In as Miners Go Out

4 AUGUST 1949

Mr Chifley: not bluffing

The unthinkable for the Labor Party has happened. Mr Chifley has sent troops into the coalfields.

Back on 28 June, the Prime Minister said only coal-miners could mine coal, but now the miners have gone too far. They have defied the Arbitration Court. They have been on strike for five weeks and they brought both Sydney and industry almost to a standstill.

There was an incredible scene in the Sydney Domain on Sunday. The Minister for Information, Mr Calwell, addressed a crowd of 20 000 workers. He called the Communists 'a screaming collection of pathological exhibits'.

He cried 'Never before have so few caused so much misery in such a short time. If it is left to me, into a concentration camp they will go. . . We will use the Army on them, the Navy on them, and the Air Force on them'.

The miners thought Mr Chifley was bluffing, but it was no bluff. The Army had been preparing for some time. The invasion of the coalfields was like a war-time tactical campaign. Mr Chifley had a special code word which he released on Monday, and at midnight 1830 troops — Army and Air Force — moved into action and occupied 12 open-cut mines. The first truckload of Army-mined coal left Muswellbrook at 12.10 a.m.

Of course, the miners said it was dangerous. The Army could not possibly walk in and take over coal mining, but they have. Amongst the troops were 1000 trained engineers; 103 of them were specialists from the Woomera Rocket Range. Army sappers started working the great mechanical shovels immediately.

The Minister for Fuel and Shipping, Senator Ashley, says the troops are working two 10-hour shifts a day and they are producing around 8000 tons a day. This is good because before the strike the miners were averaging 7900 tons a day.

Now at last life is returning to normal. The State Emergency Committee is planning to restore week-end electric trains. Power restrictions are coming off, and once again we will be allowed to turn on our hot water systems and use our electric irons.

Whether the miners had a case or not, they have received little sympathy from the *Sydney Morning Herald*, which has thundered day after day. 'Miners tyranny' has been the favourite line.

The miners, says the *Herald*, were able to wage their tyranny because they made sure coal stocks were at a subsistence level and they thought this strike would be short and sweet.

The *Herald* continued:

That shameful epoch in our industrial history is over. When the miners resume work they will not be doing so on pre-strike conditions, for their bluff has been called. The miners must be made to understand that the indiscipline of the past will not be tolerated. . . Needless strikes alone were causing an annual loss of 1,000,000 tons or more before the present stoppage.

The *Herald* thundering is not far astray. The miners don't want their jobs taken over by the Army. Already they have decided to return to work.

Patriotism and the Prizes of War

5 AUGUST 1914

Great Britain and the Empire is at war with Germany.

Our Prime Minister, Mr Cook, already has pledged our loyalty. In fierce fighting words, he said tonight: 'Our resources are great and the British spirit is not dead...Our duty is quite clear — namely to gird up our loins and remember that we are Britons'.

In Melbourne one would have thought a party had been declared rather than war. The *Age* reports:

> Scenes of wild enthusiasm were witnessed outside the newspaper office last night. All day long and throughout the early part of the evening there was a crowd extending out on the roadway reading the cables... the crowd spread right across Collins Street.
>
> It needed only a single voice to give the opening bars of a patriotic song and thousands of throats took it up, hats and coats were waved, and those who were lucky enough to possess even the smallest Union Jacks were the heroes of the moment and were raised shoulder high. Rule Britannia, Soldiers of the King and Sons of the Sea were sung again and again. The National Anthem had a sobering effect from time to time, and woe betide anyone who failed to remove his hat without hesitation. Suddenly a Frenchman got up on the steps and commenced singing the Marseillaise. The crowd grew frantic with enthusiasm. He was lifted bodily in the air shouting 'Vive L'Australie! Vive La France!'

The *Australasian* reports that a mob of 300 larrikins attacked the German Club in Victoria parade. They barged through the gate and they lashed at the windows with sticks. Then they set a piece of rag alight which they announced was a German flag, and while it was burning they jumped up and down on it, hooting threats against the Germans. They finished their little patriotic display with an all-in fight against 20 police from Russell Street.

Every leading article talks of loyalty and rallying to the cause. The *Argus* says:

> We would not descend to boasting in the presence of a stupendous crisis: still Australians would be degenerates if they could not smile in the presence of danger... Britons welcome 'The Day' with confidence that victory will not desert the flag which has braved a thousand years the battle and the breeze merely because an ambitious and desperate rival has determined to tear it down.
>
> The patience and the sincerity of the King and his advisers have failed, but their indirect effect has been to unite the Empire as it never was united before in a determination to stand beside the old land to help her through any agonies...if necessary, the last man and the last shilling.

The *Argus* reports, further, that there is great excitement in the Armed forces and men are rushing to join up, and some volunteer units are disappointed they have not yet received their call up notices.

We have seen war-time action already. At dawn today the German cargo steamer, *Pfalz*, so new she is not even on the Lloyds register, sped down the Bay. Just as she was entering the Rip, the fort at Queenscliff opened fire and a shot plunged 50 yards astern.

The *Pfalz*, very sensibly, returned to Williamstown. What happens now? We think the *Pfalz* is ours, the first prize of the war.

Mr Cook: remember we are Britons

POWs Break-out at Cowra

8 AUGUST 1944

All shops and businesses in Cowra are closed in mourning today for the burial of four Australian soldiers killed in the ugliest riot and slaughter this country has seen.

Cowra is 240 miles due West of Sydney. It has been a training camp for the AIF, and it is here that we have held prisoners of war.

At 2 a.m. on 5 August, 1104 Japanese prisoners screaming 'Banzai' and armed only with crude weapons, threw themselves on the barbed wire in a mass break-out. The slaughter has been terrible. So far the troops have counted more than 200 Japanese dead, with another 100 wounded.

The Japanese set their own camp alight. Many killed themselves by jumping into the flames. By dawn scores of corpses hung on the barbed wire and others dangled by ropes from gum trees where they had hanged themselves.

The army was aware a dangerous situation was brewing. The camp was overcrowded and the Japanese were in a very different mood to the Italians. They arrived weak and emaciated, but after months of being well-fed and even supplied with free packs of cigarettes, they became fit, arrogant and looked upon good treatment as a sign of weakness. The worried authorities decided to shift all Japanese prisoners, with the exception of officers, to Hay. At noon on 4 August, the Japanese were told to get ready to move.

That was the signal for them to strike. They had been working on weapons, nails hammered into baseball bats, mess knives sharpened and formed into bayonets, stones attached to pieces of wire...The Australians too, fearful of trouble, brought in Vickers, Bren, Owen and Sten machine guns.

When the Japanese made their charge, one guard screamed 'The bastards are coming' and just managed to get out the gate. The Japanese directed their first and main attack on a Vickers machine-gun post near the northern fence of their compound. They thought the guns in the towers could not open fire on them without killing the gunners.

So they charged into the stream of bullets coming from this gun, and overwhelmed it by sheer mass of suiciding bodies. Then they clubbed the two gunners to death. The Japanese swung the gun round to fire, but the belt jammed.

Some escaped by throwing mattresses or blankets on the wire, others climbed over the corpses of their fellows. Meanwhile guards sent down a hail of machine-gun fire, and altogether fired 28 000 bullets.

For days, thousands of Australian troops have scoured the Cowra countryside and gathered in escaped prisoners in their burgundy uniforms. Many of the POWs killed themselves in various bizarre ways. What they planned to do once they escaped is very obscure. Apparently they feared that the idea of shifting them to Hay was to have them all executed.

All Cowra, of course, is aware of the great battle and there have been many individual acts of heroism. Reporters, too, have been here from newspapers, but the entire action has been suppressed and Australia knows nothing about it.

The fear is that if it were published the Japanese would take reprisals against Australian POWs in Japan, Singapore and elsewhere.

Note: Private B. Hardy and Private R. Jones, machine gunners were awarded the George Cross posthumously.

Huts destroyed in the riot

161

Long Live the King

9 AUGUST 1902

The Coronation of His Majesty King Edward VII took place today. We are told the spectacle was magnificent and a million people lined the route to and from Westminster Abbey.

Of course the Coronation should have taken place last June. As the *Age* points out, for months we held our breath in suspense over what looked like the deathbed of the monarch, and not a few predicted that Edward VII would never put on the 'round and top' of sovereignty'.

But he made a magical recovery and as the *Age* says, never before in the world has any monarch put on the crown of an empire so majestic, never before have the bounds of sovereignty been so wide or the ties of affection and loyalty so strong. Never was there a time when the enemies of Britain were more conscious of her immeasurable strength.

In Melbourne we have had Coronation parties, we have had Coronation balls, we have consumed innumerable, sometimes highly indigestible, Coronation dinners. In Brighton the Mayor handed out Coronation lollies to the children. Practically all senior schoolchildren have scored Coronation medals, and the City Councillors all received utterly splendid gold medals in honour of His Majesty.

One wonders who paid for all this loyalty, presumably the suffering ratepayers. There have been parties bonfires and holidays in Brisbane, Adelaide and Perth. In Melbourne tonight there was an astonishing celebration attended by a huge crowd of 30 000 people at the Exhibition.

A great amphitheatre was erected outside, and hundreds of electric lights hung down from overhead, so bright they looked like 'winter moons'. The Acting Governor-General, Lord Tennyson, was there. So, too, was Lord Richard Neville, His Excellency Sir Sydenham Clarke and Lady Clarke, plus all the most important politicians.

We had patriotic tug-o-wars between the armed services. Six hundred strong members of the 1st and 2nd Battalions gave us a demonstration of war. As lights flared, and to the crash of a huge volley of gunfire, an imaginary enemy was swept into eternity.

Then we had a Highland regiment set up

The King's Coronation

camp. Suddenly they were attacked by marauding Dervishes. However the engineers set off a great explosion with gun cotton. This was coupled with a bayonet charge, which the *Age* says was the most thrilling thing of the evening. The Dervishes were decimated and many of them died with great histrionic talent.

The police then gave us a sticking up of the Never Never post office, a coach robbed by bush rangers, citizens held to ransom. But you will be pleased to hear the police triumphed utterly, order was restored and the bushrangers perished. How could it be otherwise on Coronation Day.

There were massed bands, totalling 300 bandsmen. Everyone sang the 'National Anthem' and 'Rule Britannia'.

A number of lucky colonials were invited to actually attend the ceremony at Westminster. Janet, Lady Clarke; Lady Rupert Clarke; Mr and Mrs David Elder; Mr and Mrs P.S. Grimwade; Sir James and Lady Fairfax; General and Mrs French; Mr and Mrs Macarthur; were all there.

So now we enter the Edwardian era, almost the perfect time to be a Briton. As the Lord Mayor of Melbourne, Sir Samuel Gillot, says in his message to the Throne, there is no nook of any magnitude in the King's wide dominions, save, perhaps in misgoverned Ireland alone, where the subject is not solidly loyal and submissive.

Gas Lights the City Night

10 AUGUST 1857

New city lights draw the crowds

Gaslight came to the streets of Melbourne today. At last! Hooray!

Until now we have had these wretched oil lamps that give practically no light at all. Apart from the fact that one felt downright unsafe even in Collins Street, there was always the fear you could step up to your knees in mud or slip to your doom down one of those awful gutters.

The Mayor, 60 other gentleman, plus members of the Ministry, celebrated the occasion with a grand dinner at the Criterion Hotel.

You must appreciate that gas is not completely new to us. But for an unconscionable battle over prices between the Melbourne City Council and the Melbourne Gas and Coke Company, we could have won our gas at least three years ago.

City shops have had it for a long time. The first was William Overton's splendid bakery and confectionary shop in Swanston Street. Mr. Overton made his own gas. He had a large cast-iron retort, cooked up coal inside, pushed his gas into his own tank, and, so, through to the lights outside.

The *Argus* reported on 31 July 1849:

Overton...at considerable expense, succeeded in manufacture of gas...A fine lamp, placed over his door, nightly attracts a number of persons, anxious to gratify their curiosity by gazing at the first gas lamp in Melbourne.

Mr Overton imports an extensive assortment of English confectionary, comprising Lind's comfits, black currant lozenges, white and pink candy, liquorice drops, coltsfoot rock, lovers vows, and French bonbons. The gaslight helped him do a furious trade.

We trust gaslight in the streets will do the same for the whole city. As the *Argus* says, it is 'one of the wonders of modern discovery'. Now 300 lamps have been erected between Flinders Street on the south and Victoria Street on the north, and between Spencer on the west and Spring on the east.

The *Argus* says the effect is particularly cheerful in the more central streets where we get gas light from the shops and hotels. Alas there are still 218 of the old lamps yet to be replaced.

But again the speed has not been dazzling. Sydney, for Heaven's sake, first won gas in 1841. Then there is the price of this gas, which has been the cause of such rancor. Gas companies in London charge 4 shillings and sixpence a thousand cubic feet. The Melbourne Gas Company charges 22 shillings. It is the awful cost of the coal, they claim. It has to come either from New South Wales or Tasmania.

The *Herald* is not quite as impressed with the gas as the *Argus*. It thinks the poles are too high and they tend to illuminate the trees and the roof tops.

And Melbourne *Punch* sighs wistfully:

That gleams from yonder lofty height
The lighting which the City pay,
About one shilling each per day, —
A heavy price for such a light.
That shines high up in the middle air,
Illuminates the roofs and eaves,
But in a doubtful twilight leaves
Each broad and thronging thoroughfare.

Further reading: *Circle of Influence. A History of the Gas Industry in Victoria*. Ray Proudley.

A Taste for Australian 'Twanguage'

11 AUGUST 1952

There is a splendid controversy taking place over the Australian accent.

The chances are that we could be lifted from this dreadful inferiority cringe that the way we talk is too crook for any civilised ear to hear.

At the moment you cannot get a job with the Australian Broadcasting Commission unless you speak as if you moved in the polite society of London's West End or, at least, went to school at Eton. Australian actors are told at once that their future is bleak unless they can learn to speak with the pure beauty of, say, a Leslie Howard or Laurence Olivier.

Some years back, George Highland, the Sydney Theatrical Producer, said:

The Australian twang, or whatever you like to call it, is never beautiful. It is hideous, and the thicker it gets the more hideous it becomes. People will tell you that I am a high strung or almost hysterical man. They can only form that conclusion if they have happened to see me at rehearsal, being driven mad by the Australian language, or the Australian twanguage.

I don't care what they call it. It is an abomination. It is so bad that you can't suggest it by any perversion of English spelling. You might as hopefully attempt to make a man feel the pains of cholera by spelling it.

But at last a change is coming about. Sidney J. Baker that great authority on the Australian language says:

For the best part of a century we have been afflicted with the drivellings of people who had opinions to air on the subject of Australian speech, either to damn Australians or to defend them — people who told us that we had a twang or a drawl, that we talked through our noses, that we were Cockney or that we weren't Cockney... that we were lip-lazy and tongue-lazy...

Well, at last Sydney University, in today's issue of the *Current Affairs Bulletin*, has produced a paper on the subject. It says there are two extreme points of view:

1. The development of an Australian accent is a deplorable and abnormal happening, a corrupt deviation from the line of correct English.

2. An Australian way of speech is a good and desirable thing as a sign or symbol of our national independence. It is a good thing that our speech should be distinctive.

The *Bulletin* says point one runs counter to history. One could not impose abstract standards or pick out some particular accent just because one felt this was the pure and correct one. It was impossible to get away from the speech that had developed in Australia.

As for point two, speech was communication, therefore we should not exaggerate. While we need not be uncomfortable about the Australian accent we should not exalt its individuality unduly.

Dame Enid Lyons says she is delighted with the *Current Affairs Bulletin* satement:

That there is such an 'animile' as an Australian accent and that, at his worst, he is singularly unbeautiful, no one, I think, will deny. The question is should he be killed on the spot, or merely groomed into respectability. Personally, I'm all for letting it live.

So there is a wee gleam of hope. Who knows? Perhaps one day we will have a Chips Rafferty reading the news.

Dame Enid Lyons

Dark Prospects for Night Football

12 AUGUST 1879

Major Ben Wardill, Secretary of the Melbourne Cricket Club, is fascinated by electricity.

He first saw it in 1867 during the visit of Prince Alfred, Duke of Edinburgh. Some buildings were illuminated on that occasion and they looked fine indeed.

If only the ground could be illuminated, the possibilities for night sport would be limitless. Seeing that it is winter, the Major settled on night football.

You must appreciate it is only in the last few years we have allowed football on the sacred turf of the MCG. Football, the lesser sport, was played outside on the Richmond Paddock. Until now we have adopted the beliefs of the Old Country. Footballers clumping round in their ugly boots do very poor service to a beautiful cricket ground. In 1867 we built a double-sided grandstand. At the end of the cricket season we turned the seats round the other way so that the spectators could watch the football outside in the park.

But now, you see, the Major has succumbed and we have had two night football matches inside the ground. The first drew a crowd of 12 000, and although it was a great financial success, the footballers were little more than shadowy figures in the blackness.

We had the second match tonight. The promoters borrowed a light of 7000 candle-power from the Gipps Land Railway Workshops. The match was between our two most powerful teams, Melbourne and Carlton.

It was advertised to start at 7.30 p.m., but the electricians had their problems. Electricity, you must understand, is not just a mere matter of throwing a switch. First you have to stoke your steam engine until you have sufficient power to drive your generators. That wretched steam engine took an unconscionable time to find steam.

The Melbourne Cricket Ground is frigid enough by day, let alone night. The crowd shivered for an hour until the stream of electric light came on at 8.30 p.m. Frankly, it was disappointing. It was difficult enough for the spectators to see the players and one wonders whether the players saw each other.

Here is the account that is going into the *Australasian*:

Sixteen each of Carlton and Melbourne took the field and a motley crew they were, scarcely two of a side being similarly attired. They players used a white ball, which was very attractive, but after only five minutes it blew up. This was something nobody had predicted so they had to continue with an ordinary tan-colored ball.

This made play difficult, and only when the ball passed through the banks of light could they see it. After 20 minutes Carlton scored a goal and much to the relief of everyone the promoters produced another white ball. The Carlton men adapted themselves with rare skill to the dark. They scored two more goals and had an easy win.

The *Australasian* says there are three things wrong with this form of entertainment: (a) football on an August night is a chilling uncomfortable experience; (b) night footballers need much brighter uniforms; (c) there has to be some way of improving the lighting arrangements.

But one should not worry, unless they can choose fixtures only on the night of a full moon, it is extremely unlikely that night sport will ever catch on.

Football under electric lights

165

Air Crash Horror in Canberra

15 AUGUST 1940

All Australia is in mourning. A Lockheed bomber crashed just a mile from Canberra airport. The ten people aboard were killed, and the loss to the nation is devastating.

Among the dead are Brigadier Street; the Minister for the Army, Sir Henry Gullett; the Vice-President of the Executive Council, Mr J. V. Fairbairn; Minister for Air, General Sir Brudenell White, the Chief of the General Staff; and Lieutenant Colonel Thornthwaite, one of our most brilliant young Army officers.

The crash occurred on 14 August. The bodies have been flown to Melbourne and there will be a memorial service at St Paul's Cathedral this morning. Arrangements are being made for the bellringers at St Paul's to ring a full muffled peal, beginning at 11 a.m. This peal is rarely rung, and only on the death of the nation's greatest men.

The crash occurred within sight of Parliament House and it has cast a gloom over the whole city. Messages of sympathy have come from all over the globe, including His Majesty the King and the British Prime Minister, Sir Winston Churchill.

Mr Menzies, the Australian Prime Minister said:

It is a great national calamity, in addition to grievous personal loss. Every man concerned was engaged upon an important war service. Each minister was a man of great character and intense loyalty. Their loss does not bear thinking about. Sir Brudenell White was our most gifted soldier, full of wisdom and experience.

It is even said that had the enemy chosen men to put in this aircraft, they could not have done better. Sir Brudenell White, for example, was one of the great soldiers of World War 1. It has been said of him that no single man did more to mould the AIF.

It is a mystery how the accident happened. The weather was clear and fine. The bomber was flying from Melbourne to Canberra. It had made its last circuit to check that all was clear. Then, when making its final approach, suddenly the Lockheed appeared to lose height, and failed to clear the last of the hills.

Sir Brudenell White

The pilot made a violent turn to clear some trees, the plane stalled and corkscrewed into the ground. Mrs Hitchcock, mother of Flight Lieutenant Hitchcock, pilot of the aircraft, had a presentiment of the tragedy. She was at a theatre and became so disturbed she left before the show ended. She has two other sons, also in the Air Force.

Another RAAF man killed in the crash was Aircraftsman C.J. Crosdale. His wife sent a tragic telegram tonight to her mother in Cessnock: 'Charles killed. Baby son born. Come at once'. Crosdale was one of a family of 13 sons and four daughters.

All sorts of problems have arisen. We are supposed to have a Federal election on 14 September. It may have to be delayed until 21 September. There has to be a new Army chief. Major General Northcott is being suggested. Mr Arthur Fadden, the assistant Treasurer, has been sworn in as Minister for Air, Senator McBride is the new Minister for the Army.

Mr. Menzies says he is recalling Harold Holt, who joined the AIF last April. If this happens, Gunner Holt will become Minister for Labour and National Service. Some achievement at 31 years.

The Rise of the Bunyip Aristocracy

16 AUGUST 1853

William Charles Wentworth

There is a feeling amongst some of the gentlemen of Sydney that this colony will never prosper unless we have our own aristrocracy.

Mr William Charles Wentworth is chairman of a select committee on a new constitution for New South Wales. He has recommended that the colony should have its own House of Lords, which would be a vast improvement on the present Legislative Council.

His committee says the Crown should create hereditary titles. Upon receiving the title one would have a seat for life in the House. This would not apply to the noblemen's descendants, the inheritors of the title. The Lords would elect representatives to the upper house from among their own number.

At the first reading of the Bill last week, Mr Wentworth said these gentlemen because of 'their birth, leisure and superior education' would lay the foundation for an Upper House that would be a close imitation of the House of Lords.

'Furthermore,' said he 'it would serve as an inducement to respectable families to stay in the colony and for upper classes of the United States to emigrate'.

It has caused both fury and astonishment.

One newspaper, the *Empire*, wants to know whether the ageing Mr Wentworth has gone out of his mind. 'Do Englishmen of the nineteenth century want a House of Lords, an imitation of the Parliament of King Kamehameha?...It is a painful example of the miserable dotage into which the human intellect can sink.'

We are having a whole series of protest meetings. One was even described as a 'monster gathering.' There was a protest meeting today in the Victoria Theatre. The Empire describes it as a 'triumphant manifestation of popular will'. The most eloquent of the speakers was that brilliant Irish wit, Mr Daniel Deniehy.

Mr. Deniehy asked:

Let us have a fair view of these harlequin aristocrats, these Botany Bay Magnificos, these Australian mandarins. Let them walk across the stage in all the pomp and circumstance of hereditary titles. First then in the procession stalks the hoary Wentworth. But he could not imagine that to such a hoary head the strawberry leaves would add any honour.

Next comes the native aristocrat, Mr James Macarthur; he would, I suppose, aspire to the coronet of an earl, I would call him the Earl of Camden, and I would suggest for his coat of arms, a field vert, the heraldic term for green and emblazoned in this field should be a rum keg of a New South Wales order of chivalry.

Mr Deniehy had his audience howling with laughter. There were 2500 people present at one o'clock and 4000 came and went during the afternoon. He was merciless on the unfortunate James Macarthur, who, of course, is the fourth son of the celebrated Captain John Macarthur. He manages his father's estates at Camden and sees himself, as a result of this, becoming Lord Macarthur.

But Deniehy says these people 'couldn't even aspire to the miserable and effete dignity of the grandees of Spain'. Deniehy has a name for the Australian nobility and I am afraid they are stuck with it for ever. He calls it the 'Bunyip Aristocracy'.

There is hardly a chance now of the Bunyip Aristocracy making it past the Second Reading.

Blacksmith Forges Ahead

17 AUGUST 1884

A Canadian by the name of Edward Hanlan has been making a fool of our rowers.

Quite insufferable really. When he gets in front he rows with one hand, then with the other, takes his cap off and waves to his friends. When he beat our world champion sculler, Edward Trickett, back in 1880, he even stopped and washed his face in the water.

In 1881 we produced a hefty bushman, Elias Laycock. Hanlan thrashed him, going through the same old cap waving tricks.

So this time we tried Bill Beach, a 30-year-old Sydney blacksmith, and Hanlan came to Sydney last March. He was a huge celebrity. Hanlan-mania took over. Melbourne *Punch* groaned at this worship of muscle. If a great intellect like Herbert Spencer came to Australia, nobody would notice.

Hanlan didn't mind. He was as cocky as ever. This is his training diet. Breakfast: two oranges, two chops, then stewed kidney and bread. Dinner: roast mutton, roast turkey, carrots, turnips, cauliflower with butter sauce, a large slice of plum pudding, also custard puddings with champagne sauce. Then to wash it down, a glass of stout plus a glass of champagne and stout mixed.

Well, the race took place yesterday on the Parramatta River. At the start Beach took off his shirt. 'Why take off your shirt?' said Hanlan, 'you'll need it soon'. 'I'll make you take off your shirt Hanlan, you'll have no time for monkey tricks today', replied Beach.

Hanlan had a good start and after more than a mile he was four lengths in front. The crowd of 100 000 along the bank was in deep gloom, the same old story. But then Beach started to gain. He gained and he gained, and unbelievably after 3 miles he went to the front and *won*!

The *Sydney Echo* reports:

A shout first then a yell: 'Beach wins! Beach wins!' Incredible! But true. Some hats are thrown in the air, and blown away no man cares whither. Boots and fists are driven through others. Mean leap in a frenzy of joyful excitement, clasp hands, hug each other...There are a hundred thousand throats straining! There is a roar as when a nation rejoices over a great deliverance rather than as when a crowd shouts over a race well won. The cliffs echo it, the trees vibrate it, the gale lifts and rolls it down the harbour.

Hanlan we hear did not take it very well. According to one report he burst into tears and swore he had been fouled by a river vessel. Regardless of Hanlan's tears, our blacksmith is now champion of the world.

There is no sympathy for Hanlan, Beach is the absolute national hero. There are to be banquets and dinners in his honour. He will be presented with illuminated addresses and, one hears, he has been signed by all the pharmaceutical people. For example, we read in one advertisement that whenever he feels unwell when training, William Beach takes Warner's Safe Cure Pills and he is astonished at the great benefit that follows.

Note: They raced twice again and Beach won comfortably on both occasions.

A moment of glory

Impressionists Unworthy of Serious Attention

18 AUGUST 1889

There is an exhibition of 'Impressionist' painting here in Melbourne and it has been castigated in the *Argus* by Mr James Smith, a critic of immense erudition and said even to be a friend of Dickens and Thackeray.

The paintings are by young men such as Tom Roberts, Arthur Streeton and Charles Conder.

Mr Smith says the idea of 'impressionism' is to just give a hint, a wisp of an idea:

It is as if a dramatist should give a performance on the stage of such scraps of dialogue, suggestions of situations as had occurred to him while pondering construction of a play, or as if a musician should invite people to listen to crude and disconnected scraps of composition.

But it is not art, says Smith, it is primeval chaos without form and void.

To the spectator it appears grotesque and meaningless...Of the 180 exhibits catalogued, something like four-fifths are a pain to the eye. Some of them look like faded pictures seen through several mediums of thick gauze; others suggest that a paint box has been accidentally upset over a panel nine inches by five; others resemble the first essays of a small boy.

To sum up, Mr Smith says the exhibition leaves...

...a painful feeling behind it, and causes one to despond with respect to the future of art in this colony, did we not believe with Mr W.P. Frith, R.A., that 'impressionism is a craze of such ephemeral character as to be unworthy of serious attention.'

The impressionists have fought back bravely. They pasted Mr. Smith's critique on a board outside Buxton's gallery in Swanston Street. This inspires some people to pay the sixpence to go in. Society ladies say to each other: 'Have you seen the Impressionists' exhibition? Do go, it's so funny'.

But the impressionists have one champion, Mr Edward A. Vidler of *Table Talk*. He says the Impressionists are a much abused group and many Victorian artists are holding 'coldly aloof'. Particularly he likes Arthur Streeton. He is only 22, a protege of Fred McCubbin, and an artist with a remarkable future.

Indeed, according to Mr Vidler, there had never been an exhibition like it in Melbourne. Mr Cullis Hill very kindly supplied the furnishings at Buxton's. He put drapings of soft Liberty silk of many delicate colours on the walls, so that they were knotted and drawn tastfully around the paintings. He also had Japanese umbrellas, screens and some handsome jardinieres to complete the scene. There is a piano for recitals on Wednesdays.

He said James Smith arrived at the exhibition, began taking notes, and his opening salutation to Mr Tom Roberts was 'More eccentricities?' Mr Alex Gustafson, the well-known temperance advocate and social reformer, was also there. According to Vidler 'He took a lively pleasure in sneering at anything and everything remarking that if his little boy of five could not do better than that he would hang him'.

Mr Vidler said Messrs Roberts, Conder and Streeton had to call upon all their philosophy to bear the abuse which they received. Yet most of the pictures sold. Streetons and Conders went for one to five guineas, and Tom Roberts's paintings were available for one to nine guineas.

'*Tom Roberts*' by
Charles Conder

Taking Over the Banks

19 AUGUST 1947

Mr Chifley's plan is thwarted

Two days ago Mr Chifley announced that his Government intended to nationalise the banks. The legislation is expected to go through before Christmas.

If Mr Chifley had said that Mr Stalin was coming here on a State visit and would stay at Yarralumla, he could not have caused a greater shock.

Every newspaper in the nation is pounding him with merciless editorials and it not easy to find the arguments for why he is doing this thing.

We have been told by finance editors that the cost of taking over the banks will be between 70 and 1000 million pounds, and this will be the ultimate control of you and me. Now we have the choice of nine private bank systems. If one knocks back your housing loan, there are eight others waiting in the queue with a kindly hand outstretched. But when nationalisation comes there will be just one 'Big Brother' and when he knocks back your loan, you're done.

Just look at the comments. Mr Playford, Premier of South Austalia: 'It is nothing less than sheer madness. I know of nothing more likely to destroy the confidence of the people.'

Mr Menzies, Leader of the Opposition: The time has come for Australians to defend their freedoms against dictatorship at home. This is the most spectacular move towards complete socialisation ever made in an English-speaking country. For any parallel we must go to Soviet Russia. The proposal represents a step towards complete bureaucracy with the Government in a position to give orders on all of their financial and business activities, great and small.

Mr Fadden, Country Party Leader: Nationalisation of banks will make black markets an Australian institution. By its latest revolutinary and scandalous move the Chifley Government has furthered its plan to convert Australia into a socialist State.

The newspapers are saying that the legislation has come about through a fit of pique of Mr Chifley's. Two days before Mr Chifley made his announcement, the High Court declared illegal a move by the Federal Government to obtain a monopoly of State Government and municipal banking business. The Government ruled that under the Banking Act it would compulsorily transfer all accounts of government and semi-governmental bodies from private banks to the Commonwealth Bank. The High Court rejected it under Section 48 of the Act.

But what happens now? The banks are claiming there will be the longest and most protracted legal battle in the nation's history. Mr Geoffrey Sawer, Professor of Law at Melbourne University, thinks the Government can do it. He says 'The Government has the prima facie power to nationalise banking. It is difficult to see any prohibition which can stop them. Counsel for both sides will undoubtedly think up various arguments. I think the Goverment's chances are at least four to one on'.

Mr Monk, the President of the ACTU, and Mr Cosgrove Premier of Tasmania, are among the few voices the *Melbourne Sun* quotes as being in favour of the legislation. They point out that it will help the Government control prices, keep down the cost of living and boost production in this difficult post-war period.

But the conservative forces are very nervous. The All-Australia Trade Union Congress meets in Melbourne on 1 September. There is a motion by the Sheet Metal Workers and the Agricultural Implement Makers for the Government to nationalise all key industries, not just banking, but transport, steel, coal and building.

Note: The High Court found vital sections of the Banking Act of 1947 went beyond the constitutional power of the Commonwealth and it was upheld by the Privy Council in 1949.

Harbour Span is Complete

22 AUGUST 1930

Sydney has been watching a great visual drama for months.

The two enormous spans of the Harbour Bridge have edged closer and closer together. There were sceptics aplenty. Many thought the whole structure would collapse and fall into the water. Many thought as an engineering feat it was impossible. How could they judge the construction of those two arms so exactly that they would meet, bolt for bolt, high above Sydney Harbour.

Well, they have done it. The span now is one perfect arc; two flags are flying from the creeper crane 500 feet above, proclaiming to the world that the arch of the Sydney Harbour Bridge has been joined.

There is a feeling of joy and triumph right throughout the city. The *Sydney Morning Herald* says: 'The dream that Sydney had dreamed for nearly a hundred years is a reality of steel and concrete. Hurricanes may blow and prophets bite their nails. The arch is locked — the bridge will remain'.

For the past ten days, disturbed only by the vagaries of Sydney's temperature, the process of lowering the two halves of the arch slowly progressed.

On Monday the gap between the pilot pins on the south arm and the sockets into which they are now locked on the north side decreased from 11½ inches to 6 inches. Most of this contraction was caused by rising temperatures between 8 a.m. and 4 p.m. Although the controlling cables were still further released during the night, the cold night temperatures had made the gap 8 inches wide when dawn broke on Tuesday.

So all day there was the delicate, maddening, frustrating task of juggling these mighty arms into position. The sun was on one arm and the other was shaded, so there were different rates of metal expansion.

At one moment the alignment would be correct, a quarter of an hour later there would be an error. The *Herald* reported:

Sweating in brilliant sunshine far above scudding ferry boats, men heaved their gigantic tackle, strained and thrust, and heaved again. Slowly the steel yielded to their will, and the two half-arches were in horizontal alignment. Quick-footed they made good their work with temporary clamps.

However through the night the metal contracted again and it was impossible to keep the arms together. The battle dragged on and on. Under the glare of arc lights, whistle shrilling, and telephones ringing until towards midnight, the arms began to approach each other again.

In the early morning hours human patience won. The arms touched, the pins thrust firmly into their sockets and the terrific strain of all that steel rested no longer on the cables, but on the bearings that will hold its weight for all time.

Above the sleeping city the bridge builders smiled, shook hands and then went home to bed. The job was done.

The bridge will be finished in eight months, but there is no hope of it being opened then. There is the job of the access roads and the railway tracks, with absolutely no money to pay for them. You can bet nobody will drive across that Bridge at least until 1932. And when will we have finished paying for it?

That could be a sweet continuing job for the rest of the century.

Burke's Expedition Heads for the Great 'Incognita'

23 AUGUST 1860

Mr. Burke's vast expedition into the unknown is well past Essendon and moving towards Swan Hill.

Did you ever see such a cavalcade? There are six drays, there are innumerable horses, there are 27 camels led by sepoys, and countless followers on.

The departure took place on 20 August and, according to the *Age*, no occasion in this colony ever excited such interest and even the oldest inhabitants cannot remember the like.

Mr. Burke was meant to start off at 1 p.m., but over 15 000 people gathered in Royal Park. Every conceivable type of vehicle was on the road.

It has all been made possible because some anonymous benefactor has made a donation of 1000 pounds. As the *Herald* says, if that donor was present at the departure, his heart must have leapt with joy at the thorough way everything was prepared.

The *Herald* added: 'Every feeling of patriotism evoked from that vast concourse of people was as the wide-spreading flame communicated from the torch-like glow of public spirit first held out by the "unknown".'

The boots for the men, the harness, the saddlery and even the buckets were made by prisoners at Pentridge under the strictest of supervision. No eventuality has not been foreseen. The great wagons will convert to boats so that they can be floated across water. There are special air bags to lift the camels' heads when swimming. There is a hospital camel with special stretchers to carry the sick.

If any of the parties become separated, there is signal equipment: a Chinese gong, flares and rockets. There are two pairs of leather shoes for each camel when crossing rough territory.

There are leather bags for water, and enough food for a year. The expedition is taking a biscuit composed of flour and ground meat that has been carefully designed for this expedition. One biscuit is sufficient for an evening meal. Each man has a carbon filter kit for purifying water.

The tents are the finest we have seen. They

Cavalcade sets off for the unknown

are made of the best American drill and lined with green baize. It is easy to pick out the expedition members. They wear picturesque red shirts, cabbage tree hats and flannel trousers.

The crowd made things so difficult and the confusion was so great, things did not get under way until four o'clock. The Mayor of Melbourne, Dr. Eades, made a speech, 'May God speed you' he said. He called for three cheers for Mr. Burke, three cheers for Mr. Landells (the leader of the camels) and three cheers for the party.

So off they went with Mr. Burke out front riding his pretty little grey.

Now they are moving towards the great 'incognita' where even the Royal Society cannot help them. Who knows what they will find out there.

But the *Age* says wisely that one day, even on the placid waters of the Gulf of Carpenteria, we will see great cities. It will be the task of Melbourne 'the foremost emporium' to manufacture the needs of those people, not only for Asiatic consumers but for colonies of our own people.

The *Age* and everyone else is wishing the expedition a safe and triumphant return.

Deepening Depression

24 AUGUST 1930

Ever since that ugly day, 'Black Thursday', 24 October, when the American share market collapsed, we have sunk into a dreadful depression.

Why it had to hit us so quickly is hard to understand. Wool, which used to sell for a marvelous 7s 6d a pound, has fallen to about ninepence. Before the crash we received 5s 6d a bushel for wheat, now 2 shillings.

As for share prices they are cut to a third. Take Mt Lyell. Before, 42s 9d, now 17 shillings. Unemployment is rising to an awful 30 per cent. You can walk the streets 'til the soles of your boots are through and there is no hope of getting a job.

If you live in one of the nice suburbs it is hearthbreaking, for there are knocks on the door from good looking men, virtually begging. They will cut your lawn for the price of a cup of tea or a sandwich.

The basic wage has dropped to £4 8s, but this is a laugh. Men are being forced to tear up their union tickets. A farm labourer is lucky if he gets 32 shillings a week, and a shearer is paid 32 shillings a hundred.

There are two stories in yesterday's *Age* that tell it all.

Story 1: No one who did not work amongst the poor of Fitzroy knows what an appalling amount of distress existed there, said Deaconess Young of Fitzroy Presbyterian Missions Settlement, speaking at the Kew Ladies Benevolent Society yesterday. Fitzroy was the most densely populated area in Victoria and contained 400 people to the acre. Crowds of families lived each in one room, and there were four, five and six families living in one house. The extent of poverty and distress in Fitzroy was greater than it had ever been.

Story 2: There will be no sustenance given officially at Brunswick today, but the Unemployed Committee which has been collecting on its own account will distribute supplies from its own stock. As there will not be sufficient for all, lots will be drawn. The mayor, Cr Hudson, will purchase some vegetables and supplement the stock as far as possible. A football match will be played between Brunswick and Northcote sec-tions of unemployed on Brunswick oval on Tuesday on behalf of the unemployed fund.

So where do you live? How do you survive? In Melbourne there is an astonishing area, Dudley Flats, out near Footscray, a humpy town where squatters have built themselves a village of sheets of galvanized iron and hunks of wood. There are cafes in the city that serve a greasy three-course meal for sevenpence.

If you put an advertisement in the newspaper asking for a gardener, a nightwatchman, or a serving maid, you get five hundred replies and a 200-yard queue.

The *Sydney Morning Herald* says that begging has become a feature of city life. Begging is against the law, and you can get arrested for it, but at least in gaol you get supplied with a meal. Men use their children, push them forward. 'Can you spare a coin please, Sir? I have a sick mother.'

What is the Government doing? There are dole schemes for 5 shillings a day. The *Age* this week reports that Victoria's Forests Commission is establishing camps for 3000 men in 40 parts of the State.

So there is little cheerful news, but at least the young Don Bradman is showing those Englishmen a thing or two, and there is an astonishing horse called Phar Lap.

The unemployed depend on handouts

Amazon Brigade Marches in Support of Union

25 AUGUST 1892

Women assaulting a non-unionist

Broken Hill is in a state of undeclared war. It is eight weeks since the strike started and there have been some furious battles on the picket lines.

The NSW Government has sent in 80 police and another 100 metropolitan men are on standby in Sydney, ready, if need be, to leave by the 9 p.m mail train.

There was a marvellous scene yesterday, what they are now calling the march of the 'Amazon Brigade'. The women wanted to show without doubt they are backing their men. So there was a procession through the town of 1500 women.

The procession left the Mason Hotel at 3 p.m., marched down Argent Street, then back to the Reserve. It was accompanied by a brass band with Mr Sleath, the miners' leader, out front on horseback. There was a young woman looking very splendid also on a horse.

Others marched two deep, many of them carrying babies and children in their arms. Spectators cheered and waved. When they reached the Reserve, they were met by about 3000 men.

Mrs. Rookes addressed the meeting. She was glad so many women had stuck to their colours and shown their sympathy with the cause for which their husbands, sons, brothers or sweethearts were fighting by joining in the procession. The men who had stuck out against the contract system were true unionists for it had caused the breaking up of many a family. Whilst they could get a cup of tea and a crust of bread, she hoped the men and women alike would stand out, so that in future their children might be able to boast that their parents had won the privileges they would then enjoy.

Yes, the strike is over the competitive contract system. The mines offer contracts to men at competitive rates then when the work is done they dispense with them until they are ready to hire again. The managers claim their rates up to 15 shillings a day are the best in the world, but the men want a guaranteed wage.

The mine onwers say 135 men have gone back to work. The miners say this is fiction. The number is no more than 33, and anyone who tries to get through the picket line strikes real trouble.

Yesterday William Glasson, a shift boss at the Proprietary mine, tried to get through and he was attacked by a howling crowd. He took to his heels down Argent Street South and was pursued by 300 hooting men and women. He took refuge in a furniture shop and there they threw old boots and stones at him.

The police rescued Glasson then arrested two of the miners, Francis Cox and Edward Keogh. They went before a very unsympathetic magistrate who sentenced them to three months jail with hard labour.

Another man, O.P. Johnson, a smelter boss, tried to get through. The mob chased him, punched and pummelled him until the poor fellow collapsed under a tree and fainted clear away.

The manager of the Proprietary Company, Mr. Howell, has written a letter to the *Silver Age*, condemning the strike, the fearful acts of violence, the desperate unlawful behaviour and the unjustified strike taken at a time when silver and lead prices have dropped to their lowest ever.

He suggests that these 'mad attempts to force their ideas of modern unionism' have come from America.

Whatever happens, unionism will not go away and Broken Hill will not be the same after this.

Reprisal Killings in Coorong

26 AUGUST 1840

By now you will have heard of the horrible fate of the brig *Maria*.

She set out from Port Adelaide on 7 June for Hobart Town. Aboard were Mr and Mrs Denham with their three boys and two girls, Thomas Daniel and his wife, Mrs York with her baby, and along with the crew, altogether, 26 souls.

On 26 July a message arrived from Encounter Bay that the *Maria* had been wrecked, 19 miles south-east of the Goolwa. A search party looking for survivors found the terribly mangled bodies of adults and children half hidden in the sun dunes. There were no survivors, the slaughter was complete.

Clearly Aboriginal tribesmen were responsible for this. His Excellency the Governor, George Gawler, ordered Major O'Halloran, Chief of Police, to find the blacks responsible for the murder; move the whole tribe to the scene of the crime; explain to them the reason, then deliberately and formally execute by shooting or hanging not more than two of the convicted murderers.

O'Halloran and his deputy, Inspector Alexander Tolmer, set out for the lonely beaches of the Coorong and found members of the Big Murray tribe. Tolmer reported that without exception they all wore European clothing, some of them stained with blood, and there were women's shifts that had spear holes about the breast.

After much questioning the tribesmen pushed forward two men whom they said had done the murdering. The troopers built some gallows of sheoak, which they erected over the graves of the *Maria* passengers.

All the prisoners, men women and children, formed a semicircle in front of the gallows. There was not a word or whisper from the condemned men, Mongarawata and Pilgarie. The troopers put nooses around the necks of the two Aborigines and stood them on boxes.

The crude method was to kick away the boxes, but according to Tolmer the drop was insufficient. So there was a dreadful scene with men still dangling, half-choking, toes touching the sand and their eyes glaring up at the cross beam. The Major sat on his horse paralysed, not knowing what to do. A seaman stepped

Governor Gawler

forward and said 'I beg your pardon Major, but I'll soon hang them if you will let me.'

'Do Barber, anything, but be quick.' This time they used the cross beam of the whale boat. Barber said 'Now Major when you drop your handkerchief, we'll let go.' 'Thus,' said Tolmer 'they were launched efficiently into eternity'.

Major O'Halloran, just to complete the lesson, made this announcement to the presumably incomprehending Murray tribe. He began:

Black men, this is the white's punishment for murder, the next time white men are killed in this country more punishment will be given. Let none of you take these bodies down, they must hang until they fall to pieces. We are now friends and will remain so unless more white people are killed, when the Governor will send me and plenty more policeman and punish much more severly.

However not everybody is happy about the execution. There is considerable fury and controversy in the pages of the *Adelaide Register*.

Football Kicks Off

29 AUGUST 1858

Football, an exicting free-for-all

Cricket dominates but there is a strong desire to play football in the colony.

Well, young Tom Wills, aged 23, is now Secretary of the Melbourne Cricket Club. As you know, five years ago the Government gave the club a grant of 10 acres in the Richmond Paddock.

It has come along rather well. There is a nice little club house and the Band of the 40th Regiment plays there on Saturday afternoons. So far we have had two intercolonial matches against New South Wales.

The New South Welshmen were an unkempt, rough looking lot. They did not have proper cricket gear, just drill pants, guernseys and caps, and one asks you to believe they played in bare feet or socks. Regrettably they won both matches.

Young Wills, Victoria's captain, was very lucky. His father sent him off to England where he went to Rugby school and now he has come back with all sorts of ideas.

On 10 July he wrote a letter to our sporting journal *Bell's Life*, suggesting that the MCC should form a football club to keep the players fit during the winter.

There was a match on 31 July out in the Richmond Paddock. One of the MCC cricketers, Jerry Bryant, provided the ball. Pretty chaotic, it was with parctically no rules at all. Wills wants his cricketers to survive for the summer, so he is looking for a game that does not have the hacking and savage tackling that he remembers at Rugby.

On 7 August the *Herald* announced that a Grand Football Match between Scotch College and the Church of England Grammar School would be played near the MCG, commencing at noon with an interval for lunch.

It was decided to play 40 a side, and masters would be included as well as boys. The first team to kick two goals would be the winner. But with 80 men, and the goal posts nearly half a mile apart, scoring was very difficult. It took Scotch nearly three hours to score, then Melbourne Grammar promptly returned the compliment.

By this time it was nearly dark and everyone was exhausted. They decided to complete the match the following week. The *Herald* reports:

As on the former occasion, a great number of visitors were there, some amateurs of the game, and others attracted by the novelty of the sport. A most excellently contested game was played, and for some hours the balance of victory inclined first one way then the other. When time was called no goal had been kicked.

So they called it a day again. Meanwhile the MCC members had a game on the cricket ground which resulted in a triumph for Mr Bryant's side. The *Herald* comments: 'The game of football promises, as it deserves, to be one of the popular amusements of the ingenuous youth of Victoria'.

But what about the ingenuous boys of Scotch and Melbourne Grammar? They intend to make another attempt to finish their marathon football match on Saturday, 4 September.

Note: There was still no score in the third attempt and 'two young gentlemen were wounded but not seriously'.

Further reading: *Running with the Ball*, A. Mancini and G.M. Hibbins.

Intercolonial Exhibition Marks Centenary

30 AUGUST 1870

The exhibition building

The great Intercolonial Exhibition to celebrate the centenary of the landing of Captain Cook has opened in Sydney.

The wonders of this exhibition are quite incredible. As the *Sydney Morning Herald* says today:

No man can travel through the history of inventions, or look at the patent office of England or America, without amazement at the ingenuity of man...When Cook landed 100 years back on these shores, the vessels which he commanded were mere boats compared with the mighty ships of war and commerce existing now.

A splendid exhibition building, the main hall 198 feet long and 130 feet wide, has been erected in Prince Alfred Park in Castlereagh Street. There are three triumphal arches.

However the *Herald* reporter is tremendously intrigued by the ingenious gates. They take a note every time they are opened, and furnish the propietor with an exact record with 'unimpeachable veracity' of the number of persons who pass through.

In the centre of the building there is a large fountain whose jets rise even above the level of the gallery. There is a maze of glass cases filled with all the latest in silverplate wear, furniture, arts works, busts of Captain Cook, Sir Charles Fitzroy, Sir Thomas Brisbane and others.

From the roof hang four beautifully-constructed baskets of evergreens, and down one end is a huge pagoda, set on eight pillars with walls of plate glass and filled with wax figures clad in silks, velvets and other finery. It is too big for the building, overshadows the other exhibits, and the *Herald* suggests, rather vulgar.

However you should see the modern machinery, the omnibuses, carriages, buggies, fire engines, railway carriages, pumps, ironmongery, sewing machines and all kinds of fascinating working models.

The star of the exhibition is a great credit to Mr G.E. Dalrymple of Brisbane. He is exhibiting Thomson's road traction engine, 'Pioneer', a device admirably suited for haulage on common roads. It is 8 horsepower and weighs 6½ tons.

Mr Dalrymple had it under steam today and it created great interest. It is the first of its type seen in the colony. You would not say much for its beauty, but similar engines have done remarkable things in England and Scotland. At a recent exhibition for the Royal Agricutural Society, a Thomson road steamer pulled two Fowler double-furrow ploughs, making four wide, deep furrows with amazing ease.

It also pulled four huge wagons of pigiron, 35 tons in all, up a very steep incline. It uses quarter of a ton of coal a day and there is no question that the contrast between such a machine and the common plough horse is remarkable.

There are so many other things to see: rifles, shot guns, military cannon, some excellent billiard tables provided by Messrs Alcock and Company of Melbourne. One table is made of New South Wales tulip wood, a bed of Victorian slate, and exquisite cue rack elaborately worked with spiral turnings for pillars.

The 'Countess of Belmore' sewing chair and couch, named in honour of the Governor's lady, was also much admired. A huge crowd of over 5000 went through in the early afternoon.

Fleet Misses the Party

31 AUGUST 1908

The Great White Fleet is visiting us, 16 American battleships under the command of Admiral Sperry.

It is the biggest thing that has ever happened to Melbourne and the town is bursting with people. Any person that owns a roof is accommodating three extra people.

The decorations and illuminations are beautiful beyond belief. There are six curtain arches across Elizabeth Street. By Flinders Street Station there is a superb arch with an illuminated canvas depicting the battleships. The public buildings are ablaze with 60 000 incandescent bulbs. Commonwealth Parliament has a great electric sign: 'AUSTRALIA WELCOMES AMERICA'.

Melbourne believes it is handling matters rather better than Sydney, which had the fleet last week. Melbourne *Punch* points out that Sydney did not always do the right thing. It was shameful, the number of people who had stolen the Admiral's spoons for mementos, and this was done not by the 'ignorant, untrained poor, who are not taught the nicer points of moral conduct, but by the upper crust, representatives of the best families'.

The sight of 16 white battleships sailing through the Heads all in line was an unforgettable experience. The grandest of them all was USS *Connecticut*, 16 000 tons, 74 guns, 18.8 knots, 41 officers and 815 men.

Today there was a 6-mile march by the US sailors through the city. People sat up all night to get positions. Melbourne's population is just over 500 000, but the railways reported they carried over 400 000 to town. So many people fainted in the crush, the Army brought in 200 doctors from the medical corps. There were 155 cases at the Town Hall. Why, 17 ladies even had to be stretched out in the bars at the Port Phillip Hotel.

But of all events, the most memorable was the party for the petty officers and ratings thrown by the Commonwealth Government at the Exhibition Building. A staff of 130 worked all Wednesday night and all Thursday to get ready. At 7 p.m. the tables were set and 200 dozen bottles of beer were already opened. The host, the Prime Minister, Mr Deakin, was standing by the door.

Admiral Sperry: Fleet Commander

At 7.30 p.m. all the tables were still empty and the PM was sitting down gloomily reading the newspapers. There had been a muck up, someone had confused the nights. Then suddenly there was good news. One American sailor, plump and young was outside, too frightened to come in. Smartly he was advised that the Prime Minister of the Commonwealth, 2500 diners, and a demonstration by the Metropolitan Fire Brigade were waiting for him inside.

'Guess not' said he. 'I'd have to respond, never was an orator.' The *Argus* man interviewed the sailor, who said 'Look, I just come up here to meet a shipmate. We don't want food, see. Food's cheap. Tell y'what. Them boys is walkin' the girls round town'.

That was the end. Mr Deakin, taking it well, went home. Then the Army, the Fire Brigade, and all available police were called in to clean up the food and beer. One man, said the *Argus*, had six feeds.

SEPTEMBER

HMAS *Sydney*

Who is the Pyjama Girl?

1 SEPTEMBER 1934

A deep mystery surrounds the discovery of a pretty blonde girl discovered in a culvert, four and a half miles west of Albury.

The girl wore no jewellery and was clothed in expensive canary-coloured Canton crepe pyjamas. The body is terribly battered around the head. There had been an attempt to burn it and the remains were pushed into a culvert.

There is one clue that the police believe will help them to solve the crime within 48 hours. There was a blood-stained towel with the laundry mark either R.I.W. or R.I.N, which was tied around her head.

The body was found at 9 a.m. by Thomas Hunter Griffith, son of Mr and Mrs Griffith of Delaware Station. Griffith was leading a footsore bull on the grass when he noticed something protruding from a barrel drain under a culvert.

'I thought it looked like a body but imagined I just have been dreaming', he said today. 'When I looked closer I could see that it was the body of a girl. The legs were bent and were inside the pipe, but the upper part was lying in water just outside the mouth of the pipe. The head was covered by a portion of a sack.'

Griffith immediately hurried to his home and notified Albury police. They found kerosene had been used to burn the body and the legs were charred.

The victim is aged between 20 and 30, 5 feet 2 inches in height, slim build, blue-grey eyes, blonde — might be peroxided — bobbed hair, darker at the roots, neck shaved, plucked eyebrows, pink-lacquered finger nails.

Probably the murderer dumped the girl around midnight five days ago, because the police found stocks of unused kerosene and the attempts to burn the body were not very successful. It rained heavily on Tuesday night.

The police are taking the unusual precaution of keeping the body packed in ice, and already hundreds of people have been through in the hope of identifying her. There are no girls missing in the Albury area so the police believe the girl was brought here, possibly from Sydney. Russell Street police believe it most unlikely she came from Melbourne. They have checked all their records and none fit this girl's description.

Note: The body, that of Linda Agostini, developed into one of the great Australian legends. For ten years the body lay in a formalin bath at Sydney University, while at least 18 different women were 'positively identified' as the Pyjama Girl. The spot where her body was found became a favourite spot for sightseers from Albury.

In 1944 the body finally was identified by a dentist, through her teeth, and her husband, Antonio Agostini, was arrested soon afterwards. He had battered her to death in a house in Carlton. Incredibly Agostini had been a waiter at Romano's restaurant, where the NSW Commisioner of Police habitually dined.

The jury convicted Agostini of manslaughter. The judge thought the verdict was 'merciful' and sentenced him to six years hard labour. On release he was deported back to Italy.

Further reading: *The Pyjama Girl*, Robert Coleman.

Choosing a Federal Flag

2 SEPTEMBER 1902

The Australian flag

We have a 'Federal Flag' The flag chosen has a blue background, upon which the Union Jack occupies the place of honour in the left corner. Immediately under the 'Jack' is the 'Star of Australia' with six points symbolic of the six States of the union. To the right is the Southern Cross.

The struggle for a flag has been going on for a decade. In 1893 the Australian Federation League had a bright idea. The League had the slogan 'One People...One Destiny...One Flag'.

The flag had a Union Jack in the corner, a pale blue cross on a white background, and five stars, one at the end of each arm and one in the centre. A very nice flag, but it never got anywhere.

Then in 1900 the *Melbourne Herald* ran a competition. The winner was Mr F. Thompson, a Melbourne book seller. His flag had the Union Jack in the corner. Underneath were six horizontal stripes, a stripe for each State. Then the other half was given over to the Southern Cross.

It did look rather crowded and the new Commonwealth did not rush to adopt the *Herald* design. Last year the Australian Government joined with the magazine *Review of Reviews* to run another competition.

There was £200 in prize money. *Review of Reviews* put up £75, the Government gave £75 and £50 came from the Havelock tobacco company. It was amazing. There were 32 823 entries, and they came from all over the world, Australia, New Zealand, Canada, England, USA, Malta, India, China and even the Shetland Islands.

Yesterday we had the grand opening of the Commonwealth Flag Exhibition by the Countess of Hopetoun, the wife of the Governor-General. She was greeted by the Prime Minister, Mr Barton, and Mr Drake, the Postmaster General.

Then the winning design, a huge 'Blue Ensign' carrying the Southern Cross was run up the flagstaff on the Exhibition's great dome, and out it streamed in the southerley breeze, as the *Herald* said, 'a brave and inspiring picture'.

The 'polychromatic spectacle' inside was dazzling. There was every conceivable design: flags that carried wombats, emus, possums, kangaroos, wattle, banksias, gum trees, Aboriginals, shields, spears, maps, coloured jars, stars, letters, ships, explorers, bales of wool, gold...

The winning design, however, came quite independently, from five different competitors and they will share the prize: Mr Ivor Evans, a tent maker of Melbourne; Mr John Hawkins of Sydney; Mr William Stevens of Auckland, New Zealand; Mr E.J. Nuttall, of Prahran, Melbourne; and Mrs Annie Dorrington of Perth.

The judges felt that the Southern Cross in the 'fly' was indicative of the sentiment of the Australian nation. The combination with the Union Jack was easily distinguished as a signal of distress and should be agreeable to the 'home authorities'.

However the *Herald* is most put out. It says comparisons are being made between the winning design and the *Herald* design, with the stripes. 'We venture to say that the majority of opinions expressed are in favour of the *Herald* design, which is not only thoroughly distinctive, but is beautiful in conception.

The *Herald* adds that one of their 'contemporaries' had criticised their flag for being American. 'We may be permitted to point out' added the *Herald* 'the stipes were a feature of the old East Indian Flag, which was in existence long before the Americans adopted the idea'.

Note: In 1903 King Edward VII approved the winning design. In 1909 an extra point was added to the Commonwealth star to symbolise Papua, New Guinea.

Supporters Incensed at Coleman Suspension

5 SEPTEMBER 1951

It is impossible to underestimate the grief that has swept over Melbourne. John Coleman, the champion Essendon full forward has been suspended for four weeks and will not play in the finals. Flags are at half-mast in Essendon. With Coleman they were bound to win the flag. Without, the chances are slim indeed. Geelong or Collingwood becomes the favourite.

There was an unbelievable scene at Harrison House last night where the VFL has its tribunal. There were two players involved. Harry Caspar of Carlton, who was charged with striking, and Coleman, who was charged with retaliating. Both players received the same suspension.

When Coleman heard the verdict he swayed, sank into a chair and burst into tears. He spent 20 minutes in an ante room in a state of emotional distress. Outside there was a wild crowd of supporters, shouting and screaming. Caspar was first out. They shrieked abuse at him.

Coleman was helped from the rooms by Essendon officials. Men and girls rushed forward to try to shake his hands and hug him. Coleman kept his head down and two friends who were supporting him tried to ward off the crowd.

As they tried to put him into a car, the crowd pushed against them. They staggered and Coleman was hurled against an SEC control box. He struck his head and fell semi-conscious to the footpath.

According to the *Argus* one section of the crowd cheered. There were fights, boos, and cheering. Ted Waterford, an Essendon official, managed to get Coleman into the car, where he sat motionless on the seat with his head covered.

It has been ugly right through. Jack Cannon of the *Argus* reported in Saturday's match, whenever Coleman went near the ball during the third quarter, Carlton supporters yelled 'Pull your head in you mug. Let's see you beat the tribunal this time'. After he had been awarded a free kick, a soft drink bottle was thrown at him and he was lucky to escape head injury.

When Coleman left the field, his right eye was buised and blood shot, but he played his usual superlative football taking marks as if gravity had no meaning. His tally for the game was seven goals.

Of course, the anger out at Essendon, has reached the point of mutiny. The Essendon Mayor, Cr H.J.P. Lyttle, has denounced the Tribunal's decision. The *Argus* quotes Mrs Ada Dalton, 68: 'My husband and I were frightfully upset to read the news. The lad next door was so mad he couldn't go to work to face his mates. John Coleman is only a boy, and he's such a gentlemen. Four weeks was too much'.

The *Argus* agrees. In a leading article it says it was wrong for Coleman to retaliate against Caspar, but there was a principle of justice here. Why give both men the same sentence when Caspar struck the first blow?

The *Argus* could find only one man in Essendon who was not disturbed, Tom Bence the butcher. He said 'First thing this morning I bought a lovely handkerchief. There's someone in this town who seems to need it'.

That someone has announced he may not play football again. If that happened it would indeed be a tragedy.

Coleman in action

Magnificent Funeral for Pauper Poet

6 SEPTEMBER 1922

Henry Lawson, aged just 55, has been buried. He died on 2 August. Late at night he walked out into the backyard of his house in Abbotsford, Sydney, and had a cerebral haemorrhage.

He was wearing only a singlet

He went out as he should have done, with a magnificent funeral. There was a service at St. Andrew's Cathedral and the splendid building was filled to overflowing. All the great people were there, the Prime Minister, Mr Hughes; the Treasurer, Mr Bruce; ministers like Mr Lamond, Sir Granville Ryrie and Sir Robert Garran, the Commonwealth Solicitor-General. So, too, was the Chief Justice of New South Wales, Sir William Cullen.

The Prime Minister, Mr Hughes, said it had been his privelege to know him. Lawson intimately knew the real Australia and was its greatest minstrel. He was the poet of Australia.

Archdeacon Darcy Irvine put him on a level with Kendall as the most widely known of Australian poets. Australia had only a population of five million, he said, but when we had 50 or 60 million, the human note of Henry Lawson still would be heard in the land.

Having reported all that, it is fair to ask why they allowd him to die in misery and poverty.

Henry Lawson

The *Sydney Morning Herald* ran a magnificent obituary. It reported how he was born in a tent near Grenfell on 17 June 1867. His father was a Norwegian sailor, Peter Hertsberg Larsen. His mother, Louisa, was a remarkable woman who played 'a conspicuous part in public affairs', but the *Herald* did not add that she, too, was a remarkable poet.

Lawson, said the *Herald*, suffered from a serious hearing defect, was raised in very poor circumstances and had only a meagre education. As a young man he worked at all sorts of labourng jobs. At one time he tried clerical work, but was a hopeless failure and was chided for not being able to write a simple business letter.

He had days of poverty and depression. 'I knew what it was then' he wrote 'to turn out shivering at 4 o'clock in the morning and be one of a hungry group striking matches and running fingers down the wanted columns of the freshly printed *Herald*'.

One day, seized by a sudden impulse, he began to write, sent it to the *Bulletin* and saw his work, his first verse, 'Song of the Republic' printed in October 1887. This was the start and soon his work was celebrated, known all over the Commonwealth.

The *Herald* said 'for a long time his health had not been robust'. What an understatement. His situation had been desperate. He had been an alcoholic virtually since 1902. He had been sent to Darlinghurst Jail on many occasions for failing to pay maintenance for his wife and children. Several times he was in a mental hospital.

In 1920 he was granted a Commonwealth Literary Pension of one pound a week. It did not come faintly near solving his problems or paying his debts.

Friends tried to send him off on holidays to places like Mallacoota, but it was too late. There were attempts to have the pension increased but, according to one report, this was opposed by his 'friend' the Prime Minister who did not want to spend the taxpayers' money on 'slaking the thirst of a drunkard'.

Further reading: *In Search of Henry Lawson*, Manning Clark.

Great Benefactor and Courageous Idealist Dies

7 SEPTEMBER 1934

One wonders whether there has ever been a funeral in Melbourne like the one we had today.

Sidney Myer, aged only 56, had been complaining about a tightness in the chest and he went to see his masseur. He had only recently returned from a business trip to the United States. On 5 September he left his house in Clendon Road, Toorak, at 9.30 a.m., lit a cigarette and went for a short walk around the block. The chauffeur was to follow him with the car.

He had gone just 100 yards down Woorigoleen Road when a street gardener saw him fall. His death was instantaneous. The ambulance that arrived was one he gave recently to the Victorian Civil Ambulance, just part of the £100 000 he has given to various public benefactions.

Mrs Myer and the children were on holiday at Sorrento. Dr Tonkin, a friend of the family, drove there to break the tragic news.

The public display of grief today has been amazing. At least 50 000 people lined the route from Toorak to the cemetery at Box Hill. There were more cars than most people thought existed in Melbourne.

There were more than 200 vehicles in the funeral cortege alone, and floral tributes filled eight cars. Wreaths came in a seemingly endless procession, one could look at a magnificent tribute from Sir Macpherson Robertson or perhaps the simple little bouquet left by Harry, Mr Myer's chauffeur.

There were more than 300 wreaths altogether, from the Premier, Sir Stanley Argyle; Sir Frank and Lady Clarke; Mr Theodore Fink; Sir Harold Gengoult Smith; and there were others from an Afghan hawker, a Japanese trader, and a Chinese merchant.

For the first half-mile, the Fire Brigade Band with muffled drums led the cortege. Immediately behind the hearse, Harry, the chaufferur, drove Mr Myer's car without passengers. Toorak Road was lined with cars and thronged with people. Extra trams had to be put on to bring the crowds from the city.

The thousands of Myer Emporium emplo-

Mr Myer

yees were assembled in the cemetery to honour their late chief. Most of those who joined the funeral could not get near the grave side.

A heavy black rain-cloud hung overhead as the casket was taken from the hearse. The band and the Myer Emporium choir followed one another with verses of 'Nearer, My God, To Thee'. A sea of heads was bared and bowed.

From behind, a boy stepped forward with four little bunches of flowers. The boy was Kenneth Myer, Mr Myer's eldest son. He had picked them in his own garden and they were to express the sorrow of two young sons and two daughters.

The boy placed the flowers on top of the massive oak coffin and the procession wound slowly up the hill to the grave.

The Reverend Dr Law said: 'This demonstration today is almost historic. It speaks very eloquently of the intense regard Sidney Myer inspired in those people who were acquainted with him. We are celebrating the conclusion of a great life, one which showed what can be done by those who go forth with courageous ideals'.

The Last Tasmanian Tiger

8 SEPTEMBER 1936

The last Tasmanian tiger in captivity died yesterday.

The Beaumaris Zoo, which is owned by the Hobart City Council, obtained a Tasmanian tiger with three cubs in 1924. The mother died soon afterwards. The first cub went in April 1930 with kidney disease, the second in July 1935 of pneumonia, and this one has perished, presumably of old age.

The Zoo has been trying to get another. First it offered a prize of 15 pounds, then 25 pounds and now 30 pounds, but none are forthcoming. It is a long time since anyone even saw one to be shot. Mr Wolf Batty of Mawbanna in the north-west found this wolf-like creature with stripes on its back raiding his poultry shed back on 6 May 1930 and he blasted it with his shot gun, but they have not been seen since.

One doubts if there is much interest. Yet it is an extraordinary creature. The official name is thylacine cynocephalus, meaning pouched dog with a wolf head. It has a rigid tail that does not wag. The pouch of the female opens backwards, instead of forwards like the kangaroo. This gives it greater freedom when running in the bush. It does not bark like a dog, but gives a whine described as like the sharp creak of a door.

It is a sandy-yellow colour with 15 to 20 distinct transverse stripes along the back. The most remarkable feature is its extraordinary jaws. The tiger has a huge mouth. When it yawns the sides of the upper and lower jaws do the splits to 180 degrees. They can go straight through the bones of anything it catches. It is said that the thylacine's jaws are nine times stronger than those of a doberman. But there is no record of a tiger ever doing serious harm to a human.

It is uncertain when the thylacine came to Australia, but it would have been more than 20 000 years ago. Very likely the dingo killed them on the mainland, but they survived in Tasmania where the dingo did not exist.

They always inhabited the mountainous and more remote parts of Tasmania, but they were addictive killers of sheep. Some farmers claimed they were losing 20 per cent of their stock. In 1888 the Tasmanian Government introduced a bounty scheme, £1 for an adult, 10s for a pup. It was good money for the devoted hunter.

Between 1888 and 1912 the Government paid out 2184 bounties for slaughtered thylacines. They did not have to do it any longer. Thylacines were not there any more.

Yet even though it was obvious to all that the thylacine was now an extremely rare species, they were still being captured, if possible, for zoos. Some went off to London and elsewhere. A thylacine is a good exchange for a lion, an elephant or a polar bear.

Not a great deal has been done even to protect them. The Animals and Birds Protection Board has shown some interest. In 1930 it prohibited the hunting of thylacines during December, because that is supposed to be the breeding season.

Too little, too late. Many are wondering whether the thylacine will be seen again.

Further reading: *Thylacine: The Tragedy of the Tasmanian Tiger*, Eric R. Guiler.

The Tasmanian tiger

Revenge Killing of Barrister

9 SEPTEMBER 1834

William Charles Wentworth

The *Sydney Gazette* tells us today that it has the melancholy duty to report the murder of Dr Robert Wardell.

'Our community is sadly depraved' says the *Gazette* 'but the thirst for blood is not a prominent sin. Retribution must soon overtake the callous murderers'.

The Governor has offered the astonishing reward of £100 for information that will convict the unknown villains.

Wardell was 41 years old. His great friend, William Charles Wentworth, is in a state of terrible grief. They were at the Inner Temple together in London and came out on the same ship.

Wardell was educated at Trinity College and was a Doctor of Laws, so brilliant you wonder why he ever left England. He was the lawyer from the very beginning. As soon as he arrived in Sydney he sued the owner of the ship for putting him in a wet, cold, comfortless cabin, and for denying him sufficient nourishment and refreshments on the way out.

The court gave him £200 damages and £4 16s 2d costs.

He was slight of figure, thin-lipped with a superb Roman nose. He and Wentworth went into partnership and in 1824 they launched the *Australian* newspaper. Governor Brisbane was annoyed. He said nobody had sought his permission to publish.

The adventurous pair said the law did not require any permission and in its first issue announced:

A free press is the most legitimate and at the same time the most powerful weapon that can be employed to annihilate influence, frustrate the designs of tyranny and restrain the arm of oppression.

Sometimes his leading articles were as soothing as sulphuric acid, and in 1827 Governor Darling attempted to silence him by putting him on a charge of criminal libel, but the prosecuting counsel did not have a chance against the far too clever Messrs Wardell and Wentworth.

As a barrister Wardell made a lot of money, and unquestionably, a number of enemies. He had 2500 acres at Petersham and was worth 30 000 pounds. On Sunday, the day before yesterday, he left his house on horseback to inspect the estate.

He met, it is believed, a group of escaped convicts. A neighbour and some of his servants found Wardell lying on his back dead, with a terrible wound from a gunshot in the chest. But incredibly he had not been robbed. He was still carrying his watch and 8s 6d on his person.

Mr Wentworth, overcome with grief, personally has taken over all funeral arrangements.
Note: Two weeks later three convicts were arrested and charged with the murder, two of them, John Jenkins and Thomas Tatterdale were hanged. Jenkins had been seeking revenge against Wardell for a flogging. On the scaffold Jenkins said 'Goodbye, my lads, I shot the Doctor not for gain, but because he was a tyrant. If any of you take to the bush shoot every tyrant you come across'. He refused to shake hands with fellow convict Tatterdale. 'Let every villain' said he 'shake hands with himself'.
Further reading: *Australian Dictionary of Biography*.

War a Hindrance to Sport

12 SEPTEMBER 1917

Now the war is really getting serious. The Minister for Defence, Senator Pearce, has announced that we should cut down on sport.

Today he promulgates the new regulations for horse racing. The Senator recognises that because of the importance of horse breeding we must allow a 'reasonable' amount of horse racing.

If you look at our population, already we have more horse races than any humans on earth. Sydney topped everybody with 134 races a year, nigh on three a week. In the interest of beating the Kaiser, this now is cut to 97 a year.

Melbourne had 80 races a year. This now will be 78. Brisbane had an astonishing 136. The new figure is a huge slash, down to 64. Tasmania drops from 36 to 26. Adelaide is the same, 28, and Perth for some baffling reason goes from 74 to 76.

The whole war-time attitude to sport has been interesting. In 1915 the Government made a special recruiting drive amongst sportsmen. It raised a unit called the Sportsmen's 1000. There were posters everywhere, showing a digger, arm up high, calling on the footballers, crick-

eters, athletes, boxers, golfers to join him as a mate in the greatest sporting adventure of all — killing Germans.

The Victorian Football Association stopped play for the duration, but the League determined to continue. The *Argus* has been particularly bitter on the subject. Their sporting writer, 'Old Boy', says:

Which Game? War or football! Which will you play? Many hundreds have answered the question in the only way commensurate with loyalty to the nation. Those who have not evidently place their club first, and prefer the struggle for a premiership cap before the prospect of a military cross.

And speaking of the Australian Expeditionary Force, the *Argus* said:

They were the type of Australians that love adventure, that know no fear, that could not be mere spectators. For these men no circumstances were strong enough to make them stay at home. They wanted to have a first-hand knowledge of the war, to feel the thrill of battle, to play a part in history's greatest tragedy, to see the world and feel they were doing their duty. They represented the kind of man who wants to be in the game rather than have his excitement second-hand.

However the Victorian Football League does not consider warfare on the football ground as second-hand excitement. Its president, Mr O. Morrice Williams says 'Despite the distressing times through which we are passing, some degree of harmless and healthful recreation is beneficial to everyone'.

Senator Pearce says he does not consider it necessary to take any action against football at present. However, there is too much boxing. From now on we are allowed bouts of 20 rounds only once a fortnight. As for Vaudeville shows, which are all the go, half the show must be vaudeville or pictures, and boxing bouts must not be more than ten rounds. The maximum price of admission will be 2 shillings.

We do not know what would happen if the Germans invaded Australia on a Saturday. They would have to wait at least until 5:30 p.m. We could not handle them until after the final quarter.

JOIN TOGETHER
TRAIN TOGETHER
EMBARK TOGETHER
FIGHT TOGETHER

JT JACKA V.C

Enlist in the Sportsmen's Thousand

SHOW THE ENEMY WHAT

The call to arms

Australia's First Railway

13 SEPTEMBER 1854

*The Melbourne–
Sandridge train*

Yesterday was a most exciting day for the colony, the opening of the first Australian railway.

It is called the Melbourne and Hobson's Bay Railway and runs from Melbourne to Sandridge (Port Melbourne).

The *Argus* reports:

Long before the hour appointed for the starting of the train — twelve o'clock — a great crowd assembled round the station at the Melbourne terminus, lining the whole southern side of Flinders Street from the station towards the wharf.

There were two first-class carriages and one second-class, all handsomely painted and varnished, but it was the locomotive that took the eye. It is the first locomotive built, not merely in Victoria, but in the Southern Hemisphere. It is the work of Robertson, Martin, Smith and Company and was built in ten weeks. It has six wheels with a tubular boiler, and the tender is on the same body as the engine.

The engine is only 30 horsepower but, says the *Argus* admiringly, 'its power of traction is equal to 130 tons at a speed of 25 miles an hour'.

His Excellency Sir Charles Hotham, Acting Chief Justice Redmond Barry, the Colonial Secretary, the Attorney-General, the Surveyor-General, all the right people were there and enjoyed the first trip.

An open third-class carriage contained the band of the 40th Regiment. The *Argus* says:

The first train started at 20 minutes past twelve amid the music of the band and the cheering and waving of the innumerable spectators. Its progress was at an exceedingly slow pace until the bridge over the Yarra had been crossed and then it pro-

ceeded on to Sandridge at the rate of about 15 miles an hour...Two more passages were made by the train ere all the guests were at the scene of the banquet.

Now the banquet for 300 guests took place in the engine shed, which could only be described as an enormous hall of zinc, and quite splendid for the occasion. It was handsomely decorated with evergreens and flags. The *Argus* reported justice was done to the sumptuous viands, and although there were a great many speeches, one could not hear a word from one side of the hall to the other. Then every so often 'the iron horse' steamed past to the cheers of the assembly.

After the loyal toast to Her Majesty Queen Victoria, then to Prince Albert and the Royal Family, the playing of the 'Prince Albert March', and the toast to His Excellency the Lieutenant-Governor, some interesting things were said. Mr. Goodman MLC pointed out railways were more necessary in this colony even than in America, and the time was not far distant when there would be a line all the way to the goldfields. There were huge opportunities for a railway to Castlemaine.

Mr. Thorne said 500 men were now working on the Melbourne and Geelong Railway, and such progress had been made they were within three miles of Williamstown. He said somewhat acidly, Geelong in Melbourne, was an almost unknown province, and just to get to Melbourne he had to leave Geelong the previous day and it would take him another 24 hours to return. However he hoped he would be responding to the toast of a new railway within 18 months. We understand regular trains are now running today.

Stupendous Conflagration in City

14 SEPTEMBER 1889

The most disastrous fire in the history of Melbourne hit the city last night.

The magnificent retail emporium of George and George, plus the music warehouses of Allan's and Glen's are destroyed.

The evening exodus from the city had taken place, but an immense column of smoke climbed into the sky, and as the word 'Fire! Fire!' went from street to street, the exodus changed into a return rush, and train, tram, cab, cart, or gig, every possible vehicle was crowded with people anxious to have a view of what was obviously a 'stupendous conflagration'.

Twenty-six fire brigades fought the blaze, including the Carlton Brewery Brigade and the Port Melbourne and South Melbourne Volunteers Brigades. Superintendent Stein of the Insurance Brigade turned out with two of the very latest steam-operated fire engines, 'Lady Benjamins', which had never been used before.

The *Leader* reports:
It was 6:35 o'clock when fire began to break out in the Collins Street shop. With one tremendous leap the flames gained possession of the vast buildings, and in a moment the windows of the three upper storeys burst into a glow. The intensity of the heat was almost incredible. On the ground floor the heavy revolving shutters changed suddenly from black to vivid red, then peeled and curled into fantastic shapes. All at once with a report like thunder the roof crashed down on the fourth floor...The scene from Collins Street was one of terrific grandeur.

The Lady Benjamins lived up to their expectations and put out a wonderful stream of water, but as the *Leader* put it, the fire just laughed at their efforts.

Soon the crowd gathered by the thousand. It was like a football match and the collapse of a wall would receive cheers like the kicking of a goal. Boys had a beautiful time playing in the water.

All the balconies, verandas and windows of the banks, clubs and insurance offices were occupied, and they looked like seats at the opera. The Athenaeum Club, immediately opposite, had the prime viewing position. Members could watch the fire virtually over

The Premier, Mr Gillies

their brandy and cigars. One of the viewers was our Premier, Mr Duncan Gillies.

However they did not realise how ugly it was. The firemen were too eager. They had been warned of the dangers. The rear wall of the George and George building collapsed and men were buried deep underneath. The police dug out nine men and took them to the Melbourne Hospital. The worst injured was John McLeod, blacksmith of the South Melbourne Brigade. Dr. Thomas Fitzgerald operated to relieve pressure on the skull, but he died two hours later. He was 37, married with eight children.

Then just when the fire seemed over, the roof of Allan's warehouse collapsed. Two men of the Insurance Brigade, Thomas Laite and Edward Johnson, failed to answer. Their bodies were found, terribly burned.

Note: In 1891 the handsome Block Arcade replaced the burnt out George and Georges building. Georges Store, suffering from both fire and economic depression continued operations at 89 Collins Street East, between the Baptist Church and Scots Church. It took ten years to recover.

Navy Captures Rabaul

15 SEPTEMBER 1914

The Australian Navy has captured Rabaul, plus the wireless station at Herbetshohe, and German New Guinea is ours.

There was a short and fierce battle. We lost six killed and four wounded. The Germans lost one non-commissioned officer and 30 native soldiers killed. They had 11 wounded.

The war has just started. This is the first serious engagement that has involved Australian troops. One event was particularly tragic and heroic. The Australian vessels, *Sydney*, *Warrego* and *Yarra* were involved. Their instructions were to land men at Kabakaul and then seize the wireless station.

One of the volunteers was Captain Brian Pockley of the Australian Medical Corps, 24, very good looking, splendid all round athlete. He had just graduated from Sydney University. The volunteers struck resistance almost immediately and they captured a German Sergeant Major, whom they had shot through the right hand. The German was losing so much blood it was clear he was going to die. Pockley right there amputated his hand. The German accepted this with great courage showing no sign of pain.

Pockley had just finished amputating the Sergeant Major's hand when he heard Able Seaman Williams had been badly hit, shot through the stomach, the first Australian casualty of the war. He attended to Williams and asked Stoker Kember to carry him to safety. He took off his own Red Cross brassard and tied it round Kember's hat.

That action cost him his life. He went only ten paces down the road and he too was hit. Both Williams and Pockley died during the afternoon.

The resistance was sharp and bitter but it could have been much worse. The Australians managed to surprise the Germans. Instead of moving straight up the road, they fought their way through thick jungle and outflanked the German positions. Had the Australians gone straight up the road they would have been in disastrous trouble, because it was heavily mined all the way.

Everything was done with fascinating old world courtesy. Rear Admiral George Patey aboard HMAS *Australian* sent this letter to the German Governor:

Your Excellency,

I have the honour to inform you that I have arrived at Simpsonshafen with the intention of occupying Herbertshohe, Rabaul and the Island of New Britain. I will point out to Your Excellency that the force at my command is so large as to render useless any opposition on your part, and such resistance can only result in unnecessary bloodshed...

When the fighting was all over the Admiral finally received a letter from the Acting Governor, which began:

I have the honour to acknowledge the receipt of Your Excellency's letter of today. The administration of the German Protectorate devolves on His Majesty the Kaiser in the name of the Empire. In my capacity as Acting Governor, I have not the authority to surrender the Protectorates to Your Excellency.

By this time, 3 p.m. on 13 September, the British flag had been raised at Rabaul. All available troops were present, plus the band from HMAS *Australia*. The national anthem was sung, three cheers were given for King George V and the military occupation of the territory was formally proclaimed.

The proclamation was read in pidgin for the benefit of local inhabitants.

PROCLAMATION

All boys belongina one place, you savvy big master he come now, he new feller master, he strong feller too much, you look him, all ship stop place; he small feller ship belongina him. Plenty more big feller he stop place belongina him, now he come here take all place. He look out good you feller. Now he like you feller look out good alonga him...You look him new feller flag, you savvy him? He belonga British; he more better than other feller.

Collingwood Meets Melbourne and Supporters Go Beserk

16 SEPTEMBER 1956

Melbourne has a regrettable tendency to go beserk at this time of year and never before have we had quite such a build up as that for the Grand Final between Melbourne and Collingwood.

Mr. Lou Richards picked Collingwood to win by a narrow margin.

So what happened? The biggest crowd to attend an Australian football match — 115 802 — punched, clawed, elbowed and bit their way into the Melbourne Cricket Ground yesterday.

Even that figure could be an under-estimate, hundreds more climbed over closed barriers, and who knows how many dared death to get up on the grandstand roof.

The crisis came at 12:45 p.m. when attendants closed all gates, except those into the members' reserve. Several thousand disappointed fans prowled the walls trying to get in.

They struggled with police and attendants. They smashed windows to crawl through, they levered open unattended gates and they hurled abuse at members pushing their way in. The police rushed reinforcements to the MCG when the crowd threatened to use a battering ram, but hundreds dodged the cordon, broke into the MCG bowling green, climbed a high hedge, plus a wire fence, and got into the ground.

The *Sun* reports women and children were knocked down and trampled as the crowd charged the wooden gate behind the members' stand when attendants opened it slightly to allow through the Royal Melbourne Regiment Band.

Groups of disappointed fans 'commandeered' ladders and planks to scale the walls and a few were successful. Even team members had to elbow their way through the angry, barracking crowd at the gates.

The scene inside the ground was almost as bad. The great, heaving, jammed in crowd forced thousands on to the arena to escape being crushed against the pickets. The first over the fence was the signal for a mass rush on to the ground and the police were powerless to stop them.

So there they sat, and umpire Alan Nash had to stop play while the police moved the

Alan Nash halted the game

crowd behind the Jolimont goal. Clearly the ground was filled well over capacity and one wondered about safety and health regulations.

In one not very pretty scene, Collingwood fans released four magpies. Two escaped but the other two, with wings clipped, limped pathetically across the oval.

The chief executive officer of the Olympic Games Organising Committee, Sir William Bridgeford, says these wild scenes will not be repeated on the opening day of the Olympic games. He said 'We will have an army of ushers on duty and no-one without a ticket will be allowed into the ground'. However he was pleased at the smooth getaway of the 14 000 cars parked around the ground yesterday.

Just in case you were down a mine, at the South Pole or managed to remain asleep for 24 hours and did not hear the result, Melbourne thrashed Collingwood 121 points to 48. The stars for Melbourne were Spencer, Barassi, Mithen, Dixon, Melville, Beckwith, Adams, Bob Johnson and Denis Cordner.

Looking to the Lottery to Fill Government's Coffers

19 SEPTEMBER 1953

Only South Australia is purer than we are. Otherwise Victoria is the last into the lottery business.

Tasmania has had Tattersalls since 1897. Queensland discovered the joys of the Golden Casket in 1916.

Southern prelates were horrified by ads in Brisbane shops which said:

WE TURN JONAHS INTO OWNERS
INVEST A BOB AND CHUCK YOUR JOB
THE WAY TO EASY STREET

Jack Lang, back in 1931, thought it would be great to gamble his way out of bankcruptcy so he started a lottery with the promise that all the money would go into Consolidated revenue. He was the first to give gambling absolute State grandeur with the title, the New South Wales State Lottery. West Australia succumbed in 1932. Victoria has taken much longer in its journey to sin. If we wanted to sin we always had to sin by mail, sending for tickets in Sydney, Hobart or Brisbane. Why could we not sin more conveniently? The first move came at the Labor Party's Easter conference last year. It voted for a lottery and gave a clear mandate to the Premier, John Cain.

There was an outcry from the churches. The Reverend Crichton Barr at Scots Church said 'I have seen lotteries cause the most appaling domestic misery. A lottery is equal in potential ruin to persistent drunkenness. It is an appeal to naked greed'. The Reverend Archdeacon Schofield said 'It is the sin of Judas'.

Well, Mr Cain knew that half the money for every consultation in Hobart came from Victoria and he reasoned, what objection could there be if the consultations from now on took place in Melbourne instead of Tasmania. Instead of the profits going to the Tasmania Government, they could go to Victorian hospitals.

So without telling anyone, he slipped over to Hobart and had a talk to the trustees of the George Adams estate. It was a pleasant surprise. They were thinking along exactly the same lines. If Victoria went for a State lottery then they would lose half their business.

At 9 p.m. tonight Mr Cain called a press conference and announced that the Victorian Government would give Tattersalls an exclusive licence to set up in Victoria. The lottery would have to leave Hobart to do this, and it would mean a revenue to Victoria of up to £2 million a year.

The shock on both sides of Bass Strait has been profound. Dr Reverend Irving Benson says 'It will swell the tide of paganism'. Dr A.H. Wood: 'This is an astounding revelation of the level to which Australian politics are sinking. Mr. Cain's Government is riding over the opinions of the electors of his State who have not been consulted on this outrage'.

In Hobart the news that Tattersalls was leaving after 57 years caused unbelievable grief. It was contributing a quarter of the annual tax revenues.

The premier of Tasmania, Mr Cosgrove, said frigidly: 'Mr Cain has been most discourteous in this matter. I have had no indication from him and had no knowledge that negotiations were in progress'.

So what happens now? Apparently Tattersalls will fly over their two-ton bronze barrells, plus 200 000 marbles and there will be prosperity for Victoria ever after.

Mr Lang

Party Accord on Devaluation

20 SEPTEMBER 1949

Mr Chifley decided to devalue

The American dollar is the ultimate deity of the economic world. Everyone worships it.

Importers, Australians visiting the United States, have to apply for their dollars, and they are in desperate short supply.

Struggling nations in Europe are receiving their dollar hand-outs under the Marshall Plan, but all muscle comes from the U.S. and one wonders whether eventually the U.S. dollar will buy the entire world.

The rest of the world has re-acted. It has devalued. On 19 September Britain devalued the pound sterling from $4.03 to an astonishing $2.80; the Australian pound, in concert, dropped to $2.24.

But the most amazing thing it was all done in secret and all done at once right round the Commonwealth, South Africa, New Zealand, India, Ceylon, Canada, Eire, only Pakistan held out. Now 20 other nations have followed, including France.

Even the Commonwealth Bank did not know what was happening. The British Prime Minister, Mr Attlee, called our Prime Minister, Mr Chifley, and with Cabinet concurring, an instant decision was made.

The Stock Exchange in London and the Bourse in Paris were closed for a day. When they opened today there was absolute Pandemonium. Brokers fought and clamoured for gold shares. Some speculators who believed this had to happen, have made fortunes.

Those desperately unhappy are people who are travelling in Europe and have pound sterling travellers cheques. Now they have about 30 per cent less money. The British Government has given a blunt warning: 'Cut your holiday to the time you can afford'.

Of course, it means that everything imported from America is now more expensive, machinery, tobacco, movies, cars, publications... Petrol inevitably will go up 2d or 3d a gallon.

However we are on price control. The State Prices Decontrol Commissioner, says he does not expect any increases for two or three months. 'A serious view will be taken of sellers raising their own prices' he said. 'Any rise must be authorized by the Commission'.

But then you see our prices will be more competitive. Wool, wheat, hides, minerals, will all be more attractive to the dollar area.

Reaction in the United States is mixed. New York department stores never miss an opportunity. They are running 'devaluation sales'. Gimbels is running big advertisements announcing 'England devalues the pound. Gimbels passes the savings on to you'.

The New York *Journal American* has a headline today: 'Free Trade and Cut in Pound Costly to United States'. President Truman has just cut tariffs to the lowest level in 50 years. So commentators gloomily see a flood of imports and dollar goods being eliminated from sales in many areas of the world.

Interestingly enough, there has been all-party agreement in what Mr Chifley has done. The Leader of the Opposition, Mr. Menzies, thinks the devaluation was absolutely correct.

The conservative *Argus* also approves. It says:

> The supreme achievement has been that the British Commonwealth of Nations, for the first time in history, have acted as an economic unit that we may have a decisive effect on the world in which we live. It transcends the immediate problem of the pound and the dollar.

From Moscow comes the official comment, the Capitalist world, clearly, is on the point of collapse.

The Pilfering of Parks

21 SEPTEMBER 1862

It is really outrageous. The Government is stealing Melbourne's parkland for any project it wants here and there. The taking of public land is just too convenient.

The *Argus* particularly is upset. It says: We must contrive to save our metropolitan pleasure grounds from further spoilation. If Melbourne of the next generation is to inherit her present noble provision of parks and reserves it is time to rescue them from the process of curtailment and disfigurement.

There is hardly one of those reserves that has not suffered in this way. Richmond Paddock, indeed, as the most glaring instance, has been so broken up and encroached upon, that it may be fairly regarded as lost for the original purpose.

Then the *Argus* points out that Batman's Hill used to be a fine reserve. It was the only park available for the residents of West Melbourne. Look what has happened now. The Government has handed it over as a terminus for the railways.

Mr Duffy

The *Argus* thunders:
The public may well question the right to alienate any section of the park lands from their original objects, and they have also reason to complain of even the temporary use of portions of those lands being conceded unconditionally as is the case.

The newspaper explains that a lot of land is going for cricket grounds. True it is important that we should encourage athletic games and we don't want the sort of degeneracy which we hear has become so common in America, but they are putting up the most dreadful enclosures, often 'a hideous wall of stakes' and utterly disfiguring our parkland.

Why does man always have to disfigure? Indeed if a little bit of the original wilderness had been spared, and its main features kept intact, it would constitute a park for which the denizens of a great city would be much more grateful than for any established by man's contrivance.

Particularly disturbing is the proposed sale along St Kilda Road right in the very area of the newly designated Fawkner Park. There was a deputation on Thursday to the President of Lands, Mr Duffy. Unquestionably the idea of a sale caused 'alarm' and the deputation extracted a promise that the land would go only for private villa residences. Mr Duffy said Melbourne already had more parkland than any city in the world.

The *Argus* points out this is not true. We are at a disadvantage when compared with the great cities of Europe and America. All the modern portions of London, apart from extensive parks, are dotted over with squares and large gardens attached to public institutions. 'Melbourne is singular in being destitute of squares or other large open spaces. She has no lungs in the civic meaning of the phrase.'

The deputation complained particularly about Batman's Hill being 'surrendered' to the Railway Department, as this was the site of the first settlement of the city, and it also had the important advantage of being a hill.

The *Argus* just could not believe that the Government would persevere with the idea of giving Batman's Hill to the Railways.

Wireless Telegraphy will Bring us the News

22 SEPTEMBER 1918

The Prime Minister, Mr. Hughes, now in London, has actually spoken to Australia.

The *Sydney Morning Herald* reports:
By means of a delicate and highly scientific machine the first messages received direct from England by wireless telegraphy were recorded in Sydney yesterday.

The essential feature of the apparatus was the Fleming valve, an intensely sensitive instrument, originally invented by Dr. J.A. Fleming, a noted English scientist, and since developed in conjunction with Senatore Marconi and his experimental staff. Before the war Senatore Marconi proposed personally to visit Australia, and so adapt the apparatus. This was rendered impossible by the war, Mr. Ernest T. Fisk, managing director of the Amalgamated Wireless (Australiasia), undertook the task. The messages were despatched from the Marconi station at Carnarvon in Wales and received by Mr. Fisk on his experimental instruments at Wahroonga.

The Prime Minister sent his message:
I have just returned from a visit to the battlefields — where the glorious valour and dash of the Australian troops saved Amiens and forced back the legions of the enemy — filled with greater admiration than ever for these glorious men, and more convinced than ever that it is the duty of their fellow citizens to keep these magnificent battalions up to strength. — W.M. Hughes, Prime Minister.

Sir Joseph Cook replied:
Royal Australian Navy is magnificentlky bearing its part in the great struggle. Spirit of sailors and soldiers alike is beyond praise. Recent hard fighting brilliantly successful, but makes reinforcements imperative. Australia hardly realises the wonderful reputation which our men have won. Every effort being contantly made here to dispose of Australia's surplus products. — Joseph Cook, Minister for Navy.

The *Sydney Morning Herald*, in its leading article this morning, says the first direct wireless message from England to Australia is enormously interesting, but it is no secret that we have been using the wireless for some time.

Mr Fisk

Nightly we have been recording communiques from Berlin. Also the French Navy, which claims to have the most powerful wireless system in the world, has been sending messages to Australia.

Wireless indeed has played a part in the war. Submarines have used it to intercept and locate their victims. Distressed ships have used it when calling for assistance.

However wireless is particularly useful in areas where there are great stretches of desert and no intervening communication, like Mesopotamia and Palestine. There are instances where General Allenby found it to his advantage when co-operating with the Hedjas Arabs.

As the *Herald* says, a whole new era is opening. It is really only a life time since the establishment of the submarine cable. Before that all our news used to come by ship. Newspaper representatives used to meet the ships at the Sydney Heads, or at Queenscliff at the mouth of Port Phillip.

Then the newspapers had a desperate race from ship to office to be first into print with what had taken place in Europe six to eight weeks before. The full rate for cable messages now is 3s a word. Mr Fisk believes wireless will make all the difference and we will able to reduce this to 1s a word.

So there are two exciting things to look forward to with the arrival of peace — the commercial use of the aeroplane and wireless.

Two Women Elected to Federal Parliament

23 SEPTEMBER 1943

Senator Tangney   *Dame Enid Lyons*

Lord Gowrie opened Federal Parliament in Canberra today.

It is historic for two reasons. It is the first time a Labor Government in office has actually won a Federal elelction. Mr. Scullin overthrew the Bruce Government with 47 members in 1929 but the Curtin Government in being returned has done even better with an amazing 49 seats.

But here is the interesting point. We have two female members, the first to be elected. Dame Enid Lyons is the first woman member of the House or Representatives and Dorothy Tangney is our first woman Senator.

Of course, everbody knows Dame Enid Lyons. She is the widow of the former Prime Minister, Joe Lyons. Dame Enid is the new United Australia Party member for Darwin, Tasmania. She just got there on preferences.

At the declaration of the polls, she had a classic family struggle. She had to get her five youngest children, two girls and three boys, all packed up and on the boat to Melbourne for school. Then she had to drive 30 miles to the declaration.

She campaigned mostly on reputation. She said 'I made no promises during the campaign, every minute of which I enjoyed. While my husband was Prime Minister, I think I learned most of the things about the life which for me is just beginning'.

However she has some definite views on the role of women. She said on radio at the weekend that women during the war had done well in finance, administration and industry. Some women in the future would claim the right to exploit to the full the fields of labour, but she believed the majority would find their greatest happiness as homemakers. Married women who had been receiving their own and their husband's salaries would be more than compensated for their financial loss by being reunited, making a home and rearing a family.

No man should have to compete against cheap female labour, she said.

Dame Enid says she will forgo her £500 a year pension granted by the Commonwealth after the death of Mr. Lyons.

As for the new Senator, one newspaper says:

Miss Dorothy Tangney, of West Australia, is a vivacious, bright-eyed, golden-haired woman of 32. She is a good conversationalist and emphasises she is not a feminist. The former school teacher, who holds an arts degree, gives the impression of sound ideas. Miss Tangney speaks without notes and during her campaign delivered 200 speeches and took part in 60 debates without even a sore throat.

'Education has been the Cinderella of the services and should be under Federal Control said Miss Tangney. She favoured a housing scheme with houses and gardens instead of one-room flats, and considered the Commonwealth should make money available at a low rate of interest to buy homes.

Both women, Dame Enid (UAP) and Senator Tangney (Labor), although from opposite parties, are looking forward to meeting each other in Canberra. A little unfairly tne newspapers are talking at length about what the ladies are wearing.

For example, we have discovered that Senator Tangney at today's opening of Parliament wore a long-sleeved blue crepe frock with no hat.

Pride in the Men who will March to War

26 SEPTEMBER 1914

Australia is ready

At last we are getting some evidence that Australia is actually at war. We had a march through Melbourne yesterday, 5000 troops, artillery, light horse, horse drawn ambulances, the lot.

The Governor-General, Sir Ronald Munro Ferguson, took the salute, and it was an historic occasion, absolutely no one would dare miss. The Government put on special trains and 50 000 people came into the city.

Every window, every balcony, was packed with people. So much so that just as the troops were crossing Swanston Street, there was a loud crash followed by sharp cries. A shout went up as three young women were seen to fall through the glass portion of the verandah overhanging the Collins Street footpath. The young women, two typists and a school teacher, were in a state of collapse when picked up, but not seriously injured.

The *Argus* reports:
There was the wave of a white handkerchief here and there, and the flutter of a miniature flag. But cheers and words were few — not because the crowd did not want cheer. It watched the glittering bayonets and the swinging arms seemingly fascinated, and the serried ranks of sunburned faces set a fierce joy surging through the breasts of the men and women who looked on. The dominant note of all was pride in the men who marched in the greatest parade that had ever been seen in the streets.

It was a magnificent parade too. The men who composed it looked like picked soldiers. There was no trace of the volunteer army in a single rank. But it was all typically Australian. About the Light Horsemen there was a characteristic touch, freedom and ease underlying the disciplined order of their ranks. The short ungroomed lot compared with the mounts of the crack regiments of England, but they looked as if they could be depended on to do a great deal on a very little.

And the men themselves looked of the same calibre — spare, wiry men from the hills of Gippsland and 'up country', where men and horses know each other and move as one....If some of them had looked youthful when they marched through in August, discipline had turned them into grown men.

They were all supplied with an Army ration to tide them over until they went back to Broadmeadows Camp. It was a packet of bread and jam, greeted by many of those 'grown men' with considerable distaste. So street vendors did marvellous business selling hot pies, chocolate, cake and particularly frankfurts. The Teutonic name did nothing to dampen enthusiasm for the latter article.

The *Argus* says proudly this morning:
The strength of our Empire lies in its rulers' reverence for liberty. It is men's work — grim, dour work — that all British soldiers have to do, but they go to it gladly and boldly, because they know it is honourable work, righteous work, in defence of the greatest free organisation the world has ever seen the British Empire and for the wholesome chastisement of twentieth-century Vandals filled with an unholy lust for world domination.

For Nellie There's No Place Like Home

27 SEPTEMBER 1902

Nellie Melba gave her first homecoming concert at the Melbourne Town Hall tonight. No Australian, male, female, young or old, has ever received such a reception.

She arrived in Brisbane on 17 September aboard the *Miowera*. The ship was so late, at first there were awful rumours that it had sunk.

But then she travelled South by train. Had it been Queen Victoria or her son King Edward, there could not have been such a reception. All the way there were receptions, flowers, speeches, cheering waving crowds.

When the train arrived at Melbourne's Spencer Street Station, there was top security. You needed a special ticket just to get on the platform. Even so the crush was beyond belief. Photographers had step ladders so they could get pictures. Madame Melba, like travelling royalty, had her own private railway carriage, which was filled with flowers. She grabbed great bunches of them, and throwing out her arms, tossed them to the crowd.

Some of her old school friends from PLC shouted 'Cooee'...'Hello Nellie'. Melbourne was decked out in bunting and thousands packed the streets as she started a triumphant procession. There was a band outside Allen's music store in Collins Street. It played 'Home Sweet Home'.

Not many of us knew the strain or the tragedy. Madame Melba's father, Mr David Mitchell, planned to be with her on the train, but at Albury he had a slight stroke and when she arrived there, already he was in hospital. A terrible decision had to be made, come on to Melbourne, where a whole expectant city was waiting, or stay in Albury with her father. He told her it was her duty to go on.

So she has been the reigning Queen. She made a triumphal return home to Lilydale and the *Lilydale Express* greeted the occasion by printing all in gold.

If you could be there it was the greatest night the Melbourne Town Hall has known. The police had to call in reinforcements to control the thousands of people at the corner of Collins and Swanston Streets. They began to swarm from 6 p.m. on.

So everyone waited and waited. Most people had been there for three hours by the time Madame Melba appeared on stage, just in a simple gown of classic simplicity with one rope of pearls. There she was in the middle of the platform.

It was extraordinary. Now Nellie, the one Australian known at every corner of the earth, was home. Every person in the Town Hall stood up, cheered, clapped, threw hats and programs in the air. It was a wild, wonderful tumult of welcome. It went on and on, for what seemed an eternity.

How could she perform and sing after that, after so much emotion? But perform she did. Her opening aria was the one for which she is famous and has become practically her own, the mad scene from *Lucia*.

When it was over the entire stage was deep with flowers. The cheers seemed to rock the chandeliers. Finally Nellie sat down at the piano and to her own accompaniment she sang 'Home Sweet Home'.

It was a national moment of pride and affection. The tears I think could have overflowed the Yarra.

Police control crowds at the station

'Inclement' Wragge Forecasting a Change

28 SEPTEMBER 1902

When will the drought end? We have had below average rainfalls since 1895 and now we are wondering if it will ever rain again.

Take a drive through Queensland and observe the devastation, dying cattle, rotting sheep carcasses. Back in 1891 we had 106 million sheep, now it is more like 50 million. We had 12 million cattle, now it is half that.

Everybody is trying something. For example, there is the Queensland weather forecaster, Clement Wragge. He is tall, lean and has the passion about him of the prophet. He wears huge hobnailed boots, and when he approaches it is a majestic affair. You can hear him half a block away. He is known in Brisbane as 'Wraggie the human meteor' or 'Inclement Wragge'.

He has a house in the suburb of Taringa and he has named it Capemba, an Aboriginal word meaning 'Place of Water'. He believes deeply in Aboriginal names, not imported spurious names. However apart from decorating his house with native shields and spears, there are Union Jacks everywhere. He is a devoted loyalist.

He is the first to give cyclones names. He has given them such names as Xerxes, Hannibal, Blucher, and particularly has named them after members of Parliament — Drake, Barton and Alfred Deakin all have been cyclones.

It is not always a compliment. Recently he announced Cyclone Conroy after Mr A. Conroy, the member for Werriwa. The warning went out 'Conroy, looking nasty is coming along the coast'. . . 'Conroy black and treacherous is likely to cross the Southern District' and again, 'Conroy is in a wicked humour'. Mr Conroy did not like it and called Wragge an 'advertising scientist'.

Well, Inclement Wragge has decided to live up to his name. He heard that vineyards in Italy continually were being wrecked by hailstorms. They used a device known as the Stiger Vortex gun. The explosions from the gun created rain before the water had a chance to turn to ice.

Wragge imported plans for the gun and local newspapers raised the money to have six built at an engineering shop in Brisbane's Mar-

Clement Wragge

garet Street. They are made of heavy metal, 15 feet long, and look, like ice cream cones standing on their tails.

Charleville is the worst hit drought area, so he went there, and the Queensland Railways carried the guns free of charge.

Mr Wragge was very confident. He announced 'The Warrego will behold the unique spectacle of a regular bombardment. Jupiter Tonans and his brother Pluvius will blush with astonishment'.

They waited patiently until 26 September, when the clouds over Charleville seemed perfect. Mr Wragge put the guns in two rows of three, three-quarters of a mile between each, and gave them charges of 7½ ounces of powder. At noon they opened fire with ten charges from each gun. Just one or two drops fell, then two hours later there was a slight shower.

The natural conclusion was that if a light bombardment produced a shower, what would happen if Wragge let loose with a complete Battle of Waterloo? The guns boomed and boomed. Two of them burst under the strain. Alas not a drop fell.

I think Inclement Wragge will have to try something else.

Note: Wragge was the pioneer of Long Range weather forecasting. His work was carried on by his favourite pupil, Inigo Jones, and his successor Lennox Walker is still using the system.

Mixed Bathing in St Kilda Baths

29 SEPTEMBER 1938

We have just had the official announcement. There will be mixed bathing this season at the St Kilda Baths.

As you know, women never have been allowed into the St Kilda Baths. Indeed, between you and me, it is well known that until now men have bathed in there with nothing on at all.

There has been a long history on how to handle mixed bathing. There was a belief in the early days that if males and females got into the water together, heaven knows what they would get up to.

The new fad of sun bathing, too, caused terrible trouble. It was disgusting, people displaying their skin in public. In 1912 the St Kilda City Council passed a law that directly forbade it: 'Any person bathing shall on leaving the water resume ordinary clothing, and no person shall loiter save as far as is necessary, to enable him or her to dress, run or walk in the vicinity of the beach in bathing costume'.

Oh, sex was and is, a problem. On 27 October 1914 the St Kilda Council brought out another series of regulations. The beach was divided into areas. In some spots bathing was allowed only between 4 a.m. and 10 a.m. and others between 4 a.m. and 6 p.m., but on Sundays, Christmas Day and Good Friday, it was not allowed at all after 10 a.m.

On 2 November 1914 there was a great protest meeting of local citizens and they decided that the following Sunday they would have a mass bathe. Over a thousand turned out, but it was a horrid day and the protest was a failure. We had to wait until 19 January 1917 before mixed bathing became absolutely free, with Sunday hours up to 7 p.m.

But lately we have been very worried. The year 1932 saw the backless costume. A Congregational Minister, the Reverend S.H. Cox, described it as 'the hottest thing ever introduced on the beaches'. He said it was a return to the old Paganism of the Epicureans who lived only for the pleasures of life. The costumes would succeed in attracting the prurient minded, and would affect the essential modesty of the pure woman. Girls who wore these daring, disgusting, backless costumes were not the kind to uplift the moral tone of the community, nor, when married, to teach morals to their children.

Lately the men have been causing trouble with no tops to their costumes. In 1936 it was a case of 'to roll or not to roll'. The top half of male costumes buttoned on to the bottom half, or, alternatively one could roll down the top to display a chest. Anyone who dropped a shoulder strap was liable to a fine of two pounds.

The councils now are starting to crack, although Cr Levy of Brighton has pointed out that beaches are the playgrounds for children of tender years and some men are unsightly... 'like hairy monkeys'.

But we are worried about the women with their backless costumes. The costumes are becoming very skimpy. Cr C.E. Sheppard, president of Warringa Shire in Sydney has said that over there, costumes consist of a small brassiere attached to a pair of trunks by thin cords.' 'Women soon will go into the water nude', said he.

We certainly hope nothing like that happens at St Kilda Baths.

Holiday makers at St Kilda

Tolmer and Norah Take on All Comers

30 SEPTEMBER 1846

Inspector Alexander Tolmer

Unquestionably the most amazing person in all South Australia is Inspector Alexander Tolmer.

He is bilingual in English and French, fluent in Portuguese, skilled as an artist, quite wonderful on the violin and a better swimmer than Byron. He has eloquent curls, waves, sideburns, a truly noble moustache. He is handy with his fists, arrogant, impulsive and a brilliant all-round hero.

For a policeman he is always getting up to the most remarkable escapades. The latest is the mottled grey mare Norah. He bought her off the pioneer grazier Edward Henty at his property on the Wannon River. Henty said the mare ought to be worth 500 guineas, but Norah was crazy, a killer, his men wouldn't go near her. Tolmer got her for 30 pounds.

Tolmer spent a year training her and broke her in so well he entered for the Adelaide Steeplechase over three miles on 23 September. Norah had such a build up she was the favourite. The sad truth is Norah baulked at the first jump and crept into a ditch.

At the Royal Exchange Hotel, Tolmer met a horse owner named Paxton who said 'Your horse can't gallop, can't jump, and isn't worth a damn'.

There was great laughter. The furious Tolmer said 'I bet you twenty pounds she can trot seven miles in half an hour'. The bet was not only accepted but bumped up to 60 pounds.

Oh yes, Norah was good enough to handle that, she trotted the seven miles in 27 minutes 12 seconds. Tolmer was ecstatic and had a fine night pulling the corks out of champagne bottles. Paxton then said: 'I admit she's good but I bet she couldn't do 16 minutes'.

This was very tough, but Tolmer accepted and they doubled the bet to 120 pounds. The Inspector has terrible luck. It rained and it rained. It all looked hopeless until on a visit to Glenelg he thought, why not? — the beach at low tide would make a good trotting track.

On race eve there was a hurricane, the worst in Adelaide's history. The road to Adelaide was a sheet of water and the once fine beach almost disappeared. Paxton insisted the race go ahead.

Norah had to race, sometimes through soft sand and sometimes knee-deep in water, yet on the outgoing leg she did better than expected 27 minutes 4 seconds. Going back was tougher and Tolmer had to protect his face against hailstones. Yet he reached the starting post and he went on to the seventeenth mile. This was Tolmer proving a point and his time was 55 minutes 2 seconds.

Tolmer now is wildly celebrating and he claims it is the best trotting feat by a horse anywhere in the world. Paxton is deeply shocked and disappointed, particularly as he had brought along a saddle and bridle to ride Norah home. Note: An artillery officer on leave from India offered 500 pounds for Norah, delivered safely in Calcutta. This was a fortune to Tolmer. He went to great trouble and expense to make sure her stall on the ship was well padded. Later he received a message from the shipping company. 'We regret to advise that many horses were lost in bad weather off the *Leuwin*. The mare Norah was one of the first to go'.

Further reading: *Reminiscences of an Adventurous & Chequered Career at Home & the Antipodes*, Alexander Tolmer.

OCTOBER

Melbourne racing in the early days at Batman Hill

Something for Everyone at International Exhibition

3 OCTOBER 1880

Melbourne's great International Exhibition opened on Saturday. Of course, exhibitions are all the rage. Our exhibition has been inspired by the big Paris Exhibition of 1878. There has been further incentive through the Sydney Exhibition of 1879.

However Saturday's *Herald* was quick to point out that the Sydney affair was very hurriedly got up and its overseas exhibits few and unimportant. Whereas the opening of Victoria's first international exhibition was 'a spectacle such as had never been witnessed in the history of the world in a community not 50 years old'.

We had a huge procession through the streets, out front was the Eight-Hour banner followed by all the trade unions, including such fine men as the Victorian Ironmoulders Society, the Victorian Operative Bootmakers' Union, the Sawyers and the Port Phillip Society of Boilermakers. They were accompanied by nine brass bands and 26 fire brigades.

There were ships from five navies in the Bay and the sailors lined Nicholson and Rathdowne Streets on the road to our marvellous new Exhibition building. The size of this structure is hard to believe. It cost £246 000 and, along with all its annexes, it has 22 acres of floor space.

The procession got under way at 10 a.m. The Governor, the Marquis of Normanby, was accompanied by the governors of the other colonies. Inside the great hall there were between 6000 and 7000 people for the formal opening of an exhibition in which there are 13 000 exhibitors and 32 000 separate exhibits.

If only there were space to list all those exhibits. Suffice to say there are bird cages, Turkish baths, railway locomotives, railway carriages, biscuits, top hats, hand-powered washing machines, lawn mowers, pianos, billiard tables, reapers and binders, steam engines, blunderbusses. There are galleries to depict the art of every nation and one understands the French gallery has an interesting painting, titled 'Chloe', by the celebrated painter Chevalier Jules Lefebvre.

When the vice-regal party had taken up its position on the canopied dais we looked to the

The Exhibition Building

performance of the opening cantata specially written for the occasion. Monsieur Caron, the musical director waved his baton. There were 1000 singers, the 500 females all in spotless white, arrayed before the vast Exhibition organ. The sopranos were distiguished by ribbons of blue, the contraltos by red.

Frankly the cantata was somewhat interminable but the climax came:

O Thou whose arm hath for our fathers fought
Whose guiding hand their sons hath hither brought
Lead onward till Australia's land shall rise
A greater Britain, neath these Southern skies.

Hardly anyone could hear what the Governor had to say, but there was much talk about 'legitimate pride', 'surging growth', 'wise forefathers' and 'splendid future'.

The gardens are all laid out in beautiful avenues and parterres. There are ponds, there are fountains and a scene of just wonderful gaiety. Rather expensive. For the opening day tickets were 5s and 10s, but you can get season tickets, 3 guineas for gentlemen and 2 guineas for ladies. Later you will be able to get a day ticket for a shilling.

It will be open for seven months and we believe it will make Melbourne celebrated throughout the world.

Atomic Explosion at Monte Bello Islands

4 OCTOBER 1952

Britain's first atomic explosion went off in the Monte Bello Islands at 8.03 a.m. yesterday

Immediately, a great ragged cloud sky-rocketed upwards. It reached 6000 feet within a minute and mounted to a maximum of 12 000 feet in about four minutes.

The Press observers were stationed at Mt Potter, a 300-foot coastal peak 55 miles from the centre of the prohibited zone. The explosion was different and not as spectacular as they expected.

Three minutes after the explosion the cloud was a mile wide at its centre and shaped like a ragged Z. No ground shock was felt, but a heavy air-pressure pulse smacked the mainland 4 minutes 15 seconds after the flash and, at the time two concussions were felt. The pressmen felt a slight pain in the ears from the shock.

Nearest coastal residence to the blast immediately facing the Monte Bellos is Maride Station. Joan Raynor, the overseer's daughter, was in the kitchen of an outcamp when a concussion swept the area. 'The kitchen shook like a mad thing' she said. 'Then I heard what sounded like the report of a distant gun'.

Aborigines reported 'a thunderclap hit our ears while the sky above was clear'. In Onslow, 87 miles from the explosion, a loud report, slamming of doors, violent rattling of windows and dishes, sent the inhabitants running to the beach.

The *Argus* reports that the news has given the British people a tremendous lift. All Britain is talking about 'Our Bomb', and there is natural and malicious pleasure that the Americans who denied the British atom information must now recognize Britain as an atomic partner. London's *Daily Mirror* says 'Britain is GREAT BRITAIN once again'.

Britain's Prime Minister has sent this message to Mr Menzies, the Australian Prime Minister: 'I just had news from Monte Bello Islands. Cordial thanks to you for Australia's part, ensuring success.'

There is much speculation that the British bomb, although smaller, was more efficient and better designed than the American bomb. Professor Bailey, a physicist at Sydney University even suggests that Britain could have tested the world's first hydrogen bomb. The explosion differed from the typical mushroom-shaped cloud of the American tests.

The *Herald* in Melbourne says this triumph of British science will be of big interest to Australia. 'The first call on our uranium fields will be to feed the armament plants of the democracies. Some of the resultant weapons will take their place in our defences. But we can look beyond this to the peaceful, constructive uses of the new force. In the long run, no country stands to gain more than we do from harnessing atomic power to national development.

Professor Oliphant, one of the world's leading authorities, thinks that we may have an opportunity to lead the world in the application of atomic power to industry. . . .

The other big news coming from Onslow yesterday was the birth of Rodger Burness Turpin. The Melbourne *Sun* reported Rodger Turpin was the town's 'atomic baby'. Like the bomb he was overdue. There was speculation which would be the first, the bomb or the baby. Rodger beat the bomb by some hours.

Observers view the explosion

Yarra Bursts its Banks

5 OCTOBER 1844

A more tranquil Yarra scene

Melbourne is enduring another one of those dreadful occasions in which the Yarra has burst its banks. But this time, as the *Port Phillip Herald* points out, 'It overflowed with an impetuosity not in the recollection of the oldest settler in the district'.

The rain started at 10 o'clock on Monday night. The wind was blowing from the northeast. It came down as if all Bass Strait were being dropped upon us. Then it continued on and off until daylight Wednesday.

There was no work done at all on Tuesday and now, says the *Herald*, 'the whole town bears a very sombre and dismal appearance, only slightly relieved by the occasional struggles of passengers hurrying across the overflowing streets at the imminent peril of their limbs, and their lives'.

All the lower parts of the town around William Street, Flinders Street and the wharves are deep under water. Those who dwell on the south bank, too, are in a perilous situation. The water in their houses is continuing to rise with little prospect of relief because most of the boats are on the other side.

So far, only one life appears to have been lost. The *Herald* says there is a report of a man who tried to cross the river at Richmond on horseback. Horse, saddle and bridle were seen floating down the wild, surging stream. The *Herald* hopes vainly that the report may be unfounded.

However our reporter tells us that:
in a line from opposite the British Hotel in William Street, along Flinders Street and across the river to the rising ground beyond the new road leading to the beach, the prospect is fearfully grand, one sheet of water in which the Yarra can be recognised only by the rapidity of its current...The swimming baths and the adjoining houses are almost up to their necks in water, emitting no friendly smoke. Boats ply to and fro, from house to house through the many lines that intersect Flinders Street and Flinders Lane.

One can see people carting pigs, chooks, meats from the slaughter yards, all kinds of livestock in their boats. There is one cluster of houses where the fowls are all perched up on the roof tops, most impatient towards evening about their position and 'not relishing their uncongenial lodgings'.

Then there is the big swamp by Emerald Hill, all along its edge pigs and other animals are grazing. Many people are benefitting from the disaster by gathering wood and debris which has drifted down.

However our citizens are angry heaping 'anathemas' on 'that august body — the Town Council'. They are saying that if an embankment had been formed on the margin of the river, on a level with the Queen's wharf, and extending upwards till reaching in line with Stephen (Exhibition) Street, the great destruction of property would have been prevented.

But of course, the disaster has been not just in the town. It has been equally bad in Melbourne and quite terrible out in country areas like Heidelberg. We hear that the beautiful gardens of Mr Carr and Alderman Orr are almost completely destroyed and crops at Darebin and Merri Creek have been washed away.

Paddle Steamer Reaches Albury

6 OCTOBER 1855

We are celebrating a tremendous triumph here in Albury. A paddle steamer, appropriately named *Albury*, has navigated 2000 miles of the Murray, all the way from Goolwa in South Australia.

This opens a whole new era for us. It means a direct connection to the sea. It means trade. No longer does everything have to be carted by bullock wagon.

The *Albury* is a handsome vessel, 150 tons, designed especially for the navigation of the upper waters of the Murray and she brought us a load of general cargo. The first vessel to blow steam at the Albury wharf.

The Albury correspondent of the *Sydney Morning Herald* has recorded the marvellous celebrations. He says:

Through the kindness of Captain Johnstone, about 300 persons were gratified by being taken several miles up this noble stream. The serpentine course with its eddies and currents only convinced us of the care and responsibility which attached itself in bringing a steamer 2000 miles without the slightest accident.

It was a day long to be remembered. The wild duck whizzed away on the approach of the steamer — the horned cattle would dash off as if dreadfully affrighted . . .

A paddle steamer on the Murray

A German band on board discoursed excellent music. Picnic parties were soon made up on the green sward and with the edibles prepared everyone seemed to do justice; not to those alone, but from the hilarious activity, and shouts of pleasant laughter, evidently something stronger than the crystal waters of the Murray had been partaken of.

The picnic over a dance was proposed, and right merrily it was kept up. Polkas, quadrilles, and Scotch reels followed each other in quick procession. The main saloon was cleared for dancing.

Our correspondent recalled that Hume and Hovell in 1824 crossed this river on skins sewn together, what an unbelievable advance just 31 years later, to see this noble steamer.

The hearts of the citizens of Albury, says our man, are open with excitement and joy, so right here they presented Captain Johnstone with a purse of 100 sovereigns and his officers with 30 sovereigns.

The Police Magistrate, Mr Heyward Atkins, JP, presented a testimonial and the purses. Captain Johnstone replied:

Delighted I am sure will the directors of this company be when I tell them the reception which welcomed the first steamer moored at your wharves, so convenient and so contiguous to this great emporium of commerce for the districts of the Upper Murray. On my return I hope to bring with me the originator of this vast enterprise, Captain Cadell, whose untiring efforts have brought to a successful issue this once considered Utopian scheme.

Our man says however that before the scheme is profitable someone will have to clear the river of 'the forest of snags and impediments'. Furthermore this 'grasping Government' will have to remove its restrictive system of customs. 'Never was so odious and oppressive a line of policy adopted by a professed liberal Government towards any colonists, acknowledging and glorying in the reign of Her Most Gracious Majesty, Victoria.

Our correspondent believes the denizens of the metropolis are completely unaware of the importance of developing the interior.

Alice Meets her Match in Veno

7 OCTOBER 1857

Racing day at Batman Hill

Victoria has been a colony in her own right only seven years and there is a great yearning to prove superior to mother New South Wales in all forms of enterprise.

The Victorian champion racehorse is a mare called Alice Hawthorne, owned by the rich Western District squatter, Andrew Chirnside. She has beaten with ease every other horse in the colony. The Sydney champion is Veno, an eight year old, a fine slashing horse that has won 28 races.

All right, early this year Mr Chirnside and a group of backers challenged Mr George T. Rowe, Veno's owner to a race over 3 miles on a wager of 1000 sovereigns for the winner. Sydney, you must understand, is more than 600 miles off, so it took four weeks to get a reply. But the answer was yes, providing expenses of £250 were provided. George Higgerson, Veno's trainer-jockey, converted four pigs into bacon and pork and stored other edibles to provide for his family during his absence.

The race was set for 3 October and Veno arrived by the steamer *London* on 17 July. However one must point out the feeling in the colony has been so tense over this race the situation has been most unpleasant. Alice Hawthorne's trainers were so terrified the mare would be nobbled they hired police to guard the stables day and night.

George T. Rowe complained to the Melbourne Jockey Club they had to endure every disadvantage, different ways of running, different climate, different water. Would there be any objection to giving Veno a few gallops of Flemington? Mr Rowe said 'Will my friends believe it? The request was refused' *Bell's Life*, our sporting newspaper described the refusal as 'Impertinent and unsportmanlike'.

There has been huge excitement. Visitors have flowed into Melbourne from Sydney, Hobart, Adelaide. When you consider it costs £16 return to sail from Sydney, this is amazing. The *Herald* in its editorial said:

> The passion for horses may be ridiculed, by persons of narrow minds and sedentary lives; but the feeling has ever been characteristic of the most intellectual and powerful races of mankind, and the highest form of literature and art has been inspired by the contemplation of this useful and admirable gift of the Creator.

In the midst of all this, Johnny Higgerson's 16-year-old daughter was kicked to death by a cow. However he did not allow grief to interfere with his important preparations.

On 3 October half Melbourne was on the road to Flemington. The newspapers estimated the crowd at sixteen to twenty thousand. Well, Veno started at a great pace and led to the first turn. Higgerson realizing he had the faster sprinter, pulled his horse back and Alice went to the lead for a quarter of a mile. Before they passed the stand Veno was in front again. It was obvious Alice was outpaced and Veno was never extended, an easy winner by three lengths.

George T. Rowe went crazy with excitement. He threw his hat in the air, gave a hilarious jump and fainted. Many thought he had suffered a heart attack, but no, he recovered. And would you believe there was another challenge. Two hours later Mr Rowe backed Veno, £500 to £300 to beat Van Tromp the Geelong champion. Veno won by two lengths.

There is much grief in the newspaper editorials. Today *Bell's Life* calls it a humiliation and disgrace. Our only hope now is to beat New South Wales at cricket.

£5 for *Most* Mothers

10 OCTOBER 1912

The Senate at long last has passed the Maternity Allowances Bill. From 1 November every Australian mother who gives birth to a child will receive five pounds.

Every Australian white mother, that is. The Bill states specifically that it will be paid to women who are inhabitants of the Commonwealth, or who intend to settle therein, but NOT Asiatics, or Aboriginal natives of Australia, Papua or the islands of the Pacific.

Senator Stewart of Queensland wanted to add 'negroes' to the list of exceptions, but Senator Walker (NSW) explained this was unnecessary. There were no negro women in Australia — they could not come in — and if any applied for the Maternity Allowance they would be deported.

The Bill says further that the £5 benefit is paid at birth and no more. In other words, the unfortunate mother does not earn £15 for triplets or £25 for quintuplets.

The opposition to the Bill in the Senate was remarkable. The Government was accused of cheap cadging for votes. Senator McColl of Victoria said it was 'palpably a political move. The people were getting accustomed to the Government distributing largesse for political support'.

The great majority of women, said he, were not in need of money when maternity overtook them, and no effort was made to seek out those who were. The worker was to be taxed to put money into the pockets of the well-to-do.

But it was Senator St Ledger of Queensland who really stirred the pot. He said the Bill was a sop to profligacy, and every mother who accepted the allowance was a profligate.

But what really outraged the Queensland Senator was this. The £5 will not only go to mothers who are wed, but also to mothers who are not wed. Then most outrageous of all, single women could just go on producing illegitimate children to get the five pounds.

Said the Senator:

These people are living in sin and adultery, and I object to public money of a Christian community being devoted to help such a life, even if the sin and adultery is less in Australia than elsewhere. There are vagabonds living on these unfortunate women's earnings who would not hesitate to seize the allowance, and I object to a sop being given to sin and adultery. It would be better to give the money to a good maternity home where these women could be cared for in some cases.

The *Argus* says even if it is a fly paper to catch votes this only admits that the majority of people are in favour of it. There's no question the great bulk of the people favour maternity benefits.

Indeed the sum of £5 will be a very nice gift for most mothers. There is a list in the *Age* today of the new wages being made to Railway workers. Railway repairers get a sixpence increase up to 7s 6d a day; gangers will get 9s 6d, car painters 9s 6d and the minimum wage for skilled labourers will be 8 shillings. Work that out, it is precisely £2 a week.

As for adult clerks, from now on they will get £120 a year. However this allowance is really for the mother. Only she can collect it.

Judge Flouts Convention
Bicycling on Circuit

11 OCTOBER 1883

The new spider bike, penny farthing or 'ordinary' as some people call it, is all the go in Melbourne.

One of the first to try one was Mr R.C. Bagot, Secretary of the Victoria Racing Club. Quite a character, Mr Bagot. He designed both the Flemington racetrack and the Melbourne Cricket Ground.

Well, he is a bicycle fanatic. So far, I think, he has purchased 14 of them. They are coming now in all sorts of shapes and sizes, quadricycles, tricycles, machines with all sorts of ingenious cranks.

The Melbourne Bicycle Club has been going now for five years. The annual subscription is 12 shillings and sixpence. The club uniform consists of myrtle green coat, knickerbockers, stockings and cap. Members are requested to wear the same at club meetings and when touring. White straw hats with club ribbon (green and gold) to be worn in summer. Club costumiers are Alston and Brown, Collins Street West.

Each member is requested to carry a bell or whistle and to use a lamp when riding at night.

Members are asked not to wear their uniform and badge when riding on Sundays. (The Presbyterian Assembly has condemned Sunday bicycle riding as evil and a desecration of the Sabbath.)

The president of the MBC is a Judge of the Supreme Court, Mr Justice Williams. He is a dignified gentleman with mutton-chop whiskers but there is no limit to his devotion to the bicycle. He rides it on circuit all round Victoria.

In this week's issue of *Australian Cycling News*, the Judge tells us he has one of the brand new 'safety' chain-driven machines and he had ridden his 'safety' 29 miles into Camperdown in the face of a westerley gale. 'I mounted my safety at 9.30 and reached Camperdown at 1 o'clock. You can imagine the force of the wind when I tell you I had to work nearly as hard downhill as I have on a fair day to work up hill.'

The judge continued his tour by bicycle through Warrnambool, Hamilton, Moyston, Stawell and Horsham, and was met by officials in every town before presiding over cases.

There was a bicycle guard of honour at Hamilton. 'I was met by Mr Farroll, a gentleman of six feet four inches, who was riding his 60 inch spider ordinary. I on my safety looked like Lilliput beside him on his steed'.

The *Herald* is shocked. It says:

That the whole legal profession is scandalised at the burlesquing of the judicial bench by Mr Justice Williams by going circuit on a bicycle...Fancy a judge of the Supreme Court entering a large city like Ballarat on a velocipede and being met, not by the sheriff and other functionaries, but by half a dozen other boobies on bicycles.

But *Bicycling News* rushed to his defence. It says:

I desire to point out that cycling stands at the very head of athletics in England, and that its votaries are generally of good status. In Great Britain alone there are 300,000 riders, among whom may be mentioned the Prince of Wales, Prince George of Wales, Lord Sherbrooke and two of Her Majesty's judges of the Queen's Bench. The judges mentioned frequently do their circuits on bicycles.

Tasmanian Natives Hunted like Wild Beasts

12 OCTOBER 1830

It is really total war. Relations between the Tasmanian Aboriginals and the local settlers could not possibly be worse.

One can only quote from *The Colonial Times* to show precisely the feeling of white inhabitants of this island.

We now beg most earnestly to draw the attention of all to the present situation of these poor, wretched, but infatuated savages, the Aborigines of this island...It is too late to discuss the question whether they might have been civilised...What intercourse has taken place has produced only hatred, and revenge, and nothing but removal, can protect us from incursions...

We deeply deplore the situation of the Settlers. With no remunerating price for their produce, they have just immerged from the perils of the bushrangers and now they are exposed to the attacks of these natives, who aim at their lives. We make no pompous display of philanthropy — we say unequivocally — SELF DEFENCE IS THE FIRST LAW OF NATURE. THE GOVERNMENT MUST REMOVE THE NATIVES — IF NOT, THEY WILL BE HUNTED DOWN LIKE WILD BEASTS AND DESTROYED.

Pompous display of philanthropy? There are probably only 1000 blacks on the whole island. But they have seen their hunting grounds taken, their women raped, their men abused and hideously maltreated. Sir George Arthur, the Governor, and various white administrators, have applied white law to them which they don't for a moment understand.

As you can imagine there have been plenty of incidents. On 18 May last Mr Lord's hut at the Eastern Marshes was attacked. One man there was horribly speared and the other beaten.

On 15 June the Aborigines raided a hut at Lake River and murdered Mary Daniels and her two children. On 24 August James Hooper was killed and his hut plundered of everything. On 13 September there was another white man killed by the Tamar River. On 27 September Francis Booker was speared and killed. On 28 September Mr G. Scott's house was attacked. They speared one man and killed another,

Tasmanian Aborigines

throwing his body into the river. The natives got away with everything, blankets, clothing, tobacco, and 800 pounds of flour and sugar.

There have been many other incidents too numerous to record here. It was so difficult to capture the natives, whom he considered daily became more 'bold and crafty', the Governor decided on what was really a mass hunt. He launched it last Thursday, 7 October.

He issued a proclamation that everybody was to take part, all soldiers, police, settlers, and even the ticket-of-leave convicts.

The whole affair was organised absolutely as a military operation. We hear it is costing 35 000 pounds. The operation, soldiers, masters, servants, advancing across the island is being called 'the black line'. The idea has been to drive them into the Tasman Peninsula, then perhaps to remove them to one of the neighbouring islands. Governor Arthur personally is still directing the operation and he left the unfortunate Lady Arthur in childbirth.

Even though 5000 people have taken part, so far it appears the whole operation has been a ghastly failure. Four soldiers have been killed by accident. One time a tree stump was mistaken for the enemy. Two natives have actually been captured, two were shot, and a further native was captured but escaped. Presumably there are still 990-odd Aborigines still roaming free.

Further reading: *Black War, The Extermination of the Tasmanian Aborigines*, Clive Turnbull.

Say Something Nice about Canberra

13 OCTOBER 1946

It is strange. Our national capital is terribly unloved. People keep knocking it, particularly for its ingenious lay out and its transport service.

Take yesterday's *Argus*. Mr Rupert Charlett writes:

Whether in addition to costing millions it ruined a perfectly good sheep station is another matter. However Canberra has a quaint charm of its own. For instance the poet who claimed that woman is the most unpredictable thing in creation obviously was not a patron of Canberra omnibus service. Canberra is a concerto in one movement-adagio in fact!

It is said that one person, momentarily speechless when the bus came along precisely at 9.30 a.m., as scheduled, exclaimed 'Great Scott! A Canberra bus on time'. It is also said that the conductor blushed faintly and confessed 'This is yesterday's bus, Sir'.

Clive Turnbull in the *Herald* says:

The designers who placed everything at the maximum distance from everything else had a sublime faith in the continuity of the petrol supply and disdaining vulgar things like trams and trains, left the humble citizen without any means of transport at all, except the occasional bus, which probably didn't want to go where you want to go anyway.

You have three alternatives...wait for a bus...or you may walk your 20 miles, your chart, sextant and compass slung on your shoulders...or you may decide that there is no point in going out at all and, after a lapse of 20 years, be one day discovered dead under the billiard table by a retired Colonel from Poona.

Then another *Argus* writer, A.W. Spurr, says:

Strangers especially find Canberra a maze, whose elfin mission is to torment the exalted ego in man...One merrily gyrating motorist, after bidding long and furiously to get out of the National Capital was moved to express extreme incredulity by a strangely recurring piece of statuary: 'Well, most towns have their Bobby Burns statue, but I'll go hopping if I've ever seen one before with three of them'.

But the most tragic comment came a few years ago from Victoria's Mr J.P. Jones, MLC. He said:

As I walked through Canberra I recalled a story of the memorial erected in London after the Crimean War. It bore the one word CRIMEA, and Gladstone suggested that the last letter be deleted, and placed before the other letters, thus making the inscription A CRIME. The same comment applies to Canberra.

One gentleman, a president of the Chamber of Manufacturers, Mr J. MacDougall, said on 10 January 1931 that Canberra was a ghastly failure and the longer we stayed there the greater the cost would be. He said:

It would be to the advantage of the people of Australia if the Parliament were removed to Melbourne or Sydney. I should imagine that the Melbourne people would prefer the politicians to be in Sydney.

But someone is sure to say something nice about Canberra soon. The wattle is really very nice in early Spring.

The Birth of the Liberals

14 OCTOBER 1944

We have a new political party. It is the Liberal Party of Australia.

Of course it had to come. The United Australia Party was the party of the late Joe Lyons. It was in office under R.G. Menzies. Then in 1941 it came apart at the seams and last year it was devastated at the polls.

Its name was the biggest joke. Mr Menzies might have done better had he called it the Disunited Australia Party. This week there has been a grand gathering in Canberra of all the non-Labor forces. There is the Liberal-Democratic party of New South Wales, the Liberal and Country League of South Australia, the UAP from Victoria, the young Nationalists, the Women's National League...everybody except the Country Party.

There is nothing to worry about there. Mr Menzies suggests 'full organic unity' with the Country Party could come later.

Yesterday Mr Menzies explained everything that was wrong with the UAP. It doesn't have a proper Federal organisation or secretariat. There is no liaison between Federal members and workers in the field.

There is no proper rank and file method of raising party funds. Money just comes from individual organisations. In other words the business community 'kicks in', the money does not come in democratic style from the rank and file. The new party, said he, would not be handicapped by any vested interest.

The UAP said Mr Menzies, did not have any comprehensive statement of its objectives, and, incredibly there was no means for periodically revising policy.

All that was changed today. Mr Menzies is the leader of the new party and here is its list of objectives:

- Safety for Australia from external aggression, closest communion with the Empire.
- National defence to be a universal duty.
- All members of the fighting services and their dependents to enjoy honour, security, preference and generous repatriation benefits.
- Constant employment at good wages for

Mr Menzies

all willing and able to work.
- Social provision for superannuation, sickness, unemployment and widowhood on a contributory basis free of means test and adequate medical services within reach of all.

The new Liberal Party says further that recognition of family life is fundamental to society's well being and every family should be enabled to live in a comfortable home at a reasonable cost.

However Mr Dedman, the very vocal Minister for War Organisation and Industry, is unimpressed. He says the 'interests' that Mr Menzies is rallying to his cause are exactly like those which worked for Vichy France. Mr Dedman said investigations in the liberated countries of Europe showed that the arch-collaborationists with Hitler were the financiers, the big business men and property owners, while the resistance movement had its roots in the workers.

But Mr Menzies today was buoyant. He says this is not the old UAP, the ingredients are different. It is a completely new political party with a fresh new enthusiastic organisation. He predicts it will have an exciting future.

But that glorious future is unlikely to arrive until the war is over. Meantime it is a very dull scene. The Prices Commissioner, Mr McCarthy even announced controls over ice-cream today. The fixed prices are, a halfpenny for a small scoop, a penny for a medium-sized scoop and threepence for a large. Woe betide anyone who charges differently.

The first Issue of the *Age*

17 OCTOBER 1854

The first issue of the *Age* is on sale today.

Let us run a critical eye over it. Published daily, the price is sixpence. Now sixpence is virtually the price of a three-course meal, a mighty sum of money to find every day. We would suggest only the affluent and well-to-do will be able to afford it.

It preaches a great deal and has a fine tendency to verbosity, but then so do the other newspapers, so we will not quarrel with that. The typeface is appalling, and some columns are desperately difficult to read.

However our proprietors, the merchant brothers Henry and John Cooke, ask us to be patient. Here in the colonies it is impossible to acquire fonts of type in good condition. So he is reluctantly compelled 'to wait for the arrival of several fonts of letter which are necessary to render the appearance of our journal consistent with its general pretensions'.

A column on the front page tells us:

It will be conceded that a wide field is now left unoccupied by the press of Melbourne — that a large portion of Colonial Society is unrepresented, and destitute of any organ capable of adequately expressing its views, recording its movements and doing justice to its motives.

Though not ranking with what is popularly known as religious newspapers it will be conducted with an entire and cordial sympathy with the movements of Christian men — maintaining an earnest antagonism to intemperance, and all the institutions and usages that support it.

In its literary character it is hoped *The Age* will be found to assume a higher position than that of any other existing journal in the colony... The politics will be liberal, aiming at a wide extension of the rights of free citizenship... It is to be regretted that the Press in this Colony has hitherto aimed far too low — that it has been content in many instances to become the vehicle of mere personal scurrility — has substituted venomous attacks upon the character and motives of public men for the calm and temperate discussion of public principles

...We aim at attaching to the journalism of Melbourne a higher character.

Let's see. The first issue of the *Age* tells us that is coincides with the opening of the Melbourne Exhibition and the first pages of the new newspaper are printed within the walls of Melbourne's new Crystal Palace. It would be churlish to compare it with the Crystal Palace at Sydenham opened in 1851, yet it is not one of your dull stereotyped buildings, but original and a noble achievement indeed.

Everything is on show, all sorts of colonial products and a wonderful display of colonial flora and fauna. The *Age* warns that some rare specimens of local fauna already are disappearing from the colony.

There is a splendidly researched article on the breakdown of religious groups. The Presbyterians are in front with the number of clergy 42, compared with 23 Church of England, 26 Roman Catholics and 25 Wesleyans. But as an active force, the Wesleyans are way ahead with 150 lay preachers and they have 24 churches. The Church of England has only 11 churches, the Catholics 14, and the Presbyterians 2, all others temporary.

The first issue announces that the circulation is assured, second only to the *Argus*. There is a very good range of advertisements. The best buy, one would suggest, is 50 acres for sale at Brighton, suitable for fruit growing or market gardens. Price low.

Mr David Syme

Bombala a Capital Idea

18 OCTOBER 1903

Sir William Lyne favoured Bombala

There is hopeless disagreement between the House of Representatives and the Senate on the choice of a site for the national capital.

The House of Representatives has decided on the little town of Tumut. The Senate has gone for Bombala. It is all very subtle. New South Wales has 26 members in the House of Represenatatives, so it can use weight of numbers to vote for the handiest town. In the Senate it has only six so it is outvoted with Bombala.

The House of Representative had its vote back on 3 October. A splendid array of areas went into the ballot: Bombala, Lyndhurst, Tumut, Albury, Armidale, Orange, Lake George, Bathurst and Dalgety.

Most members enthused with marvellous eloquence over sites which were in their own electorates. Mr Knox of Victoria was very keen on Albury because it was closest to Melbourne and superbly connected by rail. So, too, was the Victorian, Mr A Mclean, but it had one big failing, no port. Bombala was ideal because it was within reasonable distance of Eden, a fine seaport.

Sir William Lyne, also liked Bombala He said 'It has a dry, crisp climate, conducive to health. No doubt a little cold in winter. But for eight months of the year there is no better climate'.

'Yes, for lumbago', said Mr MacDonald Paterson.

Sir William Lyne said if Bombala were chosen, Eden could become a fine port and the centre of a great population. 'The loveliest women and the finest men were there and it would be the centre of a great race.'

The Minister for Defence, Mr Chapman, became utterly carried away. He said there was nothing to compare with the 'vivifying and health-giving climate of the Bombala heights. There is no typhoid and very little sickness, in short, only health and plenty and happiness... It's trees are simply wonderful – grand – magnificent, as every member who has visited the district must very well know'.

'They are mere shrubs' growled Mr W.M. Hughes.

Finally on the sixth ballot the members chose Tumut with Lyndhurst second. The mileages were worked out very carefully. Tumut is 389 miles by rail from Melbourne and 318 from Sydney, roughly about 12 hours from either city.

So a week went past and the Senate had a go. They discussed everything in sight. There was a worry that the rivers in the Tumut area were dry for nine months of the year.

Senator Barrett remarked 'It would be a good thing if some people were dry all the year'.

The Senators rejected Tumut; then they tried Lyndhurst. That won only six votes. They tried Albury, six for, 23 against; but Bombala finally scored, 19 for, 10 against, and they have tossed the Bill back to the House of Representatives.

Senator Dobson thinks the whole thing is a waste of time. There is no better place than Melbourne for the capital. If a new capital enriched the Commonwealth by £5 he would vote for it, but instead it will cost an enormous sum and enrich New South Wales by about £7 million. The *Argus* agrees utterly. The idea of a new capital is an indulgence when there are matters around of more practical concern.

Note: On 8 October 1908 Parliament finally agreed on a site in the Canberra–Yass area.

Prime Minister Loses his Seat

19 OCTOBER 1929

The unthinkable has happened. It was confirmed today. The Nationalist Party is in ruins and Stanley Melbourne Bruce has lost his seat.

Never before has a Prime Minister lost his seat at a general election and it is hard to believe it has happened now. The unflappable, superior Mr Bruce never before has had a set back.

He came from Toorak. He went to school at Melbourne Grammar, where not only was he school captain, but he captained football, cricket, rowing and was a cadet lieutenant. During the war he was a captain in the Royal Fusiliers and won his Military Cross at Gallipoli.

His Hombergs, always, are just right and the cartoonists adore him because he is the last gentleman to wear white spats. Good manners, elegant, and his accent so patrician invariably he is mistaken for an Englishman.

For five days Mr Bruce's seat of Flinders has been in the balance. At one stage he seemed to be gaining and he was only 75 votes behind. But now, after the counting of the preferences, it is all too clear, Mr E.J. Holloway, Labor has won by 327 votes.

The new Prime Minister is James Henry Scullin, the member for Yarra and another Melburnian, but what a contrast to Bruce. Scullin was born in Ballarat, but his formal education finished at primary school. He left to work in a grocery store. However he did attend night classes and he won prizes as a debater and orator at eisteddfods. He will have his problems. It looks as if his new Labor Government will have only two members with previous ministerial experience, Mr J.A. Lyons and Mr. E.G. Theodore.

Mr Bruce has taken his defeat with immense dignity, saying very little. Several members are so shocked they have offered him their seats. For example, Mr C.A.S. Hawker, a sheep farmer, who has won the seat of Wakefield in South Australia for the Nationalists, has offered to resign and make way for Mr Bruce.

However Mr Bruce has refused all these noble gestures. He says the idea of going back to Parliament at the expense of one of his former colleagues does not appeal to him.

Today he issued this statement.

The result of the election in the Flinders

Mr Bruce

electorate has come to me as a deep disappointment. I have represented that constituency for 11 years, and I had hoped that the degree to which I have established myself in the confidence and good will of the electors would have been sufficient to ensure my return...The electors have, however, decided otherwise. I accept their decision as the fortune of war, and I offer my congratulations to Mr Holloway upon the success which he has won.

Mr Bruce will move out of the Prime Minister's Lodge next Wednesday night. There is some speculation that Mr and Mrs Scullin will reside at a hotel. They have booked into the Hotel Canberra from Monday.

Meanwhile Mr Bruce and Mrs Bruce plan to take a long sea voyage. But he says he still hopes to serve Australia in some capacity and he will contest Flinders again at the next election.

There is much grief at his departure. Victoria's Premier, Sir William McPherson said today:

Australia today stands indebted to Mr Bruce for his self-sacrificing efforts to make her citizens prosperous and happy. Australia, through his efforts is better known today, not only throughout the Empire, but throughout the world.

Bushrangers on St Kilda Road

20 OCTOBER 1852

'Bushrangers on St Kilda Rd' by
William Strutt

St Kilda, as you know, is an utterly charming seaside village.

But it is more than that. St Kilda — Brighton is a very popular area for our market gardens and orchards. So much produce passes along the St Kilda Road to Melbourne town.

The road is in appalling condition. It becomes a desperate track almost upon crossing the bridge. Now it seems you take your life in your hands. Here is a report from yesterday's *Argus*.

On Saturday afternoon last, about half past three o'clock of a fine bright sunny day, two industrious residents of Brighton were driving in a cart along the high road leading past the St Kilda Racecourse towards the special survey.

Two men were walking before them at a little distance. They saw two or three other men with guns at their sides, apparently looking up the trees for birds. Of a sudden they found themselves surrounded; guns were placed at each of their heads, and at that of the horse. The attack was so outrageous that they thought it was a joke; but as they were addressed in the most abusive language and told that their brains would be blown out if they delayed, they got out of the cart and submitted to be rifled, the one of 25 pounds, the other of about 46 pounds.

The robbers whose horses were hung up to the trees in the neighbourhood, and who were entirely without disguise, then ordered them to proceed with their cart to the adjacent wattle scrub; a hempen halter was cut into shreds, and they were tied hand to hand with strand and ordered to sit down on the ground, two men with double-barrelled guns keeping guard over them.

In a few minutes, the two men whom they had previously seen on the road were brought in, robbed, and also tied and made to sit down. A watch was then kept up and down the road, and every individual who came up a-foot, on horseback, or in a vehicle, for two and a half hours, was stopped and robbed.

Now the *Argus* says that the five:

...scoundrels who committed the outrages on St Kilda Road have passed on to Dandenong where they are bailing up everyone they meet. In consequence of this the Executive Government is offering a reward of 2000 pounds for the apprehension of the gang and 200 pounds for the capture of each individual. Sergeant South and a party of cadets left Melbourne last nigh in pursuit of the villains.

The *Argus* is very upset at this state of affairs and makes complaints about Superintendent of Police, Mr Sturt.

Whatever may have been the efforts of Mr Sturt in this particular case, to his general mismanagement of the police is attributable a very large majority of the outrages which are prevailing. We have no personal feeling against this gentleman, whom we believe to be a well-intentioned man in the main, but it is time to speak out, when, while assured on all sides that 'there is no crime', we find a score of people tied together in a scrub, on a main line of road, within five miles of the metropolis.

Prime Minister's Wife Prepared to Shoot

21 OCTOBER 1916

There has been a sensational attempt to assassinate the Prime Minister at his private residence in Kew.

Feelings have run so high during the Conscription campaign there were dire predictions this could happen.

Mr Hughes himself made an awesome statement at the First conscription meeting in Sydney.

I am standing here tonight in circumstances which are not as satisfactory to me as they might be, but you may be sure that as long as I live I will go on with this. There is only one way to stop me going on, and that is to stop me living.

The *Age* reports that just before he left on his present trip to Sydney, a would-be murderer paid a visit to Mr Hughes's residence, a villa facing Cotham Road by Barrington Avenue. The night was extremely dark.

Mr Hughes was supposed to be home, but he had been detained in the city and only Mrs Hughes and her infant daughter were occupying the room. Both were fast asleep. It was after midnight when they were awakened by shouts and the report of a revolver fired at the window.

Mrs Hughes sprang from the bed, seized her baby, and dashed from the room into the interior of the house. She heard a rush at the side of the building and the fall of a body near the vegetable garden. Then the shout of 'Stop, or I'll fire'.

Five minutes later the policeman who had been on duty in the grounds, knocked at the door. He told Mrs Hughes he had seen this man stealthily making his way up the gravel path. He was a youngish man and he watched him force open the bedroom window. His left hand slid into the room, drew back the curtain, then saw him go for what was obviously a gun in his hip pocket.

The constable immediately fired. The man put up his hands, then turned and ran. The constable tried to fire again but it failed to go off. He gave chase but caught his feet on a low wire fence and fell.

The intruder or the 'dastard' as the *Age* calls him, jumped over a fence and disappeared down Barrington Avenue.

Mrs Hughes says she actually saw the man. It was a hideous face, and it looked very pale in the half light. I could see that the man wore a cap, and that his clothes were dark brown...I was not a bit nervous. If the constable had not been there I would have shot at the man myself. I am used to firearms as my brothers always had guns in the house for sporting purposes. I am not a nervous sort, and it is just as well, in view of the terrible letters we have received lately. When Mr Hughes came home I did not tell him what had happened. I did not want to say anything to take his mind from his work or to disturb his rest.

The *Age* says the Prime Minister has received a number of anonymous letters threatening his life. One of these stated 'Mrs Hughes and the baby will be murdered and the house burnt down'.

A Poisoner Hanged

24 OCTOBER 1894

Martha Needle has been hanged at the Melbourne Gaol. It is the second female hanging we have had there this year.

Back on 15 January Mrs Frances Knorr was hanged for murdering unwanted babies. Unmarried mothers took their babies to Mrs Knorr on the understanding she would act as a foster parent. Then she murdered them.

Martha Needle poisoned her whole family because she wanted to marry a young carpenter, Otto Juncken. Right up to the last minute Martha Needle swore her innocence. At the passing of the death sentence she stood unmoved in a deeply moved court. She stated that she was innocent and that the sentence was undeserved.

She told her friends, she told the chaplain, she told the nurse and the attendants, that she was innocent, and she was not afraid to die because she was innocent.

The *Argus* says that from the date of her arrest she changed little in her manner. She ate well, slept well and was so cheerful towards everyone who attended her that the Governor of the gaol called her 'inscrutable'.

The gaol chaplain, Rev. H.F. Scott thought she was a psychological enigma, which in all his varied prison experience he had not surpassed. There are some angry exchanges going on between the Reverend Scott and Otto Juncken. The *Argus* says Scott tried to bring Martha Needle around to a proper frame of mind 'before she approached her doom'.

He came from her cell at 9 o'clock after a most painful interview. She needed to repent. All along she had been happy with a statement that Otto believed in her innocence. Scott told her it was useless to believe this. Otto did not believe she was innocent. For a few moments, says the *Argus*, she gave way to terrible anger and told Mr Scott he was lying.

At 10 a.m. on 22 October in the presence of the sheriff, Mr Casey; the governor of the gaol Captain Burrowes, the medical officer, Dr Shields, and a few reporters, 'the wretched woman' says the *Argus* 'was led on to the drop. She stood firm and unflinching, and in answer to the usual question said "I have nothing to say".' Death followed instantaneously on the drawing of the bolt...The woman's body was buried in quicklime in the precincts of the gaol.

The *Argus* in its leader produced figures on the last moments of criminals. 'Of 64 men 25 died in a cowardly manner, while of 25 women only five showed cowardice, and one, a poisoner showed revolting cynicism'.

'Thus does history repeat itself' says the *Argus*. 'The poisosner is the worst example of the instinctive criminal. And the female poisoner is more callous and more heartless than the male offender. Her victims are usually those who by the laws of God and of man are confided to her for comfort and support. Despite her sex there is no offender whom society can with more unconcern send to the gallows.'

However in a statement to the *Argus*, Otto Juncken says this. He did not at any time tell the Reverend Scott that he believed Martha Needle was guilty...'I now leave Mr Scott to explain by what process of casuistry he can justify his conduct. Evidently the reverend gentleman knows my own mind better than I do myself.'

Martha Needle accused the chaplain of lying

Comet Flashes out of the Sky

25 OCTOBER 1934

The Comet swoops low

C.W.A. Scott and T. Campbell Black have won the Centenary Air Race.

Flying their red D.H. Comet they covered 11 323 miles in an extraordinary 71 hours 18 seconds, or just under three days.

As the *Herald* put it: 'Flashing out of the sky like a fiery particle with the roar of its engines merging into a tumult of cheers that rose from a vast waiting crowd the Comet flew over the finishing line at Flemington racecourse'.

That Comet flew on to Laverton, landed there, then Scott and Black were flown back to a big reception at Flemington. Waiting to greet them were the Lord Mayor, Sir Gengoult Smith and the man who made this air race possible, Sir Macpherson Robertson.

Sir Macpherson's normal urbanity deserted him. He cheered and cheered again, and then led the cheering once more from his position on the dais.

The crowd at Flemington began to arrive at 4 a.m. and by 3.30 p.m. it had reached fifty thousand. After landing near the bookmakers' ring, Scott and Black, perched on the hood, drove down the track in an open car, both men smoking cigarettes. They waved in response to the tumultuous applause.

The Lord Mayor said the achievement of the two fliers was marvellous. 'They have thrilled the world and the whole of the British Empire by the wonderful performance, and have earned the homage of Australia. We are proud that two Britons in a British machine have won the race.'

But now we learn of their difficulties. The two men on arrival were so exhausted they could hardly speak, and now we learn they lost an engine over the Timor Sea. Scott said of the flight:

It was a struggle like hell all the way to get the old bus through. When our port motor cut out over the last 300 miles across the Timor Sea we were punching the ship grimly through blinding rain and inky and black cloud just skimming the sea to get whatever visibility there was. I thought it was all up with us. Our chances looked so hopeless that Black and I donned our life jackets and sat waiting for the crash.

We thought it inevitable. We did not dream our starboard motor would hold under the terrific strain, but it behaved magnificently.

The *Herald* in its leader says:

This was history made at 200 miles an hour, a symbol of the new air age. Of what that symbol really means the world is but dimly conscious; but in fewer than three days the conquest of time and distance has outstripped the imagination and left men and women wondering what the future holds...

Hats off to Scott and Black! They have written their names in the scarlet of their Comet on the page of history which is reserved for great adventures, for men whom it is not sentimental even in 1934 to call heroes. They may take their place with the great Elizabethans.

There is romance in the air too. London's *Daily Mail* reports that T. Campbell Black made a proposal of marriage to Miss Florence Desmond, the actress, just a few hours before his departure from England. Miss Desmond withheld her answer, but she is now waiting to inform Black of her acceptance over the radiophone.

Frank Hardy Charged with Libel

26 OCTOBER 1950

No book ever published in Australia has caused a greater sensation than Frank Hardy's *Power without Glory*.

It went on sale in Melbourne early last month and immediately it became the talk of every bar, every office, every dinner table. Theoretically it is the story of an evil tycoon named John West, but you would have had to have been asleep for ten years not to realise West is a thin disguise for John Wren.

But it is not only Wren, the book does a fascinating job on judges, lawyers, politicians, criminals, policemen...And it is just like a crossword puzzle, part of the fun is to recognise your villain.

It went on sale for 16s 6d, but it was obvious legal action was planned so it disappeared from the nice book shops. Then you have to buy it under the counter at newsagents and elsewhere for two pounds. If you are dead lucky you can still buy a glossary with all the names converted for a little extra.

It all came to a head this week. Frank Hardy was arrested and charged with malicious libel. There is a big fuss too in the Labor Party. *Power without Glory* was printed by the same firm that prints *Labor Call*, the ALP paper, and it has a second edition with 16 000 copies ready to go.

Yesterday John Galbally appeared in the City Court on behalf of Mrs Ellen Wren, 75, of Studley Park Road, Kew, wife of John Wren Snr, 79, financier.

Mr Galbally said that the book claimed Mrs Wren committed adultery and had a child by a man other than her husband. The child was the last of Mrs Wren's nine children. He had died when three or four years old.

Mr Galbally said that Mrs Wren 'who is now approaching 80' was a woman of unblemished character. 'Although the hand that rocked the cradle has not grown weary and unsteady,' he said 'it is raised in vehement protest at this wicked lie and I proclaim 'This is the foulest libel that was ever written'. Mr Galbally continued:

This man is a Communist and it is part of a Communist conspiracy against our Government. There are other serious libels. It defames among other things the Parliament, the judiciary and the army. It imputes that Mr Justice Gavan Duffy was bribed in the Royal Commission on milk. It says of Field Marshal Sir Thomas Blamey that he ran a racket in houses of ill-repute.

As for Frank Hardy, he has been released on £500 bail. *Smith's Weekly* says he is married with two children and while writing the novel he worked 16 hours a day, earning money where he could, chiefly as a handyman and reporter for an obscure trotting newspaper.

Why had he written this book? To show that a democracy could be perverted by power hungry men for their own ends. 'I have been accused' he said 'of being anti-Catholic — my seven brothers and sisters are Catholics. I have been accused of being a Communist. I am a Communist'.

When asked if the book was based on real events and living persons, he said: 'To that question I always reply, "I made the whole thing up. But I don't expect you to believe that".'

It looks as if Frank Hardy either will go to gaol or have the best seller Australia has ever seen.

Note: In June 1951 a jury found Hardy not guilty and never again did Hardy write a novel which sold so splendidly.

Good-bye to the dear old Cables

27 OCTOBER 1940

A Melbourne cable tram

Melbourne's last cable tram ran along Bourke Street at the week-end.

It's all over. They started in 1885, provided very nearly the best tramway service on earth and carried four thousand million passengers.

Many people feel cheated. Melburnians love the old cable cars and thousands wanted to say good-bye. However the chairman of the Tramways Board, Mr Hector Hercules Bell, kept it a secret. Even members of the Board were not told until the last minute.

Mr Bell said he did this 'to foil the disorderly element'. On previous last tram occasions, the trams had been torn almost to pieces. Progressively we have been getting electric power trams since 1925 and the Clifton Hill line is the last to change over.

It had to come because of the problem of getting new steel cable. At its peak we had 95 miles of cable under the roads in Melbourne. Mr Bell said the normal life of a cable in Bourke Street was 17 weeks. Thanks to careful maintenance they had kept this one going for an extra 38 weeks and that was a record in the history of the system.

But it's all very sad. Gripman Arthur Coppledick was the veteran. In 45 years he travelled 400 miles a week, and put up the staggering total of half a million miles, all standing up.

He remembers the first time they scored full uniform. That was for the visit of the Duke of York (King George V) in 1901. Before that the symbol of authority was the peaked cap, which you bought at Lincoln Stuart's in Flinders Street for three shillings and sixpence.

Rules were strict. Boots had to be polished, collars kept clean, and clothes brushed. During the awful heat wave of 1908, the strait-laced rules were relaxed a little. The company gave permission for gripmen and conductors to remove their coats. Some took off their vests, collars and ties as well. The company panicked and rescinded the order. Heaven knowns what the men might have taken off next.

Back in the early days the cable trams were lit with kerosene lamps; two lamps inside the car and another suspended from the roof of the dummy. Sydney visitors who always liked to disparage the cable trams said it was just as well they didn't go faster than 12 mph, it would blow out the lamps.

Yet they were magnificent for moving large crowds. In the 1930s they used to move along Sydney Road to Brunswick at the rate of one every half-minute. The absolutely classic cry came from the gripman, 'Hold on for the curve please'.

Nor was it said just for fun. It was quite possible to be thrown from the side of the dummy on to the roadway. The trams always rang bells as they passed each other. Some thought this was a cheery greeting like ships passing at sea. But the real reason was to warn passengers jumping off that another tram was passing.

The crowded last trams, you will remember, always left the city at 11.30 p.m. The cable stopped soon after midnight. Those of us who live out in the suburbs can remember the sad, sinking feeling when the humming noise of the cable was not there any more 'The cable is stopped' was the common expression and you knew you had to walk home.

Now that cable is stopped for ever.

Squizzy Taylor is Dead

28 OCTOBER 1927

'Squizzy' Taylor (right)

'Snowy' Cutmore

Theodore Joseph Leslie Taylor, 42, of Richmond, better known as Squizzy Taylor, is dead. So too is John 'Snowy' Cutmore, 35, of Carlton.

At 6.45 pm last night, a man rushed into the Carlton police station and reported a man had been shot at a house in Barkly Street. They had better fetch a doctor.

When they arrived they found Cutmore dead in his bedroom. His mother, Mrs Gladys Cutmore was staggering about bleeding from a wound in her shoulder, weeping and wringing her hands.

There was mess everywhere, the walls peppered with bullet holes, cartridge cases on the floor, a smashed lamp, a smashed mirror.

It was not until 10 minutes later that they discovered Squizzy Taylor also had been shot. He staggered out of the house, fell into a taxi, saying 'I have been shot, take me to St Vincent's Hospital'. These were his last words. He died soon after his arrival.

Nobody is saying much, but the police have gathered a few details from the hire car driver, John Hall. Yesterday Taylor went on a great hunt around the hotels. For years there had been a Cutmore–Taylor vendetta, feuding over a girlfriend who ran a beer house in St Kilda.

Taylor didn't find Cutmore, so he ordered Hall to drive him to the house in Barkly Street. Cutmore was ill in bed with influenza. Police believe he was in a sitting position, he drew a revolver from under his pillow and fired at Taylor. Taylor also fired and both men were hit with simultaneous shots.

There was much wild indiscriminate firing. According to the *Sun* two bullets struck Cutmore, two pierced the wall alongside his bed, another entered the wall over his head, and a sixth shattered a lamp on a washstand while another hit the mirror on a dressing table.

At the first shot Mrs Cutmore senior ran into the bedroom, but she received a bullet through her right shoulder. There was another man with Taylor. He tried to check Taylor's flow of blood, but according to Hall, he left the car at the corner of Johnston and Brunswick Streets.

The newspapers are having their say today about Taylor. The *Argus* says:

From his youth the life of Leslie Taylor was a sordid record of criminality. Taylor who affected smartness of dress and polish in his dealings with the police force, delighted to surround himself with an air of mystery and cleverness...He came to be regarded as a master mind among criminals. This reputation was not well founded. Taylor was a criminal of ordinary mentality whose distinguishing features were his callous disregard for the lives of others, his treachery towards his associates, and his personal cowardice.

The *Herald* is even tougher:

Squizzy Taylor was a swaggering, conceited criminal fop, who glorified in the underworld reputation of being a man of courage, whereas in fact, he was a sneak with the cowardice of a sneak.

Squizzy Taylor was a little man, who dressed in a bowler hat, elegant suits, and overcoats with fine scarves. Very few people today are regretting his passing.

Kelly Sentenced to Death

31 OCTOBER 1880

The jury has found Ned Kelly guilty, and Sir Redmond Barry has sentenced him to death.

One wonders if ever there was such an extraordinary exchange between judge and the condemned. The *Argus* reported it all yesterday.

His Honour: No circumstances that I can conceive could have altered the result of your trial.

Kelly: Perhaps not from what you can now conceive, but if you had heard me examine the witnesses it would have been different.

His Honour: I give you credit for all the skill you appear to desire to assume.

Kelly: No I don't wish to assume anything. There is no flashness or bravado about me. It is not that I want to save my life, because I know I would have been capable of clearing myself of the charge, and I could have saved my life in spite of all against me.

His Honour: The facts are so numerous and so convincing...no rational person would hesitate to arrive at any other conclusion but that the verdict of the jury is irresistible...

Kelly: No, I don't think that. My mind is as easy as the mind of any man in the world

Ned Kelly in the dock

as I am prepared to show before God and man.

His Honour: It is blasphemous for you to say that. You appear to revel in the idea of having put men to death.

Kelly: More men than me have put men to death but I am the last man in the world that would take a man's life. Two years ago, even if my own life was at stake, and I am confident that if I thought a man would shoot me, I would give him a chance of keeping his life, and would part rather with my own. But if I knew that through him innocent persons' lives were at stake I certainly would have to shoot him if he forced me to do so, but I would want to know that he was really going to take innocent life.

His Honour: Your statement involves a cruelly wicked charge of perjury against a phalanx of witnesses.

Kelly: I daresay, but a day will come at a bigger court than this when we shall see which is right and which is wrong. No matter how long a man lives, he is bound to come to judgement somewhere, and as well here as anywhere.

His Honour:....A felon who has cut himself off from all decencies, all the affections, charities, and all the obligations of society is as helpless and degraded as a wild beast of the field. He has nowhere to lay his head...That is the life of the outlaw or felon and it would be well for those young men who are so foolish as to consider that it is brave of a man to sacrifice the lives of his fellow creatures in carrying out his own wild ideas...to reflect that the unfortunate termination of your life is a miserable death...

Sir Redmond passed the death sentence. 'May the Lord have mercy on your soul.'

Kelly: I will go a little further than that, and say I will see you there where I go.

Note: The prophecy was awesome. Sir Redmond Barry, after a short illness, died on 23 November 1880 only 12 days after Kelly's execution.

NOVEMBER

Archer, the winner

Conscripts will Not be Forced into Battle

1 NOVEMBER 1916

Poster supporting conscription

The conscription referendum has been lost. So now our young men will not be forced into battle.

As the voting stands today, the majority for 'No' is 89 907 votes. Victoria, Western Australia and Tasmania voted 'Yes', but NSW with a resounding 'No' vote, and a majority of 113 034, carried the day.

The Prime Minister, Mr Hughes, is bitterly disappointed. He says our 'No' vote was greeted with enthusiasm in Germany. He quoted *Vossische Zeitung* which said 'The result is the sharpest condemnation of the whole policy of Mr Hughes, who is the most noisy and abusive Prime Minister of enemy countries'.

Mr Hughes seized on that one.

Is there one man or woman who does not feel humiliated and ashamed to see in what light their action is regarded in Germany? These words of commendation from whose hands are red with the blood of our Australian soldiers; these words of jubilation from the slayers of women and children; these marks of approval from these inhuman monsters, who have, with fiendish malignity, inoculated Brithish prisoners with foul diseases, must burn themselves into the soul of every true Australian.

The *Argus*, too, is disgusted. It says:

The 'No' vote was an appeal to sloth, cupidity and self indulgence. Nearly 200,000 young unmarried men between the ages 21 and 35 were called upon to say whether or not they would go away and fight for human freedom or stay at home and take the chance of getting others to do it. All the alluring cries of selfishness prompted them to say 'No'.

The campaign was highly emotional. The trade unions and the Labor Party were behind 'No' vote but their cause received little space in newspapers like the *Argus*. Polling day was on 28 October. All hotels throughout the Commonwealth were closed on the day and the sale of liquor anywhere was prohibited.

Last-minute meetings were volatile. For example, Mr Rodgers, MP, spoke at Crossley but the meeting was packed with anti-conscriptionists. He was greeted with a fusillade of eggs and he was hit seven times.

Madame Nellie Melba personally appealed on behalf of the 'Yes' vote in Lilydale and there was a huge gathering at the Melbourne Town Hall. Mr Hume Cool told the crowd: 'Unless Britain maintains her might, Australia will not be worth 24 hours purchase. Australia should follow Nelson's line — seek out the invader wherever he is and crush him there'.

There was a march of 10 000 troops through Sydney: AIF, cadets, and the militia, better known as the 'Hughesiliers'. The march took two hours to move past and was designed, completely, to impress last-minute voters.

The *Argus* also carried a series of eloquent poems. One of the most moving was under the pen-name of Waratah:

And we're waiting, waiting, waiting:
Don't say we are waiting in vain.
Think of those lads, who are maimed for life.
Think of the Anzac slain.
Fill up the gaps, boys, let all the world see
That no matter how great was our loss
There are many more men as good as the first
Way down near the Southern Cross.

Raised Hemline Raises Eyebrows

2 NOVEMBER 1965

The VRC has been suffering from falling attendances, so there is a new craze, importing human fillies for the Spring Racing Carnival.

This year we imported Christine Borge from France and Jean Shrimpton from England. Rivalry was keen. Miss Borge, sponsored by the Wool Board, arrived on 25 October.

She walked down the gangway from her aircraft, swayed, took paces forward, then very prettily collapsed unconscious on the tarmac. Tony Lewis of the Wool Board sprinted forward and carried her off in his arms. TV cameras purred and the pictures made the front pages of every newspaper in the land.

The next day Christine asked: 'When ees the Shrimp due to arrive?' Not until Saturday, Miss Borge. She giggled 'I'd like to know how she will be beat all the publicity I've had' crowed Miss Borge.

I think it is one of those famous last words that will go down in history. The Shrimp more than made the front pages. Could I quote one story by Barrie Watts from yesterday's *Sun*:

> There she was, the world's highest-paid model, snubbing the iron-clad conventions of fashionable Flemington in a dress five

'The Shrimp' at the Cup

inches above the knee, NO hat, NO gloves and NO stockings. The shockwaves were still rumbling round fashionable Melbourne last night when Jean Shrimpton — The Shrimp — swore she hadn't realised she was setting off such an outraged upheaval at Flemington on Saturday.

'I don't see what was wrong with the way I looked.' she said. 'I wouldn't have dressed differently for any race meeting anywhere else in the world.'

For my money, she looked tremendous — but Flemington was not amused. Fashion-conscious Derby Day race-goers were horrified. 'Insulting....' 'a disgrace ...,' 'how dare she...!' If the skies had rained acid not a well-dressed woman there would have given the Shrimp an umbrella.

For hours Flemington had ached and sweltered in 94-degree heat, waiting for the late arrival of the English girl billed as the most beautiful on earth. She walked in serene and poised, dressed in this ultra-short shift she designed herself, showing a lovely amount of lissom leg unhindered by nylon. Her long hair swung about in the hot wind.'

Of course, the terrible shock was this. She had been imported by the VRC especially to present the Fashions in the Field prizes. Could anyone in their right mind declare what she had on was fashionable?

I am afraid so. Every young female in Melbourne will now want to wear skirts 5 inches above the knee. However today she was severely tamed for the Cup. Her sponsors, Dupont International, forced her to wear a very demure three-piece grey and beige tweed suit, plus hat and gloves.

She commented sadly: 'If they wanted someone conventional, they have brought the wrong person to Melbourne. I feel Melbourne is not yet ready for me. It seems to be some years behind London.'

The London newspapers have splashed the story quoting Miss Shrimpton 'wailing'...'I have been disciplined'. The *Evening News* says it is a long time since anyone in London has seen the Shrimp with bag, gloves and hat. Her image is the casual girl with wind-swept hair.

Scandal in Collingwood

3 NOVEMBER 1903

The most amazing thing in Collingwood, if not all Australia, is Mr John Wren's illegal tote.

At 136 Johnston Street there is a tea shop. If you go in there and say to the respectable-looking tea merchant that you want to put half a sovereign on the tote he will look at you innocently, 'What tote'.

No, the front entrance is round the back in Sackville Street, where there is a wood yard with a sign: 'WOOD & COAL'. This is the tote. it has agents in tobacconists and barber shops all over Melbourne, and according to the Attorney-General, Mr Isaac Isaacs, it nets Mr Wren £20 000 a year.

When you enter there is actually a pile of wood in the corner, but there is another door which leads through a wall 12 feet high and topped with barbed wire. Through here is the main betting ring. All along one side is the Tote. It is a very long structure and it looks like a cage built to retain ferocious animals. There is a raised platform about 3 feet high and behind this is a list of all the horses entered for today's racing.

In full cry it is a fantastic scene. Wren makes sure nobody is recognised at his Tote so his attendants wear cowls over their heads and gowns down to their ankles. They look like medieval torturers or members of the Ku Klux Klan.

Then behind the innermost wall, there is a secret passage about 18 inches wide, designed for a quick get-away in case of a police raid. There is also a team of savage bulldogs to be released in times of emergency.

Finally there is the Tote Room, where one makes one's bets. There's a number of these, so designed that it is impossible to see inside. Tickets are always a shilling each, but you can get 15 000 shillings invested on a single race.

Mr Wren takes 10 per cent.

No women are allowed inside, no children under the age of 15 and, as an *Argus* reporter said the other day, everything is done fairly, above board and with great efficiency. Wren owns all the houses round about and they are honeycombed with secret passages and special escape routes.

Of course, it is a public scandal. There is a Baptist Church in Sackville Street, the Reverend Carey claims he has seen 1571 people enter the tote in two hours at the rate of 13 a minute.

Closing it is easier said than done. Everyone from the Police Commissioner down has been accused of being in the pay of Mr Wren. But the preventative measures are so brilliant. As soon as the police arrive words spreads with the speed of light, so that when constables break in a miracle has been performed, there is nothing in sight, not even betting tickets. . .only fierce snarling dogs.

Today, of course, was Melbourne Cup Day. Superintendent Sharp and Sergeant O'Donnell assembled a large body of police, then marched them to Collingwood. The men did not know where they were going until they actually got there. Sgt. O'Donnell took only one man into his confidence, Senior Constable Carter, said to be the most silent man in the force.

They smashed their way into the tote with picks and crow bars. At 6 a.m. a man with an axe approached the tote and demanded admission. Innocently, he said he was the wood man. 'I work here.'

Well, 60 policemen had a fruitless day. Not a soul, not a bettor turned up. The clever Mr Wren conducted all his business from temporary quarters elsewhere, and the word is that he lost very little through the police interruption.

Brawling and Looting in Police Strike

4 NOVEMBER 1923

Mr Lawson

At least 800 of Melbourne's police are on strike. Last night it was anarchy in the city with scenes of unprecedented lawlessness.

There was brawling, there were fights with bottles. Looting was rife: 78 shops had their windows smashed. There were 200 casualties and 58 people were arrested.

The Premier, Mr Lawson, has put out an appeal for loyal citizens to come forward and so far 2000 men have enrolled. Seventy-five per cent of them are returned soldiers and a fine sprinkling of them are former light horsemen who will become mounted constables.

It all started at 6 p.m. with a brawl at the corner of Swanston and Bourke Streets. Men were fighting it out with bottles, breaking bottles of beer over the heads of whoever happened to be nearest them. Soon pools of blood spattered the roadway.

At 6:30 p.m. the brawlers turned their attention from fighting amongst themselves to attacking shops. Standing in the centre of the roadway a party of youths deliberately threw bottles at the windows of the Leviathan Clothing Company. Discarding the hats they were wearing, they grabbed new ones and rushed away wearing them.

Next they went to F.H. Kermode, jeweller, at 157 Swanston Street and there was a cry: 'Smash it in'. A semi-drunk man took a full bottle of beer, smashed in the window and within seconds the entire stock had disappeared.

And so they went from shop to shop, smashing, looting. Soon the mob was in complete control of the entire block surrounded by Bourke, Swanston, Elizabeth and Collins Streets. At 7 p.m. a party of 40 police headed by three officers marched down Bourke Street with batons drawn. At the corner of Swanston Street they charged the mob. Some hooted and jeered, some fled, but there was a pitched battle between the hooligans, which swayed back and forth all the way to Elizabeth Street.

Soon the ambulances arrived and they did a constant shuttle carrying the wounded from the riot scene to the Melbourne Hospital. Police tried valiantly to make arrests, but in many cases the struggling and fighting was so intense they lost their quarry before they had dragged them a few yards.

There was a quiet period when the looters, presumably, went off to dispose of their booty. At this time one man was about to kick in Myer's windows when he was felled by a Myer guard with such force he had to be picked up by the ambulance. So instead the mob dashed for the Monte de Piete where in the dark men greedily grabbed everything in sight, rings, watches, bracelets, jewellery.

At 9.30 they turned their attention to the London Stores using stones, bottles and shod feet to smash the windows. They stole men's wear by the armful. Some they didn't even take away. Hats were worn or just kicked down the street. Women are looting too. Some gathering skirts, cardigans, hosiery and stuffing them into capacious bags. Small boys were stealing tinned fruit, anything they could lay their hands on. It was an incredible orgy.

By 10.30 police in motor patrols had the city under control. However it remains an ugly situation. Mr Lawson is adamant and unforgiving. He has now put out an order that he will not reinstate any of the striking police. They have been false to their oaths, they violated their trust, and deserted their posts.

A Portrait or a Caricature?

7 NOVEMBER 1944

There has been an astonishing stir in the art world. William Dobell, 45, won the 1943 Archibald Prize for his painting of Joshua Smith, another artist.

Mary Edwards and Joe Wolinski, representing a group of artists, asked Sydney's Equity Court to declare that the painting was not a portrait in the terms of the prize, but a caricature.

The interest in the case has been incredible. The usually sedate Equity Court was so packed it was described as 'the biggest legal smash hit since Ned Kelly', with a complete battery of KCs, including the redoubtable Garfield Barwick for the objectors.

The first witness was Mr J.S. MacDonald, former director of the Sydney and Melbourne National Galleries and art critic for the *Age*. He said Joshua Smith of the portrait looked as if he had been cornered by the New York police and beaten with a piece of lead pipe because he wouldn't come clean. The picture was not a portrait of a human being at all, let alone a person unless the person was a freak, a fasting man.

Dr Vivian Benjafield, a Macquarie Street specialist, said Dobell's portrait was a picture of a corpse — the body of a man who had died in a peculiar position, remained like that for several months and dried up. At least ten vertebrae would have been required to produce the length of neck, whereas there were only seven in the human neck.

Dobell admitted in court that there was a slight exaggeration of Smith's arms, but said he had endeavoured to portray the character of a man whom he had learned to know thoroughly when he shared a tent with him on camouflage work. He was a man who possessed determination amounting to stubborness and it was his aim to show these things.

Paul Haeflinger, art critic of the *Sydney Morning Herald*, said:

This exaggeration you will find right through art. El Greco was such an expressionist. Rembrandt would depart from the pure physical to express emotion. In more recent times Goya, Cezanne, to some extent Picasso and Roualt have shown the same tendency.

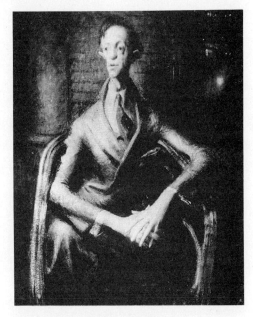

'Joshua Smith' by William Dobell

Today Mr Justice Roper gave his judgement. He found for Dobell and the Sydney Gallery Trustees. He said:

In my opinion the evidence is overwhelming that there was ground for forming the intelligent opinion that Dobell's painting was a portrait. I find it as a fact that it is a portrait within the meaning in the words in the will, and consequently the trustees did not err in admitting it to the competition.

Miss Edwards and Mr Wolinski will have to pay costs which could be considerable, as much as 1500 pounds. Mr Dobell was indisposed and out of town. He did come to hear the judgement read.

Critic Clive Turnbull writes:

This affair leaves on unpleasant taste in the mouth. There have been many similar episodes in many countries, and all of them nasty. Attacks of this kind may destroy a sensitive man. Creative artists are often hypersensitive, they are easy game for those who choose to attack them. In other countries such men are honoured. Here they can be hounded.

Burke and Wills Perish, but Archer Wins the Cup

8 NOVEMBER 1861

Melbourne has been in a state of terrible grief all the week. The news reached us by telegram on 2 November that the continent had been crossed, but both Burke and Wills were dead and one man, King, was returning to tell the tale.

All flags are at half-mast and the buildings are draped with black bunting. Prayers are being said in the churches. Thank heavens there have been a few events to relieve the gloom. There is the three-day Spring racing carnival at Flemington and yesterday we had a new event called the Melbourne Cup.

The rail to Flemington is only just opened and most of the crowd of 4000 went there by steam train. The fare was 1s 6d first class and 1 shilling second class.

There were four events, the Maiden Plate, the Two Year Old Stakes, the Melbourne Cup and the Handicap Hurdle. Not a very busy programme, but always there is plenty to do out at Flemington. There are the amusement tents, roulette, Aunty Sally, fortune tellers, and a long line of tents for food and drink. The caterers are those enterprising gentlemen, Messrs Spiers and Pond, who are bringing out next month from England, the much awaited Mr Stephenson and his cricket XI.

The Melbourne Cup was arranged by the Victoria Turf Club and there was a full meeting at the Albion Hotel on Tuesday for the Calcutta Sweep and to organise the betting. If you are a punter you must know the Albion. It is next to Cobb & Co on the north side of Bourke Street between Swanston and Elizabeth.

There were 17 starters and our champion Melbourne horse, Mormon, despite a weight of 10 stone 1 lb, was the clear favourite. The Sydney horse Archer was quoted at a splendid 10 to 1 but by yesterday he had come back to 8 to 1.

Even before the start the Cup was unnerving. The mare Twilight, bolted and did the full circuit of the course. Twilight was brought back into line again and, at the start, Flatcatcher was the first away with Archer second and the rest strung behind.

Then just as they were entering the straight for the first time came disaster. Medora fell bringing down both Despatch and Twilight. Medora was killed, Despatch had to be destroyed, and Joseph Morrison, the jockey, broke his arm. Twilight got to her feet and bolted off the course.

But Archer was untroubled. He went to the front at the river turn and coming into the straight was three lengths ahead from Antonelli and Mormon. In the home run, Archer was superb. The horse cleared right away winning by six lengths from Mormon, with Prince two lengths back third, and Antonelli fourth.

There is absolute misery amongst the punters. Few people expected this Sydney win, and there is alarm that there will be many defaulters at settling time tomorrow. You see, nothing much was known about Archer. Mr Etienne De Mestre, the owner and trainer, stabled him at the Botanical Hotel in Domain Road, South Yarra. Then Mr De Mestre trained the horse secretly in St Kilda Park.

Archer came from Braidwood, 50 miles from Canberra, and his strapper walked him all the way to Melbourne in easy stages. One wonders whether he will do it again for the next Cup.

Further reading: *Cup Day*, Maurice Cavanough and Meurig Davies. *First Tuesday in November*, D.L. Bernstein.

Railway Spans the Continent

9 NOVEMBER 1917

The line crosses the Nullarbor Plain

You can almost hear the cheering right across the continent. We now have a railway line that goes all the way from Brisbane to Perth. Of course, the promise to build the railway was made as an inducement to get Western Australia to join the Eastern States in forming the Commonwealth.

The *Argus* said on 20 October:
For nearly five years two lines of railway have been pushed farther and farther into the vast solitudes to the north of the Great Australian Bight. Today the two lines will become one, for the ends of steel will meet at last on the lonely levels of the eastern end of the great Nullarbor Plain.

The thousand miles of waterless wilderness which have cut Western Australia off from the eastern States have been bridged, and from Brisbane to Perth, a distance of 3200 miles, the capitals of all mainland States are linked by railways.

The meeting of the rails marks the completion of a task without parallel in the history of railway construction. Longer lines have been built, and lines presenting far greater engineering difficulties, but nowhere else in the world has a railway been built across a 1000 miles of waterless country, which was for nearly 800 miles absolutely uninhabited.

The battle to get this railway started back in 1870. In 1911 the estimate of the cost was 3 988 000 pounds. Work started on 31 July 1912 and so far the cost has been 6 537 971 pounds.

A huge part of the cost has been in providing water. There is storage along the line for 50 million gallons and there are 27 bores. But the miracle is this. It means that Perth is now within three days of Melbourne. That cuts the travelling time to the West by half.

Of course, the difference in the gauges is a nightmare. There is 3 feet 6 inches in West Australia. You get 4 feet 8½ inches on the East-West line at Kalgoorlie, back to 3 feet 6 inches at Port Augusta, then another change to 5 feet 3 inches at Terowie.

The first train over the line left Port Augusta on 22 October, reaching Kalgoorlie on 24 October. At the moment the line is only partly ballasted so the average speed will be only 30 mph. However when the ballasting is complete the average will be 44 mph.

The train is now in its first week of proper operation. There is great moaning about the costs in Kalgoorlie where there have been protests about the scale of fares. A first-class single from Melbourne to Perth is £10; second-class single, £6 13s 6d. Sleeping berths are an extra 19s a might first class and 5s second. Meals vary from 1s 9d to 4 shillings.

The *Sydney Morning Herald* points out it has hardly been roses all the way. There have been strikes, dismissals, commissions of inquiry, and recriminations all round. And yet
...as one looks back it seems extraordinary that during the greatest war in the world's history Australia should be able to complete her transcontinental railway while in other parts of the Empire the lines have been pulled up to provide rails and material for traffic on the European battle fronts.

Hugh Mahon, as Irish as they Come

10 NOVEMBER 1920

Anglo-Irish feelings are seething. The British Government has banned Archbishop Mannix from entering Ireland. That is bad enough, but Alderman Terence McSwiney, the Mayor of Cork, has died in a hunger strike.

This week-end 3000 people attended an Irish demonstration in the Richmond City Reserve. The chairman was Hugh Mahon, a member of the House of Representatives and a former minister.

He is as Irish as they come, this Hugh Mahon, a native of Tullamore, King's County, Ireland. He was a friend and associate of the great Parnell himself, and a prisoner in Kalmainham Jail back 1881–82.

The *Argus* report of his speech caused a sensation.

The chairman said that the outrage committed upon Archbishop Mannix would never be forgotten by the Irish people of Australia. Never in Russia under the worst ruler of the Czars had there been such an infamous murder as that of the late Alderman McSwiney. They were told in the papers that Alderman McSwiney's widow sobbed over his coffin.

If there was a just God in heaven that sob would reach around the world, and would one day shake the foundations of this bloody and accursed Empire (Loud applause). The other day he was approached by a vinegar-faced wowser who said that the police in Ireland were being shot in the back. If they were shot in the back it must be because they were running away. But there were no police in Ireland. They were spies, informers and bloody cut-throats. (Applause) He read with delight that some of those murdering thugs had been sent to their account and he trusted that Ireland would not be profaned by their carcasses. (Applause) Their souls were probably in hell, and their bodies would be sent to England. (Applause) He would not have the sweet pastures of Ireland poisoned by their carrion clay. (Applause)

The Prime Minister, Mr Hughes, was outraged by this speech. He demanded to see Mr Mahon, the member for Kalgoorlie, but Mahon refused to come, claiming a sprained ankle. Mr Hughes sent him a letter telling him he intended to move for his expulsion from the House of Representatives.

Mr Hughes is unimpressed by that sprained ankle. His secretary noted that Mahon was fully dressed with his boots on. He offered to drive Mahon by car to the Prime Minister, but still he refused to come.

Today it happened. Mr Hughes moved that Mahon be expelled from the House. His seditious remarks were in defiance of his oath of allegiance which swore that he 'would be faithful and bear true allegiance to His Majesty King George his heirs and successors'.

Mr Mahon did not attend the House. Instead he sent a very angry letter to Mr Hughes.

I have learned that you have been generous enough to imply that my absence from the House was due to lack of courage. I should have thought that the recollection of some incidents of your own career would prevent you from impugning anyone's courage... You based your speech on a report in an enemy newspaper. The epithet murderer rightly applies to a force which slays innocent people whenever they cannot find the guilty ones...I am not aware that the oath of an Australian Parliamentian ties him in allegiance to Lloyd George and his colleagues. If it did I think many members would refuse to take it.

Note: Mr Mahon was expelled 34 votes to 17. There was a by-election and Mahon again nominated, but he was defeated by a Nationalist candidate and never entered Parliament again.

Good Riddance to Sydney

11 NOVEMBER 1850

John Pascoe Fawkner

Melbourne as you must realise has a tremendous distaste for the mother city, Sydney. The Port Phillipian considers himself a superior style of person because he does not live in a penal district.

Right back to 1840 we have fought, oh, how we have fought, for separation from New South Wales. What infuriates us is the misappropriation of Port Phillip funds in Sydney. The *Argus* describes the brethren in the East as Sydney robbers.

Last November and December we had a series of protest meetings. John Pascoe Fawkner told us we were slaves under the thraldom of the robber people of Sydney. He announced there was no point in taking up muskets. There were too few of us for that. We had another power, passive resistance, and he, for one, would refuse to buy all excisable goods.

The Separation Bill went through the House of Commons on the first of August but the news, brought to us by the speediest of sailing vessels, did not reach us until today.

I can't tell you the glee, the joy, the pure bliss of being rid of Sydney. The *Argus* for example says:

A spell seems to have fallen upon all around us. Our inkstand and gum-pot have been dancing reels this hour past; our faithless lamp has persisted in staggering towards our wine glass; and thrice we have been tricked into toasting our future Victoria in a bumper of whale oil — the best news ever to reach our shores.

Immediately beacons were lit all around the town, at Richmond, Collingwood and St Kilda. There was a 21-gun salute and a balloon went up that distributed parchment slips announcing the good news.

The *Argus* continued:

We unhesitatingly assert that there never was an occasion in which the residents so readily, so cheerfully and so unanimously united in giving expression to their joy. Every house was illuminated. Even in the most dirty hovels in the most dirty of all the dirty lanes in the city followed the example of their neighbour and gave some token of rejoicing.

There are fireworks, gunfire and barrels of tar blazing in the streets. The buildings in Elizabeth, Bourke, Swanston and Collins Streets are bedecked with bunting and great transparencies, many of them far from kind to Sydney.

The Bush Inn sports a fascinating series. One shows the Sydney dragon disgorging all the money stolen from Melbourne. This regurgitation was brought about by a stab in the stomach from a spear labelled 'separation'. Another shows Britannia addressing her children, Sydney and Melbourne. 'You are naughty children, I must separate you. Phillip make sure you act like a man. Sydney, make sure you don't interfere with the boy'.

Robert Ferguson, the linen draper in Lonsdale Street, has a transparency depicting Sydney as a decrepit old man, wailing over his loss. Port Phillip, though, looks magnificent, like a rich English Earl. He has a bag of gold at his side and he says 'Through my youth you have fleeced me, now I give you a last adieu'.

The mighty celebrations are planned to go for a week, and there is not the slightest doubt here that this new colony, in all respects, eventually will become far superior to New South Wales.

Sydney Sinks the *Emden*

14 NOVEMBER 1914

Watching the stricken Emden

The German cruiser *Emden* is ashore at the Cocos Islands, a complete wreck. The victor is our cruiser HMAS *Sydney*.

It is a complete triumph for our Australian sailors. Messages of congratulations are coming in from London, from Canada, from New Zealand and all around the Empire.

The *Emden* was a mystery raider. Already it had sunk 19 merchant ships. On 9 November the *Emden* arrived off the Cocos Islands, landed 40 men, three officers and four Maxim guns. Three boats went ashore. The German commander, Captain Mueller, could easily have shelled the wireless station into submission.

But he did not. This gave the Cocos manager a chance to send out emergency signals. While the Germans were ashore wrecking the station and all its instruments, the *Sydney*, pouring smoke, appeared on the horizon.

Emden did not wait to pick up its shore party, immediately it moved to do battle with the Australian. *Emden's* shooting at first was excellent. It hit the *Sydney* killing three RAN sailors and wounding another fifteen.

But *Sydney* returned an accurate and deadly fire, and the *Emden* salvos became totally inaccurate. *Emden* lost two funnels and a mast and the entire after section was ablaze. The action lasted an hour, until the *Emden* was in such a helpless condition its only choice was to run up on the beach.

The *Emden* has 200 killed, 30 wounded. The Captain is captured and unharmed, so, too, is a nephew of the German Emperor. The German landing party, took the opportunity, while the sea battle was on, to commandeer a schooner with two months provisions, and escape.

The interesting part is the old world courtesy displayed by both sides. The Germans when they landed were most considerate to the Cocos Island staff and did them no harm. We learn too in the *Sydney Morning Herald* that when the *Emden* captured merchantmen, the German took the crews off their ships before they sunk them, then treated them well.

Indeed there is the extraordinary story of the *Gryfevale*, 4437 tons, which Von Mueller met near Calcutta. The commander noted that *Gryfevale's* captain had his wife aboard. So he spared the ship, put the crews of other captured ships aboard, and sent a message to the captain's wife. 'Dear Madam, — In the name of the Emperor of Germany I hereby hand back your husband's steamer.'

The national euphoria is something to behold. This is the first action for our Navy and it has proved our absolute skill and valour. The High Commissioner for Australia, Sir George Reid, said 'The sea breed is all right. It is never more all right than when Australians are on Australian ships under the white ensign with the Australian flag at the jackstaff'. He added that the treatment meted out by the *Emden* to captured ships showed there were still two kinds of Germans. He could only hope that a large number of the gallant sailors had been rescued.

Newspapers everywhere are paying tribute. London's *Daily Telegraph* says 'In a Nelsonian spirit of humanity, after victory every assistance was rendered to the *Emden's* survivors. Australians may be proud of the manner in which their navy has been blooded.'

Boxing Hero Wins World Title

15 NOVEMBER 1952

In 139 whirlwind seconds at Johannesburg, Australian Jimmy Carruthers has become the first Australian-born boxer to win a world title.

He twice hammered world bantamweight champion, Vic Toweel, out of the ring for a count of nine, then left him helpless on the canvas. Twenty-eight thousand fans gave a mighty roar of applause for the new champion.

Ken Moses of the *Argus* spoke to Carruthers tonight by radio telephone. Carruthers said:

All I could see in front of me was Vic's bleeding face and the world title, so I kept hammering him. I took the fight to him from the start and he never had a chance to settle down. The bell went and I went straight across to him and landed a solid left cross to his chin.

It staggered him, he reeled back to his corner with his eyes glazed. I could hardly believe it. I followed him and got on top of him, pummelling him all the time.

I could see I was doing damage. I had cut his left eye, and skin was missing from his lip and nose.

I moved in again. I let him have two more left crosses, and he went sailing through the ropes. His feet shot into the air and he landed on the reporters' table and rolled over. They told me later he came back at the count of nine, but I wasn't counting I was just waiting for him.

A few moments later I had him out of the ring again. Again at the count of nine he was up, then I switched my attack to the body. He kept grabbing me, but I shook him off every time. I knew the time for the round was running out. I prayed it would not end before I had him.

He wanted a rest, and the spell before the second round was what he was waiting for. I said to myself 'This is it Jimmy' and I gave it everything I had.

I let fly a hail of punches. He struggled to his hands and knees but he had no chance of raising any further. I don't know how many times I hit him. He might have hit me, but I never felt a punch.

In Sydney, Carruthers's wife, Myra, wept with relief after speaking to her husband by radio telephone. She had been without sleep for 34 hours. She and a group of friends stayed up all night to hear the fight broadcast. Then she found her phone was out of order and she had to call from a neighbour's house.

'Jimmy told me' she said 'he is completely unmarked and he is like a dog with two tails'.

Under the terms of the agreement there has to be a return bout within 90 days, but next time, says Carruthers, it will be different. He will get 40 per cent of the gate and Toweel will get the 12 per cent.

A hero's homecoming is planned for Carruthers when he reaches Sydney on 1 December. Plans are being made to drive him in triumph through the city streets.

Jimmy Carruthers (right) leaves the ring after the bout with Vic Toweel

Cable Trams Set Melbourne Agog

16 NOVEMBER 1885

Wonder of wonders, at last, at last, cable trams have been running in Melbourne for five days and they really work.

You must forgive the elation. The battle has been long and agonising. We have won the cable trams largely due to the astonishing enthusiasm and patience of an American, Francis Boardman Clapp.

Mr Clapp first came here in 1857 and ran Cobb & Co's Melbourne to Ballarat line. But he believed Melbourne was perfect for street railways and cheap public transport. He thought it appalling when he had to pay half a crown to take a cab from Melbourne to Richmond.

In 1869 he formed a horse drawn omnibus company. These omnibuses ran to Carlton, Richmond, Collingwood and North Melbourne. Marvellous. It meant that if you lived in these suburbs you didn't have to suffer the business of keeping your own horses and stables.

The omnibuses were a big financial success, but Clapp's dream was to put in a proper power-operated tramway. An expatriate Englishman, Andrew Smith Hallidie, came up with this fascinating invention, a tram hauled by cable, and gave the idea to San Francisco in 1873.

Well it took the redoubtable Mr Clapp 20 years to unravel State, city and municipal jealousies. There was the terror that railways in the streets would take business away from Government trains; terror that trams running down Bourke, Flinders and Collins Streets would interfere with business; terror that he would make too much money out of it. The objection was even raised that a tram could never cross Elizabeth Street because it was so much of a public drain.

The question of who owned the public streets was a delicate one, and who would do the repairing? After a thousand compromises Clapp got there, conceding that the trams would revert to Government after 21 years, and his profit, if any, would not be more than 10 per cent.

As you can imagine, setting up 43 miles of a cable system is a gigantic operation. You have two rails with a hidden trench in the centre along which a continuous cable runs. The tram has a grip mechanism which grabs. When gripping the cable the tram is hauled along the road. When the driver wants to stop he releases the grip and applies the brakes.

Very simple, but the excavation works are huge. Last week using great teams of powerful horses, the engineer, George Duncan, laid the first cable. This tram line runs from Spencer along Flinders Street, up Wellington Parade, to Bridge Road, finishing at the Hawthorn Bridge.

The trams started running on 11 November. Just at the moment there are only five trams operating, between 8.30 and 6.30 p.m., and they are coming to a stop at every street corner. The speed is an average of six miles an hour, the same as the omnibuses, but it will be doubled soon.

The reason for this is the drivers are still training, but within a few weeks trams will run at night, more trams will come in and there will be a service every two minutes. A short trip is a penny, the whole route, threepence.

Passengers are advised they must get on or off only on the rear platform of the car. Failure to follow this advice, says the company, is a fruitful form of accidents.

All Melbourne is agog. Everybody wants to travel on this new form of transport.

Further reading: *Governing the Metropolis*, David Dunstan. *The Tramways of Australia*, Samuel Brimson.

Emus *V* Army

17 NOVEMBER 1932

Sir George Pearce

The Emu War, one of Australia's more regrettable military campaigns, is in full cry.

It all began several months ago. Wheat farmers in Campion, Western Australia, 180 miles east-north-east of Perth, claimed they were being invaded by an army of 20 000 emus. They appealed to the Government for help.

Sir George Pearce, Minister for Defence, despatched the 7th Heavy battery RAA under the command of Major G.W.P. Meredith. His second-in-command was Sergeant S.M. McMurray. They were equipped with two Lewis guns and 10 000 rounds of ammunition.

The campaign opened on 2 November and the Army scored 12 kills on the first day. But by the second day war correspondents were beginning to sound a note of disillusionment. The West Australian correspondent wired:

It would be perfect shooting country if only the quarry were content to be passive victims. Each mob has its leader, always an enormous black-plumed bird standing fully six feet high, who keeps watch while his fellows busy themselves with the wheat.

The way the birds can carry the wound caused by a nickel encased 303 bullet is astounding. Frequently the burst of machine gun fire will hit the brown mass of hurrying birds, causing a few to go head over heels, and others will falter but keep going. One small mob fired at today appeared to go unscathed but half a mile down the track, two were found in dying condition. One had been shot clean through the neck and another through the body. Only a hit in a vital spot will stop the birds.

On the third day Major Meredith's patrol encountered a huge force of 1000 emus, all bunched together with no hope of escape. They started to open fire, a dozen birds fell and the Lewis gun jammed. He had expended 2000 rounds with no great result. The Major told correspondents:

If we had a military division with the bullet carrying capacity of these birds, it would face any army in the world. They are like Zulus, whom even dum dum bullets would not stop.

Fourth and fifth day, nothing achieved, blazing sun with temperatures over a 100 degrees. Sixth day, thirsty emus were coming closer and the Army cornered 50 at a waterhole and opened fire. There was a terrible confusion of wounded flapping birds, struggling to escape. The Army men went in and clubbed to death with waddies those that were not killed outright. Score of kills:50.

Eighth day there was a call for a ceasefire with Campion farmers furious. 'City pussyfoots' said Mr G.J. Lambert, a local MLA.

However Sir George Pearce has had to endure a difficult time in the Senate. One member shouted 'The emus have won every round so far.' Another asked who was responsible for the farce of hunting birds with machine guns? A third was curious to know whether a campaign medal would be struck for all who took part in the campaign.

Sir George reported today that 300 emus had been killed. Charles Barrett, the naturalist, commented how sad, what a waste it all was. The birds in London would fetch £85 a pair.

Note: A month later the Premier of WA asked the Army to return, which they did. This time their tactics were better. They waited in ambush for the emus and their kill rate was higher.

237

Luxury Train Makes its Debut

18 NOVEMBER 1937

The Spirit of Progress

Victoria has a marvellous railway train, the Spirit of Progress, as modern and as speedy as anything in the world.

It has none of the ugly knobs, bulges, exposed pipes of normal steam engines. It is utterly smooth, streamlined and painted a dashing blue with a gold flair down the sides.

It had its debut to the public yesterday on a special official run to Geelong. Over 1000 people gathered at Spencer Street station to see it off and overhead were two aeroplanes, one of them the veteran *Spirit of Melbourne* DH4 biplane which had to battle desperately to keep pace with the speedy land machine.

The *Age* says:

The train's reception as it passed the Newport workshops, where it had been built during the past 21 months, was enthusiastic. Almost all the employees stopped work to watch their train gather speed on the way to Laverton.

And how it responded. Fifty, sixty, seventy miles an hour were passed by the locomotive, named after the pioneer who first landed in Victoria 103 years ago...73 miles an hour against a headwind was reached at Lara...

Inside the train, the 300 invited passengers found it hard to realise they were travelling at more than 70 mph. There was practically no noise or vibration, the air circulated gently at an even temperature of 70 degrees, and all windows were sealed.

Pastel-tinted carpets, panelled walls, seats upholstered in varied shades of leather; and in the parlour observation car, flowers, lounge chairs and settees all told of the new era in Victorian rail travel. There is splendid use of Australian timbers: panels of flowery walnut and jarrah are in the smoking compartments, royal walnut in the first class ladies' compartment, silver silkwood in the second, and ribbon walnut in the other compartments.

With a following wind the express reached 79 mph on the return trip. It was only prevented from reaching even higher speeds by cows that wandered over an open crossing between Newport and Laverton.

Before the train left, the Premier, Mr Dunstan, performed a launching ceremony by opening the door of the parlour car with a gold key. He said Victoria now had one of the finest trains in the world. He had travelled on most of the important railways overseas, and for beauty, utility and comfort, he had seen nothing to equal the *Spirit of Progress*. 'Long distance travel in the future' said he 'will be more of a pleasure than a test of endurance for passengers'.

Mr R.G. Menzies, who represented the Prime Minister, said his special interest in the train lay in the fact that the first discussion regarding the train took place with Mr Clapp when he was Victorian Minister of Railways.

The newspapers say the new train is the answer to the challenge of rivals in the transportation field and it does great credit to the chairman of the Railway Commissioners, Mr Harold Clapp.

But what happens now? Next week the *Spirit of Progress* goes into service between Melbourne and Albury. The New South Wales Railways Commissioners have promised to put on two luxury sleeper cars to match the Spirit, but they will not be air conditioned. One hopes that New South Wales will come up with a similar train soon.

'Oppy' Cycles from Fremantle to Sydney

21 NOVEMBER 1937

Hubert Opperman is a marvel, the endurance man of all time. What has he done? He has ridden a bicycle across the continent in 13 days 10 hours 11 minutes.

He set out to break Billy Read's record ride from Fremantle to Sydney. He covered the 2751 miles in 18 days, 18 hours. Oppy rode a Malvern Star and, of course, Malvern Star sponsored him.

Bruce Small of Malvern Star covered the nation with progress sheets. It had the exact time Billy Read arrived in each town, and there was a blank column in which you could write the precise second Oppy got there. One also received a map of the route and it told us 'Hubert Opperman is the greatest and most renowned rider the world has known'.

Oppy started by dipping his bike in the Indian Ocean and he rode 268 miles from Fremantle on the first day. The road across the Nullarbor you can imagine. Oppy was terrified of riding at night for fear of losing the track. He could not plough through the sand so he got off his bicycle and walked. For 100 miles the sand surface was so heavy he could average only 4¾ mph.

He slept about three hours a night, and the going was so tough he says he felt like a fly walking across fly paper. Bruce Small played some tricks on him. After Oppy had been asleep for only 20 minutes, Small would tell him he had been in bed for eight hours and mechanically off he pedalled again. But Oppy is a man of awesome integrity. He was determined to ride every inch, so much so that if he finished his ride for the night at the rear of the caravan, he did not start the next day from the front. He insisted on going back to the rear.

The hardest part of the ride was coping with the civic receptions. At Ballarat 2000 people were waiting at the City Hall, plus a civic reception. At Flemington they were so thick he had to get off his bike. There were 10 000 at the Post Office and 20 000 outside Parliament House, where the Premier of Victoria, Mr Albert Dunstan, was waiting to greet him.

Several times Oppy fell asleep while riding and crashed off his bike. Even the driver of the caravan that was following him fell asleep at the wheel near Goulburn. It went off the road, down a bank and was saved from turning over by a fence. Opperman went from Seymour straight through to Marulan, NSW, without a break, 29 hours continuous riding.

He arrived in Sydney at 10.51 p.m. and over the last 20 miles the traffic was packed tight. He was escorted by hundreds of cars and hundreds of cyclists. The traffic came to dead standstill along George Street and up to the GPO. Here he received his final civic reception. He has broken the record by better than 5 hours.

Adventurer Lucky to be Alive

22 NOVEMBER 1883

At last there is a message in the *Age* today from George Ernest Morrison. Twice speared by natives he is incredibly lucky to be alive.

This 21-year-old son of the headmaster of Geelong College is an extraordinary adventurer. Three years ago he walked 750 miles around the coast to Adelaide. Much of that country, of course, is quite uninhabited.

Next he went to North Queensland, got himself a job as an ordinary seaman on a recruiting lugger, and wrote articles for the *Age* on the Kanaka trade, the near black slavery on the sugar plantations. Last year he went to the Gulf of Carpentaria and walked back, following the route of Burke and Wills. He reached Cooper's Creek in an amazing 123 days, after walking 2000 miles.

The *Argus* in most disparaging tones, said it was the curious purposeless feat of a swagman. Others thought differently. Had Burke and Wills travelled as light as Morrison they might have found their job easy.

Last July, sponsored by David Syme of the *Age*, he set out from Port Moresby on an expedition to cross New Guinea. In his despatch sent from Cooktown and published yesterday Morrison writes:

We could not get on with the natives. They saw the weakness of our party, and took advantage of it...Our camp was always more or less surrounded by natives, waiting an opportunity to make a raid...In spite of our vigilance we had axes and tomahawks stolen, and a native sneaked off in open daylight with one large red blanket. The natives ultimately regarded our firearms as harmless instruments of noise, and crowds of men were in the habit of coming with spears, clubs and shields and motioning to us to go back.

Morrison was reluctant to shoot to kill. One native stole a vitally needed scrub knife. Morrison waited until the native was almost out of range then fired, inflicting, he believed, little injury.

The others in the party thought this a terrible mistake, a further sign of weakness. They had travelled a 100 miles into the centre, every bush seemed to bristle with spears. Morrison was out front, leading his horse, when he was hit with two spears. One went into his stomach and the other into the corner of his eye.

His white assistant, Jack Lyons, came running up and found him covered in blood from head to foot and vomiting more blood.

Morrison says:

When Lyons came up he thought I was mortally injured. To save my life he resolved to abandon everything to bring me down to the coast...he could not return by the way we had travelled as we knew the natives were waiting for us.

We retreated, leaving our stores, and escaped from the natives to nearly perish from starvation. For eight days I had not a morsel to eat, but the change of air healed my wounds. Lyons, by the exercise of extraordinary courage and endurance, brought us safely into port. For nine days Lyons was entirely without food, and but for his marvellous stamina I should now be rotting in the New Guinea bush.

Further reading: *Morrison of Peking*, Cyril Pearl.

Driving Out the Demon Drink

23 NOVEMBER 1923

The Federal in its heyday

The noble era of the coffee palaces is almost over. The Federal Coffee Palace secured its licence yesterday and from now it will be stained by liquor. It is the Federal Hotel.

In the 1880s coffee palaces were all the rage. There were dozens of them in Melbourne, Sydney, Adelaide, Brisbane. The Sydney Coffee Palace opened in 1881 and, according to the *Bulletin*, its object was to wean the youth of the city from sinful restaurants with superior quality milk, waitresses and fresh butter. The weaning didn't work. It sold out, alas, to a publican in 1884.

The coffee palaces were really the idea of the Hon James Munro who had the dream that if all hotels became coffee palaces then the demon drink could be driven from the land. His greatest effort was the Grand Hotel in Spring Street. In 1886 he formed the Grand Coffee Palace Company, bought and extended the Grand Hotel, and at the opening banquet made a never-to-be-forgotten gesture.

There he was in his frock coat. He wore a

blue ribbon indicating that he was a member of the Total Abstainers' Blue Ribbon League. He took out a box of matches, and announced: 'Well, gentlemen this is what we think of the licence' then set it on fire. It was now the Grand Coffee Palace and the next day the newspaper advertisements announced the sale in the refreshment rooms of tea, scones, beef-tea, malt extract and fresh milk.

The Federal Coffee Palace, the greatest, the most exotic hotel Australia had seen was built in time for the International Exhibition of 1888. It had six accident-proof lifts, its own ice plant in the basement, gas light on all floors and even electric bells.

The coffee palaces all fell on desperate times. The Federal could only keep going by sneaking in liquor on the quiet and selling it to boarders at wholesale prices. At the annual meeting of 1890 the directors complained bitterly they were spending up to £2 a day on cooling liquor from which they derived no profit.

For nigh on 30 years the Federal tried to get a licence but the Government at this time was reducing licences rather than handing them out. The *Bulletin* commented:

> The Federal Coffee Palace has come to be the most humorous of all the Melbourne monuments erected to the Land Boom greed and pharisaical snuffle for there the shareholders...sacrificed their deeply lamented asset on the altar of Public Morality.

When Mr Munro burned his licence the Grand Hotel went into desperate financial straits and did not recover any prosperity until 20 December 1920, when it received back its licence and re-opened as the Hotel Windsor.

A new era of prosperity should open now for the Federal. Our one remaining coffee palace is the Victoria Coffee Palace in Little Collins Street, which is a favourite of country families, and for church conferences and temperance luncheons.

Note: In 1967 the Victoria Coffee Palace displayed an ugly drop in profits, and just like the Federal and the Grand of old, the shareholders voted at once to acquire a licence. So the last of the coffee palaces succumbed.

'Honest, I Was a Riot.'

24 NOVEMBER 1954

Roy Rene 'Mo', Australia's greatest clown is dead. His funeral was yesterday.

In theatreland news of his death flew from mouth to mouth, and old hands began telling their Mo stories.

Herald critic, H.A. Standish, says:

He had only to come on to the stage leer at the audience and say 'Strike me lucky!' to start gales of laughter that were puzzling to newcomers. Mo was a vulgar comic, but he numbered amongst his wildest admirers, people who wouldn't have a bar of 'blue' lines from lesser men.

'You little trimmer!' he would say — and it became hard to remember whether he had taken the phrase from Australian slang or contributed it. 'Honest, I was a riot'…'Curse my fatal beauty!' so they went on, with the splutter and the leer, and the grease paint whisker.

When Mo published his book of memoirs Sir Ben Fuller wrote in the preface:

Roy, in my estimation, is one of the world's greatest clowns and had he gone abroad would quite easily rank with Grock, George Robey, and other eminent buskers. I can safely say after an association with Mo, of over 40 years, that he hasn't got an enemy in the business.

Sir Ben told he once tried to prevent vulgarity on the Fuller circuit, and he posted a notice forbidding performers to use the words 'damn' and 'hell'. He asked his manager to note how many times Mo used the forbidden words.

Mo knocked off in the middle of a scene with his partner, Nat Phillips, said 'Excuse me Stiffy', walked over to where his manager was doing his recording angel act in a box and said 'Damn, damn, damn, hell, hell, hell. Have you got that down, George?'

Then he went on with the show and Sir Ben gave him up as a bad job.

Mo was born Harry Van der Sluys in Adelaide in 1892, the son of a Dutch immigrant. Until he was eight he was taught by nuns at a Dominican convent. As a boy he had a good soprano voice and sang at Adelaide's Theatre Royal. He continued as a soprano until his voice broke then became a comic singer and dancer. He used the name 'Boy Roy'. He be-

Roy Rene

came a little too old for the 'Boy' so he changed it to Roy Rene after a famous French clown. His first big success was at the Princess Theatre in Sydney when he took to saucy songs. He sang 'Yiddle on Your Fiddle' and did a Jewish monologue 'Levinksy at the Wedding', which he learned from a Jewish comedian, Julian Rose.

Sir Benjamin Fuller saw the show, engaged him for a New Zealand tour, where he added the whisker make-up and also the distinctive Australian slang that he used for the rest of his career. 'Fair go mugs'. I'm a wake-up to you, Alec.' 'You little be-yew-ooty.'

The funeral service was at the Woollahra Chevra Kadisha Memorial Hall. Mo's wife, actress Sadie Gales was there with his son Sam and daughter Mylo. Many famous names in show business were present, Queenie Paul, Leo Sterling, Rita Pauncefort, Bert Lamond, Hal Cooper, Eddie Desesmer, Maria Diamond, Minnie Love, Willie Fennell, Hal Lashwood, and Ernest 'Freddy McFrog' Dunn, 104, a contortionist who worked with Mo for 40 years.

Electric Lamps Light up the Night

25 NOVEMBER 1882

Melbourne's Spencer Street Railway Station has been wonderfully lit up this week. Night times have been almost as bright as day.

We have to thank the Australasian Electric Light Power, and Storage Company. It arranged with the Railways for the lighting.

The *Argus* reports that this company is represented in the colonies by Sir Julius Vogel and it has the patent rights for the Brush arc and the Lane-Fox incandescent lights as well as the Hopkinson's dynamo machine.

The company put in 16 arc lights of 2000 candle power each, and 50 incandescent lamps of 50 candle power, all fed by dynamo and a 25-horse power steam motor. The lights included seven globes, which lit splendidly the entire platform for the Williamstown trains, many others were at advantage points and there was also a conspicuous and effective globe outside the Commissioner's door.

There was a special demonstration of the lighting for the Minister for Railways and Public Works, Mr Thomas Bent; the Attorney-General, Mr James Munro; and invited guests.

The *Argus* says 'The display was generally considered to be highly successful all round. The illumination on the platform was interfered with somewhat by the moonlight, but it was nevertheless exceedingly effective, while the incandescent lamps shed remarkably bright clear rays'.

The Minister's room was brilliantly lit for the occasion and there was a fine supper with champagne. Sir Julius Vogel first proposed the toast to the Queen, then the Government.

Mr Bent in responding said:

Since I have been at the Railways I have done what I can do to study the comfort and convenience of the public, and to foster in the department scientific progress. No one, seeing what the gentlemen present have seen this evening, would deny the great superiority of the electric light over gas, and it is clear that the electric light is going to be a grand thing in the colony. (Applause)

I trust that before long incandescent lamps will be used in the trains, and I believe that eventually electricity will be used as the propelling power in trains.

Mr Munro, a very cautious gentleman, said no one had referred to the cost. Electric light, of course, was a brilliant success, but not everyone was satisfied it would pay.

Sir Julius Vogel made nonsense of this matter of cost.

Some people are timorous about going in for speculation in the electric light because of the improvement which must be made. Such ideas will quench all enterprise. We must be sure that the organisations which obtain a start in this matter keep an eye on the centres of scientific investigation.

For instance we would pay a man four pounds a week to attend to a dynamo for an experiment, and the same man and machinery would serve an entire neighbourhood. The cost of electricity, compared with gas, will cheapen very greatly in country neighbourhoods. Electricity, unlike gas, does not require coal and the engines can be fed with wood. I concur with the view taken by Mr Bent as to the illimitable future open to electricity. Let them bear in mind how young electricity is.

Arrangements for electricity at Spencer Street Station will be completed next week. According to Sir Julius, after the passing of the Electric Lighting Act by the Imperial Parliament, many towns in England are now showing their intention of moving to electricity on a basis which could prove very remunerative.

Hargrave takes Flight

28 NOVEMBER 1894

Mr Hargrave

Lawrence Hargrave has made some extraordinary experiments with flying and he is writing a paper about them for the Royal Society.

However nothing has appeared in the newspapers. Hargrave is dismissed as an eccentric, and the Chancellor of Sydney University, Sir Normand MacLaurin, has announced: 'men will never fly'.

He is so wrong. The 44-year-old Hargrave has done it already. He is a clever man with a very clever father. Hargrave's father, John Fletcher Hargrave, was Attorney-General of NSW, then Puisne Judge of the Supreme Court. He apprenticed Lawrence to an engineering firm at sixteen, Lawrence then became an assistant at the Sydney Observatory.

There he studied air currents and became fascinated by the idea of human flight. He studied the movements of fishes, insects, birds, and he was intrigued that fish when diving turned their tails in a certain curve. He went even further in studying three-dimensional movement. He looked at worms and built a giant model of a worm to find out how a worm writhed, dipped and turned.

In 1884 he started building what were really model aeroplanes. He made them out of light cane and tissue paper. One which had flapping wings flew 98 feet. Then he put in motors, rubber bands, compressed air, and steam, which drove a crude form of a propeller.

In 1889 he invented the rotary aeroplane engine. He wrote:

I conceived the idea that a three-cylinder screw engine could be made by turning the boss of the propeller into an engine, thus allowing the cylinders to revolve on the crankshaft, the shaft and crankpin being stationery and the thrust coming direct on the valve-face.

Next he went to work on lifting surfaces. He discovered a remarkable thing. A wing with a curve in it had twice the lifting power of a plain flat surface. Last year he built a box-kite, two rectangular cells separated by a distance of 21¼ inches. The upper and lower surfaces of the kite, convex on top and concave below. This gave marvellous lifting power.

On 12 November last he performed his most amazing experiment of all. He went to Stanwell Park. There he used four kites, one above the other, moored his rope on the sea shore and made a cradle for himself under the lowest kite.

The wind freshened to nigh on 19 mph. This lifted him off the ground. He measured the pull at 180 pounds. Then came a strong gust of 21 mph. Hargrave soared up to 16 feet and he was flying. He measured the lift at 240 pounds.

Hargrave writes:

The particular steps gained are the demonstration that an extremely simple apparatus can be made, carried about and flown by one man; and that a safe means of making an ascent with a flying machine, of trying the same without risk of accident, and descending, are now at the service of any experimenter who wishes to use it'.

Note: Lawrence Hargrave was the true inventor of the box-kite flying machine. In 1903 Wilbur Wright wrote to Hargrave asking permission to use his patents. Hargrave replied there were no patents and wished him every success. Wilbur's brother Orville made his historic flight at Kittyhawk in 1903.

Free Banquet turns into Free-for-all

29 NOVEMBER 1867

Prince Alfred

Yesterday was one of the more violently orgiastic days in the history of Melbourne.

The Goverment decided to celebrate the visit of HRH Prince Alfred Ernest Albert, the Duke of Edinburgh, second son of Queen Victoria, with a Citizens' Free Banquet in Richmond Park by the Yarra.

It was thought 10 000 would feast and 10 000 would watch. The Sunbury wine growers donated 600 gallons of claret and the Collingwood Brewery gave 600 gallons of beer. There were 500 loaves, 70 tons of potatoes, 120 000 pound of meat, 5000 pies, 4500 pounds of plum pudding, plus fish tarts, cakes, lollies, buns, fruit...

There were 50 fires to cook the food, nearly a mile of tables decorated with flowers and ferns. Wine was pumped through two splendid fountains, one raised high and connected to a siphon pump.

The following disaster was caused by the Duke. Had he shown good manners all would have been well, according to the *Argus*. He was invited to come at 1 p.m. to open the affair, and ultimately he was turned away when approaching the gates at 3 p.m.

Rather than the 20 000 expected, the crowd grew to a ravenous 60 000, which even 250 police could not control. The first barrier gave way at 1.30 p.m. Women shrieked, others fainted. The long tables were rushed and in a few minutes there was nothing left of the vast store.

The *Argus* described the scene:

Loaves bedabbled in the mud, and joints with only half the meat cut away, and covered with dust lay there. Boys catching hold of fresh loaves tore them to pieces like wolves. The long rows of barrels of ale had been rapidly disposed of by the simple process of beating in the heads of the casks and dipping out the liquor in the readiest way.

In the tent appropriated for the committee there were a few cases of porter and champagne. This got abroad and soon the mob collected. At last as everybody foresaw, there was a great rush and the tent was pulled down over the heads of the committee and most of the contents appropriated as loot, long before the police could interfere.

There were cries of 'WINE, WINE, WE WANT WINE'. Louis L. Smith, chairman of the banquet committee, said it had been decided not to give away the wine but reserve it for the poor...One man climbed up, pulled the spigot out of the 500 gallon vat and out came the wine drenching all who were near. Another thirsty man climbed the tree where there was a cask to supply the fountains. There he cut the pipes and sprinkled wine over the heads of the crowd.

For nearly half an hour the wine was running. People came running with every possible container. By 5 p.m. hundreds of men and boys were reeling through the crowd. Some were saturated from head to foot and enjoyed themselves by abusing the gentry.

The *Sydney Morning Herald* commented that it was really only to be expected.

It must be remembered that in Melbourne there is a large number of the vilest of the vile — remnants of old convict systems — the gathering of old seditions and of all those abominations which are heaped upon new countries.

No Chance of Saying No

30 NOVEMBER 1917

The Prime Minister, pelted with rotten eggs, emerged from a fist fight yesterday with bleeding knuckles.

The Prime Minister, Mr Hughes, for some time has been furious with Thomas Ryan, Premier of Queensland. Ryan was an arch advocate of the 'No' vote in last year's conscription referendum.

Now it is on again. There is another conscription referendum on 20 December. But you have no hope of getting a 'No' story into the newspapers because Billy Hughes will censor it. On 19 November Premier Ryan delivered an anti-conscription speech.

But he did not get it into the newspapers. The Commonwealth Censor stepped in. Ryan's next move was to give his speech in the Queensland Parliament, have it recorded in Hansard, then he had 10 000 copies printed for free distribution.

The Censor seized the first batch of the pamphlets at the General Post Office. From there on we had a battle between Prime Minister and Premier, both exploiting their various powers. The Censor, Captain Stable, with Army men, raided the Queensland Government Printing Office. The printing office was closed and access to the rear guarded by State Police. Ryan was outraged that his authority as Premier should be usurped by the Commonwealth.

Ryan took out a writ against the Commonwealth for this action and Hughes made a counter action against Ryan for 'making a false statement of fact' and 'for conspiring to effect a purpose that is unlawful under the laws of the Commonwealth'.

Mr Hughes was returning South by train yesterday. The train stopped at Warwick, where he planned to address an open-air meeting on the platform.

The *Brisbane Courier* reports:

The moment they saw the Prime Minister they commenced hooting and groaning and hurling vile epithets at him...An egg thrown from the crowd just missed him and broke on the platform railings. The odour it gave off quickly cleared a space about it. A second one, better aimed, broke upon the Prime Minister's hat and knocked it off. There was a howl of jeering

Mr W.M. Hughes

laughter which drowned the cries of 'shame'.

But the thrower of the egg did not enyoy the triumph long. A returned soldier hurled himself upon him and in a second a free fight was in progress.

The *Courier* reports fists were flying everywhere and the PM was in the thick of it. Although he was being jostled by men twice his size, he emerged with blood on his knuckles.

Hughes told Senior Sergeant Kenny of the Queensland Police to arrest the egg thrower. The Sergeant took no action. Hughes then told him he was Attorney-General of the Commonwealth and he wanted an arrest. The Sergeant replied he was an officer of the Queensland Government and he recognised no other authority.

The egg thrower, P.J. Brosnan, finally was arrested and charged with disturbing the peace. The Prime Minister can only be described as livid. He has sent a furious telegram to Mr Ryan detailing his treatment. Mr Ryan sent a frigidly polite letter in return.

Note: Even after all the censorship the 'No' vote won the referendum and as a result of the egg treatment Mr Hughes formed the Commonwealth Police.

DECEMBER

Edward with Mrs Wallis Simpson

Swimming is a Delicate Matter

1 DECEMBER 1902

*Bathing at the turn
of the century*

There has been a terrible to-do over wanton bathing at Manly.

On the surf beach at Manly, like everywhere else, bathing is allowed only at night. Swimming normally is a very delicate matter. It is best to keep the sexes apart. The normal practice for a lady is to have a bathing machine, a box on wheels which is trundled right into the water and the dip can be taken with the utmost discretion.

At Manly the rules have not changed much since the 1830s. All surfers have to be out of the water by 7 a.m. and a man gives a signal with a large dinner bell.

Last September on a hot Spring day, some yachtsmen decided to cool off with a swim. When they came out police were waiting for them. They were arrested and taken to the local lock-up. The charge — they had broken the local by-law by swimming after 7 a.m.

Mr. W.H. Gocher, Editor and Publisher of the *Manly and North Sydney News*, was outraged. The law, said he, was an absurdity. In the next issue of his newspaper he announced that he would test the law by 'bounding in for a bathe on the morrow'.

And so he did. Mr Gocher wrote:
It was the most enjoyable bathe of my lifetime. But nothing happened. Very few people were about. No posse of police came flying down with drawn batons to the water's edge to yell out to me come forth and be arrested. There was no mighty concourse of citizens to cheer me as I came

shooting in on No. 4 breaker, breathing salt spray and defiance.

Actually one passer-by stopped for a second and asked who the lunatic in the water was, that's all. Mr Gocher was a little depressed that so little notice was taken of him.

The council meeting was the next Tuesday and Mr Gocher received no sympathy. The Mayor, Alderman Quirk, MLA, said that he would not tolerate all-day bathing on the beach. Before he did this he would pull down all the sheds, and every Alderman but one agreed with him.

So Mr Gocher tried again, and again and on the third occasion he had his triumph. He was arrested. Mr Fosbery, Inspector General of Police told Gocher that no magistrate would convict him, but men would have to take care to wear neck to knee costumes and the ladies would have to take care not to expose their bosoms.

Today there is a letter from Mr Gocher on the Council table calling for all-day bathing. It has been 'received' with no action taken. There is also a letter from Mr A.G. Cambridge complaining about bathers misconducting themselves on the Ocean Beach. That's been more than received. The Council decided to call the police to stop such misconduct.

Note: Mr Gocher finally succeeded on 2 November 1903. Bathing is now allowed after 7 a.m. provided everybody over the age of eight years wears a neck to knee costume. Penalty for offenders is fixed at not more than one pound.

The First Hippy Drop-out

2 DECEMBER 1973

Beatrice Miles died today. Even though she drove police, magistrates, taxi drivers and many others to the point of fury, all Sydney loved her.

Bea Miles said it in court, proclaimed it as often as she could:

I am a true thinker and speaker. I cannot stand or endure the priggery, caddery, snobbery, smuggery, hypocrisy, lies, flattery, compliments, praise, jealousy, envy, pretence, conventional speech and behaviour and affected artificial behaviour upon which society is based.

Bea Miles was the scourge of taxi drivers and the agony of cinema proprietors. For 20 years she never slept in a bed and she was in court 195 times. Always she gave her name as 'Bea Miles, student, NFPA'.

When asked the meaning of NFPA she would say 'No fixed place of abode, of course'. Bea Miles was born at Ashfield, Sydney in 1901. She was sent to the very exclusive Abbotsleigh private school where she graduated with first class honours in English and Bs in Latin, French and Modern History.

She went on to Sydney University, but you might describe her as the first of the hippy drop-outs. She began to gather fame in the late thirties. By that time she was known to every taxi driver, every tram and bus conductor in Sydney. Her philosophy was that all public transport should be free. Many of the old hands treated her kindly for the character she was; others fought her, man-handled her, took her to the police.

Despite her 13-stone bulk she was brilliant at getting a door open and flopping into a cab while it was moving. If the taxi driver was violent she could be superbly violent in return. Her neatest trick was to bend back the taxi doors until the hinges snapped. That sort of behaviour cost her a jail sentence of three months in 1957 and six months in 1958.

In January 1955 she approached a King's Cross taxi driver, John Clifford, and asked him to drive her to Perth. This time she did pay. The cost of the fare was a shilling a mile and at the end of every 100 miles she would reach into her purse, pull out £5 and hand it over. It cost her nearly 700 pounds. There were no hotels.

Clifford said 'Bea could sleep on rocks, or anywhere'.

Bea had an extraordinary knowledge of Shakespeare. Quote almost any line of Shakespeare to her and she would carry on and finish the verse. She had a regular spot outside the Public Library where she stood with a sign around her neck: 'SHAKESPEARE POETRY RECITALS. 3/-, 2/-, 1/-, 6d'. For her top fee of three shillings the listener could have. 'The Man from Snowy River'. Her poetry reading was so good she entered the Sydney Eisteddford in 1947 and 1948. In 1948 she received 79 marks out of 100 for her reading of *Measure for Measure*.

In 1964, a diabetic and suffering from arthritis, she became too sick and old for the NFPA life. There was not a home for the aged in Sydney that would take in such an odd ball, and although a declared atheist since she was 21, she went to the Roman Catholics Little Sisters of the Poor at Randwick. She would point to one of the sisters, Mary Rebecca. 'There you are, she's a pet. The best girl in the place. Give me a bit of time and I'll make her the best atheist'.

At her funeral she has asked for a band to play 'Waltzing Matilda' and 'Tie Me Kangaroo Down Sport', and she wants a ribbon over her coffin with the words, 'One who loved Australia'. All that will be done.

Beatrice Miles: the first hippy drop-out

Sydney Missing, Presumed Lost

5 DECEMBER 1941

HMAS Sydney

HMAS *Sydney*, Australia's finest warship, has been lost in action.

The Prime Minister, Mr Curtin, has made the following statement:

Information has been received from the Australian Naval Board that H.M.A.S. *Sydney* has been in action with a heavily armed merchant raider, which has been sunk by gun fire. No subsequent communication has been received from H.M.A.S. *Sydney*, and the Government regrets to advise that the ship must be presumed lost. Extensive search by air and surface units to locate survivors continues.

The Prime Minister added that although the action took place some days ago, an announcement could not be made earlier for strategic reasons and there was just a remote possibility that the *Sydney* might still be afloat.

The action took place 300 miles west of Carnarvon on the evening of 19 November German sailors from the raider *Kormoran*, now prisoners in Western Australia described the action.

Flying the Norwegian flag, we approached within half a mile of the Australian warship and silenced her big guns with our first salvo. Although in a sinking condition, the Australian ship replied with a broadside and set us ablaze.

Mr Curtin in a further statement says:

The *Sydney* was on patrol duties when she encountered the German. The initial advantage lay with the German since she

was disguised as a merchant ship, and her identity had to be established before she could be attacked...

With dusk falling, the *Sydney* had to close with the suspect to established identity. As soon as the raider was convinced her identity would be known she opened fire simultaneously with the first salvo from the *Sydney*.

The raider's salvo hit *Sydney* full on the bridge, putting the control system out of action. *Sydney* kept on fiercely with independent firing. *Kormoran* was ablaze, the men abandoned ship and subsequently it blew up.

From their boats the Germans watched the *Sydney* disappear over the horizon. She was on fire and that was the last they saw of her.

The casualty lists today give names of the entire compliment of the cruiser. The captain and all his crew are listed as missing. There is great grief in Sydney, the city which gave the lost cruiser its name.

'Loss of H.M.A.S. *Sydney* is the biggest heartache the people of Sydney have had in the war', said the Lord Major of Sydney, Ald. Crick.

The Catholic Archibishop of Sydney, Dr Gilroy, said:

We have always been proud of this ship that bore the name of our city, and we gloried in the valour of her officers and men. We may be confident that those who perished died for their country as they lived for it — brave and courageous patriots.

HMAS *Sydney* cost £2 100 000 to build, and replacement cost is put at three and a half million, but there is a surge of patriotism everywhere. We want *Sydney* replaced. A fund has opened all over Australia. For example, the Lord Mayor of Melbourne, Cr. Beaurepaire, has opened the fund in Melbourne and £50 000 has been promised already with G.J. Coles at the top of the list with £5000.

Everybody wants to be in it. During settling at the Victoria, Mr. J.J. Liston made an appeal to members and raised £1600 pounds within a few minutes. This is good but getting a new *Sydney* built might be another matter.

Fearful Affray at Eureka

6 DECEMBER 1854

There has been a dreaful tragedy at Eureka in Ballarat. Heaven know what will happen next, but today His Excellency, Sir Charles Hotham, has declared Martial Law with instructions for immediate suppression of the rebellion.

The *Age* today sums up the universal feeling: At length the dreadful and fateful hour in the destinies of this singular colony has fully come; and the sounds that announce it are the sharp reports of death-dealing rifles ringing through the ranges of Ballarat. That terrible crisis, which has been for so long a time impending over us like some black portentous cloud, has now burst upon us; and its first appalling effects are those read in the lists of the killed and wounded in that fearful affray on Sunday morning.

It seems still incredible. While reading the mournful record, the mind refuses to believe that those scenes were really enacted within a few miles of Melbourne, and the actors in them were our fellow colonist.

Our appeal is now made — not to the power of the brute force at the Command of the Government — but to the good feeling, the manliness, the sense of justice, the bravery, the Christian principle of the diggers; we entreat them in the name of all that is human, all that is sacred, for God's sake — to suspend the strife instantly.

The news reports coming in are so scattered it is hard to assess what is really happening, but the representative of the *Geelong Advertiser* writes:

Several parties have been to Eureka and returned with fearful tales of the state of things there. One gentleman says he counted 21 diggers dead in the trench behind the barricades and that some of them had been removed. The total he says was 25. Of the military I learn that there are three killed and a few wounded, including one of the officers who has had his leg broken by some means.

Parties who have been about all the morning have just now come into the office with such reports as would make the blood boil in any man's veins. The affair is alleged

Sir Charles Hotham

to have been not an attack, but a downright massacre; the unarmed and unoffending were more punished that the real armed party. An instance — a man happened to smile at one of the horsemen — he was instantly fired at.

Men, aye, hundreds of them, who were 'conservatives' up 'til now, feel irritated. All parties having lights in their tents after 8 o'clock p.m. within musket shot of the sentries, are to be fired at. We are really under martial law even now. There are at present 125 prisoners taken and in the camp.

The soldiers are by all considered to have done their duty rightly, as they were ordered. The troopers are accused of being cowardly and merciless, especially towards the unoffending parties.

Note: The final count was 34 miners killed, and six government men killed. General sympathy was with the oppressed diggers and no jury could be found that would convict the men who were arrested.

Further reading: *Lucky City (Ballarat 1851–1901)*, Weston Bate.

Oil Strike at Exmouth Gulf

7 DECEMBER 1953

Mr Walkley walks down Pitt Street

All Australia is in a state of euphoria. There was an oil strike at Exmouth Gulf on 4 December.

Exmouth Gulf is 600 miles north of Perth. Announcement of the strike came first from the headquarters of the Standard Oil Co. of California. Ampol confirmed it in Sydney.

The announcement said oil was found at between 3605 and 3620 feet. During a 25-hour test, oil flowed at the rate of 20 barrels — about 640 gallons — an hour through a quarter-inch pipe.

The Stock Exchange went beserk. Ampol Exploration 5 shillings shares, paid to 2 shillings, jumped from 13 shillings to 6 pounds 15 shillings and yesterday they hit 7 pounds 10 shillings.

Brokers' offices were besieged with cables, telegrams and telephone calls. Under the glare of huge arc lights as movie cameras shot the scene, the Sydney Exchange had its most feverish day's trading since the gold boom days of the early 1930s. All day the broking scene was pandemonium. Huge crowds packed the vestibules eagerly reading lists as they were posted.

Many brokers had what the newspapers called a 'juicy meal'. One broker after the morning call bought 3000 Ampol Petroleum for 13 shillings and threepence and he was able to sell them a few hours later for fifty shillings.

Mining men said yesterday that it was a miracle that the drilling company should strike oil at its first stab at the shallow depth of 3605 to 3620 feet. In the U.S. oil zone, only one bore in 10 proves profitable.

There is a picture on the front page of Melbourne's *Sun* depicting Mr H.C. Walkley, managing director of Ampol, walking down Pitt Street, Sydney, wearing a red 10-gallon hat. The caption says: 'THIS IS THE HAPPY MAN'.

When Walkley was at Exmouth Gulf three months ago, a party of Pressman presented him with the hat in appreciation of his hospitality. He promised them he would wear it in a walk down Pitt Street on the day the drillers struck oil in Australia. He kept his promise.

At the Ampol office in Flinders Street Melbourne, the staff cheered when they heard the news. A member of the staff said 'Everyone from the executives down to the office boys had a hug for the person they were working with. Already the staff are beginning to talk about the Christmas bonus'.

The Prime Minister, Mr Menzies, was cautious at first, but then he said:

This is a very important development. We have always realised that the discovery of oil in Australia in large quantities would have a tremendous bearing upon our internal economy and upon our international financial situation.

Senator Spooner, Minister for National Development, said it might turn over a new page in Australia history.

Ampol's chief, Mr Walkley, said last night that more wells would be drilled in the Exmouth Gulf area as soon as the experts had properly evaluated scientific data. They would continue drilling the present hole from 10 000 to 12 000 feet.

Some people are expressing caution, but right now it is like the day after the Melbourne Cup. Those who backed the winner are grinning from ear to ear.

Note: The euphoria was short-lived. Exmouth Gulf after its glorious beginning failed to live up to its expectations.

Spofforth our 'Demon' Bowler

8 DECEMBER 1882

We had the welcome home at the Melbourne Cricket Ground yesterday for Mr W.L. Murdoch's triumphant touring XI. Never will we forget our extraordinary victory at the Oval where F.R. Spofforth our 'Demon' bowler took 14 wickets for 90 runs.

Unquestionably it was one of the most spectacular processions Melbourne has seen. The first part of the programme was a torchlight procession composed of 700 firemen from Melbourne's fire brigades. They assembled at the Burke and Wills monument in Collins Street at 7:30 p.m. At 8 p.m. they lit their flambeaux and the march started.

The Australian XI occupied two drags in the middle. There were crowds all along the footpaths, the upstairs of houses were occupied and there were people on the roofs.

There were bands. There was the band from HMVS *Cerberus*, the strength of the Victorian Navy; there were the bands of the Emerald Hill, Sandridge, and West Melbourne brigades, and the band of the Fitzroy Lifeboat Crew. The procession moved down Collins Street, to Elizabeth, to Bourke, to Spring then to the MCG.

'Peace hath her victories no less than war' said the *Australasian*, 'and the view from Jolimont, the procession with glittering points of light, as it wound its way from Spring Street down the steep descent was especially imposing'.

At the MCG all was ready. The Electric Light Company kindly gave a special display of electric light, provided by an 8-horsepower steam engine. Mr Tillett, the fireworks expert, was there with some marvellous equipment. When Murdoch's men drove into the MCG, the volunteer bands struck up 'See the Conquering Hero Comes' and Mr Tillett lit a device which crackled out WELCOME HOME in luminous letters.

The players made their grand tour of the MCG then they stopped in front of the main grandstand. Here Mr E.S. Watson of the Cricketers' Association presented each man with a gold medal. This medal is the size of a five shilling piece. It has the words 'Victorian Cricketers' Association' and the Victorian coat of arms on one side, and on the other a formal inscription. Spofforth's medal has these words:

Presented to Mr F.R. Spofforth
In commemoration of the brilliant
performance of the Australian
team in England 1882.

The crowd cheered after each presentation, then came the fireworks display. There were rockets, catherine wheels, stars, and the heavens were laced with streams of gauzy fire. There was one device that displayed 'SUCCESS TO CRICKET' and another which wound up the show 'GOOD NIGHT'. The entertainment finished just after 10 p.m.

However Melbourne *Punch* says caustically: You must sometimes think the cricket fever is overdone, especially when the reporters tell us in tedious minuteness how this ball was snicked and how that cricketer held his bat. Perhaps we shall be informed some fine day, what tweed your trousers are made of (imported naturally) how you wear your hat, sideways or at the back of your head, where you purchase your shirts and whose hotel you drink in. Were you Premier of the colony you could not be better known. Everybody courts your acquaintance, and to not know you, not to have 'shouted' for you, or even not to have known anyone who has known you or seen you, are very heinous offences in the eyes of the young Australian born.

Illegal Fisticuffs

9 DECEMBER 1854

Tom Curran

Prize fighting, of course, is illegal in the colonies. Polite journals like the *Argus* and the *Sydney Morning Herald* treat it with contempt and never deign to mention fisticuffs in their pages.

Sporting journals think differently. Recently *Bell's Life* in Sydney said furiously nothing could ever stop it.

The excuses are that such contests excite ill-feeling, and may result in serious casualties. Oh! most benign and protective judicial act! What a pity it does not more fully embrace all other British national pastimes under its guardian wing!

Bosh! Bosh! say we to all those milk and water philanthropists.

Well, it does indeed go on all the time. The fights take place at lonely spots around Sydney Harbour or Port Phillip. It is a delicate matter advising the location of the bout to the thousands of enthusiastic fans, but, incredibly it is done.

The fights are extraordinary, a bout of four or five hours is nothing. On 2 January 1847 Bill Davis met Bungarabee Jack and fought him bare knuckle for four hours 22 minutes over 188 rounds. At the end of that time Bungarabee's face was a blood-pulped ruin.

Only rarely do the papers report the effect that bare knuckles can have on a man's face, but after a 100 rounds there is not a square inch of facial flesh that is not cut up, carved and swollen.

Now we hear reports that on 7 December there was the longest fight the Australian colonies have ever seen. Jim Kelly fought Jonathan Smith for £400 and it took place at Fiery Creek near Daylesford, Victoria. Kelly, an Irishman was 24, and Smith from Norwich was 33.

Rain poured down but this did not deter anyone. A great flow of traffic poured out from the diggings, a long line of carriages, carts, men on horseback, and on foot.

They set up a ring on a lovely piece of ground four miles from the Fiery Creek Road. The crowd was thick all around and so many people were up on branches that the surrounding gums were more laden than Christmas trees. It was the biggest 'rush' since the diggings opened.

A round lasted until a man was knocked off his feet, so the first round was an all time record. It went for two hours with much sparring, backing and feinting. The fifteenth was another long one — it lasted for an hour, with both men, puffing, heaving out slow motion blows and not causing much damage. Meanwhile the crowd contented itself by drinking bottled stout and eating sandwiches.

In the sixteenth round Kelly let go with a powerful left and right on Smith's ear and the blood began to flow. This would provide a little interest but it was a slow motion affair, so slow that Smith dropped his arms, Kelly folded his and they looked at each other for five minutes.

By the seventeenth round they were both exhausted. The crowd was hissing and telling them to get on with it. Kelly taunted his opponent: 'Come on. Are you going to fight? It will never come off if you don't'. Smith let go with a left. Kelly countered with a right, then Smith faltered and to the astonishment of everyone, he gave in.

The fight had lasted six and a quarter hours.

Shock and Grief greet Abdication

12 DECEMBER 1936

It would be difficult to underestimate the shock and grief that has come with the announcement that King Edward has abdicated.

Oh everybody knew that the King had been dallying with Mrs Wallis Simpson. But never for a moment did we think it would come to this. The newspapers have displayed very good manners, pretending almost that it was not happening.

They have, until now, virtually ignored all cabled stories about the romance. The formal announcement came through to Canberra at 2 a.m. yesterday. Parliament House was ablaze with light all through the night and members rushed there to see what was happening.

Yesterday morning the Prime Minister, Mr Lyons, gave the King's message of abdication on the wireless and said:

I feel sure that I am voicing the sentiments of every Australian when I express the profound regret at the step which His Majesty King Edward has taken. We must all wish that he had acted otherwise.

It is sad that a reign begun in such auspicious circumstances should end so soon and in such a manner...when the Commonwealth Government urged him to reconsider his decision, I spoke, I knew for every Australian. With the deepest sadness in our hearts we bid King Edward VIII, farewell.

There were formal announcements yesterday in all the Commonwealth Parliaments. The Senate for example, solemnly and gravely stood at attention while the Leader of the Government, Sir George Pearce, read the King's message of abdication.

The *Age* says:

As far as this country's influence is effective the unparalleled Royal crisis must not be permitted to leave any weakening influence on the monarchical system or on the throne that cements the British Common-wealth of Nations...The qualities required of a patriotic people are cool courage and patience. There is no justification for alarm, and no warrant for any interruption of normal life and business.

The *Herald* points out bluntly that Mrs Simpson is an American-born woman, married twice with two husbands still living. It says 'The King's marriage to Mrs Simpson in such circumstances as would make her Queen of England had never been possible to contemplate. Such a marriage would have irreparably degraded the throne'.

Smith's Weekly thinks differently. On the front page it has large romantic black and white portraits of Edward and Mrs Simpson with the glowing words:

To lose him would be a calamity. He is the greatest rallying-point of patriotism history has known. For to him accorded what no king since the birth of time has been given — the hearts of the free peoples of the mightiest Empire that ever was or ever will be.

The *Bulletin* shows its old 1890s cynicism. It says the hearts of flappers and the editors of flapper-papers might be moved by 'LUV' but history would not. History would just say that at the age of 42, in a time of national disquiet, Edward VIII abandoned his empire, his church, his crown and his house for an infatuation for a double-divorcee.

But just think of other more mundane matters. A whole series of postage stamps and coins have to be abandoned. The public service has a small mountain of Edward VIII notepaper. Then a far greater mountain of diaries, calendars and such are obsolete because they all bear the wrong date.

But we will overcome this, already the flapper-magazines are going beserk with photographs of the new, before unnoticed, young Queen Elizabeth.

Indomitable Aeronaut Parachutes Down

13 DECEMBER 1888

We have just received reports in Sydney of the extraordinary achievement of Mr J.T. Williams.

He has made a descent from a balloon by parachute. Until last week Mr Williams, a watchmaker, was comparatively unknown in Sydney. Now he is famous.

The *Sydney Morning Herald* reports:
Mr Williams is a quiet, unassuming man, 33 years of age, scarcely five feet six inches in height. For a considerable time he has been making small experiments with the parachute with a view to demonstrating that it is possible to afford the aeronaut a means of escape in times of danger. The private trials have been so successful he determined to make a public ascent on Saturday from the Ashfield Recreation Ground.

The balloon was the well-known Gem and the gas was supplied from ordinary sources through a special six-inch main. The parachute bore a resemblance to the top story of a chinese pagoda. It consisted of two rings, one about fourteen feet and the other four feet in circumference. These were covered in fine chinese silk, the smaller ring being at the top and being partially uncovered to permit of the free passage of the air.

Police were present and a rumour was afoot that they had been ordered to stop the ascent, but they were there only to warn Mr Williams of the grave risk he was running.

At 6 p.m. all was ready. Attaching his parachute to the net of the balloon by a piece of silk, so that it might be readily broken away, Mr Williams took the end of the ropes and stationed himself in a sling in the spot usually taken by the orthodox car. Mr Williams told the crowd he was absolutely confident of his skills and even his insurance company might have no fear of having to make a payment to his executors. There was not the slightest cause for alarm.

So off he went. He rose very rapidly to a point half way between Homebush and Ryde, getting higher and higher every moment. He had been up scarcely seven minutes at a height between 4000 and 5000 feet when he detached himself from the balloon.

The first balloon flight, France 1783

The *Herald* reported:
Almost immediately, the parachute opened out and amid the ringing cheers of the spectators,the plucky adventurous little man was observed to be slowly descending. The enthusiasm among those who had witnessed him leave the ground, many of whom were all too fearful that he would never return alive, knew no bounds, as the parachute spread out like a huge umbrella. Cheer after cheer was given and these increased more and more as the indomitable aeronaut endeavored to guide or work his life preserver in order to make the drop as closely as possible to the place where it had started.

Eventually Mr Williams reached the ground at a spot about a quarter of a mile from Homebush. He described his fall afterwards as being very slight, and nothing more than a jump from a high wall would be. When he left the balloon he pulled the valve and the monster dropped at Greenwich on the Parramatta River, and has been recovered in a good order.

The experiment was certainly a pronounced success.

London-Melbourne Flight a Triumph

14 DECEMBER 1919

As you know the Prime Minister, Mr Hughes, is keen to prove that the aeroplane is more than a curious novelty. He offered £10 000 to the first aviators to fly from London to Australia in less than 30 days in a British built machine.

The Adelaide brothers, Captain Ross and Lieutenant Keith Smith, have done it, aided by their mechanics J.M. Bennet and W.H. Shiers. They flew in their huge bi-plane, a Vickers Vimy, powered by two Rolls-Royce 380-horse-power engines. They did it in 27 days 20 hours. They are now recuperating in Darwin.

Oh, but they suffered. The Vimy is a bomber-aircraft with an open cockpit. The early part of their flight was through storms, sleet and hail. Their limbs were so numb they could hardly fly the plane. Their sandwiches were frozen solid.

The noise of the aircraft was so loud they could communicate only with notes. Their only navigational aid was a compass, and mostly they had nothing but road maps to find their way.

The mechanics Bennett and Shiers are delighted to have made the trip, but they say they would need £100 000 pounds to do another. They could not sleep in the aeroplane because of the noise and the cold. Then on land they had to work through the night trying to service it. The plane carries nearly a 1000 gallons of fuel. This they had to pump out of four-gallon tins and 20 000 gallons were used during the flight.

At Ramadie, near Baghdad, there was a near hurricane and 50 soldiers spent the entire night holding it down. At Calcutta hawks flew into one of the propellers causing severe damage.

At Sourabaya the Vimy landed on reclaimed ground and sank right down in the mud. It took seven hours work to dig it out and before they could take off, 200 coolies laid down a quarter of a mile of bamboo matting.

Now that they have arrived the Smiths are very happy indeed. They believe the route has commercial possibilities. Of course, it would be necessary to have different aircraft and different crews for all the various stages. There have been big celebrations in Darwin at the Victoria Hotel. Nobody is allowed to get together or congregate because of the terrible influenza epidemic. But this time regulations have been abandoned. When they arrived they were carried shoulder high from their aeroplane and the Administrator called for a citizens banquet.

The *Sydney Morning Herald* asks:
Is flying now really safe and certain for the future as a means of ordinary commercial traffic and communication? After the armistice civilian flying received a great impulse in England, and was declared by the initiated to be as safe as motoring. Insurance people still do not think so. The catastrophe to the squadron of machines which was sent from England to Egypt — seven out of 11 were wrecked over the north coast of Africa--is still fresh in our minds...

It probably amounts to this — that where the pilot eliminates, or takes the fullest precautions against all risks that he can counter, the dangers of accident are greatly diminished.

Plugger Wins and Retires Richly Rewarded

15 DECEMBER 1901

Plugger Bill Martin, 42, won the Austral Wheel Race on the MCG this week-end. Please be impressed, this is one of Australia's biggest sporting events, and it has taken place every year since 1886 when a grand piano worth £200 was the first prize.

Plugger Bill, Irish born out of Detroit, has flowing red hair and a fiery temperament to go with it. He has raced everywhere, USA, West Indies, South America, Africa, Spain, Portugal, Germany, England, New Zealand...Heaven knows how many times he has been disqualified. He even went to jail in 1897 for beating up an Adelaide cyclist with his fists.

But everyone loves him. The *Sportsman* shouted his glory in verse:

When we went to see the cycling on the
Melbourne Cricket Ground,
How we hollered and shouted as the
Plugger whistled round.
With his 'trilbies' both a-movin' as quickly
as you like,
And his youthful hands a-grippin' both the
handles of his bike.
With his auburn hair a-floatin' like a banner
in the breeze
With his quarters up to heaven, and his
head between his knees;
With his body all a-wobblin' and his fea-
tures stern and set-
Well, the Plugger made a picture I never
will forget.

The Austral has become so big it now is like the Melbourne Cup complete with bookies, betting ring and all. Some MCC members are not too happy about it. No longer does the hallowed ground have a nice amateur atmosphere.

The *Sportsman* says never was there a more perfect day, and never was there such a brilliant crowd. Plugger arrived appropriately on the steamer *Austral* and stayed at the Austral Hotel.

The crowd was 30 000 and the takings £1307 pounds, an MCG record for any sport. Plugger rode a remarkable race. He won by 15 yards and he was only the third rider in the history of the race to win from scratch.

The *Argus* says there was great excitement and tremendous enthusiasm when Plugger crossed the line and there was no doubt about the popularity of the win. But there is trouble over this race. The pay-out in the ring is estimated at nigh on £8000, a record for any cycling race anywhere. There is a rumour that the famous gambler, John Wren, plunged on Martin.

One rider, F.S. Beauchamp, was suspended for life for acting as Plugger's pacemaker. There was also an inquiry at the Port Phillip Hotel. Seven riders, each were asked if they had taken bribes all denied it and the inquiry was inconclusive.

Note: Did Plugger win fairly? We will never know, but the May 1907 edition of *Lone Hand* says Plugger had 19 opponents in the race and all but one ran dead. Plugger had a settlement at his hotel. He had a pile of notes and sovereigns on his bed. He had a loaded revolver beside him then called in the cyclists, one by one, paid them off and gave them a receipt to sign.

Plugger at last had made enough money to retire.

Cyclists at the turn of the century

Women Revel in Right to Vote

16 DECEMBER 1903

Miss Goldstein

Women, for the first time, voted in Federal elections today. The Government urged women to vote between 10 a.m. and 12 noon and 2 p.m. and 5 p.m. The working men would want to rush the other hours.

But it was all a huge success. As the *Age* put it, for years there has been this parrot cry:'But the women don't want the vote'. Ah, but in every booth you could see their satisfied smiles, their eager and confident looks. They trooped along to the booths from 8 a.m. and by noon women voters far out-numbered the men.

In the fashionable suburbs elegant carriages all day trundled along to the polling booths. Conservative ladies were rounding up their female friends offering them rides in the hope that they would vote.

The press was very interested in Miss Vida Goldstein, the famous feminist. The *Age* reports: At all her meetings Miss Vida Goldstein has urged upon her hearers so earnestly the advisability of voting early that it was expected she would back up her precept by her own example.

But Cr Jeffries was not prepared to find her, as he did, waiting in the rain at 7.20 a.m. yesterday morning. She was the first to enter and record her vote at 8 o'clock, and probably holds the distinction of being the first woman to exercise her franchise in an Australian election. At any rate Cr Jeffries was so impressed with the incident that he intends to preserve the ballot box in which Miss Goldstein dropped her papers, and in it place the names of the clerks at the table. The plain white box is to be handed down to posterity, and — perhaps — will be an object of curiosity in the Smithsonian Institute of Australia 1000 years hence.

The real patriotic spirit was exhibited by an old Scottish body who had a vote in Melbourne. She had been 85 years in this world of politics and promises, and it was the first time she had ever had a say in an election. One energetic canvasser drove up to her door in a carriage, and announced he had come to take her to the polling booth.'Na, na', responded the old dame as she put on her bonnet and sturdily set out on her journey. 'It'll no be for me to ride. I've waukit that far for ma pleasure mony a day, so I'll just gang there on foot for the guid of ma countree'.

There is likely to be a great number of informal votes. Until now you just put a line through the names that didn't appeal. Today we are asked put a cross beside our favoured candidates. A pity, there was a certain satisfaction in ruthlessly running a pencil through names of politicians one could not bear.

Some women waited outside, shy, too terrified to come in. Some asked embarrassed policemen inside the booth whom they should vote for. Several had arguments with their husbands, husbands aghast at wives who were not going to vote the way they had expected.

The *Age* says that at one suburban booth: a sweet young thing, all frills and furbelows, rustled in, and was gallantly conducted to her right table by a properly impressed major domo. Arrived there, she smiled sweetly upon the assistant returning officer, lisped a name, smiled again and received papers from an overcome official, who barely escaped giving her five for the Senate and none at all for the Representatives.

The *Argus* however is concerned. Although women have been very responsible in their voting, it fears that with their own interests, like temperance, they may turn politics into entirely new channels.

Prime Minister Feared Drowned

19 DECEMBER 1967

The Prime Minister, Harold Holt, is missing, feared drowned.

He disappeared after swimming far out in rough surf at Cheviot Beach near Portsea on Sunday, 17 December. Inspector L.J. Newell, in charge of the search, said last night: 'I regret to say I do not hold out much hope for him now'.

Mr Holt went swimming with a friend, Mr Alan Stewart, 30, of Armadale. Mr Stewart found the surf difficult and left the water. He said Mr Holt appeared to be swimming strongly when he disappeared. He ran a quarter-mile back to the car and drove to the Quarantine Station to give the alarm. TAA and Ansett-ANA helicopters and Naval and civilian divers were brought into the search immediately.

Mr Holt went into the water, just in his bathing suit. He was wearing neither wet suit nor flippers.

Cheviot Beach is almost at the tip of Point Nepean, two miles inside the very private Quarantine Station. There are 500 yards of sand protected by a jagged reef. It is a favourite swimming spot for Mr Holt, but dangerous, and this week-end it was attacked incessantly by huge ocean waves.

A distraught Mrs Zara Holt was rushed from Canberra on Sunday. She flew to Melbourne in a special RAAF plane and then transferred to a Commonwealth car which took her to Portsea.

Mr McEwen, deputy Prime Minister, will be sworn in as Prime Minister today. He will hold the post until the Government parties elect a new leader, probably in the New Year.

Churches of all denominations are praying for Mr Holt. Mr McEwen issued a statement: 'We will pray that despite the grim situation the Prime Minister may still be found alive' and his press secretary, Tony Eggleton said 'It is a very slender hope, but I believe, Mr Holt may have got ashore somewhere'.

President Johnson of the United States, according to the US Embassy, is deeply concerned and upset. He has asked for reports day and night. The Queen has been in touch with Canberra by telephone and has asked to be kept fully informed.

The Leader of the Opposition, Mr Whitlam

Harold Holt

has postponed his six-week tour of South-East Asia. He said 'It is almost impossible adequately to express my sense of shock and grief. Even at this stage I share with the Deputy Prime Minister and all our fellow Australians the prayerful hope of a miracle'.

The Liberal Party is in turmoil. Party officials are stunned. There is no obvious choice for a new leader. The newspapers are saying there are five possibilities: Mr McMahon, the Treasurer; the External Affairs Minister, Mr Hasluck; the Defense Minister, Mr Fairhall; the Labor Minister, Mr Bury, and the Education Minister, Senator Gorton is a rank outsider.

The *Age* comments:

Harold Holt died unfulfilled, as a man and as a Prime Minister. Behind him was a long and honorable record of distinguished service to his nation. Yet there was much ahead of him. We will never know how much. He had been Prime Minister for a relatively short time...It may well be that Australians will only now feel the full measure of Harold Holt's quality; only now when his Government and his party looks for a successor from a field of contenders, who, with one or two exceptions, have never been regarded as Prime Ministerial material.

Fighting Phylloxera

20 DECEMBER 1881

It can only be described as disaster for the Victorian wine industry and one wonders where it will end.

For a start the Geelong district is no more. Fifteen vineyards have gone, uprooted and destroyed. The Government passed legislation today, which means that any vines, planted or growing within 20 miles of the Geelong Town Hall can be torn out at the direction of the Minister.

The problem is phylloxera, a bug so tiny you can barely see it with the naked eye. The theory is that it came to England and France on rooted American vines some time between 1854 and 1860. The devastation was so terrible it very nearly destroyed the great vineyards of France.

We did not take it seriously here and continued to import vines. The Victorian Minister for Lands, Mr J.J. Casey, for example, said he was at a loss to understand how vines and cuttings after travelling 16 000 miles from Europe could still carry the disease.

He gravely underestimated the vigour of the little bug. It all began on 8 November 1877. Mr Henry King, the lessee of a vineyard at Fyansford, near Geelong, noticed the row of five vines which had a very sickly appearance. A week later they looked worse. He dug up the roots and examined them under a magnifying glass. At first he found nothing, but he lifted up a piece bark and then discovered an insect, phylloxera.

Others were having the same trouble. Charles Craike, a neighbour to Henry King, had vines that were dying. Other sufferers were the vineyards of Hammerly, Hopton and Darley. How had all this happened? A possible suspect was Charles Wyatt's Frogmore nursery. His foreman had imported vines from Chelsea in England back in 1870.

In January 1878 the Department of Agriculture gave the order for the destruction of the first vineyards. Poor Charles Wyatt was quite overwhelmed by his tragedy. He was away on an extended visit to Tasmania. He only knew his vineyard had gone when he read about it in the newspapers. He said he had 150 varieties of vines, some Japanese and American wild vines, entirely resistant to phylloxera.

A goverment committee has produced a report. It reports that all sorts of remedies have been applied. Some have tried bi-sulphide carbon. In one instance a grower completely inundated his vineyard, but nothing worked. The official report states: 'There appears, so far, no remedy or cure for this disease...A reward of 12 000 pounds offered in France for the discovery of a practical and effective remedy remains unclaimed'.

There are rumours that the deadly scourge is spreading to Bendigo. New South Wales and South Australia have passed regulations prohibiting the importation of vines and cuttings from Victoria. It is having an appalling effect on the reputation of Victorian wine. Some cure will have to be found.

Note: The Government took the drastic measures at Geelong to protect Rutherglen, the greatest Victorian wine area. However phylloxera struck Rutherglen in 1897. A combination of economics and the bug ruined the growers. In the early 1890s Rutherglen had 5600 hectares under vine. In 1906 there were less than 2800 hectares left.

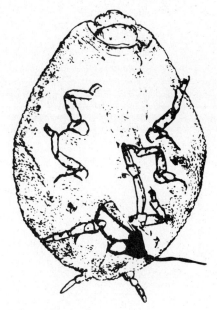

Phylloxera bug

Not a Drop of Water to Save Burning Homes

21 DECEMBER 1909

There was a fierce, hot northerly wind in Melbourne yesterday. Its effect in Williamstown was devastating.

The *Argus* reports:

A block of wooden villas, over 200 yards in length by 100 depth, was swept out of existence, nothing remaining save several tottering chimney stacks. Over 30 dwellings were destroyed.

On such a day it was only necessary for a house to be touched by the flames and it went up like tinder. When the flames had roared down Verdon Street each villa, once the fire reached it, lasted only 20 minutes.

The fire started at 23 Verdon Street in the house owned by Richard Salt. Just like nine out of ten Monday fires, it began in the wash house. Mrs Salt lit the copper fire and began washing. She left the wash house for a moment at 11 o'clock and when she came back the place was in flames.

Mrs Salt and her brother-in-law came running, telephoned the fire brigade, which arrived even before the flames had hit the wash-house roof. But when they turned on the water not a drop came out. The reticulation in the area was utterly feeble under the strain of a 1000 taps, on a day when the temperature was over 100 degrees.

Even modern equipment is useless without water

Nine men with buckets did not touch that fire. The flames ran along the grass to a large workshop in the rear. In a moment it was alight. A few minutes later it hit the house next door owned by Mr Alexander Page, and so it went, from house to house .

What was happening was inevitable, and along Verdon Street and Railway Place owners frantically pulled their furniture out into the street.

The ridiculous part was cinders from the fire blew right across the railway line and set fire to six houses in Railway Place. So easy it would have been to save those. But there was not even a horse trough from which to pump water.

The astonishing array of errors continued. The chief officer of the Fire Brigade, Mr H.B. Lee, rushed from the city in his motor car. A constable pulled him up and charged him with breaches of all traffic regulations. The constable accused him of driving at 30 miles an hour.

'I was doing 30' said Mr Lee 'simply because I could not do 40'.

Mr. Lee, understandably, is furious. He said:

This has been absolutely the worst day on record from a fire brigade point of view. What has happened at Williamstown might have happened in any part of Melbourne. The Metropolitan Board states distinctly that by their act they are compelled to supply enough water for domestic purposes. If there had been a full domestic supply — never mind about enough water for fire brigade purposes — we would have stopped those fires. I tell you that before Williamstown had the water laid on it was better protected, that's because every one of those houses had a tank from which to draw water.

But Williamstown was not the only area that suffered. There were fires at Abbotsford, Hampton, Ballarat, Tatura, Charlton and Albury. Indeed one of Mr Lee's fire engines was rushing to Hampton when it smashed one of its springs on the rough road and moved no further.

It made no difference. There would have been no water for the steamer to pump anyway.

Troops silently Steal Away

22 DECEMBER 1915

The War Office in London announced yesterday that all our troops had been evacuated from Gallipoli. It leaves one with mixed feelings. First, one of immense relief, but second, was it all for nought?

After all, there were 200 000 Allied casualties and of these 25 000 were Australians. *Age* correspondents cable from London:

The news of the abandonment of Anzac and Suvla is the sensation of the day. The newspapers were hurriedly bought up as newsboys with placards dashed into the streets.

The newspapers are unanimous in emphasising the great services rendered by the Australians and New Zealanders. They are printing vivid stories of their doings, and are reproducing diaries giving the dates of the principal events on Gallipoli.

The *Times* says:

The ease with which the withdrawal was effected will bring intense relief. It was a wonderful organising feat, which will be found as extraordinary as the heroic landing of the immortal 29th Division, and the glorious Australian and New Zealand corps, who share the chief honours of some of the noblest and most tragic pages in the history of the British Empire.

As early as last October the Generals started discussing evacuation, but there were 83 000 men, 5000 animals, 2000 vehicles and 200 guns to be moved. There were terrible fears that as they left they would be at the mercy of the Turks and casualties could go from 25 000 to 40 000. They even had 12 000 hospital beds ready in Egypt.

It was the weather that finally forced a decision. On 27 November came the worst blizzard in 40 years, English, Australians, and Turks alike suffered a deluge of water and snow. The freeze was worse than the shelling. The Allied Army lost a tenth of its strength, some frozen to death, some drowned and some incapacitated through frostbite and pneumonia.

The withdrawal was a miracle of good organisation. It was all done at night by subterfuge. The men left their trenches, deadening the noise by feet wrapped in sacking. Stores and equipment were disembarked but mules

Troops in Anzac Valley

always came back with empty boxes, to make it appear they were really loading, not unloading.

They didn't fire after dark to give the illusion to the Turks that this was the usual practice. No tents were pulled down and the last remaining troops kept up a furious rattle of gun fire. On the very last night they even invented devices to operate self-firing rifles; some had a complicated arrangement of weights provided by water dripping from kerosene tins; others had fuses and candles which burned through a string and released a weight on the trigger.

But it all appeared to work. The Turks had no idea they were going. Either that or they too had a feeling of relief and wanted it to be all over.

But it was a sad business for the Australians. They were startled when told it was time to leave. Many of them went to the graves of their friends and erected new crosses. One soldier even remarked 'I hope they won't hear us going down to the beaches'.

Further reading: *Gallipoli*, Alan Moorhead.

White Australia, the Law of the Land

23 DECEMBER 1901

Mr Barton (later Sir Edmund)

The Governor-General will sign the Immigration Restriction Bill tomorrow and the White Australia policy will be the law of the land.

This, obviously, is the desire of nine out of ten Australians, but it has been very tricky. The Prime Minister, Mr Barton, did not want to make it too obvious.

Word has come through from Whitehall. The British Government, already involved in a war in South Africa, in trouble in China and fearful of the Russians, does not want to offend the Japanese.

So the Immigration Bill, very cunningly, calls for the exclusions of any person who fails to write out a passage of 50 words in the English language dictated by the officer. Or further, any person who in the opinion of the minister is likely to become a charge on the public.

Mr Barton last month changed the English language to any Europen language, because he felt it would keep out good German and Danish farmers.

Well matters have been very delicate. The Governor-General, the Earl of Hopetoun, was reluctant to sign it, because the Japanese are upset. The Japanese Consul in Sydney complained: 'I have received a cable message from His Imperial Japanese Majesty's Government stating that they consider the bill clearly makes a racial discrimination, and requesting me to express their high dissatisfaction...'.

The debate has gone on since last August and it has been fascinating. Many members were outraged at the subterfuge of this dictation business. Wanting to be a White Australia was what it was all about. Why didn't we say so?

Mr J.C. Watson, the Labor Leader raised the question: Did we desire that our sisters or one of our brothers be married to these coloured peoples? A few years ago business men looked upon Chinese or other coloured undesirables as men who could be very well tolerated, because their labour was cheap, but when it was found these Orientals possessed all the cunning and acumen necessary to fit them for business affairs, there was a marked change about the 'heathen Chinee'...'In each and every avenue of life we find the competition of the coloured races, insidiously creeping in', said he.

King O'Malley agreed. You don't just keep out the ignorant coloured people. The more educated the more dangerous they become. 'It will not keep out the Indian "toff" who becomes a human parasite preying upon the people of the country'.

Many members gave the warning; bring in Asiatics and coloured races and they would carry with them all the vile diseases of the East, including the terrible curse of leprosy. Mr Ronald, the member for Southern Melbourne, said whenever an inferior race tries to blend with a superior race it drags the latter down to its own level. There was proof of this right back to before Christ.

Passionately he cried:

Let these people come in here and our race will become piebald in spite of our efforts to prevent it. Let us keep before us the noble ideal of a white Australia — a snow-white Australia if you will. Let it be pure and spotless...Let us tell these foreign races that when they can live up to our social and moral ideals we shall welcome them; but never let us try to blend a superior with an inferior race.

Almost all members agree with the idea, it is just the dictation test that is worrying.

Black Fighter Exacts his Revenge

26 DECEMBER 1908

We have just created history in Sydney, the first world title fight between a black man and a white man.

Hugh D. McIntosh, staged the fight between the Canadian, Tommy Burns, the white heavyweight world champion, and Jack Johnson, of Galveston Texas, the black champion of the world.

The fight took place in the open air stadium at Rushcutter's Bay before a crowd of 20 000. Mr McIntosh, a real go-getter, built this stadium as the biggest thing of its kind anywhere.

He was crafty. A black-white title fight has been out of the question in the US. John L. Sullivan and Jim Jeffries always drew the colour line. Jack Johnson, a very amiable man back home and a good Methodist, has been trailing Burns all over the world, trying to draw him into a fight. He claims Burns snubbed him in London, so the black fellow was bitter indeed.

All right, McIntosh enticed Burns to Australia and offered him the colossal sum of 6000 to fight Johnson. Johnson received only 1000, but he would have fought Burns for nothing.

Never before has a fight attracted such attention. Sydney today has been jammed solid with people. Jack London, the American author is here to see the bout, and Mrs London, was the first woman to be admitted to a title fight in Australia.

When Burns stepped into the ring there was a deafening cheer from 20 000 throats. The *Bulletin* says they came to see the black contender beaten to his knees. But when they met in the ring it was an awesome sight, Johnson, superbly built, a black tower of a man, five inches taller and two stone heavier than Burns.

'Aaal right Tahmmy' said Johnson, giving a grinning display of gold teeth. He threw a left to Burns's ribs, then a right. Burns sank a left into Johnson's stomach, but then Johnson swung an upper cut which lifted Johnson off his feet and left him sitting on the floor.

That was the decisive blow. Burns never quite recovered. 'Ahh, poor little Tahmmy' jeered Johnson. 'Don't you know how to fight Tahmmy? They said you were a champion.' Johnson amused himself by stiffening his abdominal muscles and letting Burns punch at them.

Burns did actually hurt Johnson in the fourth round with a left to the heart and a right to the jaw, but that was all. Johnson could have knocked him out any time but mercilessly he applied slow torture as if he were getting revenge for everything that had ever been done to black people.

Burns's face was all puffed on one side and his jaw hung down as if it had been broken. 'Jewel won't know you when you get home, will she?' said Johnson. Jewel was Burns's wife.

In the fourteenth round Burns seemed to make a slight recovery, but Johnson rained blows on him. Down went Burns and with astonishing courage he staggered to his feet. Johnson swept in, hit him again, and was about to shoot another blow when a Superintendent of Police waving his riding crop, shouted 'Stop Johnson'.

The fight was over.

Tommy Burns is offering no excuses for his defeat but the cocky Mr Johnson doubts if Burns can do anything. For 20 pounds wager he is prepared to beat Burns at cycling, running, swimming, tennis, baseball, gold fossicking, bowls, sculling, piano, guitar, fiddle, banjo, car racing and even archaeology, his hobby.

Jack Johnson

Victoria's Extravagant Victory

27 DECEMBER 1926

Jack Ryder

Victoria has just beaten New South Wales in the annual Christmas cricket match. Very satisfying really, we won by an innings and 656 runs.

It all began last Friday and by 6 p.m. this was the scoreboard: Woodfull, c. Ratcliffe, b. Andrews, 133. Ponsford, not out 334. Hendry, not out 86. Sundries 20. 1 for 573.

Ponsford did what nobody has ever done before, made 300 runs in a day. His 300 came up in 285 minutes. There were 22 893 spectators to see him do this, a splendid crowd for a Shield match. Victorians adore seeing NSW go down, so 22 000 were back again first thing on Saturday. Oddly enough Ponsford did not last long, he was bowled by Morgan for 352.

But that wasn't all. In came Jack Ryder, who made 295 with six sixes. He scored his first 100 in 115 minutes, his second in 74 minutes and his last 95 in 56 minutes. His sixes were prodigious. One very nearly smashed the clock on the Smokers Stand. Ryder was very nervous. He thought he would be in fearful trouble if he damaged the clock. Oddly enough there is a prize for doing that. Had he hit it he would have won a case of champagne.

The hitting went on and on. Victoria was all out for 1107, a world record for first-class cricket. The newspapers printed photographs of the scoreboard and also put in a photo of the gloves of A. Ratcliffe, the New South Wales wicket-keeper, the man who had to stay there for 1527 deliveries, an iron-man performance.

Arthur Mailey, the NSW and Test spin bowler, has the rather unnerving figures of 60 overs no maidens, 4 for 362. He is producing both stories and cartoons for the newspapers. He says:

Ryder in particular played a splendid innings... After he had cruelly hit me into the members' reserve Andrews said, 'Put a man there; that's his weak spot.' It was rather a pity that Ellis was run out at the finish, for I was just striking my length.

Very few chances were given, although I think a chap in a tweed coat dropped Jack Ryder just near the shilling stand. Here I would like to thank the spectators who fielded so well. They never let up during their long stay on the other side of the fence.

Of course we would have done much better if the scoring board had been up to date. There was only room for eight bowlers' names and I am sure the wicket-keeper, who appeared to be the most agile person on the ground, would have gone right through the Victorian team.

Mailey, if nothing else, has gained great mileage out of this match. He also said:

A well-known Victorian cricket statistician told me this morning that no other alleged bowler had ever had so many runs knocked off his bowling in an innings. He shook my limp hand. I am still wondering whether it was a congratulatory grip or even one of thanks. He is a statistician who makes a hobby of recording uncommon performances.

New South Wales scores were paltry, even miniscule; first innings 221 and 230 for the follow on. Now we think Australia should just use Victoria for the Test side. You don't need anyone else.

One Survives Steamer Sinking

28 DECEMBER 1893

Never have we had a worse Christmas, hail, rain, mountainous seas, weather so frigid we have needed fires to keep warm.

The *Herald* displayed news on its office window today that there had been a fearful tragedy, the 243 ton iron steamer, *Alert*, had gone down off Cape Schanck near the Port Phillip Heads.

There were 15 people aboard, but only one survivor, Robert Ponting, the cook. As we understand it, the *Alert* was on its way from Bairnsdale to Melbourne. When they approached the Back Beach at Sorrento, the ship was hit by mountainous seas, which put the fires out. Captain Mathieson ordered everyone on deck with life jackets, but a few minutes later an enormous wave hit the ship, it capsized and sank.

This happened at 4 o'clock in the afternoon. There was a crew of 12 and three passengers all of whom drowned, except the remarkable Robert Ponting. He clung to a cabin door and was in the sea all night until 5 or 6 o'clock in the morning. For hours he looked at the Cape Schanck light, unable to get near it and all the time getting colder and colder.

It was dawn, around 5 a.m., when he felt himself ashore, staggered up the sand and collapsed. He lay there until 11 a.m. when Mr. J. Douglas Ramsay with his wife and sister on a stroll along the beach, discovered what they thought was a dead body. He was almost covered with sand, there was sand in his nostrils and he appeared stiff and cold.

They called for help, forced brandy down his throat. One of the ladies took off her jacket and wrapped it round him. A Mr Stanton was out walking his dog, a large St Bernard, Mr Stanton persuaded his dog to nestle up close to Ponting to give him warmth. It was a strange sight to see a huge dog lying close to an apparently dead man.

But the effect of the warmth was obvious. After 10 minutes Ponting opened his eyes and drew a long breath. In a delirious state he kept asking 'Where is my life belt?'

It was two hours before Constable Nolan of Sorrento and a rescue party arrived. Police carried Ponting up the steep cliff and through the thick scrub, which in places is almost impassable. Then they conveyed him by buggy to the Mornington Hotel, Sorrento, where he is recovering from his frightful ordeal.

It is a very sad Christmas story. Most of the crew had large families. Mr James Newton, a saloon passenger, was a Treasury clerk at Bairnsdale and very popular. He had bought a railway ticket to Melbourne, but at the last moment decided instead to take the *Alert*.

Mrs Ponting, who lives at Albert Park, was standing at the door of her house when a 'considerate neighbour' called out to her: 'Have you heard the news?'

'What news?' said Mrs Ponting.

'Why the *Alert* is wrecked and all hands lost.'

'Oh God, my poor husband' shrieked Mrs Ponting. Frantic she raced into the city to be greeted with the news that her husband was the one survivor. She is leaving by the *Hygeia* this afternoon to join him in Sorrento.

Cape Schanck Lighthouse

Paying Politicians Opens the Door to Riff-raff

29 DECEMBER 1870

Mr W. Degraves

Some Queensland members of Parliament, the representatives for Claremont and Rockhampton, have actually been paid money, but today Victoria created history. Parliament passed a Bill that will give members of the Upper and the Lower House £300 a year.

Agitation for payment for members has been going on since 1859. The Legislative Council rejected the Bill in 1861, 1865, 1867 and 1869. The terrible fear has been that if you pay people to sit in Parliament you will get the crudest, most dreadful, type of riff-raff, creatures concerned only about money.

The Hon. W. Degraves said in the Council: If we had payment for members, I have no doubt we should have political loafers introduced in large numbers, and that they would keep the country in a state of uproar from one year's end to another and I think it is a downright attempt to loot the Treasury. It is a disgrace to the country. If I found any man voting for a measure like this I would not take his bill for five and twenty pounds.

Mr G.P. Smith said in the Assembly, look what would happen if you gave politicians the enormous sum of 300 pounds a year. 'I believe it would have the effect of creating a class of professional politicians. Of all classes of men, I believe that the most despicable is a class of professional politicians — a class of men who trade on politics, and live by politics.

Mr Henry Wrixon, often called 'Righteous Wrixon,' said 'Give money to politicians and you get the poor and meansless, who have not succeeded in prosecuting any business successfully.'

Melbourne *Punch* says contemptuously that MLA are the letters members of Parliament are entitled to put after their names. It means Multus Loquens Asinus.

On the other hand, the real feeling is what hope has the working man ever of getting into Parliament if there is no pay. The *Argus* believes this. Payment for Assembly members will bring in a new blood, but it is absurd to pay Council members. Here membership is based on possession of property. Soon you will have a situation where one House will hardly be recognisable from the other. The members were signing their own death warrant.

'The Legislative Council' thundered the *Argus* 'is now an excresence on the Constitution and must be lopped off. Payment of members will raise the character of the Assembly, and in the same proportion lower that of the Council'.

Ah, but to get it through the Legislative Council the Government has legislated to pay members for three years only as a trial run to see what happens; to see whether it causes some dreadful fall in standards.

Note: The trial bill had to be renewed in 1874 and 1877 restirring a ferocious acrimonious battle. In 1877 the Legislative Council rejected the Bill entirely. Melbourne *Punch* commented: 'The disastrous system of payment of members has brought to the surface of political life a whole tribe of needy, seedy and greedy adventurers, to whom 300 pounds per annum is positive wealth, because it is six times as much as they could earn by their own industry, even supposing they had the aptitude or the inclination to aim at obtaining an honest livelihood', Payment for members did not become a permanent thing until 1886.

Buckley Makes for the Bush

30 DECEMBER 1803

Lieutenant-Colonel Collins

There has been a Christmas break-out of prisoners from the camp at Port Phillip.

It always happens; the convicts thought things would be particularly lax at Sullivan Bay with the officers full of wine and good cheer.

The Lieutenant-Governor, Lieutenant Colonel Collins, out of the goodness of his heart gave an order that the Commissary would issue for Christmas a pound of raisins to each person in the settlement (women and children excepted).

But there was a good indication something was about to happen. Right on Christmas Eve there was a raid both on the commissary and the hospital tent. Provisions, a rifle and even a pair of boots were stolen.

Heavens knows why anybody would want to escape. It is all forbidding bush and mountain. The nearest settlement is at Port Jackson and that is 600 miles off. But some are under the illusion if they can get there, China is not much further.

Five men were brought back on 16 November last. On the seventeenth Collins decided on a public declaration of his commission as Governor. The convicts received new clothes, the Marines were all paraded in splendid scarlet and white. The convicts gave three cheers and the military men fired three volleys.

Part of the ceremony was the lashing of the convicts. Each of them received 100 lashes on their bare backs and their screams coupled with the cries of the seagulls. Watching Aboriginals, no doubt, were puzzled by these examples of white man's civilisation.

The camp chaplain, the Reverend Robert Knopwood, who was usually quite immune to a good flogging was disturbed. He wrote: 'The day would have passed off with the greatest joy, but His Excellency was obliged to punish the five deserters that were brought to the camp to deter others from deserting.'

On another occasion escapers returned to camp so starved, so ill, Collins decided they had suffered enough, a perfect example to the others. But now it has happened again. One of the men is William Buckley, a giant of a man, 6 feet 5 inches.

He is a bricklayer, and for the three months he worked on building the magazine. He had four years in the Army and received a nasty wound on his right hand while fighting the Republican French in Holland. He claims that he got into bad company while on leave and in 1802 he was charged at the Sussex Assizes with having stolen two pieces of Irish cloth worth eight shillings. He was sentenced to death, but this was commuted to transportation for life.

Over Christmas Day, five convicts, including Buckley and Knopwood's own servant, Daniel McAllenan, escaped. A fifth, was shot in the stomach and badly wounded.

Now discipline has all changed. There is a new curfew. Prisoners who had been allowed to build their own bark huts have to return to camp and live in tents like the rest. There are tough new restrictions on hunting for crayfish. Life at Sullivan Bay will be harsher than ever from now on.

Note: McAllenan returned after five terrible days. The others perished except for William Buckley who lived with the Watourong Tribe for 32 years and gave himself up to the settlers of infant Melbourne in July 1835.

Further reading: *Convicts Unbound*, Marjorie Tipping.

Currency and Measurements

Currency

12 pence (d) = 1 shilling (s)
1 pound (£) = 20 shillings
Sovereign = former English gold
coin worth 1 pound sterling
1 guinea = 21 shillings
(In 1966, at the time of conversion
to decimal currency, 10 shillings
was deemed to be worth 1 dollar,
and 1 shilling was deemed to be
worth 10 cents.)

Linear Measure

1 inch = 2.54001 centimetres
12 inches = 1 foot
3 feet = 1 yard
5280 feet = 1 mile
(1 mile = 1.60935 kilometres)

Square Measure

4840 square yards = 1 acre
(1 acre = 0.405 hectare)
640 acres = 1 square mile
1 square mile = 2.59 square
kilometres

Weights

16 ounces = 1 pound
(1 pound = 0.45359 kilogram)
14 pounds = 1 stone
2240 pounds = 1 ton

Liquid Measure

1 pint = 20 fluid ounces
(1 pint = 0.568 litre)
2 pints = 1 quart
4 quarts = 1 gallon

Index

INDEX